AN HISTORICAL INTRODUCTION TO MODERN CIVIL LAW

For
my Father,
Jane and Hannah

An Historical Introduction to Modern Civil Law

THOMAS GLYN WATKIN
Reader in Law
University of Wales, Cardiff

Ashgate
DARTMOUTH
Aldershot • Brookfield USA • Singapore • Sydney

Published by
Dartmouth Publishing Company Limited
Ashgate Publishing Ltd
Gower House
Croft Road
Aldershot
Hants GU11 3HR
England

Ashgate Publishing Company
Old Post Road
Brookfield
Vermont 05036
USA

Ashgate website: http://www.ashgate.com

British Library Cataloguing in Publication Data
Watkin, Thomas Glyn
An historical introduction to modern civil law. - (Laws of the nations series)
1. Civil law - Roman influences 2. Civil law - History
I. Title
346'.009

Library of Congress Cataloging-in-Publication Data
Watkin, Thomas Glyn, 1952-
An historical introduction to modern civil law / Thomas Glyn Watkin.
p. cm. --(Laws of the nations series)
Includes bibliographical references and index.
ISBN 1-85521-851-8 (hardback)
1. Civil law--History. I. Title. II. Series.
K585.W367 1999
340.5'6'09--dc21 99-36051
CIP

ISBN 1 85521 851 8 (HBK)
ISBN 0 7546 2100 6 (PBK)

Printed and bound in Great Britain by MPG Books Ltd, Bodmin, Cornwall

Contents

Preface

The last fifty years have seen a progressively closer relationship developing among the nations of Europe, and the last three decades have seen the United Kingdom becoming involved in that process. In legal practice and in legal education, this has led to a growing demand within the common law jurisdiction of England and Wales for lawyers with a knowledge and understanding of the laws and legal systems of the other European nations. By and large, the other countries involved are part of that family of legal systems which are heirs to the civil law tradition of continental Europe. Lawyers from England and Wales who encounter the legal systems of their continental neighbours are inevitably impressed by the underlying similarities which still exist among the national legal orders which have resulted from the codifications of the last two centuries.

It is therefore ironic that there has been a steady decline in the teaching of civil law within the university law schools of England and Wales during the very years in which circumstances have led and are still leading to a situation in which it is no longer sufficient for lawyers to be conversant with the structures of their own legal system alone, but also need some knowledge of those of their nearest neighbours. Even more remarkable is the fact that the role of Roman law within the law curriculum has almost always been challenged as being irrelevant to the modern practitioner. Whereas a previous generation of university educated English lawyers would have had at least some acquaintance with the general form and content of the civil law as a result of having studied its Roman ancestor, in the very years in which such information would have been of most practical use to them, that happy circumstance has ceased to obtain.

The result is that, whereas a generation ago the need was for texts which would link knowledge of Roman law in the ancient world to the legal systems of the modern states by telling the tale of its development into the mediaeval and early modern *ius commune*, the need today is for an account of civil law which will make good the deficit incurred by the neglect of the Roman achievement as well as tracing how the contribution of the ancients was recognized and embraced during the intervening centuries by the various schools of civil and canon law, and also how the civilian tradition encompassed and absorbed many features from the legal arrangements of the Germanic world and other legal orders.

The present work is intended to assist the reader who seeks an historical explanation of the similarities which exist among the civil law countries of contemporary Europe. It is not intended to furnish a narrative history of European civil law from ancient Rome to the present time. Instead, it focuses upon the development of those parts of the civilian legal heritage which are important to an understanding of contemporary civil law systems, while supplying sufficient information regarding the general history of the civilian tradition to make those developments comprehensible. From there, a reader with a deeper interest should be able to progress to the wealth of more advanced literature which exists in many languages.

This book was written during the course of a year's study leave from Cardiff Law School. I am indebted to the University and the Law School for that sabbatical period and for the opportunity to develop over many years my teaching and research interests in legal history and civil law. Not least I have benefited from being able to visit universities in several civil law jurisdictions with funding from Cardiff Law School and the ERASMUS and SOCRATES programmes of the European Community. During the course of my study leave, I was particularly helped by a generous grant from the Academic Purposes Awards Fund of the Society of the Public Teachers of Law for which I am very grateful.

I am grateful also to the many colleagues at Cardiff's partner universities in Europe and farther afield who have always extended a warm and helpful welcome to me when visiting their institutions. I wish particularly to record my thanks to Professors Andrea Padovani and Alberto Cadoppi of the Università degli Studi di Parma; Professors Rudolf Carpanini, Giovanni Cordini, Dario Mantovani and Luciano Musselli of the Università degli Studi di Pavia; Professor Mariano Abad of the Universidad de Oviedo; Dr. María Isabel Alvarez Vélez of the Universidad Pontificia Comillas de Madrid; Professor Dr. Reiner Schulze of the Westfälische Wilhelms-Universität Münster; Professor Hirokatsu Kato of Surugadai University and Professor Yasunori Kasai of Niigata University. I am also greatly indebted to my colleague at Cardiff, Mr. Kazuhiko Niijima, for accompanying me on my visit to Japan, and to his wife, Chiemi, and their family for their hospitality during my visit. Over the years, colleagues, friends and students at Cardiff and elsewhere have encouraged my endeavours in this field; I cannot mention them all by name but they all deserve the warmest thanks, as do Mr John Irwin and his staff at Ashgate Publishing who have facilitated the book's production and completion. I alone am responsible for any shortcomings or errors.

Finally, my thanks are due once more to my wife Jane for proof reading the final manuscript and compiling the indexes. She and my father endured this book's long gestation period as well as my frequent absences abroad while it was being researched and written. To them, and to my daughter Hannah who was born as the book was nearing completion, this work is rightly and lovingly dedicated.

Thomas Glyn Watkin
Cardiff
December 9th, 1998

Introduction

Civil law, like common law, has a variety of meanings. Sometimes, within a particular legal system, civil law is differentiated from criminal law, in which case it refers to the rules of private law which regulate the relationships of individuals one with another rather than with the State. Again, within a particular legal system, it can be used to differentiate all those rules, including those of criminal law, which apply to the civilian population as opposed to those which apply to military personnel, in which case civil law is opposed to military law. On the international scene, the words civil law can be used to distinguish all of the rules of a particular legal system - private, criminal and military - as opposed to those which belong to the international legal order, civil law as against international law. Finally, civil law can be used to demarcate those systems of law which are derived from Roman law, or which have their roots in that system, as opposed to those which have their origins in the common law of England - civil law contrasted with common law.[1]

It is with this last sense of the words civil law that this book is concerned, that is civil law as that family of legal systems which have their origins in the law of ancient Rome, and which have since been developed and shaped in the universities and legal systems of continental Europe during the mediaeval and early modern period. It is a system of law which would probably today be unrecognizable to lawyers from the time of the Roman republic, but modern civil lawyers looking back to that time are able to identify the similarities and continuities which have maintained the family resemblance over almost three millennia. It is a law which has therefore served the needs of a community in the ancient world which expanded from being a city state in central Italy, first to dominate the Italian peninsula and from there the whole of the Mediterranean basin together with much of northern Europe and the Middle and Near East, forming the greatest empire that the world at that time had ever seen. Within the context of that initial development, it maintained its validity as the legal system of the Roman citizenry despite the geographical expansion of empire, despite the extension of the citizenship to peoples of various races and tongues, despite the change from republican to imperial government, despite the removal of the capital from Rome to Byzantium, despite the change in religion from paganism to Christianity and despite the replacement of Latin with Greek as the principal language of the imperial administration.

After the collapse of the Roman empire in western Europe, although Roman civil law continued to operate in the eastern Byzantine empire, its hold on the west weakened, but it was to re-emerge in the university law schools of Italy and later France as the prime subject of legal study in the eleventh and twelfth centuries. From this academic revival, the revived learning of Roman law influenced first the legal culture of the western catholic Church and then the legal arrangements of many of the secular societies of western Europe. Having achieved, together with the Church's canon law, the position of being the so-called common law, *ius commune*, of continental Europe, colonisation of the Americas, the Indies and many parts of Africa by continental European nations led to this civil law being in effect exported to parts of the world which had not merely not been part of the original Roman empire but of the existence of which the Romans would have had no inkling. Moreover, the subjection of this civil law to rational systematization and criticism during the seventeenth and eighteenth centuries led to its codification in written texts during the nineteenth century to serve as the law of the individual states which had utilized the *ius commune*. The considerable convenience of laws reduced to systematic codified forms has further increased the system's attractiveness, so that it has been freely adopted by many modern states which knew neither the imperial power of Rome nor that of its modern European successors.

Thus it is that the ambit of civil law in the modern world is much greater than that of Roman rule in ancient times. Today, modern civil law systems exist in the greater part of continental Europe - in France, Germany, Belgium, the Netherlands, Italy, Spain, Portugal, Switzerland, Austria and, on the Asian frontier, Turkey. Across the Mediterranean Sea, civil law has been influential in providing much of the law codes of the countries of North Africa, including Morocco, Tunisia and Egypt. In the Middle East, it has proved its worth to states such as Syria and Jordan, and farther south in Africa, former French, Belgian and Portuguese possessions employ civil law codes as the bases of their respective legal systems, in countries such as Zaire, Angola and Mozambique. In Central and South America, the picture is even clearer with every single nation from the Mexican border with the United States southwards having a legal system which belongs to the civil law family.

Somewhat surprisingly, even in the United States and Canada, there are still areas where civil law operates. In the United States, only the modern state of Louisiana continues to enjoy a civilian system based on French law, while in Canada, the province of Quebec retains a civil law system as part of its distinctively French inheritance. Both of these instances reflect the desire of those who have once enjoyed the benefits of civilian jurisprudence to retain the system even where it is at variance with the dominant legal culture of the society in which they live, the United States and Canada being predominantly common law jurisdictions. Across the Pacific, one finds societies which have not retained but actually adopted the civil law as the basis of their legal orders. Japan is probably the clearest example of such adoption, but civil law systems are also to be found in Indonesia and the Philippines.

Some countries have managed to accommodate both civil law and common law elements to a substantial degree within their legal systems. South Africa is the prime exemplar of this phenomenon, although the same is true of Sri Lanka and to a certain extent of both Japan and the Philippines, while Scotland also affords an instance of a jurisdiction in which the heritage of the common law and that of the civil law have been blended into a system which arguably enjoys the benefits of each.[2]

Thus far, the concept of the civil law has been described in terms of its historical origins and geographical extent rather than in terms of its form and content. The question must be asked therefore what elements within a legal system distinguish that system as being part of the world-wide civil law family. Several features deserve mention.

One of the hallmarks of modern civilian systems is that its legal rules are predominantly written. The lawyers of ancient Rome distinguished laws as being either written or unwritten, *ius scriptum* or *non scriptum*.[3] Although Roman law in the ancient world was never in truth codified, written texts played a large part throughout its history, from the Twelve Tables in 450 BC to the compilations of the emperor Justinian in the sixth century AD. In the formation of modern civil law, the *Corpus Iuris Civilis* of Justinian is undoubtedly the written text which has played the most significant part. Today, the laws of every civil law country are found in part in codes, which seek to present the rules relating to different departments of the law in a systematic and comprehensive form. Indeed, the fundamental private law source in civilian jurisdictions is the civil code, dealing with the questions of who may have rights (the law of persons) and over what those rights may be exercised (the law of things). The law of things is today regularly divided into distinct sections - the law of property (what can be owned) and the law of obligations (what can be owed). Within each of these divisions, the code deals systematically with questions such as how property and obligations are acquired, what forms they may take, how they are transferred from one person to another, and how they are terminated. A separate code, the code of civil procedure, will deal with how rights and duties are enforced by the legal system in question. The rules of criminal law will be contained in a separate Penal Code and the criminal justice process in a code of criminal procedure. Some systems deal with the relations of businessmen in a separate Commercial Code, thus drawing a distinction between legal relationships of a predominantly mercantile nature from contractual obligations entered into by ordinary citizens as part of their everyday life rather than as entrepreneurial endeavours. The key factor to emphasize about these codes at this stage is that they bear witness to the fact that in civil law jurisdictions the law is predominantly written law.

That the law is written highlights another important factor in relation to these systems, that is that the primary source of law, some would argue the only true source of law, within them is enacted law. Law-making is seen as being the exclusive task of the legislator. Herein lies, as will be shown, something of an anomaly, for the jurists of ancient Rome distinguished enacted law, *lex*, from law generally, which they described as *ius*. They would have been surprised to be told that only legislation, that is *lex*, properly amounted to law in the sense of *ius*. The word *ius* in Latin does not just mean law; it can also mean right, and is connected etymologically with *iustitia*, the Latin word for justice. The word *ius* therefore means law, but with a distinct overtone that it is law in the sense of what is right and just rather than what is merely enacted. The interplay between the two words and their respective meanings opens up possibilities for debating whether an enacted law is really law if it is not just. In other words, the test of whether an enacted law is valid is not necessarily a formal questioning of whether it has been duly passed by the legislature. It may also be possible to challenge it on the basis of whether its content is just and therefore lawful. Modern lawyers in the common law tradition find this a difficult issue, preferring to regard the question of whether an enacted law is just as being ethical or moral rather than legal.[4] The problem is compounded by the fact that the Roman distinction between *ius* and *lex* has survived in the languages of those countries with civil law systems, while English, the predominant language in most common law countries, does not mirror the subtlety. Thus, for instance, the French speak of *droit* as opposed to *loi*, the Italians of *diritto* and *legge*, the Spanish of *derecho* and *ley*, and even the Germans - whose language is not based on Latin but who have inherited the civilian legal vocabulary - of *Recht* as opposed to *Gesetz*.

Thus, the civil lawyer is heir to a legal tradition in which law is seen as being a particular manifestation of a greater order of which it is a part not the whole. The law of a particular country, its civil law in a narrow sense, is only a part of a greater legal order. The Roman jurists used the words *ius civile* for the proper law of a particular people, while recognizing that some laws were common to all mankind. This latter body of law was at times described as the law of nations, the *ius gentium*, but at other times as being part of the law which was common to all creatures, the natural law or *ius naturale*. Christian thinkers saw this latter concept as being a part of the divine order, a manifestation in nature of the divine will, a God-given law which mere human legislation could not revoke and ought not to contravene.

It is important to realize that this perspective is built into the vocabulary and terminology of civil law systems. It is not surprising therefore that within the nations which share this overarching view of human affairs, it has become common for law-makers to ground their law-making activity in a formal recognition that the basic substance of legal rights and duties is not created by law but rather that it is the task of law to recognize those basic rights and to protect and promote them. Thus, there appears another hallmark of civil law systems, namely that they possess written constitutions, that is written fundamental laws, a development of the natural law school of jurisprudence of the seventeenth and eighteenth centuries. The constitution or basic law is not just an enactment of the legal rules and mechanisms for making, amending and revoking laws; rather it is a statement of those rights and duties which belong to legal subjects not as citizens of a particular State but simply as human beings, fundamental human rights which are not of the law's creation but which law exists to uphold, protect and advance. All other laws are then required to conform to this basic law and derive their validity and indeed their legitimacy from it.[5]

Written constitutions are in fact an articulation of the previously implicit notion that man-made laws, enactments, must conform to a more fundamental concept of law which does not derive its validity from human law-making activity. This raises the question as to what is to occur if in a particular State laws are enacted which transgress such express or implied fundamental law. In the last century, civil law countries have been in the vanguard of those jurisdictions which have developed mechanisms for adjudicating upon this very question - whether a particular piece of legislation offends against the fundamental law of the State. Another hallmark of civil law systems therefore is their possession of a constitutional court or some such body to hear and determine such matters.

The existence of such a body, with jurisdiction to police the work of the legislature itself, gives concrete expression to a principle set out in the constitutions of many civil law countries, namely that sovereignty - ultimate power within the State - resides in the people, not in the government or the legislature. The State is seen as existing to protect and promote the interests of its subjects and cannot therefore be allowed to offend against those interests. Accordingly, a body such as the constitutional court exists to uphold that view and enforce it, even against the legislature or the executive of a State. It can force the highest powers in the State to respect the fundamental law. No power within the State can be regarded as above the law; all derive their legitimacy from the law.

In that all other legal enactments are regarded as being subordinate to the constitution, it follows that their purpose is to a greater or lesser extent to carry the principles and policies of the constitution into effect. This they do in a number of ways. For instance, if the constitution recognizes the right of a person to own property, then the State must promote that right by supplying legal rules which allow its subjects to acquire property. Such rules will be part of the civil code, and will set out what ownership means, how it is acquired, how it is transferred from one person to another, and how ownership terminates. These rules will provide the subject with the legal framework within which he or she may enjoy the fundamental right to property enshrined in the basic law.

It will not be enough however to provide such rules for acquisition, transfer and termination. The law must also provide for mechanisms to resolve disputes about the ownership of property and the means by which those who are owners according to the law may enforce and protect their rights. These rules will be found primarily in the provisions of the civil procedure code, where the State will provide tribunals within which those seeking to have their rights declared and enforced may obtain legally binding determinations. Methods of safeguarding property from threatened danger will also be found there and remedies for invasions of property rights which have actually occurred. Methods may also be provided for safeguarding rights by registration, although these methods are often dealt with in the civil code itself.

The State's interest in its subjects' rights does not however end with their protection and enforcement in the civil code and the civil process. If a right guaranteed by the State has been transgressed or invaded, then to that extent the State has failed in its purpose of protecting the subject who has suffered that wrong. A State based upon upholding such fundamental rights can be neither indifferent nor inactive in the face of such conduct, and will define the circumstances in which it will respond to such conduct by depriving the perpetrators of some or all of their rights in consequence of their unjust behaviour. The circumstances which will justify such a response are set out in the criminal code, each crime being in effect a definition of conduct entitling the State to interfere in what would otherwise be the protected fundamental rights of a wrongdoing subject. The extent of the interference which the State is allowed to make amounts to the punishment considered just for the crime as defined. Moreover, as it is according to this perspective a fundamental injustice for the State to invade a subject's rights in this way unless the subject has indeed contravened the State-protected rights of others, the State must provide mechanisms to ensure that no subject is wrongfully deprived of their rights. This it does by creating a criminal justice system, set out in its code of criminal procedure, providing for the means by which crimes are to be investigated, prosecuted, tried and punished, together with the manner in which a period of punishment is monitored and any discretion regarding it exercised.

The pattern of carrying the principles and policies of the fundamental law into effect by means of subordinate legislation in the form of codes and providing tribunals or courts to adjudicate disputes concerning the rights thereby protected and also to enforce those rights is again a hallmark of the civilian systems. Each body of law ideally is meant to be contained in a code, and for each code there is a court or a system of courts to adjudicate upon it and enforce the rights and duties pertaining thereto. Thus, the fundamental law is contained in the constitution and this is policed and enforced by the constitutional court. Private law rights are enshrined in the civil code, and these are protected and enforced by the ordinary or civil courts. Crimes are defined by the criminal code, and the criminal courts exist to adjudicate upon such infractions and punish the delinquents. When the State makes administrative laws to further its activities in protecting and promoting the fundamental rights of its citizens, its administrative activities may be policed and enforced by special administrative tribunals or courts. The pattern is reproduced in relation to virtually every substantial body or department of law. Each body of law has its written text and courts with jurisdiction over it.

The courts which exercize jurisdiction over the various bodies of law exist in order that the citizens may be able to protect and enforce their rights. The State in effect must provide these tribunals if it is to effect its fundamental responsibility to protect and promote the rights of its citizens. Thus, the courts are not open to the citizens as a matter of grace or favour on the part of the State. It has rather a duty to administer justice, and therefore justice must be available to the citizen in tribunals which are convenient in terms of location and accessibility. The administration of justice is therefore markedly decentralized in civil law countries, with courts of first instance, in both civil, criminal and administrative matters, established in every city and nearly every major town. Justice is available usually within a day's travelling distance to and from the party's home, judged in terms of the period when rail transport was the norm.[6] Even appeal courts are to be found in every regional capital, that is every major city. Such decentralization, of course, has its price, and one price is the risk that the law becomes fragmented and regionalized, different interpretations and expectations growing up in various parts of the country. To prevent this, civil law jurisdictions have a final court of appeal, usually in the nation's capital, which exists solely to hear and determine points of law in order to ensure that legal interpretation and application remains uniform throughout the national territory. Such final courts of appeal, or perhaps more properly review, are generally called the Supreme Court or Court of Cassation, and their existence is another common feature of the civil law landscape.

While the courts have the function of interpreting and applying the law, it is not regarded as a part of their function to make law in any way. Law-making is the function of the legislator, and for the courts to have any law-making role would offend against the principle of keeping the legislative and judicial functions distinct, a principle jealously guarded in civil law jurisdictions. Thus, although it is inevitable that in interpreting the law particularly, the courts are bound on occasion to supply detail to legislative enactments which the legislator had not foreseen, the decisions of the courts do not constitute a binding source of precedent as do the decisions of the higher courts in common law countries. Nevertheless, the recorded decisions of the courts in civil law countries, especially those of the court of cassation, have considerable persuasive force as examples of how the law is being interpreted and applied so as to remain uniform throughout the national territory. The decisions of the courts are referred to as their *jurisprudence*, and this is regarded as a secondary source of law, being of persuasive force. Court decisions however never amount to a justifying reason why the law should be applied or interpreted in a particular way; rather they illustrate how a legal rule is being applied and interpreted and show how consistency may be achieved.

As well as ensuring that a particular rule is applied and interpreted uniformly throughout the country, civil lawyers also place a high value upon ensuring that each rule is interpreted and applied so as to conform with the other provisions of the legal system taken as a whole.[7] Individual rules must cohere within the system taken as a whole and that systematic unity must be maintained. In achieving this synthesis, the contribution of legal scholars and academics is highly valued. Just as in ancient Rome, where the opinions of those learned in the law were regarded as a source of law in themselves, so also in modern civil law systems, the writings of legal scholars are regarded as of considerable persuasive force, in indicating how the laws comprising the system are best interpreted so as to further the cohesion and systematic unity of the system taken as a whole. This feature is yet one more hallmark of the family of civil law systems.

These then are some of the hallmarks of modern civil law systems, the features by which such systems can be identified in the modern world. The question therefore stands as to where these concepts, ideas and structures have their origins. Modern civil law as has been said is rooted in the law of ancient Rome and many of the features which are hallmarks of the modern civil law have their starting point in Roman law. However, although their origin may lie there, their modern appearance has been greatly affected by the process in which those original Roman ideas have been developed during the intervening centuries when the rules of Roman law have been continually refashioned to serve the needs of successive generations and societies. It is the purpose of this book to identify in the history of the civil law the strands which one finds today woven into the fabric of the modern civil law. By examining the history of civil law from Roman times through to our own it is intended to show how modern civil law has been shaped as the ideas, concepts and structures of the Roman legists and jurists have been reworked, woven and rewoven into the garment of European jurisprudence. It is not intended to provide a comprehensive, narrative history of civil law in either the ancient or the modern world. Such a task would be way beyond the scope of the current volume. It is intended rather to trace the growth of those elements which are today the component parts of modern civil law from their beginnings through the various phases of their development. At the time of their inauguration, it may have been quite impossible to foresee their importance to us today; it is only with hindsight that one can identify the salient elements in a particular legal tradition. Not all of the elements which are of importance in modern civil law systems are derived from Roman law: some have their origins in the legal traditions of the Germanic peoples and in feudalism; some have developed from the innovations made by the canon law of the western Church, albeit that that system was itself based on decidedly Roman legal foundations. It is hoped to show how despite the vicissitudes of the intervening centuries, the arsenal of legal concepts provided by the Roman jurists remains identifiable in the modern civil law, and also that they remain amongst the most serviceable of building materials and designs for the fashioning and developing of further legal orders for the new millennium.

Notes

[1] The phrase, common law, also has this variable usage. As well as being used to differentiate those systems derived from the law of England from those rooted in the civil law of Rome, it is also sometimes used to distinguish rules of English law which are derived from decided cases from those which have a legislative origin, and amongst case-law rules, common law rules are further distinguished from those rules which are derived from the exercise of the Chancellor's equity. A separate distinction is also made between common law rules in England, meaning English private law, and the criminal law of the kingdom.

[2] See, on South Africa, R. Zimmermann and D. Visser (ed.), *Southern Cross: Civil Law and Common Law in South Africa* (Oxford, 1996), and, on Scotland, R. Evans-Jones (ed.), *The Civil Law Tradition in Scotland* (Edinburgh, 1995).

[3] See Justinian, *Inst*. I. 2. 3.

[4] See H.L.A. Hart, 'Positivism and the Separation of Law and Morals' (1958) 71 *Harvard Law Review*, 593, reprinted in R.M. Dworkin (ed.), *The Philosophy of Law* (Oxford, 1977), pp. 17 ff.

[5] The United States, although overwhelmingly a common law jurisdiction, has such a bill of rights - indeed, one of the very first. If speaking of a constitution as a fundamental law from which all other laws derive their validity, it is quite correct to say the United Kingdom has no constitution in this sense.

[6] Almost all the modern civilian systems coincided with the coming of the railways.

[7] In the common law, this was termed *convenience*, the coming together of the various decisions. Thus was it often said that the law was more prepared to tolerate an injustice in a particular case than an inconvenience. See C.N. Doe, *Fundamental Authority in Late Medieval English Law* (Cambridge, 1990), pp. 161 ff.

PART I

SOURCES AND INFLUENCES

1 The Roman Republic

1 The Sources of Law

Both the main texts for contemporary knowledge of Roman law come from the period following the end of true republican government in ancient Rome. They are Gaius' *Institutes*, written by the jurist of that name during the second century AD, and the legal compilations ordered by the emperor Justinian during his reign in the sixth century of the Christian era.[1] Both texts list six sources of law. These sources were not all of equal importance throughout the twelve hundred years which separate the traditional founding of Rome in 753 BC from the reign of Justinian at Constantinople from 527-565 AD. The six sources of law as listed by both Gaius and Justinian are: *leges*, the laws enacted by the assemblies of the Roman people; *plebiscita*, laws enacted by the council of the plebs alone; *senatusconsulta*, being, strictly speaking, the advice of the senate; *constitutiones principis*, decisions of the emperor; *magistratuum edicta*, edicts of the magistrates, and *responsa prudentium*, the opinions of those learned in the law. These will now be discussed in the context of the development of law-making as part of the constitution of ancient Rome, this chapter dealing with the republican period and the next two with the centuries of imperial government.

Rome knew four main phases of government during the twelve centuries described above. From its foundation in 753 BC until approximately 510, it was ruled by a succession of kings, so that this epoch is called the Regal period. Thereafter, from the expulsion of the last king in 510/509 BC until the accession to power of Augustus in 27 BC, Rome was a republic. Although Augustan propaganda asserted that his actions in assuming power in 27 BC amounted to his restoration of the republic, his accession is generally regarded as the start of imperial rule, firstly in the form of the emperor acting as first citizen or *princeps*. This period is from that designation called the Principate and lasted until the reign of Diocletian (284-305 AD), when formal acceptance of the emperor's absolute rule was institutionalized, inaugurating a period called the Dominate, which lasted in the West until the fall of the Roman empire in the fifth century and in the East continued into the thousand year history of the Byzantine empire.

2 Assemblies, Law-Making and the Republican Constitution

The verifiable history of Roman law in the ancient world begins and ends with a text. Given that one of the features identified as typical of civil law systems in the Introduction was the tendency for law to be written, the fact that the known history of Roman law starts with a written text is significant. The text in question is the Twelve Tables, and this legal compilation which stands at the beginning of Roman legal history dates from 450 BC, in the middle of the first century of republican government.[2]

Firm evidence for legal institutions and their development before that time is scant, sufficient for interesting speculation but not enough for reliable conclusions to be drawn. Rome was believed to have been founded by Romulus in 753 BC, who became the first of the city's seven kings. History at this point is firmly rooted in legend, the story of the foundation of the city by the twins Romulus and Remus, who had been saved from the Tiber and suckled by a she-wolf, being particularly well-known. In the eyes of subsequent generations, each of the kings embodied particular characteristics: Romulus was a warrior hero; his successor Numa was a priest-legislator, who founded the traditional Roman religion; the sixth king, Servius Tullius was credited with settling the Roman constitution.[3] In later centuries, this meant that any religious practice the origins of which were lost in the mists of time tended to be ascribed to Numa, and likewise any constitutional innovations to Servius Tullius. The first four of the seven kings were Latins, but the last three - Tarquinius Priscus, Servius Tullius and Tarquinius Superbus - were of Etruscan origin, the Etruscans being the people who at this period inhabited that part of central Italy lying to the north of Rome across the River Tiber.

There is however evidence to suggest that it was the coming of the Etruscans to Rome which transformed the fortunes of the city during the course of the seventh century BC. Until that time, Rome appears to have been no more than a settlement based on two hills - the Palatine and the Esquiline - looking out over the flood plain of the Tiber towards the sea. It enjoyed, but had not capitalized upon, an excellent geographical location, commanding the lowest bridging point on the Tiber on the land route linking the Apennines to the sea. The settlement was however agrarian, the people driving out their flocks and herds in the mornings and regrouping within the hill-top settlements for the night.

The Etruscans on the other hand were craftsmen and traders rather than mere agriculturalists. Far from invading Rome, they would appear to have infiltrated the existing society and galvanized it for economic development. It is believed that they constructed a forum, in which the peoples from the various settlements could trade amongst themselves and with others; a temple, where a common cult could be developed to integrate the various tribes; and a stadium for sporting activities, in which the groups of inhabitants could compete on terms of friendly rivalry. In other words, there was an early recognition of the power of trade, religion and sport to unite disparate social groups.

Two other features of Etruscan life should perhaps be noted. Firstly, unlike the original Latin settlers, the religion of the Etruscans was based upon sacred writings, that is there was a reverence for a textual tradition. The Romans' religion is thought to have been a reverence for and reliance upon co-operation with the forces of nature, and not to have made use of either sacred texts or images. Secondly, the Etruscans would appear to have tended to demarcate sharply between an upper and a lower class in their social arrangements, a division not previously believed to have existed at Rome. Both of these factors were to be important in subsequent events.

It is perhaps against this background of Etruscan integration into the Latin settlement, that the role of the first of the Roman popular assemblies is best understood. The Roman people had three popular assemblies, the earliest of which was called the *comitia curiata*. It bore this name in that it was composed of thirty *curiae*, these being divisions of the Roman people upon tribal lines. Indeed, it is said that the *comitia* was composed of three tribes - the Ramnes, Luceres and Tities - each tribe being subdivided into ten *curiae*. Some writers hold that each *curia* was composed of ten *gentes*, the *gens* being a group of families which bore the same name, *nomen*. Each Roman had at least three names: a personal name or *praenomen*; a gentile name, the *nomen*; and a family name, the *cognomen*. Thus, for instance, Gaius Julius Caesar bore the personal name, Gaius, but had the family name of Caesar and belonged to the *gens Julia*, hence bearing the name Julius. Likewise, Marcus Tullius Cicero's family name was Cicero, but he belonged to the *gens Tullia*. The *gens* remained of importance for much of Roman history, for instance enjoying the ultimate right of succession to a member's property upon death if there were no other heir.

Voting in the *comitia curiata* was by *curiae*, and this may well indicate that in the earliest assembly certain acts which crossed the original tribal divides required the consent of the whole community. The only functions which are known historically to have been performed by this *comitia* were the approval of wills, which of course changed the normal order of succession upon death, and the approval of certain adoptions called adrogations, which also altered the status of a family or *gens* member. These functions are not the kind one would today expect to find carried out by a legislative assembly,[4] but probably give an important clue as to the type of transaction which this *comitia* performed and the kind of transaction which was held at the time to require community approval.

It is also significant that the *comitia* was composed of divisions of the people based upon their original tribal origins, not their social status or geographical residence. Loyalties, it may he guessed, were based on family and clan interest. It was this foundation which was disturbed by the constitutional reforms attributed to Servius Tullius in the sixth century.

Servius Tullius is credited with the creation of a new assembly of the people, the *comitia centuriata*. This assembly differed from its predecessor in that it was composed not of *curiae* but of *centuriae*, centuries or hundreds, familiar to most modern readers as divisions of the Roman army. Indeed, the *comitia centuriata* was an assembly of the people based upon military array. In its final form, this assembly was composed of 193 centuries, into which thc adult malc population was fitted according to their ability to equip themselves with military equipment. This ability was assessed in terms of their wealth. The wealthiest citizens were those who had fortunes sufficient to equip themselves as cavalrymen or knights, *equites*; those with lesser fortunes were required to furnish themselves with varying levels of equipment for service in the infantry as footsoldiers. The infantry were grouped into five classes based on wealth. The very poorest were grouped into five centuries of baggagemen, buglers and the like. There were, in its final form, 18 centuries of cavalry, 80 centuries in the first class, 20 centuries in each of classes two, three and four, and 30 centuries in class five. Moreover, in each of the infantry classes, the centuries were divided into seniors and juniors, the juniors being the men young enough to undertake the fighting, while the seniors were required to remain in the city to guard it.

A straightforward arithmetical calculation will reveal that the *equites* and first class of the infantry provided the majority of the centuries in the *comitia centuriata*, and as voting was by centuries, this meant they had political control within it. Here perhaps is a relic of the clear social division of rich and poor which was a legacy of Etruscan rather than Latin social arrangements.

The earliest *comitia centuriata* however did not have 193 centuries and witnessed even greater social division. The earliest version of this assembly is believed to have consisted of only six centuries of cavalry and the first class of infantry, called simply at this time the class, *classis*, and consisting solely of the wealthiest members of the community. It did not increase in size until the siege of Veii at the end of the fifth century and did not reach its full proportion until even later. It may be for this reason that Servius Tullius is credited with the creation of yet another voting assembly, the third of the Roman popular assemblies, the *comitia tributa*. This assembly consisted of divisions of the people called tribes, but these tribes were not racial but more in the nature of geographical divisions of the populace. Each citizen was allocated a place in a tribe, there being four urban tribes and a larger number of rural tribes, eventually totalling 35 in all.[5] It is believed that this *comitia* was concerned with administrative rather than political affairs.

One thing however is very clear from the composition of both of these assemblies, and that is that in them, differentiations based upon racial origin has given way to a new-found unity among the Roman people. In both the *comitia centuriata* and the *comitia tributa*, the members were all united by their being first and foremost Roman. What divided them now was, in the case of the *comitia centuriata*, their social class or wealth or, in the case of the *tributa*, their place of residence. The emergence of these assemblies marked also an emergence of a specifically Roman identity among the citizens, transcending earlier loyalties based on tribal origins.

However, the new arrangements contained within them the seeds of future divisions and discontents. These problems were to manifest themselves following the revolution which ended the regal period and inaugurated the republic.

The last of Rome's seven kings, Tarquin the Proud, Tarquinius Superbus, was expelled from the city having pursued the policies of a tyrant. Following his expulsion, it was decided to avoid the pitfalls of monarchical government by establishing a republic within which ultimate political power, *imperium*, would no longer reside in one man but would be shared. Further, such shared power would not be given to the magistrates for life but only for the space of one year. Thus, there would be two checks upon the power of the leaders: collegiality, power would be shared between them, and annuity, the principle that they held office for only a year. The magistrates who were to wield this power, who eventually bore the name of consuls,[6] were elected annually by the *comitia centuriata* and had to be from this wealthier class, that is patricians. Thus, the humbler citizens, the plebs, were excluded from the highest political office in the community.

While the kings had governed, it is likely that they did so with the benefit of advice from the senate, which at that time would have been a royal council. The composition of the senate at this time is uncertain, but some believe that it was composed of the heads of the 300 *gentes* represented in the *comitia curiata*.[7] The king would have had the authority to convene the various assemblies, as well as having the ultimate political power, *imperium*, to lead in times of war and preserve peace at home in the city. With the expulsion of the king, *imperium* passed to the consuls, who now led the armies in time of war, had the power to act against insurrection at home and to convene the *comitia centuriata* and the *comitia tributa*. As was the case with the kings, the consuls were expected to govern with the advice of the senate, to which former consuls were now admitted after their year of office. Membership of the senate had become partly hereditary and partly by appointment, although certain functions may have been reserved to the hereditary caste. Either magistrate could veto the acts of his colleague, the power of *intercessio*.

The *comitia centuriata* had the power to pass *leges*, that is to enact legislation, but this power was limited to deciding whether individual proposals should be passed. The members of the *comitia* had no right to introduce legislative proposals into the assembly. Only the magistrates could do this. In other words, the legislative initiative was a separate matter from the decision phase of the legislative process; the consuls had the legislative initiative, the assembly the power of decision. Nor did the assembly have any right to debate or amend the proposal. The deliberative stage was in effect one for the senate. A magistrate who wished to promote a bill would present it first to the senate. The senate had no power to pass it, but they would give their opinions, individually or collectively, upon the proposal.[8] The magistrate could amend it in the light of these comments. In addition, during the republic, the practice developed of the magistrates giving the people notice of proposals which were to come before the assembly at least three weeks before the assembly convened. Such informal *contiones* allowed some popular imput into the process. In 98 BC, this process was formalized by the *lex Caecilia Didia*.[9] The assembly then voted on the proposal by centuries. If the law was passed, it bore the name of the consul or consuls who proposed it; thus, a law proposed by a consul from the *gens Valeria* would be called the *lex Valeria*, and so on. The year was also recorded according to the consuls who held office during it.

In this legislative system, one sees already the separation of the legislative initiative, the deliberative phase and the decision-making phase.

One other feature deserves mention. Even after a law had been passed by the assembly, it was necessary for it to be vetted by the hereditary members of the senate to confirm that it did not contravene good custom. In this, there is a distinct flavour of the idea that for a *lex* to be valid, it must not only have been duly enacted in formal terms, but also that its substance must not be contrary to law in the sense of *ius*, what is right or just. The giving of the senate's authority to an enactment, the *auctoritas patrum*, confirmed this. Eventually, this authority was given before the assembly was convened.[10]

The problem with the system described above is that it places political power unmistakeably in the hands of the patrician class, who supply the members of the senate, the chief magistrates and the membership of the *comitia centuriata*. Although the plebs are represented in the *comitia tributa*, the fact that legislation can be passed by the other assembly which is binding on all citizens in effect excludes them from a say in government. Indeed, if it is true that the *comitia tributa* was meant to deal with administrative rather than political decisions, in effect the plebs were denied a voice on the major policies of the community. Within a generation of the foundation of republican government this grievance erupted into direct action, with the plebs withdrawing from the city in what has become known as the first secession of the plebs. They withdrew to the Aventine Hill.

This occurred in 494 BC, and the upshot was that their grievance was recognized and remedied by the creation of a special plebeian magistracy, the Tribunate. Every year, the *comitia curiata* would elect tribunes to represent the plebeian interests in the community. The tribunes were to have the right to provide assistance to any person below the rank of the *classis*, that is *infra classem*, to prevent their unjust molestation or punishment, and could lawfully summon the assistance of the plebeian population to accomplish such an intervention, any person withstanding such a move being forfeit to Ceres. Any tribune could also veto an enactment of the *comitia*, thus ensuring that legislation which ignored the interests of the plebeian class could be abrogated. This was the tribunician power of *cessio*, quashing legislative enactments. There therefore emerges a popular right to veto duly enacted legislation deemed contrary to the popular interest.

Although the tribunes of the people, the *tribuni plebis*, had this right of veto, they did not have any right to initiate legislation. However, within a generation of their introduction, meetings of the plebs were taking place, in all probability to inform the tribunes of what was deemed to be the popular interest. From 471 BC, these meetings appear to have acquired a formal recognition in that the plebeian body becomes known as the Council of the Plebs, the *concilium plebis*. It is believed that this body was composed of the plebeian members of the *comitia tributa*, meeting apart from the patricians. In other words, it was based on the newer, geographical tribal divisions of the population.[11] This body was later to have the power of passing laws, *plebiscita*, binding not only upon the plebs but the whole Roman population, but that development lay in the future.

What is however fairly clear is that the grievances of the general population against the patrician hierarchy were not completely assuaged. The next episode in this rivalry involved a second secession of the plebs, but is presented by the Roman historians as being the result of concerted action rather than internal discord. It concerns the production in 450 BC of the first Roman legal text of importance, the XII Tables.

According to the tradition recounted by the historians, the XII Tables were the result of a commission of ten men, the *decemviri*, who were appointed to produce a written code of law for the Roman people. It is said they carried out a survey of the laws of Rome's neighbours and of states further afield in the Mediterranean world in order to select what was best in legal practice for the governance of the Roman people. It is also claimed that they were particularly influenced by the Athenian laws attributed to Solon. While it is probably the case that the Romans were influenced by the Greek practice of writing down their laws, a practice of which Rome would have become aware through contact with the Greek settlements in southern Italy, it is almost certainly the case that the laws in the XII Tables are a reduction to writing of Rome's own customs. What was novel was not their substance but their written form.

This gives rise to the question of why at this time the laws were reduced to writing. Although no firm answer can be given, it is widely suspected that the move was connected with popular discontent concerning knowledge of the laws and customs. If the laws were known only to a hierarchical caste, then the ordinary people were at an obvious disadvantage, particularly newcomers to the citizenship.[12] The XII Tables are therefore most likely to have been a reduction of the existing customs to writing in response to popular demand.

The Tables were produced in two stages. The original commission of ten produced ten tables, but their work was regarded as incomplete and also perhaps biased in that all ten commissioners were patricians. Another commission of ten in the following year added a further two tables bringing the number up to twelve. Some of these commissioners were plebeian, and some of the customs contained in these additions resulted in the second secession. One of the main bones of contention was the rule that there should be no intermarriage between patricians and plebeians, thus shutting the door on social advancement through matrimony. The second secession of the plebs led to reversal of this rule by the *lex Canuleia* of 445.

The XII Tables mark a significant moment in the development of civil law in that there emerges for the first time that hallmark of civil law systems, a written text, upon which legal and juristic discussion and interpretation would in future focus. However primitive some of its provisions, its significance for subsequent legal development is undiminished.

That there was considerable internal disquiet around the time of the production of the XII Tables cannot be doubted. During the years when the *decemviri* worked on them, the normal constitution was in suspense, to be restored in 449. However, it had become obvious that two magistrates could not, unaided, perform all the executive functions at Rome. Therefore, in 446, new magistrates were appointed to assist the consuls, particularly in regard to their financial responsibilities. These were the quaestors, whose office was to become regarded as the first rung on the ladder of a magisterial career, even giving the holder a seat in senate.[13] Three years later, in 443, censors were appointed to take from the consuls the task of carrying out the five-yearly census of the citizens, to place them in their appropriate classes and tribes for membership of the assemblies and to admit those qualified to membership of the senate. The censors held office only for the months in which they performed their task and were usually very senior and respected statesmen. They were also custodians in their work of the values of the Romans, in that as well as promoting citizens to the senate, they could also demote them and place a black mark, the *nota censoria*, against the name of those who by their conduct had rendered themselves unfit to hold public office. The office of censor, however, recognizes, like the *lex Canuleia*, that the class system of Rome at that time was not to be static. There was to be the opportunity for upward mobility and downward decline within political society, and the task of judging merit was taken from the patrician consuls.

It is also significant that previous to the creation of the censorship, a development took place which in effect allowed plebeians to exercise consular power without occupying an office reserved for patricians. Instead of appointing two consuls, the State was instead led by military tribunes with consular power, sometimes three, four or even six in number. This arrangement was followed with considerable regularity from 444 right through to the passing of the *lex Licinia Sextia* in 367 which reformed the magisterial structure.

Before that time, however, Rome experienced a period of intermittent but protracted war, most notably against Fidenae from 437-426 and against her neighbour Veii from 406-396. This latter engagement took the form of a lengthy siege of Veii requiring an increase in Rome's military resources, so that the number of cavalry centuries in the *comitia centuriata* was increased to eighteen and the infantry was also expanded by recruiting persons who would previously have been *infra classem*. Thus, membership of the *comitia centuriata* was widened and social divisions diminished.

However, following the final capture of Veii, Rome was to suffer one of the most appalling disasters in her history. In 390, the city was sacked by the Gauls, a Celtic tribe who had moved south through the valleys of the Apennines, and even the Capitol was burned. Following this catastrophe, Rome had to make a fresh start, and undoubtedly the needs of adversity produced a unity among the population. The new arrangements were to serve Rome well for several centuries during which she not only recovered but proceeded to become the master of south and central Italy and from there of the Mediterranean and parts of northern Europe.

3 The Constitution of the Later Republic

The greatest changes which took place in the year 367 concerned the structure of the magistracy. By the *lex Licinia Sextiae*, henceforth one of the consuls was always to be a plebeian. This was a significant step in unifying the Roman people. Moreover, new magisterial offices were created in the shape of the praetorship and curule aedileship.[14] Like all the lesser magistrates, these had *imperium*, but were allotted a particular sphere in which to exercise it, namely their province. The consuls has full *imperium* in all areas and their acts could not be vetoed by the lesser magistrates while the acts of the lesser magistrates were subject to the consular *intercessio*. The praetor's province was to be in charge of civil jurisdiction within the city, including the administration of justice, so that this magistrate is of particular importance to Roman legal development. The curule aedile was a new office. Previously, there had been aediles who were plebeian magistrates assisting the tribunes much as the quaestors assisted the consuls. The new curule aediles were however elected by the entire *comitia tributa* and were entrusted with the administration of public roads and transport and the running of the markets, so that they played a significant role in the development of the law relating to sales. Eventually, there was to develop a staged magisterial career, the *cursus honorum*, by which those aspiring to state office progressed from being quaestors through the three chief magistracies in turn - aedileship, praetorship, consulship - with minimum ages applicable to each office and minimum time periods between the enjoyment of each.[15]

The *cursus honorum* was so called because each magistracy was regarded as an honour, *honos*. This word came to bear considerable legal significance through the work of the praetor and to a lesser extent the curule aedile. When a magistrate stood for office, it was customary for him to outline in a sort of manifesto the policies that he would follow during his year in power. On election, the successful candidate would then issue an edict directing in effect that those policies be now followed by those under his authority. In the case of the praetor, this edict would describe the situations in which the praetor intended to allow legal actions during the coming year. He had no power to alter the law or to contravene it, but he could supplement it by exercise of his magisterial power. Thus, he could indicate circumstances in which actions allowed by law would not actually be given because to do so would be inequitable; he could describe circumstances in which the law did not intervene but in which the underlying principles made it fair to provide a remedy or in which an existing remedy required extension to meet the justice of the case. He could not alter the law of the citizens, the *ius civile* or civil law, but he could grant remedies according to this law, *secundum legem*, or in situations going beyond its strict letter, *praeter legem*. He could not go against it, *contra legem*. Although his extensions did not amount to enactments of the people, such as *leges* or *plebiscita*, he acted on the authority of the people in that he was their elected officer. The rules which therefore emanated from his activities were regarded as a source of law, albeit a different type of law from that to be found in the XII Tables and the enactments. This law was called the *ius honorarium*, because it was founded upon the power of a magistrate. The curule aediles also issued an annual edict which did much to develop the law relating to sales in the market place.

Like the consulship, the office of praetor was held on an annual basis. It would obviously be very inconvenient if each incoming praetor engaged in a total *volte face* regarding the policies he intended pursuing. Somewhat inevitably, the incoming praetors retained much of the substance of the edicts of their predecessors when issuing their own. Thus, the edict of the praetor achieved a large measure of stability, developing as one incumbent gave way to the next. The provisions of the edict were in large measure handed on from one praetor to another, so that the edict became known as the *edictum tralaticium*, the traditional edict, or even *edictum perpetuum*, the perpetual edict.[16] Again, the same was true of the aedilician edict.

The praetor was to play a highly significant role in the development of the civil law, *ius civile*, to meet the needs of the citizens of Rome as the city rebuilt itself, psychologically as well as physically, after the destruction wrought by the Gauls. Part of the new strategy for increased security involved building up links, commercial as well as military, with surrounding areas, and during the remainder of the fourth century, Rome became a major player on the central and southern Italian stage. This involved her in forging alliances against powers outside of Italy altogether, including against Carthage, one of the greatest Mediterranean powers at that time. It was as a consequence of the wars which Rome began to fight against Carthage during the third century that she emerged as a Mediterranean and not just an Italian power. It was also as a result of these Punic Wars that Rome acquired her first provinces outside the Italian mainland, namely Sicily and Sardinia.[17]

The century following the rebuilding of Rome after the sack by the Gauls saw the emergence of Rome as an important commercial centre. This meant that substantial numbers of foreigners came to the city to trade, which set a challenge for the city's developing legal system. Hitherto, Rome had relied in the main upon treaty relations with other cities to regulate trade and commercial contacts. Thus, for instance, during the fifth century, Rome had been involved as a partner in the formation of a federation of Latin cities, the citizens of which enjoyed very full citizen rights in each others' cities when visiting or even staying there to trade. This had perhaps led to the recognition that the laws of other cities were in part similar to those of Rome, which may have inspired the comparative study of other legal orders which tradition claims preceded the publication of the XII Tables. Regardless of the historicity of that account, it is known that the Romans recognized that there were some laws which were apparently common to all societies and not peculiar to a particular social group. Every society, the jurists of later ages were to write, were governed partly by laws which were peculiarly their own and partly by laws which were common to all mankind. These latter laws they termed the law of the nations, *ius gentium*.

This concept reinforces the notion mentioned earlier that law, in the sense of *ius*, that which is right or just, is not something which a particular social group creates for itself. Rather it pre-exists the group's existence and the group's own legislative enactments must conform to this higher law in order to be valid. The concept of the *ius gentium* emphasizes this approach. Eventually, under the influence of Greek philosophy, the Romans would also identify a law of nature, which nature teaches all animals, the *ius naturale*, a natural order in which human societies have a share but which they either cannot or should not contravene. The original meaning of *ius gentium* has much the same implications. The need for the senate's grant of the *auctoritas patrum* for enactments, and the activities of the praetor in developing his supplemental *ius honorarium*, both point in the same direction, the need for enacted law to conform to an overarching concept of what is just and right.

With the influx of foreigners to Rome during the third century, it was not possible to limit rights to trade to those who came from cities with which Rome enjoyed a special treaty relationship. Accordingly, some provision had to be made for accommodating their legal needs. This was achieved in 242 with the creation of a second praetor, whose province would be legal relations between citizens and foreigners, or between foreigners resident at Rome. Such relationships were outside the provisions of the civil law, so they came to be regulated under the terms of the edict issued by this second praetor. His province of activity was demarcated from that of the older praetorian office in that the original praetor now came to be called the urban praetor, *praetor urbanus*, while the new praetor was called the peregrine praetor, *praetor peregrinus*. This title derived from the Roman term for a foreigner, peregrine, one who has come across the fields, *per agros*.[18] Some believe that the activities of this praetor in developing a system of law applicable to cases involving a foreign element influenced quite substantially the subsequent development of the law of actions between citizens as regulated by the urban praetor.[19]

Both praetors were elected annually, and a further two were created to govern the provinces of Sicily and Sardinia in 227. The number was increased to six in 197 when a further two praetorships were created to govern the two new provinces in Spain. All six were elected annually, the province of each being determined after their election by drawing lots.

One further change in the republican constitution needs to be discussed before moving on to consider the interpretation and application of the law. That is the role of the *concilium plebis* in legislation. It is clear that by the year 287 BC, the plebeian assembly had acquired the right to legislate for the whole citizenship, and not just for the plebs. Three enactments are mentioned with regard to this development: the *lex Valeria Horatia* of 449; the *lex Publilia Philonis* of 339, and the *lex Hortensia* of 287. The prevailing modern view is that these enactments gradually increased the powers of the assembly. Before 449, it could only elect the tribunes and pass laws binding on the plebs, but in 449 it was enacted that *plebiscita* would bind the whole citizen population provided their terms were approved by the senate. This is an interesting view because it extends senatorial control over the justice of enactments of the whole people to a control over the justice and apparently the policy of enactments made by the commons. It also suggests that the senate was now seen to be the body representative of the patricians, who could introduce legislative proposals into the assemblies through their magistrates, but were content to allow the plebs to introduce proposals through their magistrates in their own assembly subject to a senatorial right of veto which appears to mirror the tribunician veto in the patrician-dominated bodies. Thereafter, in 339, the senate reduced this requirement to endorsing *plebiscita* introduced into the council by plebeian officials, in that other magistrates would have discussed their proposals with the senate beforehand. In 287, the final restriction was apparently removed and the *concilium plebis* emerges as a full-blown legislature of the Roman people at a time when internal divisions among the citizens had become of far less significance when compared with the distinction between citizens and foreigners.

4 Application and Interpretation of the Law

When the senate considered whether an enacted law should receive the *auctoritas patrum*, according to what has been said above, it was in fact considering whether the *lex* conformed to the requirements of *ius*, was law in the sense of what is right and just. It may therefore be asked by what means this would be established.

Undoubtedly, on occasion, it would be a question of whether the statute offended against the age-old custom of the ancestors, the *mores maiorum*. Innovative laws, however, would be a different matter. Some means of testing whether what was proposed was pleasing to the gods or not was required, as was also needed for every public act from the appointment of a magistrate to the declaration war. In each case, it was customary to take the auspices, to see whether or not these outward and visible signs of the gods' wishes were favourable to what was proposed. At Rome, this was primarily done by observing the flight of birds.

In essence, the question was one of whether proposed human activity conformed to the divine will. To answer the question, some method was needed by which communication between the divine and the human could be achieved. The creation of such lines of communication was the responsibility of priests, called in Latin *pontifices* which means literally bridge builders. From regal times there had existed at Rome a college of pontiffs headed by the Pontifex Maximus. Originally, this body had the responsibility of interpreting the law, so as to ensure that its interpretation was in conformity with the will of the gods and therefore truly *ius*, that is just. The college was, until the end of the fourth century BC, composed entirely of patricians.

Again, therefore one encounters a patrician monopoly, this time not of executive government or of law-making, but of legal interpretation. Nevertheless, this gave the patrician pontiffs much power. To break that stranglehold, in 304 according to tradition, one Gnaeus Flavius published the manuscript held by his master, the former censor Appius Claudius, containing the pontifical secrets regarding the actions which might be brought at law. The text became known as the *ius Flavianum*, and it is widely believed that Appius Claudius may have encouraged his secretary's leaking of the document. The upshot was clear and consonant with other developments in that, in 300, by the *lex Ogulnia*, plebs became admissible to the college of pontiffs.

Within a half century, Rome had acquired its first plebeian Pontifex Maximus, one Tiberius Coruncanius who had previously been consul in 280. He appears to have gone yet further in popularizing legal knowledge, for the second century AD jurist Pomponius records that Coruncanius was the first to teach law publicly at Rome and to offer his services as a legal adviser. Within a century, the provision of juristic advice would appear to have been completely severed from the control of the pontiffs when Servius Aelius produced a legal commentary called the *Tripertita*, which dealt systematically in its three parts with the law of the XII Tables, interpretations of it and the bringing of actions at law. This is credited with being the first treatise on the civil law.

During the second century BC, the juristic interpretation of law continued apace. The jurists of this period were known to their successors as the *veteres*, and it was under their influence that the four distinctive juristic functions of giving advice, drafting forms and documents, and assisting in litigation - *respondere*, *cavere*, *scribere* and *agere* - developed.[20] Of these, the first mentioned was by far the most important. Those who had become learned in the law, *jurisprudentes*, could be called upon to give advice in a number of contexts. Private clients could approach them as they would a modern lawyer for advice in relation to a dispute or with regard to the conduct of a legal transaction. As well as giving advice, the jurist might also concoct the appropriate verbal formula for the party to use in the transaction in question, verbal forms being very important in Roman legal affairs at this time. This is what is meant by *cavere*. The jurist might also be called upon to draft a written document to evidence a legal transaction, what is meant by *scribere*. Finally, he might be asked to assist the client in the process of litigation, but not usually as an advocate. Those skilled in the art of rhetoric would act as advocates in litigation and would not normally be skilled lawyers. Instead, the jurists would be on hand to see that the forms of litigation were observed properly and in order, what is meant by *agere*.

Central to all these tasks however was *respondere*, the giving of advice, and this was not always or even in the main to private clients. Not only were advocates in ancient Rome not usually trained lawyers, neither were judges or magistrates. Magistrates, such as the praetor, were politicians and statesmen not professional practitioners, although some might have legal knowledge. The vast majority however did not and therefore stood in need of legal advice when framing their edicts and performing other law-related tasks. Thus, jurists could be called upon to advise praetors and aediles on the content of their edicts, particularly with regard to innovations. Moreover, although litigation in republican Rome commenced before the praetor, the praetor was not a judge in the sense of being one who decides questions of law or of fact. Instead, the work of the praetor was more in the nature of settling the pleadings of the parties and identifying what matters were actually in dispute between them. Once, it was clear what issues were actually in dispute between the parties, the function of the praetor was then to assist them in reconciling their differences. This he would do by asking them to choose a person acceptable to both of them to settle the matters in dispute. They would choose who was to act as the judge, *iudex*, to settle their differences. If they could not suggest a name, the praetor would ask them choose one from his *album*, white book, although the choice remained theirs. They would then swear an oath to abide by the decision of their chosen judge, so that the judge's decision was binding upon them by virtue of their agreement and not by public authority. The praetor would then remit the case to the judge to hear the arguments, assemble the evidence and decide the issues. The judge again would not generally have any legal knowledge; he would more likely have been chosen for his probity and common sense.

At both stages of this procedure, jurists could be called upon to advise. Thus, the praetor might wish to know whether in these circumstances he should give an action to the plaintiff or what defences on the part of the defendant the judge should properly take into account. He might require advice as to whether an action available by law in similar circumstances should be extended to cover the instant case or whether to do so would be contrary to law. The judge, when the case was remitted to him, might have points of law as well as of fact to decide and to decide points of law he would undoubtedly request the assistance of a jurist. Likewise questions concerning the admissibility of certain forms of evidence, the competence or compellability of witnesses, the propriety of transactional forms which the parties had utilized in property transfers and the like, would all require the judge to seek juristic guidance.

One other major activity of the jurists deserves mention and that is education. As with other professions, it was understood that they would admit into their presence young men desirous of learning the law and who would benefit by being present at their consultations. Jurisprudence was a gentlemanly pursuit, and the jurists did not charge for their services. Their skills were handed on to their successors by this process of informal education. Alongside this activity, jurists began to write treatises on the law. Following the work of Sextus Aelius at the start of the second century, legal literature began to flourish. Its progress was not unconnected with the increase of Greek influence at Rome and in particular the vogue for Greek philosophy, including the systematic example of Aristotle. During the second century, juristic works were composed by Marcus Porcius Cato and his son of the same name, and then in the second half of the century by three of the republic's most famous jurists, all of whom wrote treatises discussing the law rather than merely compiling enactments and interpretations. They were Manlius Manilius, Marcus Junius Brutus and Publius Mucius Scaevola, whom Pomponius esteemed as a group to be the founders of the civil law. Brutus' work took the form of a dialogue with his son, a sure sign of Greek philosophical influence, but the first really great work of Roman jurisprudence was that of Quintus Mucius Scaevola, son of Publius, who wrote the first systematic treatise on the civil law in eighteen books, identifying institutions and dividing them up into types, *genera*.[21]

With his work, juristic study of the civil law emerges as a science. It is said that he once rebuked a young advocate for his lack of knowledge of the law. The young man responded by becoming a legal scholar in his own right. He was Servius Sulpicius Rufus, the first to attempt a commentary on the praetor's edict. He wrote over 180 books on the law, including understandably some corrections to the works of Q. Mucius. The first full commentary on the praetorian edict was written in the closing decades of the republic by Rufus' pupil, A. Ofilius.

5 Conclusion

By the end of the last century of the republic, Roman law had developed many of the features which remain hallmarks of the civil law systems. In legislation, it had effectively distinguished at a very early date the different roles of those who initiate, deliberate and decide upon legislative enactments. It had also produced a form of legislative scrutiny to ensure that enactments did not offend against fundamental principles of the community's life as well as procedures for vetoing legislative enactments which were contrary to the popular will. In the magisterial edicts, there had emerged a responsible and accountable method of shaping the law to meet the needs of a changing society within the arena of litigation, and the peregrine praetor had devised procedures for allowing cases with a foreign element to be heard at Rome. Finally, in the systematic treatment of the law by jurists, Roman law began to be seen as a system, capable of rational and scientific presentation. The jurists also commenced that important relationship between legal learning, practice and education which was to prove of lasting importance in the future of civil law.

Moreover, despite the severance of law from formal religion with the taking over of interpretation by the jurists from the pontiffs, the idea that human law was only a manifestation of an immutable, higher concept of right or justice was not lost. Jurisprudence remained, as Ulpian was later to write in the third century AD, the science of the just and the unjust, the knowledge of things human and divine.[22]

Notes

[1] Until the early nineteenth century, only Justinian's compilations were thought to have survived, Gaius' *Institutes* being known to have existed but no text of them

having survived in anything like a complete form. In 1816, the German scholar Niebuhr discovered an almost complete text in the cathedral library at Verona in Italy, where it had survived in the form of a palimpsest, that is a manuscript which had been reused, another text having been written over the original. Subsequently, further fragments were found buried in the sands of Egypt in the 1930s, which fragments supplied some of the deficiencies of the Veronese palimpsest.

[2] The text with which Roman legal history ends in the ancient world is the *Corpus Iuris Civilis* of Justinian.

[3] The traditional list of the kings of Rome reads as follows: Romulus, Numa Pompilius, Tullus Hostilius, Ancus Martius, Tarquinius Priscus, Servius Tullius and Tarquinius Superbus.

[4] A modern comparison would be the need for a private act of parliament to secure a divorce *a vinculo matrimonio* in England and Wales prior to 1857.

[5] There is a division of opinion about the original number and how they were expanded. Some believe that there were originally fifteen rural tribes, with two being added in 495 BC. Some believe there to have been sixteen originally with only one being added in 495. In any event, it is known that there were twenty-one tribes in all by that date and that fourteen more were added as Rome's influence in Italy and the size of the citizen body increased between 387 and 241 BC. The total number did not increase thereafter, but stayed at four urban and thirty-one rural.

[6] Originally they were called praetors, but this name was given after 367 BC to the magistrate who administered justice at Rome, when the chief magistrates became known as consuls. To avoid confusion, the post-367 titles are here used throughout.

[7] See H.F. Jolowicz and B. Nicholas, *An Historical Introduction to the Study of Roman Law* (3rd Ed.; Cambridge, 1972), p. 31.

[8] The senior senator always spoke first, a precedent which gave the *princeps* pre-eminence in the imperial period.

[9] In this is seen the origin of bill procedure with its three readings, one to publish a proposed change, one to discuss it and one to vote upon it.

[10] In 339 BC, by the *lex Publilia Philonis*.

[11] There is a difference of opinion regarding the chronology of these developments. Some argue that the *concilium plebis* antedated the *comitia tributa*, the latter developing out of the former: see E.S. Staveley, *Greek and Roman Voting Assemblies and Elections* (London, 1972), 129 ff. Some indeed believe that both the *comitia tributa* and the *comitia centuriata* were post-Regal constitutional developments.

[12] At least one and possibly two new tribes were said to have been added to the population in 495. While the original immigrants might have been prepared to settle for a position of relative disadvantage with regard to knowledge of the laws, those born at Rome and who had now reached maturity were less likely to do so.

[13] From the time of Sulla (81-79 BC).

---

[14] It should be remembered that until 367, the chief magistrates had borne the name of praetor. These now became the consuls, while the term praetor was applied to a lesser magistracy.

[15] The minimum ages arose from a law passed by L. Villius in 180 BC, although the establishment of the *cursus honorum* itself is attributed to an earlier unattested law of 197. See M. Crawford, *The Roman Republic* (Glasgow, 1978), 76 ff.

[16] This phrase was to acquire another meaning after the edict was codified by Salvius Julianus on the instructions of the emperor Hadrian. See below, pp. 41 ff.

[17] The first, second and third Punic Wars were fought between 264-241, 218-201 and 149-146 BC respectively. Sicily and Sardinia became provinces in 227 BC.

[18] It is the root of the modern word *pilgrim* in English, *pélérin* in French, *pererin* in Welsh. The original Latin word for a foreigner, *hostis*, came to mean enemy; the original made no distinction between friendly and unfriendly foreigners, but the assumption about them all is clear.

[19] For more on this see chapter 13.

[20] See Cicero, *De Or.* I. 48. 212; *Pro Mur.* IX. 19.

[21] See for instance Gaius, *Institutes*, I. 188, where five kinds of *tutela*, that is guardianship, are distinguished.

[22] See Justinian, *Inst.* I. 1. 1, and Digest I. 1. 10.

2 The Principate

1 The End of the Republic

The history of the last century of the Roman republic is basically one of the steady decline of the institutions of republican government. The authority of the magistracies and the assemblies in particular diminished quite spectacularly so that on more than one occasion, most notably under Marius, Sulla and Julius Caesar, Rome seemed poised to become a dictatorship.

There was indeed provision within the republican constitution for a dictator to be appointed. Contradictory as this may appear, the availability of dictatorship in an emergency had been a feature of republican government from its early years, but it was a dictatorship defined by the constitution, what might be termed a constitutionally-limited dictatorship. This form of dictatorship could be resorted to in an emergency where the sharing of power by two consuls was not thought to be in the best interests of the community. It was open in such circumstances for a dictator to be appointed to hold office for six months. Although he could be re-appointed, his powers while unlimited in scope were curtailed in terms of their duration. This was not the sort of dictatorship which was emerging at Rome in the last century BC.

The cause of the decline in the republican institutions is not difficult to understand. The mechanisms of republican government had been developed to serve the needs of a city state, all of whose citizens were normally resident within a relatively small radius. As a result of the expansion of Roman rule and influence, first large portions of Italy and later great sections of the Mediterranean lands and the countries of northern Europe had fallen under Roman hegemony. Strictly speaking, the consuls as chief magistrates should govern the whole area of Roman influence. In practice this was an impossibility in an age in which overland communications were necessarily slow and sea communication, while speedier, subject to the vicissitudes of the weather.

The expedient which Rome adopted to overcome the problem of how to govern the empire it was acquiring was to harness the abilities of those men who had already proved their worth in service of the state at home. Thus, those who had already held the chief magistracies at Rome would be granted pro-consular power to govern a particular part of the empire, the province in which they would exercise their *imperium*. This power would be granted for only a fixed period after which the pro-consul would be expected to account for his governance at Rome. Pro-consular power included command of the army in the province as well as governmental functions relating to keeping order and encouraging trade.

There had developed therefore during the second century BC a clearly defined career in public life at Rome. The aspiring statesman would seek to hold in turn the main magistracies at home, beginning with the office of quaestor, and progressing through being aedile and then praetor to the consulship. This was the so-called *cursus honorum*. All former magistrates became members of the senate and their families thereafter would be expected to follow their forebears into public service. After the consulship, distinguished elder statesmen could aspire to be censors and there was also the honorary position of Pontifex Maximus. However, the coming of empire opened up new opportunities which offered in terms of glory and material rewards much more than a successful political career at home. A proconsul who waged successful wars of conquest on the boundaries of the empire would win not only the gratitude of his native city but also the wealth that would flow from the spoils of war and the immense political influence that would result from returning home with a conquering army which, when disbanded, would form rather more than the nucleus of popular support.

Political progress at home was relatively smooth for the aspiring statesman while the chief magistracies remained at two each in number. Each year the two aediles could look forward in due course to becoming praetors, and the outgoing praetors could expect in the fullness of time to become consuls. However, when the number of praetors was increased to four in 227 and then to six in 197, this meant that for the first time there was likely to be intense competition in rising to the highest rung of the domestic political ladder, the consulship. Aspiring statesmen were rapidly converted into ambitious politicians. To secure election required acquisition of sufficient support in the popular assemblies and very soon the necessary popularity was being in effect purchased by the candidates through the provision of games and circuses for the people. These became more and more lavish as competition grew keener, and more and more expensive for the candidates. A political career had become a financially hazardous undertaking.

Given that members of the senatorial class were not permitted to engage in trade, a familiar chasm opened between the professional, land-owning political class and businessmen. Although the latter would often have much larger fortunes than their senatorial brethren, they would be content with the social status of *equites*. They would not aspire to political office and the senate. On the other hand, their financial support might well be crucial to a political candidate so that the *equites* could wield immense influence behind the scenes. Moreover, the need for money caused many senators to seek ways of circumventing their exclusion from commerce in order to enhance their own fortunes, or else they would have to resort to borrowing from their wealthier but socially inferior fellow citizens.

The upshot was that it cost a lot of money to obtain political office of any sort, for the people expected lavish expenditure to obtain their support. This expenditure in turn could be undertaken in the belief that the expense would eventually be recouped by making a fortune for oneself and one's supporters when governing a province. Many governors became rapacious, resorting to unlawful methods to make money while running provinces. Many of the political trials of the last century of the republic bear witness to this phenomenon.[1] It was even said that a governor needed to make three fortunes: one to pay his electoral expenses; one to cover the costs of securing his acquittal on the inevitable charges of extortion, and one to enjoy in his retirement.[2]

Attempts were made during the second century BC to regulate the *cursus honorum* so as to alleviate the problems of competition. As well as laws passed against bribery, minimum ages were enacted for the chief magistracies - 36 for aedile, 39 for praetor, 42 for consul - together with a rule that one could not progress from one rung to the next without an interval of two years.[3] It was also forbidden to be consul on more than one occasion, but exceptions were made usually for the most powerful of persons. In any event, those who had enjoyed the greatest successes and made therefore the largest fortunes during their tenure of a provincial proconsulship would have the wealth and influence at their disposal to promote the careers of their family, friends and supporters, so that they could exercise great power without the need of holding office themselves. Thus, political power was separated from magisterial office.

The expansion of empire also wrought changes with regard to the citizenship and the popular assemblies. Rome was extremely jealous with regard to the grant of citizen status. Some colonies established in Italy and other lands might be granted the right of citizenship, but it was more common for such colonies to be given the more limited right of Latinity, which allowed their inhabitants to trade with the Romans using the contractual forms of the Roman civil law but did not extend to other civic rights. Foreigners generally had to proceed while at Rome under the provisions of the *ius gentium* as set out in the edict of the peregrine praetor. In the provinces, the provincial governors also had authority to issue an edict, and justice was administered to the inhabitants in their relations with the occupying power according to the terms of this document. The rights given, while perhaps based on the law of the citizens, fell far short of granting the provincials citizen rights. Individuals might be granted Latin or citizen rights as a special favour or in reward for services rendered to the Roman people.[4]

It was in the neighbouring territories of Italy that this jealous refusal to extend the citizenship first gave rise to discontent and insurrection. The Social War of 91-88 BC ended with the Romans having to concede citizenship to all the inhabitants of Italy south of the River Po, a grudging grant forced from a far from gracious giver. However, the grant necessarily complicated the composition of the popular assemblies at Rome. All the new citizens had to be placed in tribes for the purposes of their voting in the *comitia* and the *concilium plebis*. Realistically, moreover, the citizens who were not resident in the city were not in practice going to be involved in electing the magistrates or passing legislation. In effect, therefore, it was the city mob which had to have its support bought with games and bribes. The popular assemblies were no longer representative of the citizenship.

This increased in turn the influence of the senate, for new men who came to Rome with the wealth to further political ambitions would, if successful in reaching even the first rung on the magisterial ladder, become members of the senate. The senate began to become more representative of the citizenship geographically than were the popular assemblies, albeit once more it was the political upper class which was represented there. During the last century BC, legislative proposals placed before the senate appear to have acquired the status of law once approved by that body without reference to the *comitia*, and Cicero certainly regarded enacted laws as capable of being made by either the *comitia*, the *concilium plebis* or the senate. One wonders whether the absence of a tribunician veto was now taken as sufficient to indicate popular approval.[5] If that was so, it was to be a valuable precedent.

The senate was not, however, strong enough a body to withstand the growing power of the victorious generals returning from their wars of conquest with plentiful political and if necessary military support at their backs. One by one, characters such as Marius, Sulla, Pompey and Julius Caesar came to enjoy virtually unrivalled power within the state. One by one, they fell from that power through intrigue, conspiracy and the assassin's knife rather than through the strength of the republican forms of government. Intermittent civil war throughout the last half century of the republic regularly threatened the security of the Roman state. When after the assassination of Julius Caesar and after defeating the forces of his main rival Marcus Antonius, Octavius Caesar assumed supreme power at Rome, the task before him was as obvious as it was difficult, namely to restore stable government to the city and its empire. The policy by which he achieved this was subtly presented to appeal to the conservative instincts of the Romans as the restoration of the republic.

2 Augustus and the Foundation of Imperial Government

The year 27 BC is regarded as ending the period of republican government at Rome and marking the start of the reign of Rome's first emperor, Octavius Caesar, better known by the title awarded him of Augustus.[6] Augustus' policy was to present himself as first citizen, a first among equals and a father to his people, rather than as a kingly monarch, for the Romans' detestation of monarchy, rooted in their pride in the institutions of the republic, was famous. Accordingly, he presented his style of government as a restoration of the republic, and the propaganda description is not without foundation. Augustus assumed certain offices, all of which had existed during the republic, but which by being combined in one person gave that person supreme power. Thus, he was given tribunician power for life. This meant that he could intervene to protect any citizen and legitimately call upon the people to support him in this, and also that he could veto the enactments of any assembly of the people as well as having himself the right to convene the *comitia tributa* and the *concilium plebis* and present legislative proposals to them. He could also convene the senate. At Rome, he was periodically elected consul, which gave him the right to quash the acts of any other magistrate and to convene the senate and the *comitia centuriata*, although he appears not to have wished to hold the consulship permanently, trusting rather to his influence in assuring the election to that office of candidates favourable to his policies. Outside of Rome, he was given proconsular power for life, amounting to a full grant of *imperium* in the provinces. Where other proconsuls actually governed those provinces, his power was greater and was described as *maius imperium*. The provinces of the empire were divided into two broad categories, senatorial and Augustan. Proconsuls went as governors to the former; the latter were governed by delegates of the emperor, *legati*. His proconsular power was effective within the city also. The same powers were allowed his successors, and expressly conferred on Vespasian in 69 by senatorial decree, the *lex de imperio Vespasiani*.

Effectively, Augustus therefore had in his magisterial roles both the legislative initiative and the tribunician power of popular veto. The deliberative phase belonged to the senate. Here, he was from the first regarded as *princeps senatus*, again a role recognized in the republic. The *princeps senatus* was always called upon to speak first in any discussion of legislative proposals or on the election of officers. Accordingly, the imperial will would be made clear before any other senator spoke. In effect, Augustus would appear to dominate the senate by his influence, *auctoritas*, rather than by his power, thus again preserving the forms and theories of the republic but encasing within them the powers of an absolute monarch.[7]

In reality, the senate was completely subservient to the imperial will and became a rubber-stamp for imperial initiatives. If the emperor proposed a project, the remaining speeches in the senate were bound to be in favour if any were made at all. Those made were probably aimed more at ingratiating the speaker with the ruler than with advancing policy. Gradually, it even became customary for the emperor to send a representative to the senate to read to the assembled senators his speech, and some laws were actually referred to as being based on that speech, *oratio*, rather than upon the senate's advice let alone the popular vote. The assemblies themselves met less and less often until they went out of existence. In as much as the first citizen spoke for all the citizens as tribune, if he did not veto a law, then the people must wish it. Therefore the imperial and the popular will were equated and it came to be said that what was pleasing to the first citizen had the force of an enacted law, *quod principi placuit legis habet vigorem*. The senate's advice indicated that it was not contrary to *ius*.

The senate itself was undergoing a profound change regarding its composition. As Roman citizenship came to be extended to communities rather than just individuals in various parts of the empire, so loyal servants of the emperor as much as of Rome (not that any such distinction was admitted) were rewarded with seats in the senate. In the republic, admission to the senate was a matter for the censors, and so it remained in theory during the first century of the Principate, although in practice it was of course an imperial gift. Only those who had held magistracies were admitted unless co-opted, and imperial permission was needed to stand for election to the magistracies. Augustus' successor, Tiberius (14-37 AD) removed magisterial elections from the *comitiae* to the senate, and, at the end of the first century AD, the emperor Domitian (81-96) neatly united theory and practice by having himself appointed a permanent censor, so that senate membership was lawfully under his control. Domitian was the last of the three Flavian emperors, his father, Vespasian (69-79), and his brother, Titus (79-81) being the other two. During their reigns, the composition of the senate became markedly provincial, Italians making up for the first time less than half the number. Under Trajan (98-117) and Hadrian (117-138), there was a steady influx of Spaniards and then of Africans, with only some thirty senators left with Roman republican pedigrees. By the end of the second century, during the reign of Septimius Severus (193-211), the senate was largely recruited from equestrian families in the provinces, with few senatorial families reaching back more than two generations. The senate had however become representative of the upper classes of the empire rather than of the city or even Italy. That the senate represented the empire rather than just Rome or Italy by the start of the third century was fitting also in that it was in 212 AD that the emperor Caracalla extended Roman citizenship to the free inhabitants of the whole empire.

The senate had begun its life as the advisory council of the Roman kings, and had continued in that role with regard to the consuls under the republic. Augustus had increased its membership from 300 to 600, but, although it progressed to be a representative assembly with law-making powers, albeit under imperial control, it was no longer the body to which the ruler turned for advice. In this regard it was succeeded by the emperor's own *consilium*, a body composed entirely of imperial appointees upon whose loyalty and wisdom the *princeps* felt he could rely. Just as the emperor's private *consilium* replaced the advisory role of the senate, so also there developed an imperial civil service which gradually ousted the magistrates with regard to their executive functions. The main imperial offices were the prefectures, of which the most important was the post of praetorian prefect, the head in effect of the imperial civil service. In charge of the city of Rome was the *praefectus urbis*, while police and emergency services - such as firefighting - were in the charge of the *praefectus vigilum*. Supply of food, especially corn, to the city was also of constant importance and a source of some anxiety; this was the province of the *praefectus annonae*. These officials gradually assumed the importance which the republican magistracies had once enjoyed, but they were all filled by imperial nomination and held at the emperor's pleasure. By the time of the Severan dynasty (193-235), it was not uncommon for leading jurists to occupy these high positions in the imperial service; indeed, the famous jurists Papinian and Ulpian both held the praetorian prefecture - and ultimately paid for the honour with their lives.

As well as the prefects, jurists also came to occupy some of the important secretaryships within the imperial service. Amongst the most important of these was the office of *magister a rationibus*, an accountancy post which dealt with the affairs of the imperial purse or *fiscus*. Under the republic, Rome's public finances, the *aerarium*, had been under the control of the senate in the care of the quaestors. Although the *aerarium* continued to exist, the *fiscus* gradually became the more important institution and the *magister a rationibus* became the imperial finance minister. Juristic skills were in demand in the departments *ab epistulis*, which dealt with queries from imperial officials in the provinces, and *a libellis*, dealing with petitions from private persons, often on points of law. There were also offices relating to appeals from imperial tribunals, *a cognitionibus*, and the keeping of records regarding imperial appointments and grants, *a memoria*. The first of these merged with the office *a libellis*. The importance of these offices increased sharply during and after the reign of Hadrian.

The period of the Principate therefore began with an attempt by Augustus to combine in his person the powers previously intended for several magistrates and institutions, and by the strength of his personal authority to make the constitution work. From the first, the *princeps* in reality was an absolute ruler, but one who chose to exercise his absolute powers through the channels by which they had passed in the age of the republic. Augustus and his successors were forced, however, to develop alternative administrative structures in order to maintain their ability to exercise that authority, and as time went by, those structures became in effect the actual institutions of government by a process which with hindsight appears inevitable. It was during the second century that this transformation was steadily accomplished and, equally inevitably, it affected both the methods of law-making and the sources of law in ancient Rome.

3 The Sources of Law in the Principate

Of the six sources of law listed by Gaius and Justinian, two, *leges* and *plebiscita*, declined immediately upon the accession to power of Augustus and had ceased to be of any importance by the close of the first century AD. Their function had always been to decide upon the acceptability in terms of policy of proposals initiated and deliberated upon by the magistrates and the senate respectively, so that their passing marks the introduction of a new decision-making method with regard to legislation rather than an entirely new legislative method. What was left on their demise was the interplay of the emperor and the senate in the legislative process, the former having the initiative by virtue of the magisterial offices he held together with the tribunician right to speak on behalf of the people at the decision-making phase, while the senate retained the deliberative function, albeit under imperial sufferance. It is this combination of rule by emperor and senate which leads to government during the Principate being referred to as a dyarchy as opposed to monarchy, rule by the emperor alone.

For the first two centuries of the Principate, the senate has all the appearance of having become the legislative assembly of the Romans, and if one thinks of a legislative assembly in terms of being a parliament, a place where proposals are discussed, this is what it was. Laws which were made by this route had their validity attributed to the advice of the senate and were called *senatus consulta*.

Already, however, at the close of the republic, much legal development took place not by enactment but by the gradual growth of procedural practice in the edicts of the magistrates, particularly that of the urban praetor. The coming of imperial government affected this source of law too. The concentration of political power in the hands of the emperor gave but little room for innovation by others. It would have been a brave magistrate who sought to amend his edict other than in accordance with the imperial will. Given that most magistrates owed their positions in any event to imperial favour and nomination, the holders of offices such as that of urban praetor had in effect become servants of the emperor in all but name. The result was that little further development of the magisterial edicts took place, so that the *edictum tralaticium* was handed on unchanged from year to year.

Its ossification as a living source of law was finally recognized by the emperor Hadrian in the second century. Hadrian's reign is a significant turning point in the history of Roman civil law, and perhaps the major development that occurred during it was his decision to codify the edict. He gave this task to one of the most distinguished jurists of the day, Salvius Julianus, who recast the edict in a form which subsequently remained unchanged. The form he gave it would appear to have achieved presentational elegance as well as a large measure of comprehensiveness. He included those edictal statements of the republican magistrates which were still in force, and after each added the appropriate *formula* for commencing litigation on the issue. He also included where relevant a statement of the civil law rules upon which the edict's provisions were based or which they supplemented or corrected, again together with the relevant procedural *formula*. Salvius Julianus, or Julian as he is often referred to, in effect produced a codified statement of the living *ius civile* and *ius honorarium* of his time. He supplied a new text upon which discussion of Roman law would turn for some centuries, just as previous discussion of the civil law had focused on the law of the XII Tables. Thereafter, the phrase *edictum perpetuum* was taken to refer to the edict in its final form as codified by Julian. It was to jurists of the Principate what the XII Tables had been to their republican counterparts, the text which was to form the basis of their study and exposition of the law. Civil law remained the law embodied in a text. A tradition to this effect was developing.

According to Justinian's sixth century account, Julian's *edictum perpetuum* was enacted in 130 by the authority of the senate together with a clear statement that any amendment to its provisions in future should only be made by imperial legislation.[8] If correct, this clearly signifies Hadrian's appreciation of what the actual position now was in respect to law-making and his determination to place the new method on a regular footing. Edictal development of the law had been the chief means of legal innovation and amendment during the late republic. It was no longer consonant for any magistrate save the emperor to wield such power. Accordingly, such development of the law was now reserved to him and that by agreement of the senate, guaranteeing the propriety as well as the wisdom of the move.

Hadrian appears to have been one of those rulers who have a genuine and deep-seated interest in legal affairs.[9] His reign marks a significant stage in the introduction of jurists into influential positions in the imperial service. Hadrian began to prefer men of equestrian rather than senatorial rank as advisors in his *consilium*, and these men sometimes included the leading jurists of the day who begin to take over responsibility for the imperial offices *ab epistulis* and *a libellis*. These offices were to be of great importance in the making of imperial laws.

Augustus had not claimed for himself any general law-making powers. He ensured that his legislative proposals were successful through his control of the existing legislative machinery. Nevertheless, as a magistrate, the emperor was entitled to issue edicts, as his republican predecessors had done, and the emperors did indeed as occasion demanded utilize edicts to introduce general legal innovations. Thus, Caracalla's *constitutio Antoniniana*, granting the Roman citizenship to virtually all the free inhabitants of the empire,[10] was legislation by edict.

Imperial law-making was not as a rule that dramatic. It took place in the context of what can perhaps be termed routine government and administration. Its form was usually a response to some query, appeal or request for instructions from private individuals, imperial officials or governmental bodies.

Where the request for guidance came from a municipal council or governor within the empire, the emperor would normally reply by letter, *epistula*, issued from the office *ab epistulis*. The guidance might relate to a problem of administration, but could involve a point of law. A legal opinion or interpretation given in such manner was hardly a binding authority, still less an enactment, but it was of course given by imperial authority. Copies of such letters were retained by the *ab epistulis*, and formed a source of interpretative precedents.

Provincial officials might sometimes ask for instructions with regard to particular problems in their province.[11] The emperor could reply to these in the form of orders, *mandata*, instructing the officers, who were his delegates, as to how the problem should be tackled. Although strictly speaking, such orders only related to the matter in hand and had no validity outside of the province to which they were issued, nevertheless a body of imperial precedent again developed from these *mandata*, primarily in the area of public law.

Replies to petitions from private persons did not usually take the form of letters, but of annotations at the bottom of the petition submitted. Again, the petition might be a request to clarify a point of law of importance to the petitioner. Replies made in this form, *subscriptiones*, were issued by the office *a libellis*, and copies were again retained forming a body of persuasive, if not technically binding, precedents for use on future occasions. *Subscriptiones* and *epistulae*, both being sorts of reply, are referred to generically as *rescripta*.

The emperor could also be approached to act as a judge in a dispute between citizens, either at first instance or as a tribunal of appeal. If the emperor did so act, he would issue his judgement by means of a decree, *decretum*. While again technically this was not a precedent but only binding upon the parties to the instant case, if the issue had been solved by reference to a general principle stated in the decree, or the decree in applying the law gave an interpretation of it, such general principles or interpretations would be of great persuasive force when similar points arose for decision elsewhere. It was not uncommon for other judges to refer such points of law to the emperor for decision, to which he would reply giving his determination of the legal point at issue. Such replies were in the form of *rescripta*, and only binding in the instant case. Sometimes the judge would even set out one possible set of facts, and the imperial solution would only apply if the facts were then found to be the case.

In all of these instances of imperial legal activity, the question arises as to how the emperor instructed himself with regard to the law. It is here that another important change in Roman legal arrangements during the Principate becomes significant, the change in the role of the jurists. The replies of those learned in the law, *responsa prudentium*, occurs in both Gaius' and Justinian's list of legal sources. During the republic, the jurists acted as advisers to the magistrates, private clients and judges, but with the advent of imperial rule, one of their most important functions was to give legal advice to the *princeps*. Indeed, this became the principal activity of some jurists and was to become the sole activity of some leading jurists during the second and third centuries. The ablest jurists by that time would actively be pursuing a career in the imperial service.

When asked how to interpret or apply a particular rule of law, the emperor would turn to a jurist for advice.[12] He would obviously be able to call upon the services of the ablest jurists available. The opinion embodied therefore in an imperial rescript or decree would often be that of one of the jurists, confirmed by the emperor, who might also have directed the resolution of any policy questions involved in deciding upon the interpretation or method of application.

The temptation must however have been great for a litigant to pray the imperial opinion in an attempt to settle authoritatively a disputed point of law. It may have been to prevent unnecessary recourse to imperial opinion that Augustus introduced a privilege which has been the subject of much discussion and speculation, the *ius respondendi*. This right was a patent given to jurists to give their opinions with the authority of the emperor. It may have been issued so as to make it unnecessary for litigants to bother the emperor in person in order to obtain a definitive legal ruling in relation to their problems or disputes.

The privilege does not appear to have been one that was widely dispersed during the first century of the Principate, but the emperor Hadrian nevertheless acted to overcome some difficulties in its operation. Given that the opinion of the emperor was only technically binding in the instant case, it might be asked whether the opinions of the jurists could be binding unless directed at the particular case in question. Rather more difficult was the question of what a judge was to do if on a particular point juristic opinion was divided, so that jurists of eminence could be found to support both sides of a case. Hadrian's solution was to decree that where the opinion of the jurists was at one, that was to be taken as a correct statement of the law by the judge, but if juristic opinion was divided, the judge could choose which line to follow. In either case, therefore, recourse to the emperor would only be necessary on points of law which were novel or undecided.

Hadrian's direction indicates several things about jurisprudence at that time. Firstly, he clearly has confidence in the jurists to supply the correct answers to legal problems. He recognizes that they are founts of legal knowledge. Pomponius writing in the second century was to claim that the knowledge of the jurists was the true source of the civil law, *ius civile*, elevating their interpretation above enactments and decisions. This marks a restatement of that notion of law as being something more than the rules which people enact to govern themselves. Under Hadrian, the senate was losing its role as guardian of that concept of law as what is right, *ius*, which role was passing to the jurists who advised the emperor both in his *consilium* and in his other legal work. The jurists had become the guardians of that legal tradition which had once been in the custody of the pontiffs and which Ulpian in the following century would describe as being "the knowledge of things human and divine".[13]

Hadrian's directive also witnesses to the fact that it was not uncommon for juristic opinion to be divided, and there had indeed been during the first century AD some notable divisions of opinion concerning certain legal rules between two rival schools of jurists at Rome, the Sabinians and the Proculians. There has been much controversy concerning the nature of these schools of jurists.[14] What is clear is that they took their names from two jurists of the first century, Sabinus and Proculus, but that neither of these was the founder of the school which bore his name. The Sabinian school instead is said to have originated with Capito, a jurist known to have been a supporter of the Augustan regime. The Proculians on the other hand are traced to Capito's contemporary, Labeo, a convinced opponent of imperial rule. One of Sabinus' successors as leader of the school which bears his name was the eminent jurist, Cassius, from whom the Sabinian school is sometimes referred to as the Cassian. The two schools differed in their opinions on a variety of issues, so that it sometimes appears that their differences were based less on principle than a competitive spirit, perhaps honed in the service of clients with opposing claims. As many of their disputes turned on interpretations of the praetor's edict, some believe that Julian's codification brought their rivalry to an end, though others believe it subsisted until the early years of the following century.[15] Julian himself belonged to the Sabinian persuasion.

From the reign of Hadrian onwards, the leading jurists gravitated towards imperial service where it was now possible for them to aspire to very high office. By the end of the century, they were not only holding the important posts of the secretaries *ab epistulis* and *a libellis*, but were also within reach of the praetorian prefecture itself. Papinian was the first of the jurists to actually reach that position during the reign of Septimius Severus. He was a close friend of the emperor, accompanied him on his visit to Britain and is said to have held court for him at York. It is claimed that his assessors at that time were two of his pupils, Ulpian and Paul, at least one of whom was destined to become praetorian prefect. Papinian was put to death by the emperor Caracalla in 212 AD, reputedly for failing to approve the emperor's assassination of his brother, Geta. Ulpian, who served the emperor Alexander Severus (222-235), was murdered by his own guards in 223 during a revolt; Paul, who had been a pupil of Cervidius Scaevola, chief legal advisor to the emperor Marcus Aurelius (161-180), as well as of Papinian, served the same emperor.[16] Modestinus, the fourth great jurist of this generation, sometime *praefectus vigilum*, survived until 244.

The period from Hadrian to Alexander Severus is deemed the golden age of classical jurisprudence, largely due to the achievements of the men named above. Papinian was particularly gifted in relating his solutions of problems to general principles, and had much to do with the development of pithy legal maxims, of immense use in guiding the direction of legal interpretation, application and development. Ulpian is famed for his clarity and economy of expression. They, and the other jurists of this period, continued to give legal advice, but their main work was in framing legal responses on behalf of the emperor. Much of the literature of this period therefore takes the form of collections of the *responsa* of the leading jurists, as well as literature reflecting their disputations on legal questions, *quaestiones*. The great classical jurists were also however prolific writers, assembling great commentaries on the law as well as treatises on individual aspects of it. The subjects of the great commentaries were the *ius civile*, often based on its discussion by Sabinus in the first century, together with commentaries on the edict of Salvius Julianus. Ulpian's commentary on the edict ran to 83 books; Papinian's to 80.

The jurists continued to play an important role in the education of their successors. As well as admitting them to disputations and writing the great commentaries and monographs, a specifically educational form of literature had also been developed based on the models of instruction in the art of rhetoric. Such texts were called *Institutes*, and several examples of the genre are known to have been written during the second century. The most famous and the most important are those of Gaius.

Gaius is one of the great names of the classical age of Roman jurisprudence, but unlike Julian, Papinian, Paul and Ulpian, hardly anything is known about his career. He certainly held no office in the imperial service and did not have the *ius respondendi*. Remarkably, even his full name is a mystery; only his *praenomen*, Gaius, is known. His reputation however is high, and the affection in which he was held great. To the jurists and legislators of a later age, he is "our Gaius", *Gaius noster*.[17]

His great claim to fame is the composition of the *Institutes*, probably completed during the reign of Marcus Aurelius. In it, Gaius presents an account of Roman private law according to what is now called the institutional scheme, a scheme probably of his own devising. It was destined to be the model for the presentation of civil law thereafter. Gaius' plan is to deal firstly with those who have rights and duties under the law, then to discuss the things over which those rights and duties may be exercised, and finally to consider the means by which those rights and duties may be enforced. He deals respectively with persons, things and actions, in a manner which is readily familiar to civil lawyers of every succeeding age, all of whom will have been educated according to the scheme he devised. It is a remarkable legacy. His systematic approach continues, as, for instance, he divides, in dealing with the law of things, things which can be owned from those which are owed, and considers in turn what ownership is, how it differs from possession, how it is acquired, transferred and lost. The order and lucidity of the arrangement is breathtaking in its simplicity if one remembers that it had never previously been achieved.

4 Conclusion

The period of the Principate contains the classical age of Roman civil law, the high water mark of civilian learning in the ancient world. This claim rests almost exclusively upon the work of the jurists, those learned in the law, during these centuries. Their writings and their shaping of the law through their influence as legal advisers to successive emperors created this achievement. The institutional scheme of Gaius, the principled overview of Papinian, the elegant lucidity of Ulpian, all contributed to shaping the legal development of their age but also the legal culture of the next two millennia. It is an awe-inspiring achievement.

In other respects, the Principate may not appear so attractive an age in the evolution of the civil law. The achievements of the Roman republic in discriminating between those who were to initiate legal proposals, those who were to discuss them, and the methods of securing popular approval while insisting upon the moral propriety of enactments, all appeared to wither in the face of the absolute rule of an all-powerful leader. There can however be no concealing the historical fact that the absolutist maxim *quod principi placuit legis habet vigorem* had a considerable future before it. Regrettably, in many ages and not least in the succeeding centuries in Rome, the subtle difference between asserting that what pleased the leader had the force of law in the sense of an enactment, *lex*, not in the sense of what is just and right, *ius*, was lost. With it perhaps was submerged the concept that law is something more than rules which govern a particular community but rather is part of a natural order to which such rules should conform or even must conform to be valid.

However, if that notion survived, it survived in the work of the jurists. The idea expressed by Pomponius that the civil law existed primarily in the interpretations of those learned in the law refutes the idea that law is just the command of an all powerful ruler. Gaius begins his *Institutes* with the time-honoured distinction between the *ius civile* and the *ius gentium*, the law which a people makes for itself and the law common to all mankind. It was in shaping private law not public law that the classical jurists made their great contribution, and this remained in substance largely unaffected by the change to imperial rule. In that the jurists sat on the emperor's council, they may well have influenced legal developments in all departments in accordance with their professional view of justice and fairness; it cannot be for nothing that Papinian is said to have sacrificed his life rather than consent to the murder of Geta.

Finally, one further feature of this age is worth careful note. In it, as at the end of the republic, the jurists focussed their attention primarily upon written texts. During the Principate, the focus of attention may no longer have been the XII Tables but it was still a text, the Edict of Salvius Julianus. Civil law was becoming very definitely a law based on texts and upon juristic commentaries expounding those texts. It was equally clearly not a law based on decided cases, although references to the highest judicial authority were seen as a method of deciding disputed points of law, which decisions could be taken as illustrative of general principles.

Notes

[1] For instance, Cicero's prosecution of Verres in 70 BC.

[2] See M. Crawford, *The Roman Republic* (Glasgow, 1978), p. 172.

[3] Laws of 197, 180 and 151 BC; see Crawford, *The Roman Republic* (Glasgow 1978), p. 76 f.

[4] For details see A.N. Sherwin White, *The Roman Citizenship* (2nd Ed.; Oxford, 1973).

[5] See Cicero, *Topica*, V, 28, cited by O. Tellegen-Couperus, *A Short History of Roman Law* (English Ed.; London & New York, 1993), p. 50.

[6] The title *Augustus* is derived from the Latin verb *augere* meaning to increase. It denotes the increase in the fortunes of the State achieved by the emperor.

[7] See H.F. Jolowicz and B. Nicholas, *An Historical Introduction to Roman Law* (3rd Ed.; Cambridge, 1972), p. 44.

[8] *Constitutio Tanta*, 18. The accuracy of Justinian's account has been doubted by A. Guarino in, for instance, *Storia del diritto romano* (4th Ed.), p. 460 ff. See W. Kunkel, *An Introduction to Roman Legal and Constitutional History* trans. J.M. Kelly (2nd English Ed.; Oxford, 1973), pp. 92-93 and n.

[9] His idea of a day off was to sit in the gardens of his villa at Tivoli outside of Rome listening to and deciding appeals.

[10] *Dediticii* were excluded, as these were non-Roman inhabitants living within the empire who were resistant to Roman rule, and forbidden to approach within a hundred miles of Rome upon pain of enslavement.

[11] A particularly famous example is Pliny the Younger writing to Trajan with regard to how to treat the Christians in his province of Bithynia; see Pliny, *Ep*. X. 96, 97.

[12] It was rare for the emperor to be a jurist, although Nerva (96-98) is an example of one who was and who came from a distinguished legal family.

[13] There is a similarity here to the notion that the common law was contained in the bosom of the judges.

---

[14] Beliefs are divided as to whether they were influenced by rival philosophies of Greek origin, differing political attitudes or simply distinctive juridical approaches to the law. See chapter 11, note 33.

[15] Some disputes appear to have remained unresolved however until the time of Justinian, e.g. *specificatio*. See below, chapter 11, pp. 240 ff.

[16] It is disputed that he was praetorian prefect: see Tony Honoré, *Ulpian* (Oxford, 1982), pp. 43 f.

[17] Much speculation has taken place concerning his life and career: see A.M. Honoré, *Gaius* (Oxford, 1962); J.C. Ledlie, 'Gaius' in Sir John MacDonell and E. Manson, *Great Jurists of the World* (Boston, 1914; reprinted New York, 1968), pp. 1 ff.

3 The Dominate

1 The Crisis of the Third Century

Marcus Aurelius was regarded by subsequent generations as the model imperial ruler. His reign saw a period of peace and prosperity which typifies the second century AD. The orderly arrangement and systematic presentation of Gaius' *Institutes* seem to mirror the age in which they were written, a time which allowed for reflection and mature thought. As satisfying as the connection between the spirit of that age and the jurist's achievement may be, it is in an equal degree cruel and unacceptable that a man of breadth of vision like Papinian and a thinker of such clarity as Ulpian should both have met violent deaths, one for upholding the virtues of justice against murderous tyranny, the other at the hands of those rebelling against lawful authority. Yet, their end is as typical of the century in which they lived as is Gaius' work of his age.

Ulpian was assassinated in the service of Alexander Severus, and his imperial master went to his death in the same manner in 235. For a third century emperor to die a natural death was a considerable and rare achievement. During the half century which separates the killing of Alexander Severus and the accession of Diocletian to the imperial throne in 284, over twenty emperors came to power, almost all of whom were killed in office. That Diocletian managed to retain power for over twenty years and retire from office is a telling testimony to his achievements.

The cause of the anarchy which engulfed Roman government at this time was not new. A stable rule of succession to the imperial dignity had never been found. Augustus at the very start of the Principate had had great difficulties in finding a successor. His idea was to nominate the next *princeps*, but one by one his chosen nominees predeceased him, so that he was succeeded by his son-in-law, Tiberius. Tiberius also managed to nominate his successor, Gaius - nicknamed Caligula, but on his assassination it was the army who made Claudius ruler. Thereafter, an uneasy relationship developed between the emperor's right to nominate a successor, the senate's right to approve his choice, and the army's power to bestow the title by sheer military force, and likewise to dispatch any holder of it of whom they disapproved.

During the second century, the Antonine emperors[1] achieved a measure of stability by indicating their chosen successors clearly by adoption of them as their sons. Thus, Hadrian ensured a smooth transition to Antoninus Pius, who likewise ushered in the reign of Marcus Aurelius. For all his virtues, that emperor made the error of resolutely favouring a blood successor despite his son's obvious failings, and it was Commodus' reign (180-192), ending in assassination, which in a way started the rot of the third century.[2] The adoption principle was however sufficiently strongly established for Septimius Severus, after taking the imperial title by force in 193, to arrange for his posthumous adoption by Marcus Aurelius so as to legitimize his claim.

From 235 until 284, however, the army in effect made and unmade emperors as they chose, the imperial title and the lives of those who held it depending almost entirely upon shifts in the balance of power within the military establishment. The empire was weakened and suffered a series of disasters at home and abroad. War and disease rendered the lot of the citizens a sorry one. Firm government had to be re-established if the empire was to survive.

2 The Reforms of Diocletian

It was the army which brought Diocletian to the imperial title in 284, but they brought to power a general determined to restore stability to Roman government. Diocletian realized that if he were to achieve that goal, it was necessary to reorganize the administration of the empire from top to bottom, and at the top something had to be done about the recurring problem of the order of succession.

Diocletian's answer to the problem of the succession was inspired in part by the practice of his predecessors and in part by the institutions of the republic. He realized that an orderly succession to the imperial title required the acceptance of the successor by the army and the senate during the reign of the preceding emperor. There had to be no doubt that there was someone who had a right to succeed, so that it became a duty to see that that person succeeded. A large part of the problem had been that no-one was perceived as having a right to succeed, so that the succession was not due to anyone as a matter of right, *ius*, as opposed to a matter of his predecessor's wish, *voluntas*. For the future, each emperor was to bear the title of *Augustus* as in the past, but now, throughout his reign, each Augustus was to have an heir apparent, who would bear the title of *Caesar*, another of the imperial designations. The emperor and his successor would both therefore be clearly set apart from other powerful personages at every stage of a reign. There should never be a moment at which an Augustus was without a designated successor, a Caesar.

If the inspiration for this innovation was the Antonine model of adoption, which also clearly demarcated the chosen successor, albeit transformed from a matter of choice to a matter of office, the influence of the republican constitution can be discerned in the other aspect of Diocletian's reform regarding the imperial title. He introduced the principle of collegiality into the imperial office. Just as during the republic there had been two consuls of equal dignity, each having *imperium* in all matters throughout his year in office, so Diocletian provided that there should be two Augusti to rule the empire, each of whom would uphold the power of the other. Unlike the consuls of the Roman republic, these Augusti were not subject to any restriction of time upon their rule, but could hold office for life once they succeeded to the imperial title, although Diocletian himself significantly chose to abdicate his powers in 305, perhaps wishing to illustrate to the full the benefit of having a designated successor in waiting, in that even an Augustus could step down when weary of the burdens of office or unable to continue through illness or old age.

In later years, the two Augusti were to be seen operating in different spheres of influence geographically, one in the East and one in the West. This was not however Diocletian's intention. The two Augusti were each to have power throughout the empire, although for administrative effectiveness, one would be resident in the East and one in the West. Each however held sway throughout the Roman world, but innovations were to be subject to the approval of his imperial colleague. Each Augustus was to have his own Caesar, so that succession to the office of each should be assured.

Beneath the Augusti and the Caesares, there was a general reorganization of the whole of the government and the administration of the empire. The Principate had been based upon the institutions and structures of the republic and there had been no integration of them with the new imperial institutions. This meant for instance that some provinces of the empire continued to be classed as senatorial provinces, being governed by proconsuls, formally appointed by the senate but in truth imperial nominees. In addition, there were the provinces of Caesar, those directly under the control of the *princeps* in theory as well as practice. These were governed by imperial legates, and had a different administrative structure. Republican magistrates continued to be appointed alongside their imperial counterparts, although in reality all power flowed from an imperial rather than a popular or senatorial source.

Diocletian was prepared to overhaul these structures entirely and replace them with governmental institutions and structures which reflected the reality of imperial rule. He divided the empire into provinces, which were not coterminous with the provinces which had previously been shared between the senate and the emperor. The new provinces were generally smaller in size, and there were 163 in all throughout the empire. Each province was to be under the control of a governor, a *praeses*, who was the head of the provincial state. The *praeses* however was not a military but a civil governor, for Diocletian was determined to separate control of the army from civil administration. This would ensure that those with political and governmental experience were not also supported by the loyalty of the troops as had previously been the case, while successful generals would no longer have experience of civil affairs as previously, such that their ambitions might turn in the direction of the imperial throne.

The 163 provinces were grouped into larger regions, called dioceses or vicariates. These in turn were grouped into four praetorian prefectures. In future, the praetorian prefect would be the chief officer of the emperor in a certain part of the empire, and the vicars who had jurisdiction in the vicariates or dioceses were delegates of the praetorian prefects although they were appointed by the emperor. There was therefore a hierarchical structure of government leading from the provinces, through the dioceses and the prefectures, to the Augustus and his Caesar. It was however perfectly open for vicars or even provincial governors to contact the emperor directly on matters relating to their work.

The head of each tier had in effect full jurisdiction within his sphere of operation. It was therefore within the competence of every governor to administer the law and to hear and determine disputes within his territory. Such jurisdiction of necessity involved having the authority both to make administrative regulations with regard to the carrying out of imperial laws within the particular conditions of the individual province, as well as having to interpret legal rules from time to time as part and parcel of their application. While it was not unusual for provincial governors to have legal training now that they were no longer military men, there existed in such arrangements the danger that decentralized administration of justice would lead to fragmentation of the law itself, as different interpretations might be reached in different parts of the empire. To counter this threat, it remained open for governors to obtain definitive rulings on points of law from the emperor, and litigants who were dissatisfied with the decision of an official in their case were allowed to appeal to the emperor directly or to the vicar or the praetorian prefect.[3] If either of the latter officials was appealed to, a further appeal to the emperor remained possible. These structures, as well as the terminology of province and diocese, were to be of immense importance to the subsequent organization of the western Church and to the development of its canon law jurisdiction following the conversion of the empire to Christianity during the fourth century.[4]

As well as this radical reform of the structure and government of the empire, Diocletian also reconstituted the imperial council. The *consilium* of the Principate was transformed into the *consistorium* of the Dominate, another title which was to have a distinguished future before it in the legal arrangements of the Church. Members of the *consistorium* fell into two main classes: those holding high office and those who had held high or important offices in the State. The current office holders included the *quaestor sacri palatii*, who took over from the praetorian prefect of the Principate the role of Minister of Justice. The previous offices of *a memoria*, *a libellis* and *ab epistulis* were now referred to as the *scrinia* and came under the oversight of the *magister scriniorum* who was a member of the *consistorium*. The heads of the three departments were not members of the *consistorium* while in office, but there is evidence that they became members upon retirement.[5] Also members of the *consistorium* were the financial managers of the new dispensation, the *comes sacrarum largitionum*, who ran the *fiscus*, and the *comes rerum privatarum*, who dealt with the imperial estates, the *res privatae*, technically the emperor's own patrimony but in effect supplying the privy purse. The non-official members were referred to as the *comites spectabiles consistoriani*. The word *comes* means a comrade or fellow, here of the emperor, and again foreshadows the future when the great feudal nobles would be the counts or *comites* of their king or the later imperial rulers of Europe. There was a *consistorium* in each half of the empire.

The title *consistorium* replaced that of *consilium* to emphasize the changed nature of the institution as well as its changed membership. The *comites consistoriani* did not sit in the presence of the emperor as had their counterparts on the *consilium*; they stood. This was to emphasize that the emperor was a different sort of person to his councillors. The emperor was no longer the first citizen or the first senator; he was their imperial master. Diocletian clothed the Roman emperor in all the trappings and ceremonial of Oriental divine kingship. His purple attire, the form of address, posture in the imperial presence, even the colour of ink with which he wrote, all emphasized the otherness of the imperial personage. This was to encourage awe and reverence of the emperor, and to place any interference with his person into the category of sacrilege. The word *sacer*, meaning sacred or holy in the sense of being set apart, was much used of the emperor and imperial institutions. It was meant to mark a new beginning, in which the often violated emperors of the third century gave way to inviolate rulers in the fourth. Whatever measure of success Diocletian's reforms were destined to enjoy, they were bound to have a profound effect upon the sources of law and the process of law making during and after his reign.

3 Sources of Law during the Dominate

Diocletian's acceptance that the emperor was now an absolute ruler meant that for the future there could be no doubt as to where the legislative power within the empire lay. What was pleasing to the emperor had the force of enacted law. The emperors continued to make law as previously, partly by general enactments in edicts, which would be published via the praetorian prefects to every provincial governor, partly by *decreta* in which the emperor gave his judgement in cases which came before him either on appeal or at first instance, but still in the main by way of *rescripta*, replies to requests from officials and private persons for clarification of points of law. These *rescripta* were carefully preserved in the imperial records but not generally published. They were by far the most voluminous source of legislation in the third, fourth and fifth century. The new structure for administering justice within the empire which Diocletian instituted increased considerably the requests from provincial governors and other local officials for clarification or determination of legal questions.

The growth in the volume of imperial legislation coincided with a sharp decline in the quality of juristic interpretation and writing. This was mainly due, without doubt, to the political turmoil of the middle years of the third century which must have made a juristic career in the imperial service much less attractive to the ablest intellectuals in Roman society. During the fourth and fifth century, this decline continued, particularly as there was by that time an alternative field of activity of great prestige for those wishing to pursue an intellectual life, namely the Christian Church. Theological questions of great subtlety replaced those of jurisprudence as the staple diet of intellectual discussion. The toleration of the Christian faith within the empire proclaimed by Constantine in 313 in the Edict of Milan, following that emperor's conversion to Christianity, allowed men of intelligence and ability to pursue an ecclesiastical career openly, and this tendency was accentuated after Christianity became the official religion of the empire under Theodosius I in 378.

The result of the increase in legislative activity by the emperor, mainly through rescripts, coupled with the decline in juristic quality was a deterioration in the standards of the law itself. One of the prime difficulties was the problem of ascertaining what the law actually was on a particular point given that it was dispersed in the mass of imperial legislation. The return to orderly government under Diocletian appears to have inspired two jurists of ability to attempt a remedy to the problem of how to deal with the undifferentiated mass of imperial constitutions which had accumulated since the time of Hadrian and which had not been properly assimilated since the end of the classical age of Roman jurisprudence a half century previously. Gregorius and Hermogenian both produced during the reign of Diocletian ordered collections of imperial legislation, in the main rescripts, to assist those seeking to determine what the law was on a particular matter.[6] Both works are called *codices*, not because they are codes in the modern sense of systematic, comprehensive legislation on a whole area of the law, but because they were written on individual sheets of parchment bound together in book form and not on papyrus rolls as hitherto had been used. The *Codex Gregorianus* was composed in 291 and the *Codex Hermogenianus* followed in 295. Neither has survived in its entirety; little of the former survives at all, but more of the latter is extant. Both were independent productions; they were not in any sense official collections and had no legislative force.

The *Codex Gregorianus* was the larger of the two and arranged its material in books, subdivided into titles. Each title dealt with a particular legal topic, and within each title the constitutions assembled were presented in chronological order. The order of the books and titles followed the traditional arrangement of the *digesta* produced by the classical jurists. While the arrangement is orderly therefore it cannot be described as systematic in the manner in which Gaius' *Institutes* followed a logical programme of presentation. It was however an arrangement which would have been readily accessible to those trained using the works of the classical authors. It also perhaps emphasizes a continuity within the sources of law themselves, in that the classical jurists had based their work in the main on the Edict of Julian, and it had been clearly stated at the time of that work's promulgation that alterations to it could be made only by imperial legislation. To collect imperial legislation in an order referable to the text of the Edict was therefore very sensible.

The *Codex Hermogenianus* followed the same presentational method, but was divided into titles only, and not into books. It was also a large work.[7] Its purpose appears to have been to supplement the earlier compilation of Gregorius by assembling Diocletian's own legislation since the earlier work was published. The size of the *Hermogenianus* is therefore a tribute to Diocletian's law-making activity. There is evidence that both works were subject to some updating after their initial compilation, and in the case of the *Hermogenianus* this continued into the second half of the fourth century.[8]

The volume of rescripts being issued continued unabated in the fourth century but their status as a source of law came into question. Influential litigants were able to obtain rulings favourable to themselves with considerable ease, and the decline in juristic skill meant that conflicting or dubious interpretations would cast the law into confusion if each such pronouncement were treated as authoritative. The binding nature of rescripts other than in the cases in which they were obtained was questioned, and at the end of the fourth century the emperor Arcadius was moved to rule that they had no binding authority. In 438, the Roman senate was moved to reiterate more than twenty times a plea that laws should no longer be made in response to individuals' petitions. This latter request was made during a significant period in the history of later Roman law, the reigns of Theodosius II and Valentinian III, the former emperor in the East, the latter in the West.

The reigns of these emperors are legally significant for a number of reasons. Most importantly, perhaps, it was Theodosius II who ordered the production of an official collection of imperial legislation, the *Codex Theodosianus* or Theodosian Code. Unlike the previous compilations of Gregorius and Hermogenian, this collection of extant laws was official, but it was only part of the enterprise upon which Theodosius embarked in 429. His original intention was to collect all the general laws of the emperors from Constantine (311-337) until his own time, and then to extract from that and the Gregorian and Hermogenian codes all the enactments that merited retention, together with extracts from juristic writings that ought to be preserved. He appointed a nine man commission to execute this task, but the enterprise was not a success and had to be abandoned in 435 in favour of the more straightforward task of assembling imperial legislation from Constantine's time to the present. This was entrusted to a commission of sixteen who completed their work by 438. The end-product was the Theodosian Code which was promulgated as law in both the eastern and western parts of the empire.

Interestingly, Valentinian III promulgated the Code in the West by means of an *oratio* to the Roman senate, and it was in this year that the senate made its plea for no more rescripts, perhaps believing that the law was now sufficiently certain as to render them unnecessary. Twelve years earlier, Valentinian III had also used the time-honoured legislative method of an *oratio* to the senate to promulgate another law made by himself and Theodosius II in attempt to end legal uncertainty. This was the Law of Citations of 426. It was meant to deal with the problem of uncertainty arising from divergence of opinion on points of law in the writings of the jurists.

Hadrian, it will be recalled, faced the same problem in the second century, but in a much less acute form. His solution was to state that if the jurists agreed, their opinion was to have the force of law, but if they disagreed, the judge should be free to decide the matter for himself. To some extent, the Law of Citations is modelled on this approach, but its solution is more complex just as the problem it addressed was more severe. It was during the centuries separating Hadrian from Theodosius and Valentinian that the bulk of juristic writing on Roman law had occurred, including virtually the whole of that of the classical age. The problem which faced the imperial judges of the fourth century was what to do when faced with a plethora of juristic opinions advocating different solutions to a problem. The solution supplied by the Law of Citations was to limit the number of jurists whose works could be cited. Only the works of five jurists were to be admissible as of right: the classical jurists of the Severan age - Papinian, Ulpian, Paul and Modestinus, and somewhat surprisingly the writings of the (by comparison with the others) undistinguished Gaius. As well as these five, the writings of other jurists cited by one of the famous five were to be admissible, and if there were a difference of opinion among the juristic writers, the opinion of the majority was to prevail. If there were no majority view, then the opinion of Papinian was to be adopted, and only if Papinian were silent in such circumstances was the judge to be free to impose his own solution.[9]

Although both the Law of Citations and the Theodosian Code were promulgated in the West by an *oratio* to the senate, there can be no doubting that in both the eastern and western parts of the empire the legislative initiative and the decision to enact a law lay with the imperial will. Theodosius II, however, did make provision for some deliberation of legislative proposals. In 446, he provided that legislative proposals should be debated in both the senate and the imperial *consistorium*. When both bodies had discussed a proposal and settled its text, both had then to agree that text before it was read to the *consistorium* and then passed to the emperor for enactment. Although this process should be thought of as consultative rather than legislative, it foreshadows some legislative methods in civil law countries today,[10] although it is far from clear to what extent if any it influenced actual legislative practice in late antiquity. In the sixth century, the emperor Justinian was to issue laws under his signature together with the countersignature of the *quaestor sacri palatii*, another practice which has its corollaries in the legislative practices of modern states.

There is much in the legal development of the first half of the fifth century which foreshadows the work of Justinian in the sixth, the work which marks the culmination of the development of Roman law in the ancient world. However, there is much also which indicates a continuity with the achievements of earlier ages. There had however been some significant breaks with the past during the two centuries which bridge the gap between the reigns of Diocletian and Justinian, and before the latter's achievements are recounted, something must be said of the changes that had taken place in the Roman world of the fourth and fifth centuries.

4 The Roman World from Diocletian to Justinian

Although the structural reforms to the government of the empire made by Diocletian were destined to be of great importance in the future ecclesiastical and civil government of Europe, his plans for a college of emperors and a resulting stability in the rules of succession to the imperial office enjoyed little success in the short term. After his retirement in 305, it was not long before his co-Augustus, Maximian, was involved in disputation concerning the succession and within a decade Constantine had established himself as sole ruler of the whole empire. After the reigns of Constantine and his sons, co-emperors did again emerge, but not as Diocletian had intended with joint authority throughout Roman territory.

Instead, from 364, Valentinian and Valens ruled respectively as emperors in the East and West, and despite a brief re-unification during part of the reign of Theodosius I, under his sons Arcadius and Honorius the empire was divided for the last time into eastern and western parts.

Diocletian had also moved the capital of the western portion of his empire from Rome to Milan, a more accessible centre of administration at the time of his reign. He also established a capital in the east, at Nicomedia, but the greatest change in the siting of the seat of administration came during the reign of Constantine with the founding of a new city on the banks of the Bosphorus in 330. Constantinople was named after its founder and was, as Byzantium, to remain an imperial capital for over a millennium. It was established as a new Rome in the East, with similar civic and governmental structures. When Diocletian had reformed the empire into provinces, vicariates and praetorian prefectures, Rome was not under the jurisdiction of the praetorian prefect of Italy nor of his *vicarii*. Instead, Rome remained under the control of an official who was directly answerable to the emperors, called suitably the *praefectus urbis*. He was the chief magistrate of the city and continued to have a *praefectus vigilum* and a *praefectus annonae* under his jurisdiction. The Roman senate, as has been shown, continued to meet, but was primarily concerned with the municipal government of the city. Constantine repeated these immunities, offices and structures in his new foundation at Constantinople. Thereafter, the eastern capital was in reality the dominant imperial centre of the Roman world. This inevitably affected the language and culture of the empire, and arguably also its laws.[11]

The reign of Constantine also marks another major change in the Roman empire, namely the emergence of Christianity as an officially tolerated religion. The emperor having himself been converted to the faith, he promulgated legislation making the faith lawful as in the Edict of Milan of 313. Other than a brief return to paganism under Julian (361-363), the empire thereafter remained Christian, Christianity becoming the official religion of the empire under Theodosius I in 378. This step had considerable influence upon various departments of the law, particularly marriage, inheritance and parental power.

The conversion of the empire to Christianity gave the Church an ever increasing role and influence in Roman society. Although Rome was no longer the secular capital of the empire, not even in the West, as the seat of the Papacy it began to enjoy a new-found importance and prestige. Throughout the empire, bishops became respected figures in civic as well as ecclesiastical life. They were permitted to have jurisdiction not only over the clerics in their cities, but also over the disputes of baptized Christians generally if both parties, or even one of them, so wished.[12] Constantine and later emperors regarded it as their duty to maintain the unity of the Church, so that the great Councils of the fourth century were summoned under the emperor's authority.[13] The administrative structures and terminology devised by Diocletian, of provinces, dioceses and vicariates, survive in the Church to this day.

The privileged position of the clergy in terms of being within the jurisdiction of the Church courts rather than the ordinary courts of the State mirrored other such privileged occupations. The military, civil servants, tenants of imperial lands and members of the city guilds of Rome and Constantinople were allowed their own courts.[14] In this, there is a foretaste of the special jurisdictions which were to be a feature of mediaeval law, and there are many features in the legal developments of this period which foreshadow the Middle Ages. The growth of *colonarii*, technically not slaves but nevertheless tied to the land, anticipate the mediaeval serfs, and the taxation in kind by which the army was supported can be seen to bear similarities to the payment of feudal dues.[15] In the field of legal practice, Constantine introduced a corps of notaries into his civil service to keep the minutes of his *consistorium*.[16] Greek influence is believed by some to have reduced the law's reliance on formal ceremonies and increased the importance of writing as evidence of legal transactions.[17]

By the turn of the fourth century, not only was the empire becoming more Greek in its orientation, the lands of the West were beginning to be lost to invading tribes from northern Europe, particularly the Goths. In 410, they sacked Rome under their leader Alaric, and Rome was to suffer the same ignominy at the hands of the Vandals in 455. Although the fall of the western empire is usually dated to 476, the year in which the last emperor in the West, Romulus Augustulus, abdicated, in truth there had been no recovery of independence from the barbarians since the middle years of the century. Although Rome remained the seat of the Papacy, the imperial capital was now very definitely Byzantium. Although Justinian (527-565) succeeded in recapturing parts of North Africa, Spain and Italy from the invaders during his reign in the East, the only reconquered territories which remained under Roman, that is Byzantine, government permanently were those parts of north-east Italy around the city of Ravenna which to this day bear in the name of their region evidence of their imperial recapture, namely the Romagna. Although Justinian's reconquests supply a part of his fame, they do not compare in terms of the permanence of their legacy with his achievement as a law-maker.

5 Justinian and the *Corpus Iuris Civilis*

As well as restoring to his empire the lost lands of the West, Justinian also wished to restore to his subjects what he regarded as being a rightful part of their heritage, namely the benefits of living under the rule of Roman law. The problems which Theodosius II had failed to solve a century earlier were to be tackled much more successfully by his sixth-century successor. Justinian was determined to reduce the confused and confusing mass of imperial legislation and juristic opinion which composed Roman law at the start of his reign into an ordered and accessible whole. To this end, he appointed in 528 a commission led by Tribonian, his *quaestor sacri palatii*, and Theophilus, professor of law at Constantinople, to produce a code, an official collection of imperial legislation, which when published would supersede all previous enacted laws and alone have validity as a collection of imperial legislation. This code, very little of which has survived and which is known as the *Codex Vetus*, was published in 529.

In the following year, Justinian set an enlarged commission the more demanding task of producing an ordered compilation of that portion of the law which was contained in the writings of the jurists. This was a vast endeavour, entrusted to six commissioners: Tribonian and Theophilus once more, but now joined by another civil servant, Constantinus, and a colleague of Theophilus from the Constantinople law school, Cratinus. The other two commissioners were the professor of law at the other great imperial law school at Beirut, Dorotheus, and his colleague, Anatolius. They were aided in their task of reading all the extant juristic literature by a team of advocates from the Constantinople bar. Although it was claimed that the work was expected to take ten years, modern scholarship indicates that it was known from the outset that the work would be finished in 533.[18] The end product is known as the Digest or the *Pandects*. Both titles reflect its achievement. It is a digest in that a vast mass of juristic writing was reduced to more manageable proportions; *Pandects* reflects the comprehensiveness of its coverage. The whole work, which is in length one and a half times the size of the Bible, is composed of fifty books divided into titles. The titles provide the true system of the work in that they follow the order of the earlier juristic digests and therefore the order of the second century Edict of Julian. Under each title are arranged systematically excerpts from the writings of the jurists, together with attributions to their works.[19] The writings of the classical jurists predominate, especially Ulpian, Paul, Papinian and Julian. The commissioners did not however settle disputes by counting heads or following the Law of Citations. They were to select the best opinions and the imperial will was utilized to settle some difficulties in the course of the compilation.[20] It was claimed that the finished work contained no contradictions or errors, and it was given the force of law. Henceforth, it was to be the only source used for citing juristic opinion, so that in reality all law was now enacted law, and no commentary on the text was to be allowed.[21] Obsolete laws were said to have been expunged; outdated laws were meant to have been adapted to contemporary needs.[22]

Although the completion of the Digest was an achievement which had eluded previous generations, it was also apparent that this was not a work which was suitable to place in the hands of young men setting out to learn the law. Realising this, Justinian set three of the commissioners, Tribonian, Theophilus and Dorotheus, to produce a much shorter work, suitable as an introduction for students. This task they undertook early in 533. The work which they completed by the end of that year, so that it was promulgated and given the force of law at the same time as the Digest, was modelled on Gaius' *Institutes* and bears the same title. It is in four books, unlike Gaius divided into titles, setting out the law in excerpts borrowed from but not attributed to the classical jurists, according to the lucid, orderly, systematic arrangement devised by Gaius in the second century. It was destined to be the beginners text on Roman law for many centuries to come.

The changes wrought by Justinian to the law in settling some of the long-unsettled juristic disputes during the compilation of the Digest meant that much of the law in the *Codex Vetus* was already out of date. Accordingly, in 534, Tribonian and Dorotheus, together with three advocates, were instructed to prepare a revised version of the code bringing it up to date. This, the *Codex repetitae praelectionis*, was completed and published by the end of that year. It replaced the *Codex Vetus* and is composed of twelve books, divided into titles, following the order of the earlier codes and therefore of the Edict. It was given the same authority as the Digest and the *Institutes*. The three works were to be known to future generations, but not until the close of the Middle Ages, as the *Corpus Iuris Civilis*, the body of civil law.

Justinian's law-making did not end in 534. Further legislation was enacted by him, and this had to be collected in supplements to the main work called novels, *novellae*, that is new laws. The same title had been used for collections of new laws made as supplements to the Theodosian Code in the fifth century, for instance during the reigns of Marjorian and Marcian.

6 Conclusion

The period of the Dominate completes the history of Roman law in the ancient world. The history ends where it begins, with a text. From the XII Tables, through the *edictum perpetuum* and the codes of the Dominate to the *Corpus Iuris* of Justinian, there is a constant need to reduce law to a written form. Justinian's compilations raise the status of the text to be the only source of law; it is the first manifestation of the belief that a ruler can produce a code which will provide the only source of law needed by a society, a law which does not need interpretation or commentary. The same reign witnesses the futility of that faith with the need to legislate further in the Novels.

The Dominate also sees the emergence of the Christian Church as a force in the legal firmament, and the development of a hierarchical courts system which was to prove vastly influential in the future development of civil law. The concept of the absolute ruler whose will was law also had a future before it in the civil law world, as had the use of writing and the employment of notaries in transacting legal business.

There can however be no doubt, in terms of legal history, what is the most significant event in this period. It is the composition of the *Corpus Iuris Civilis*, for this was to be the hub around which the entire history of civil law in the mediaeval and modern world was destined to revolve.

Notes

[1] These were Antoninus Pius (138-161), Marcus Aurelius (161-180) and Commodus (180-192).

[2] In the immediate aftermath of Commodus' killing, Pertinax became emperor for three months, and, on his demise, Didius Julianus became emperor by purchasing the imperial dignity when it was auctioned by the praetorian guards. Unsurprisingly, he did not retain his purchase for long, Septimius Severus seizing and retaining the title by superior military force.

[3] For a fuller account of the structures for the administration of justice under Diocletian's reforms, see chapter 13.
[4] See chapter 15.
[5] See Justinian, *Code* 12. 19. 8.
[6] There is a dispute about the dating of these collections. See H.F. Jolowicz and B. Nicholas, *An Historical Introduction to Roman Law* (3rd. Ed.; Cambridge, 1972), p. 463 f.; cf. Jolowicz, *Historical Introduction* (2nd Ed.; Cambridge, 1952), p. 482.
[7] One reference is given to the 120th constitution collected under the 69th title.
[8] For additions to *Gregorianus* in 295 and *Hermogenianus* as late as 364-365, see Jolowicz, *Historical Introduction*, p. 482, and Jolowicz and Nicholas, p. 464 n. 4.
[9] The Law of Citations has been much criticized for its preference for quantity of juristic opinion above quality. This is in some measure unfair. Had Theodosius' project to give legislative force to a selection of imperial enactments and juristic opinions reached fruition, the Law of Citations would have been a short-term measure which operated only for a decade. The failure of Theodosius' original project of 429 and the production of the Theodosian Code instead meant that it remained in operation for a century. What was therefore perhaps designed as a holding solution while the 429 project got underway was left in force for a much longer period than was intended.
[10] Spain for instance and Italy. See chapter 14.
[11] There has been considerable dispute over the extent to which Greek influence shaped legal developments during the fourth and fifth centuries: see L. Mitteis, 34 *Zeitschrift der Savigny-Stiftung für Rechtsgeschichte (Romanistische Abteilung)* 413 f; S. Riccobono, 'Punti di vista critici e ricostruttivi a proposito della dissertazione di L. Mitteis' (1928) 12 *Annali del seminario giuridico di Palermo* 500 ff; Jolowicz, *Historical Introduction*, 517 ff.; Jolowicz and Nicholas, pp. 469 ff.
[12] As provided by Constantine in 333; see A.H.M. Jones, *The Later Roman Empire 284-602* (Oxford, 1964), p. 480.
[13] Beginning with Constantine's own summoning of the Council of Nicea in 325.
[14] See A.H.M. Jones, *The Later Roman Empire*, pp. 484 ff.
[15] See A.H.M. Jones, *The Later Roman Empire*, p. 65; Jolowicz and Nicholas, *Historical Introduction*, pp. 437 ff.
[16] See A.H.M. Jones, *The Later Roman Empire*, p. 103.
[17] See Jolowicz and Nicholas, *Historical Introduction*, pp. 509 ff, and the references to the dispute in n. 11 supra.
[18] See Tony Honoré, *Tribonian* (Ithaca, New York, 1978).
[19] These attributions have proved invaluable to modern scholars, notably F. Bluhme and O. Lenel. The former utilized them to develop a theory of how the Digest commissioners worked and compiled their text, while the latter used the references to reconstruct the lost text of the *edictum perpetuum*. See F. Bluhme, 'Die Ordnung der fragmenten in den Pandektentiteln' (1820) 4 *Zeitschrift für geschichtliche*

Rechtswissenschaft 256 ff; O. Lenel, *Das Edictum Perpetuum* (3rd. Ed.: Leipzig, 1927).

[20] The Fifty Decisions which have not survived.

[21] *Constitutio Deo Auctore* 12; *constitutio Tanta* 21.

[22] This gave rise to the quest for interpolations as well as fuelling the enthusiasm of the Humanist school; see chapter 6.

4 The Dark Ages

1 The Germanic Invasions

The Dark Ages is the unflattering description given by certain historians to the period between the fall of the Roman empire in the West and roughly the turn of the first millennium. An historian of the civil law might facetiously claim that it is in fact the period between the fall of the western empire and the rediscovery of the benefits of Roman civil law in the eleventh century. It is certainly the period during which the Roman juristic achievement was of hardly any influence in the law and government of western Europe.

Before the deposition of Romulus Augustulus in 476, Germanic tribes from the north of Europe had settled within the boundaries of the western empire and in fact were in control of much of it. At first, they were happy to accept a federated relationship with the Romans, accepting in theory that the authority of their rulers was recognized by if subservient to the Roman imperial power. This may have given the Germanic leaders a sense of prestige and consolidated their authority over those of their subjects who were of Roman rather than Germanic stock, but the reality increasingly was that the newcomers were in control. The Germanic tribes who had travelled as far south as the shores of the Mediterranean at this time were the Goths: western Goths or Visigoths, who occupied much of what is now south-west France and Spain, and eastern Goths or Ostrogoths who occupied some parts of south-east France and the Italian peninsula.

Already, at the start of the fifth century, control of the western empire had been passing from the titular rulers to barbarian generals who actually wielded power. Pressure and danger from the north had inspired the emperor Honorius to move the western capital from Milan to Ravenna. By the end of that century it was to be the capital of a barbarian kingdom. Odoacer's deposition of Romulus Augustulus was the assumption of a kingship which was in reality already his; it was the fiction of his being the servant of the western emperor which ended. Fourteen years later, Theodoric became king of the Ostrogothic kingdom which he was to rule from Ravenna until his death in 526.

It was in response to this loss of control in the West that Justinian launched his campaigns to recover the lost lands of the western empire to Roman rule. His generals Belisarius and Narses enjoyed considerable success, the former recapturing Ravenna itself in 540 and the latter going on to recover most of northern Italy by 561. Justinian attempted to promulgate his laws in the West, first by the so-called *Edictale Programma,* issued shortly after the capture of Ravenna, and somewhat more confidently by the Pragmatic Sanction of 554. However, the eastern emperor's conquests were short-lived, the Lombards successfully invading northern and central Italy and establishing their kingdom there in 568. Parts of southern Italy and the exarchate of Ravenna did remain under Byzantine control.

Justinian's laws did not however have long enough to take root among the people of Italy who still thought of themselves as Romans living according to Roman law. The Roman law by which they lived, and according to which their legal advisers had been educated, was the law of the Theodosian Code. This was even more the case with regard to the Romans who had found themselves living under Visigothic rule in the lands of southern France and Spain.

The Lombards were to remain in control of most of Italy until the Frankish conquest under Charlemagne in 773-774. The Franks, under their leader Clovis, had already defeated the Visigoths at the battle of Vouillé in 507, during which the Visigothic king, Alaric II, lost his life. Thereafter, the Visigothic kingdom was virtually confined to Spain, with its capital moved from Toulouse, now in Frankish hands, to Toledo. The Visigothic kingdom flourished however during the sixth and seventh centuries, but met with a sudden and almost total disaster when, in 711, the Islamic Moors invaded Spain from Africa. Within the space of weeks, the Visigothic kingdom crumbled, leaving the Moors in control of virtually the whole of Spain other than some mountainous areas in the Pyrenees and a narrow coastal strip in the north in Asturias. From this base in Asturias however, Pelayo was able to resist the final onslaught of the Moors in 718, and his victory at Covadonga marked the beginning of the process of reconquest which was to take almost nine centuries.

Meanwhile, the Moorish advance had taken the forces of Islam into the kingdom of the Franks, and there they were not stopped until the victory of Charles Martel over them at Poitiers in 732. Charles was the mayor of the palace, that is the chief minister, of the Merovingian king, but actually had more power than the king he served. In a familiar manner, the descendants of the mayor eventually took the royal title itself, and it was from Charles

Martel that the great ruler of the Franks, Charlemagne, was descended. From his name comes the dynastic designation of Carolingian Franks. Charlemagne it was who was to conquer the Lombard kingdom of Italy and have himself crowned by the Pope on Christmas Day in the year 800, in an attempt to revive the imperial title in the West, albeit now as Holy Roman Emperor.

2 The Barbarian Law Codes

During the centuries which separate the fall of the Roman empire in the West from the creation of the Holy Roman Empire of Charlemagne, many of the barbarian rulers provided their subjects with written statements of the laws under which they were governed. To some extent, these edicts, as they were often called, were imitations of the legal provisions which some of the later Roman emperors had made for their citizens, in particular the Theodosian Code. The word *edict* appears to have appealed to some of the earliest rulers in that it reflected well upon their status within the empire, being akin to the edicts issued by Roman magistrates and governors in the provinces within which they exercised their powers.

The earliest of these barbarian laws is the Edict of Theodoric. This was thought for many years to have been issued by Theodoric, king of the Ostrogoths (490-526), but is now generally believed to be the creation of a Visigothic ruler of the same name. It was issued *circa* 460, and reflects the existing relationship of theoretical dependence of the Visigothic ruler upon the titular Roman emperor. It is a simplified version of passages drawn from the codes of Gregorius, Hermogenian and Theodosius II, with a heavy bias towards the procedural and the penal elements of the law. Its Roman law is so lacking in sophistication compared with the originals and the subsequent work of Justinian that the Roman law it exemplifies has become known as vulgar Roman law.

Euric, king of the Visigoths (466-484), also issued a law code for his people. Parts of this enactment have survived in the form finally given it by his successor Leovigild (569-586). It is generally maintained that Euric's laws were meant to govern only his Visigothic subjects, and was not intended to extend to those within his kingdom who considered themselves Roman citizens and therefore continued to live according to Roman law, or at least what they remembered of it.[1] Alaric II, who was king of the Visigoths (484-507), also issued a law code which is known as the *Breviary of Alaric* or as the *Lex Romana Visigothorum*, the Visigothic Roman Law. It bears this name because it has generally been thought to be a code produced by Alaric for those of his subjects who were Romans, so as to complement Euric's provision for his Visigothic subjects. The *Breviary of Alaric* is again a work of vulgar Roman law, drawing heavily upon the Theodosian Code, later imperial enactments and some juristic sources, most notably a much simplified version of Gaius' *Institutes*.[2] The influence of Vulgar Roman law can also be found in the laws issued by Gundobad, king of the Burgundians (474-518), known as the *Lex Burgundionum*.

Alaric died at the battle of Vouillé, defeated by Clovis, the Merovingian king of the Franks. It was under his rule that there was produced sometime between 507 and 511 an agreed written text of the Frankish law code known as the Salic law, the *Pactum legis Salicae*. This appears in part to have been influenced by the laws of Euric. Clovis' production of an agreed legal text for the Salian Franks appears to have inspired the production of further such texts for the customs of the tribes living in what is now Switzerland and southern Germany - the *lex Alamannorum*, in Bavaria - the *lex Bauiorum*, and along the banks of the Rhine - the *lex Ripuaria*. Although the idea of reducing the laws to writing shows a degree of Roman influence, mediated by the example of the Visigothic and Salic rulers, the substance of these laws is Germanic, with considerable emphasis on compensation payments for wrongs committed, although there is occasionally clear ecclesiastical influence in some quarters.

Following the death of Alaric at Vouillé, the Visigothic kingdom became centred in Spain, and its rulers continued to add to the law code inaugurated by Euric. Towards the end of the sixth century and at the beginning of the seventh, documents were drafted to govern transactions which evidence for the first time an intermingling of the Germanic legal customs of the Visigoths and the rules of Roman law remembered by the Roman elements in the population. These forms were collected, probably during the latter half of the second decade of the seventh century and are known as the *Fórmulas Visigóticas*. They are the first sign of that uniting of the two legal traditions which marks the development of a new communal identity. This was taken further during the reign of Kindasvinth (642-653), with the abrogation of the *Breviary of Alaric* and the introduction in its stead of a new code of law which was to apply equally to both the king's Visigothic and Roman subjects. The work is known as the *Liber Iudiciorum*, and was revised under Kindasvinth's immediate successor, Reccesvinth (653-672) and under Ervig (680-687) and Egica (687-702). Ervig's edition, which has survived, was entitled the *Forum Iudicum*, or in Spanish, the *Fuero Juzgo*. It was to play a massively important role in the subsequent history of Hispanic law. It is a fusion of Germanic and Roman legal material: the Germanic predominating on matters relating to marriage, family property and family relationships; the Roman element being most clear on succession, prescription and contractual obligations.

One of the factors which made for the fusion of the Visigothic and Roman legal traditions was the conversion of the Visigothic rulers, and therefore their subjects, from the Arian heresy to catholic Christianity.[3] This occurred during the reign of Reccared (586-601), who reissued Euric's code. Thereafter, the Church encouraged the application of common laws to all the king's subjects, some of which were issued at Councils held periodically at Toledo.

The same feature can be discerned in the development of Lombard law in Italy. The first legal enactment made after the fall of northern and central Italy to the Lombards in 568 was the Edict of Rothari (636-652) issued in 643. The title of edict was probably chosen in imitation of the legislative work of the praetorian prefects, and the Lombard laws are indeed set out in Latin and betray Roman influence also with regard to attempts at systematization, definition and explanation of the laws. Much of the content is Germanic, although from the outset the Lombard laws were intended to apply to all subjects, Roman as well as Lombard, although with regard to matters not dealt with in the edict, subjects were free to follow the legal system of their origin. Rothari's edict was introduced in direct imitation of Roman codifications and made provision for subsequent amendment by the king's successors. Amendment did indeed occur, most notably under Liutprand (712-744), when not only were considerable additions made but there is clear evidence of the growth of Roman and ecclesiastical influence. Thus, for instance, Liutprand admits females to succession rights and allows gifts for religious purposes. Under the eighth-century Lombard rulers, the purpose of law also veers in a distinctly Christian direction.[4]

It was however during the eighth century that Lombard rule in Italy came under attack from the Franks. This was the result in part of the Papacy feeling threatened by the expansion of Lombard power into southern Italy and into the Exarchate. Pepin III therefore invaded Italy and forced the Lombard rulers to recognize him as their overlord. He granted the Exarchate to the Pope as a papal fief. In 773-774, however, Charlemagne, king of the Franks, again invaded Italy and on this occasion supplanted the government of the Lombard kings, whose sphere of influence was thereafter reduced to the duchy of Benevento in the south. The Franks had emerged as the most powerful group in western Europe, as Spain was at this time in the hands of her Moorish conquerors.

3 The Carolingian Empire

Charlemagne was crowned Holy Roman Emperor of the West by the Pope on Christmas Day, 800. The Pope's conferring of the title upon the Frankish king manifested a claim which the Papacy was to maintain for several centuries, namely its right to confer the imperial title in the West. It based this claim on the so-called Donation of Constantine, asserting that when that emperor had moved his centre of government to his new capital of Constantinople in the East in 330, he had given to the Bishops of Rome the right to provide for the imperial succession in the West.[5] Thus was brought into being the tension between the Pope and the emperor as to who was the ultimate source of legitimate power in western Christendom.[6]

The Carolingians were to make several important changes in the legislative practices of the lands they governed. The laws of the barbarian rulers discussed above were made in assemblies of the people, reminiscent of the *comitiae* of early Rome. These assemblies were general meetings of the population at which not only would the customs of the people be stated and possibly reduced to writing, but also disputes among the populace would be settled and if necessary the customs elaborated or even changed in order to effect such settlements.[7]

To reflect the fact that the laws were agreed by the people, they were sometimes described among the Franks as *Pacta*, agreements or bonds, therefore alluding also to their binding nature. The *Pactum legis Salicae* is an example, as also is the earliest form of the *lex Alamannorum*. In both of these cases, it was the people who stated the laws for themselves in the presence of their leader, but in other cases, the leader himself might have the legislative initiative and state the laws which could then be approved by the people. Such was the case with both the Lombards and the Burgundians, the Edict of Rothari having been made and amended in this way. The leader might call upon the elders of the group to frame the legislative propositions that he would put to the people, again recalling the original role of the Roman senate in the law-making of the early republican, and possibly of the even earlier regal, period.

In such circumstances, the people themselves rather than their rulers were the source of law and had the law-making and law-applying power. The laws they made were therefore only applicable to the members of the group. A person's social life proceeded according to the law of the group to which he belonged and not according to the place in which he lived. Such legal arrangements are described as being personal systems of law rather than territorial systems, and rules had to be devised regarding what was to occur when relationships between members of different groups, whether friendly or conflictual, were involved. Some maintain that this personal approach was generated by the fact that the barbarian tribes who occupied the western empire did so in circumstances in which they were moved to allow the original inhabitants to continue to live according to their remembrance of Roman law, so that it was the existence of Roman vulgar law and the attachment of the Roman elements of the population to it that gave rise to the system of personal laws in the aftermath of the fall of the western empire.

Charlemagne found himself ruling an area in which many such systems of personal law prevailed and in which it was not therefore possible to convene his subjects let alone expect them to agree upon a common set of customs. Here occurs therefore during the ninth century a centralization of law-making power in the hands of the emperor and his court, which may have been inspired in part by the example of his Roman imperial predecessors as well as being in part forced upon him by circumstance. In any event, the emperor began to legislate by means of issuing what are known as Capitularies. The word had been used by the Lombard kings of their additions to their edict, but perhaps more significantly it was used by the Church for the recording of the decisions of its councils which, in Charlemagne's time, were passed to the emperor to become part of his legal requirements from his subjects. Thus, the alliance of ecclesiastical and secular government went hand in hand with the beginnings of imperial legislative power.

Some of the capitularies are therefore of an ecclesiastical nature, others secular. Both sets were however primarily concerned with the relationship between the ruler and his people, it being part of his duty to uphold the faith. Among the secular capitularies, some were of general application throughout the emperor's dominions, others only applied to parts of it, according therefore to the previously separate kingdoms and peoples over which the Frankish dynasty now held sway. However, the emperor's subjects no longer attended the popular assemblies in the manner in which their ancestors had done in previous generations. Instead, few only attended, and they in the main were those who held offices of responsibility under the emperor. *Missi dominici*, officials of the emperor, now presided at the assemblies and were in attendance at meetings of the imperial court. That assembly therefore moved closer to being a royal council, with the emperor's officials representing the lands they governed. On their return, they would promulgate the legislation, copies having been authenticated by imperial officials after the texts had been approved. Authentication of approved texts had been a feature of earlier legislation too, including the *Breviary of Alaric* and the Edict of Rothari.

In order to be able to provide for the needs of specific groups, indeed nations, within his empire, Charlemagne needed to be aware of what their diverse customs were. Thus it was that very early in his imperial reign, in 802, he required that each people should submit to him an agreed text of their customs, their elders playing an important role in formulating the texts which the popular assemblies were to agree. From the compilations made on this occasion derives much subsequent knowledge of the laws of the period. Although the customs contained in these redactions had on occasion been reduced to writing before, nevertheless Charlemagne's collections often supply the first extant evidence of their contents. From the imperial initiative of 802 emanate the Laws of the Saxons and the Frisian Code of the people occupying the lands which today form the Netherlands. Among the Franks, as well as supplying additions to the *lex Ripuaria*, Charlemagne's collection probably furnished the earliest texts of the Thuringian Code and that of the Chamavi, the *lex Francorum Chamavorum*, the laws of the Franks living in the Hamaland.[8]

All of these customs were the personal laws of the tribes whose lives they governed, but Charlemagne also ruled over vassals who were subject to his governance as a matter of personal submission. His imperial power was therefore not confined to upholding the laws and the peace of those whom he governed as a matter of duty; he also claimed the loyalty of the subjects he governed on a personal basis. The *ban* or fine imposed for breach of the emperor's peace was not solely or primarily a penalty for transgressing the order which he was bound to uphold; it was also a penalty for offending against the ruler to whom personal allegiance was owed. In all of this, there are shades of the feudal arrangements which were to emerge into the limelight upon the demise of the Carolingian empire.

The transformation of the assemblies into councils of royal ministers not only affected the legislative procedures of the period; judicial activity was also changed. Whereas previously, the people as a whole had exercised the judicial function, this was no longer sustainable in the face of smaller attendances. Accordingly, Charlemagne required those who were informed with regard to the customs to sit as popular judges, called *scabini* in Italy and *schöffen* in Germany, to declare, interpret and apply the customary laws in determining disputes among their people.[9] Whereas previously, the people as a whole would play a role in adding to their customs in the context of dispute settlement, it now fell to these popular judges to develop the customary law by judicial pronouncement, *sine fraude, secundum Deum*,[10] emphasizing not just the integrity of their work but also that it should accord with that law which overarched human law-making, and which now was regarded as being divine law as expressed in Scripture and developed in the teachings of the Church. The notion that human law must conform to a higher law to be valid was still therefore present, but the Church was making claims to be the interpreter of whether it achieved that standard or not.

Charlemagne also established a central court for the empire, the *Aula Regis*. The decisions of this court were of persuasive force throughout the empire, giving a lead to the more local courts in the manner in which they interpreted imperial legislation and local custom, ensuring the influence of imperial authority and thereby the values of the western Church. This again militated against the personality of law, so that gradually matters such as the penalties for wrongdoing and the validity of marriage ceased to be determined according to one's personal status and were instead respectively matters for the public law of the empire or the canon law of the Church.[11]

4 Feudalism and Revival of Learning

On his death in 814, Charlemagne's empire went into a period of gradual but steady decline, in large measure caused by absence once more of a satisfactory rule of succession. Following Frankish custom, his lands were divided amongst his heirs, inevitably leading to competition for predominance. This allowed the more individual and confident lands to assert their relative independence. Italy was one of these, so the assembly at Pavia, the old Lombard capital, was able to claim successfully that while imperial laws might be introduced by the emperor, they needed the assent of the people for enactment. This viewpoint was successfully maintained against Lothar in 832.

The failure of Charlemagne's successors to maintain their authority at the head of the empire meant an increase in the power and influence of the imperial appointees who held the various fiefs as *missi dominici*. They also were able to assert their independence and in 877, Charles the Bald conceded that they might enjoy their benefices heritably, thus creating what was to become an hereditary class of feudal lords within the empire. These in turn were able to extract oaths of loyalty from their followers in return for grants of land. The weaker the emperor, the stronger the position of the local princes, counts and dukes who held their lands of him.

There had already been signs of this emerging feudalism under Charlemagne himself, but by 900 it had advanced considerably. One of its effects was to put an end to the personal nature of legal status, for the population now lived according to the law of the lord under whose protection they had placed themselves and their land. The custom of the tribe gave way to the custom of the lordship. Law became territorial rather than personal.

This development had an important impact upon the role of the judges who staffed the lords' courts. Although they might still be representatives of the people, they were no longer in a position to state the relevant customs from their knowledge alone. Stating the custom of the folk gave place to recognizing customs which were valid. Here, for the first time, a measure of legal expertise became important, as customs were expected to be not just practices of the community, but practices which were in accordance with divine law, the law of the Church and natural law, otherwise they were bad. In addition, it became the norm to require the customs to be approved, either by the ecclesiastical or the secular authorities. Judges needed to know which customs were approved. The core however of feudal law lay in the compacts made between a lord and his vassals concerning their landholding from him and the duties each was under. This was to become the learning of feuds, and a specific area of legal knowledge.

Under Charlemagne there had been a steady growth in the encouragement of learning. Schools were established at the great ecclesiastical centres of the empire and in the greatest monasteries. The increasing involvement of the Church in secular affairs since the conversion of the barbarian kings to Catholicism as opposed to Arianism led to a need for skilled learned men to serve the secular rulers and to ensure that their policies and enactments furthered the Church's mission and did not offend against the principles of Christianity. The Church's virtual monopoly of learned skills such as reading and more especially writing made the clergy ideal servants to secular lords in what were to be termed clerical tasks. Education was also something which the Church could provide to ensure a succession of able persons to serve both the Church and the State.

The main subject of study in the cathedral schools and the monasteries was theology, but the monastic copyists also produced manuscripts of the classical writers of ancient Rome. Through their work, much of the learning of classical antiquity survived into the later mediaeval and indeed the modern world. Learning turned very much upon the reading and interpreting of texts. In theology, the Scriptures in the Latin translation produced by St. Jerome (347-420) were central, followed by the works of the Fathers of the Church - Jerome himself, St. Ambrose (340-397), St. Augustine (354-430) and St. Gregory the Great (540-604). Their works were studied with great reverence as being revelations of the word of God, and copied in order that that revelation of truth might be more widely disseminated. Collections of the decisions of the Church Councils, both ecumenical and local, also began to be made.

In the Lombard imperial city of Pavia, the cathedral school rose to great eminence and the laws of the Lombard people began to be studied there. These were in part derived from the *Lex Romana Visigothorum* but also from collections of enactments of the Lombard rulers from Rothari onwards, together with the capitularies of the later Holy Roman Emperors. Study was also undertaken of the Lombard customs. The relationship of Lombard and Roman law was the subject of a work from the early eleventh century called the *Liber Papiensis*, produced by a judge of the imperial court at Verona, Walcausus, which suggests that such persons were in need of a literature to guide their activities. The growth of legal literature and legal education were to go hand in hand once more as in the Roman republic, together with division of juristic style and opinion, some Pavian jurists, the *antiqui*, preferring to stick to studying the vulgar Roman law, while the *moderni* favoured mixing Roman and Lombard legal studies. It has been argued that it was here that the first steps were taken in developing a methodology of legal study which was to lead to the great flowering of jurisprudence in Italy in the coming centuries.[12]

5 Conclusion

Although the Dark Ages did not produce a legal culture comparable to the ages preceding or succeeding them, they are not without their legal significance. The progress of the Germanic peoples, the reduction of their customs into writing and the contact of those customs with the remnant of Roman law in western Europe and the developing canon law of the western Church, all introduced into European legal culture forces which were to be of great importance in the shaping of the laws and legal institutions of Europe thereafter. The Germanic customs threw into the melting pot of early mediaeval legal development very different conceptions of family relationship, the status of women, family rights in property and the rights of family members to inherit upon death. They also reintroduced into government notions of popular participation which had fallen into desuetude in ancient Rome and, under the influence of the Lombard kings and then the Frankish emperors, developed further the importance of authenticated documents as a reliable source of evidence in legal transactions. The use of popular judges in dispute settlement and their jurisdiction to declare custom and to adjudicate upon its suitability prefigured the importance of the judicial role in future legal development, and gave rise also to a new legal literature and a new need for legal education. The reduction of customs to writing and the collection of legal enactments met this need in part, but also led to the study of these texts and their methodical comparison with the sources of knowledge of other legal orders including Roman law.

Although the legal material which this age left in its wake does not compare to the classical remains of the Roman world, nevertheless its cruder materials were of great strength and were to prove serviceable as building blocks in the next stage of European legal development.

Notes

[1] This has been challenged by those who say it was a general code - see E.N. Van Kleffens, *Hispanic Law until the End of the Middle Ages* (Edinburgh, 1968), pp. 67 ff.

[2] Again, it has been argued it was meant to apply to all of Alaric's subjects, Roman and Visigothic; see Van Kleffens, loc. cit., supra.

[3] Arianism was a heresy which refused to accept that God the Father and God the Son were equal, but rather maintained the inferiority of the Son whom, it was said, had been created by the Father. The Goths and the Vandals had been converted to Christianity when Arianism was very influential in the Roman empire, although it had been condemned as a heresy at the Council of Nicea under Constantine (325).

[4] See for example the preambles to the laws of Rachis (746) and Astolf (755).

[5] Written evidence to support this claim was duly furnished according to the prevailing need for documentation. At the Renaissance this was recognized to be a 'forgery', but the opprobrium attaching to this term makes its use inappropriate. The 'forgers' were responding to the demand that written proofs be furnished, and were creating acceptable evidence of facts they believed to be true.
[6] The so-called Investiture contest is referable to this.
[7] See C. Calisse et al., *General Survey of Continental Legal History* (Boston, 1912; reprinted New York, 1968), p. 36. Similar such assemblies can be found until the thirteenth century in Scandinavia; see *General Survey*, pp. 540, 546.
[8] See *General Survey*, p. 57 for an account of the geographical location of these systems of law.
[9] These replaced the *rachimburgi* in Frisia.
[10] See *General Survey*, p. 77.
[11] See Council of Treves, 895; discussed in *General Survey*, p. 68.
[12] See Charles M. Radding, *The Origins of Medieval Jurisprudence: Pavia and Bologna, 850-1150* (New Haven & London, 1988).

5 The Rebirth of Civil Law

1 The Digest and the Glossators

The history of civil law in the ancient world began and ended with the production of a text: began with the XII Tables and ended with the Codes, Digest, Institutes and Novels of Justinian. It was with the rediscovery of one part of the latter compilation that the history of civil law in the mediaeval and modern world commences, marking the next phase in the development of civil law. Whereas the Code and Institutes of Justinian had been known in the West during the intervening centuries, the Digest had not. The Digest was the largest section of Justinian's work and contained the wealth of juristic opinion preserved from the classical age of Roman jurisprudence. It appears to have been rediscovered in Italy during the eleventh century.

The manner of its rediscovery is uncertain, but a famous story is attached to the event. According to tradition, a scholar named Irnerius was asked a question concerning the meaning of the Latin word *as* in the saying of Christ recorded in the Gospel of St. Matthew: "Are not two sparrows sold for a penny?" The coin mentioned in St. Jerome's Vulgate translation is the Roman *as*. Irnerius searched diligently for information concerning this coin, and found it much referred to in a manuscript previously little regarded in any sort of study. The manuscript in question was the only surviving manuscript copy of the Digest in western Europe. It was at that time in the cathedral library in Pisa, but was removed from there to the library of the church of San Lorenzo in Florence following that city's military victory over the Pisans in 1406. It is still in the library of that Florentine church from which it is known as the Laurentian manuscript.

Irnerius was a scholar in the city of Bologna, which was emerging as a notable centre of learning in the tenth century. From the cathedral school at Bologna was to arise the first university of western Europe. The prime subject of study in all of the cathedral schools was theology, but prior to studying the Scriptures and the Fathers of the Church, students were expected to undertake a general study of the liberal arts. These were formed into two groups: an initial group of three, consisting of grammar, logic and rhetoric, and thereafter a further group of four, arithmetic, geometry, astronomy and music. The group of three was called the *trivium*; the group of four the *quadrivium*. These were taught in the *studium generale* or Faculty of Arts. Only after completing their studies in these general areas, or at least in the *trivium*, could young men progress to more advanced studies in theology or by this time medicine. Bologna was to add another option to these subjects of advanced study - law.

Study of law was not new. It was already taking place as was noted in the last chapter at the cathedral school in Pavia.[1] However, legal studies lacked an element which the subjects of the *trivium* and of theology and medicine possessed, a central text of unrivalled authority upon which serious study could be concentrated. In theology, this was the Bible in the Vulgate translation; in grammar, logic and rhetoric, there were also ancient texts of great distinction, including Latin translations of some of the works of Greek philosophers such as Plato and Aristotle, as well as the works of Latin authors such as Cicero. During the twelfth century, further works by both Plato and Aristotle were to become available for study as a result of the Reconquest of Spain from the Moors. The Moors knew of works by Aristotle which were lost in the Christian West, but which had been translated into Arabic by Islamic scholars. These works were now further translated into Latin from the Arabic. This happened at a time when ecclesiastical contact with the Greek east was declining as a result of the orthodox break with the Papacy in 1054.

While the theologians, philosophers and grammarians had their texts, the lawyers had nothing of equivalence. At Pavia, there had been attempts to assemble legal texts, such as the *Liber Papiensis* and the *Lombarda*, but these compilations were not seriously comparable with the materials studied by the theologians and philosophers. The rediscovery of the Digest supplied the lack. It gave students of the law a text upon which to focus their study; a text the antiquity and authority of which put it in the same class as the writings of Plato or Aristotle or the Fathers of the Church, if not quite of such distinguished provenance as Holy Writ.

The Digest bore on its face the great claims made for it by Justinian and his compilers. It was to be in total concord and to exhibit total consistency. There were to be no repetitions, no contradictions, no superfluities of content or style. The emperor had ordered legal perfection, and that is what he claimed to have achieved. The Digest was an ordered compilation, aimed at presenting a comprehensive selection of the Roman jurisprudential achievement. In the realm of law, it was the jurists' nearest equivalent to the

Bible. If the Bible was the revealed truth of God, then the Digest was human reason reduced to writing; it was *ratio scripta*, written reason.

To understand the manner in which the Digest and the other parts of the emperor Justinian's compilations were received and studied at Bologna, this reverence for the text has to be grasped. Learning generally was text oriented; legal learning could hardly be different. In the context of the civil law tradition however this marked both a continuity and a precedent for the future. The Roman jurists had centred their work upon texts; firstly the XII Tables and then the praetor's edict, particularly in its final form of the Edict of Julian. The mediaeval jurists were therefore following their classical predecessors in fixing their sights upon the explication of a text, but in doing so they gave this tradition a new stimulus and a fresh impetus, which was destined to present the world eventually with the legal codifications of the nineteenth and twentieth centuries.

The rediscovery of the Digest inspired several generations of scholars at Bologna to devote their energies to a complete understanding and mastery of what they perceived to be *the* legal text. The Digest, it was thought and accepted, manifested not just a legal system but legal perfection. The claims made for it by its imperial author were accepted and therefore if there were repetitions, they were for a purpose; if there appeared to be contradictions or errors, such appearances were due to deficiencies in the reader and not the text. Greater understanding and more careful analysis it was believed would overcome such apparent blemishes.

Irnerius himself was the first of the Bolognese scholars to undertake this task of revealing the full majesty of the Digest. The technique which he adopted, which was to be continued by his pupils and successors, was to explain the text by means of glosses, annotated comments upon words, phrases or entire legal rules. These glosses were first written above or below the words being explained, between the lines of the manuscript. They are therefore called interlinear glosses. As the extent of the glosses increased, they could no longer be inserted interlinearly and were removed to the margins of the manuscripts, and finally when not even marginal glosses could accommodate the immense learning which the scholars had accumulated in the glosses, they came to dominate the pages of the manuscripts, being written all around the texts which they explained. Often, the text would be so well known that it would be omitted from some manuscripts altogether.

The scholars who elucidated the Digest in this manner were known as the Glossators, and their work dominated the study of civil law at Bologna for two centuries, during which time the accumulated glosses extended until they were longer than the Digest itself. They were finally integrated into a vast total gloss of the whole work in the thirteenth century by the jurist Accursius. His final complete gloss is called the *Glossa ordinaria*, the Ordinary or Standard Gloss. It was treated with much the same respect as the Digest upon which it was based, as it was thought to be the setting in which the precious stone of Roman jurisprudence was best appreciated.

The intellectual process by which the Glossators worked was not unique to them at this time. Their method was similar to that being employed by theologians and philosophers, particularly those in the nascent universities of northern Europe, particularly at the cathedral school of Notre Dame in Paris. It was there that Peter Abelard had enjoyed great success as a teacher of logic in the early years of the twelfth century. Abelard had dared to recognise publicly that even in the Scriptures and the writings of the Fathers there appeared to be contradictions. He emphasized that these contradictions were only apparent, that is in the eye of the beholder, but nevertheless he was prepared to give examples of them. In his groundbreaking work, *Sic et non*, he presented apparent contradictions in the writings of the Fathers as pairs of statements which needed to be reconciled. He then proceeded to use the techniques of logical argument, in particular the method called dialectic, to demonstrate how the apparent contradictions could be reconciled and each statement be seen to be correct in relation to the other. Abelard ran the gauntlet of being charged with heresy, and was twice accused and once convicted. His great success as a teacher and daring as a thinker won him the hostility of his ecclesiastical superiors, but he is a seminal figure in the development of that school of mediaeval philosophy which is called Scholasticism, which was to reach its apogee in the thirteenth century in the works of St. Thomas Aquinas.

Some believe that the achievement of the northern theologians influenced the work of the southern jurists; others hold that the process may have been the reverse; perhaps the developments were simultaneous manifestations of the intellectual spirit of the age. In any event, north and south of the Alps, in theology, philosophy and jurisprudence, it was believed that the apparent imperfections in perfect texts could be overcome by the use of human reason. Texts revealed truth, wisdom and justice - truth in the Bible; wisdom in the ancient philosophers; justice in the works of Justinian; full understanding of their respective revelations was achieved by reasoning upon their content. Confidence in the use of reason was a feature of the intellectual life of the age; the men who exemplified its use enjoyed celebrity, even if they recognized that they were only gathering the harvest for which others had laboured, "pygmies on the shoulders of giants".

The Glossators developed four main methods of overcoming contradictions in the text of the Digest. Each was a reason, *ratio*, for limiting the application of a rule of law so as to avoid or overcome an apparent conflict. It might be that the one rule was intended to operate in one place, the other in another - *ratio loci*. It might be that one of the rules was limited to its particular period - *ratio temporis*. There might be a logical distinction between the fields of operation of the two rules - *ratio significationis*, or it might be that one rule was that for general application and the other an exception - *ratio dispensationis*. These four techniques are grounded in the application of reason to the texts so as to exhibit their true meaning and application. They are therefore examples of what modern civil lawyers would call the logical interpretation of a legal rule. They go beyond the merely literal explanation of the meaning of a word or phrase, which is what the first interlinear glosses set out to achieve. Reverence for the text, that is belief that it is not inherently flawed, married to a set of techniques which explain its terms and, by the use of logic, tease out its underlying system, are a legacy of the Glossators to future generations of civil lawyers.

Irnerius was succeeded in his work at Bologna by four of his pupils, known as the Four Doctors - Jacobus, Martinus, Hugo and Bulgarus. They were among some of the most celebrated scholars of the school of the Glossators. One of the most famous was Azzo, whose lectures were so well attended that he had to give them in the large square in front of the basilica of San Petronio in Bologna. Students flocked to Bologna from all over Europe to study the new discipline of civil law, believing that it would further their career in the Church or in the service of secular rulers. Manuscripts of the Digest and other parts of the Justinianic compilations had to be hand copied and were therefore costly. Students preferred to learn the texts by heart and merely copy down the glosses which they heard at their lectures. Eventually, they would take the law which they learned and the legal skills which they acquired back with them to their homes in the various parts of western Christendom.

The great achievement of the Glossators arose from their belief that the texts which they studied could not be inconsistent. Each part must blend with every other. The Digest was a legal jigsaw to which the Gloss was the solution. Underlying this was the belief that the law it contained was ordered and systematic; once understood, it was both coherent and comprehensive. This belief that, for laws to be fully understood, human reason must reveal their underlying system was to inspire some of the Glossators' contemporaries to turn the light of their legal learning upon other bodies of legal rules.

2 Gratian and the Emergence of Canon Law

One of the first bodies of contemporary law to benefit from an application of the glossatorial technique was the law of the Church. Ever since the conversion of Constantine, when secular rulers had begun to take a positive interest in the Christian faith, the Church had in effect legislated on matters relating to its doctrines, worship and clerical and lay discipline. Certain topics, for instance, marriage, had been claimed as being particularly if not exclusively the preserve of the ecclesiastical authorities.[2] The rules of Church life had been promulgated in the form of canons, that is rules, issued by the early ecumenical councils. These were regarded as being binding upon the Church universally, but Church affairs in individual provinces and dioceses were also regulated by canons passed by synods or councils composed of the clergy from the area in question. Important councils had, for instance been held, in Arles, Lyons and Toledo.[3] It was from the canons passed at these assemblies that the law of the Church came to be referred to as canon law.

Canon law in the west also recognized the law-making powers of the Bishop of Rome, the Pope, as the only holder of an Apostolic see in the western Church. This primacy was in the Dark Ages coupled with the papacy's specific claims to have been given a measure of secular authority in the west by the Donation of Constantine. Papal decrees were therefore also a source of canon law, inferior to the canons of ecumenical councils, but of validity throughout the western Church. Individual bishops also had powers to make decrees binding on their own clergy, as did archbishops in their respective provinces.

The crowning of Charlemagne as Holy Roman Emperor in 800 marked an important moment in the relationship between the Church and secular government in the west. It inaugurated a partnership of secular and spiritual power. The decline of the empire as a significant political unit by the end of the ninth century and the growth of feudalism with its emphasis upon the independence of local lords also weakened the position of the Church. The feudal magnates of the tenth century, sometimes including the emperor, saw the Church as being under their territorial jurisdiction. If they built a church or founded a monastery, they wanted the right to choose the priest or nominate the abbot. If their territory included a bishopric or an archbishopric, they felt that the ecclesiastical office ought to be in their gift. They were resistant to the idea that any wrongs were excluded from their secular jurisdiction by reason of the nature of the act - because it was a sin, or by the nature of the wrongdoer - because he was a cleric. Disputes therefore arose concerning the ecclesiastical and secular jurisdictions, beginning with the question of which was the superior and which the inferior, and ending with the compromise solution of where to draw the boundary between the two spheres of interest.

These questions were to bedevil the politics of western Europe for several centuries. In the eleventh century, they formed the basis of the so-called Investiture Contest between the Pope and the Emperor. This concerned who was to invest a bishop with the symbols of his temporal and spiritual authority. In England, they formed the core of the troubles between King Henry II and Archbishop Thomas Becket. They were problems which affected every level as well as every locale of feudal jurisdiction.

In the middle of the eleventh century, the Papacy set its sights upon achieving a reform of the Church to ensure its independence of secular power. For two centuries and more, a line of reforming popes, many of them lawyers or at least of a legal turn of mind, undertook the work of reform. They began with Leo IX (1048-1054), but advanced considerably during the reign of his disciple, Hildebrand, who was Pope as Gregory VII (1073-1085). To enable the work of reform to be undertaken successfully required that the existing laws of the Church should be both available and accessible. This was all the more important in that part of the programme of reform involved subtracting from the secular jurisdictions matters of a spiritual nature and creating alongside the courts of secular lords and princes ecclesiastical tribunals to deal with such matters at the very least.[4]

It was during the eleventh century that two of the earliest collections of canon law were made. These were the works of Burchard, Bishop of Worms, in the early years of the century, and of Ivo, Bishop of Chartres, during the latter half. Burchard's *Decretum* is a collection of over 1,700 extant canons of the Church in twenty books, each dealing with a particular topic. The arrangement of the canons within the books is not apparently ordered. The work was however of great use as a source of canonical material to later writers. Ivo compiled at least two works, one of which was also called *Decretum* and contained well over 3,000 canons in seventeen books, making it an unwieldy tool for serious research. He followed it, perhaps by popular demand, with a collection of about 1,000 canons, more carefully chosen, divided into eight books, called his *Panormia,* and this was his more influential work. This also contained a prologue setting out guidance on the interpretation of the canons which was to prove of great value to later writers.

The works of Burchard and Ivo were primarily collections of canons, arranged only into groups according to subject matter. There was no attempt to create a logical or progressive arrangement. This was where the influence of the developments made by the Glossators at Bologna was of signal importance. The order of the Digest was not something which was apparent to the twelfth century scholars, for it followed the order in which the Edict of Julian had dealt with its subject matter. Following that order would have made the work accessible to those for whom that order was a part of their legal tradition and learning. The Glossators however sought to overcome the disorder of the texts from their standpoint by means of the Gloss. The same technique of identifying apparent contradictions, superfluities and inconsistencies, and explaining them by means of the use of dialectic reasoning, could be employed to elucidate other systems of law. The first task would be to collect the sources; this men like Burchard and Ivo had done. The next stage was to turn upon them the light of human reason so as to allow order and comprehensiveness to be achieved.

This was the endeavour undertaken by Gratian, a monk who had studied at Bologna under the Glossators. It was he who produced in the early 1140s the first great attempt to expound the underlying system of the canons of the Church. This he did in a work which is known as his *Decretum,* but which he himself referred to as the Concordance of Discordant Canons, *Concordia discordantium canonum.* The title encapsulates effectively the author's purpose and methodology. Henceforth, the civil law of ancient Rome had a competitor in terms of the legal system which students and scholars at Bologna and elsewhere could study, the canon law of the Church. Indeed, from Gratian's time onwards, it was customary for law students to undertake the study of both laws, *uterque ius,* and to take a degree in both.

Unlike Roman civil law, the law of the Church was a living system, in the sense that it was constantly being added to and adapted to fit the contemporary world.[5] Following the publication of Gratian's *Decretum,* the flow of ecclesiastical legislation did not abate, so that additions to the *Decretum* were needed. These duly appeared in five instalments at the end of the twelfth and the beginning of the thirteenth century. Bernard of Pavia produced the first, *Prima,* in around 1190. He distributed his additions under five headings - *iudex, iudicium, clerus, connubia, crimen* - dealing respectively with ecclesiastical persons with jurisdiction, procedure, the duties of the clergy, marriage and wrongs. The divisions were to prove most influential in future compilations. The *Secunda* was produced officially prior to 1215 by John of Wales to follow the *Prima*, although the part called *Tertia* compiled by Peter of Benevento was already in existence in 1210. The *Quarta* contained the decretals of Innocent III made after the compilation of the *Secunda* and also the canons of the Fourth Lateran Council of 1215, while the *Quinta* continued the collection with decretals of Honorius III for the period 1216-1226.

The first major addition to the *Decretum* of Gratian however came in the year 1234 when Pope Gregory IX instructed the great Spanish canonist St. Raymond of Peñafort to compose an official addition to the *Decretum* to replace the five works described above. This Raymond did, following the arrangement of Bernard of Pavia's *Prima*, and the whole work, known as the Decretals of Gregory IX, or the *Liber Extra*, was sent with the *Decretum* to the universities of Bologna and Paris, in clear recognition of the work's status. The work was subjected to a full gloss by Bernard of Parma, at roughly the same time as Accursius' *Glossa ordinaria* was completed.

Further collections of canonical material were added in 1298 and 1317. The former, known as the *Sext* because it added to the five divisions of the *Extra*, was issued by Boniface VIII, and the latter, issued by John XXII consisted of the legislation of Clement V and is known as the *Clementinae* for that reason. These, the preceding works and other legislation not incorporated into them, called *Extravagantes*, were to become known in the sixteenth century as the *Corpus Iuris Canonici* in response to the title of *Corpus Iuris Civilis* which had by that time been acquired by Justinian's codifications.

3 The *Libri Feudorum* and other secular compilations

Obertus dall'Orto was an imperial judge in the city of Milan. He sent his son, Anselm, to study law at Bologna during the twelfth century. Anselm, so the story runs, was amazed to discover that the law he was taught at Bologna made no connection with the law his father administered in his native city. Accordingly, he is said to have asked his father to commit to writing the laws and customs administered by him in his daily, judicial duties. The result was the work known as the Book of Feuds, the *Libri*

Feudorum. It was subsequently recast by one Ardizo, and finally in the time of Accursius divided into books, titles and rubrics, in the manner of the Digest, and glossed by the great jurist himself. It was indeed placed by the jurist Hugolino into the body of law taught at the law schools, by being incorporated therein as a new tenth *collatio*, following the nine *collationes* composed of Justinian's Novels, together with enactments of the more recent Holy Roman Emperors.[6]

Whether the original composition of the *Libri Feudorum* is connected with the school of Bologna or not, there is no disguising the fact that its final form witnesses to the juristic urge to give laws generally the glossatorial treatment. It is surely also significant that the work is attributed to the year 1150 approximately, within a decade of the same having been done for canon law. The legal knowledge and skills being taught by the Glossators at Bologna were attracting young men from all over Europe, who believed that study there would further their careers in the service of either secular rulers or the Church. The pan-European nature of learning, scholarship and education was assisted by the use of a common language, Latin, both in the literature and for instruction. Rulers and ecclesiastics impressed by the fruits of their learning when they returned were not backward in seeking the services of scholars from Bologna to give instruction at schools and universities in their own lands. Thus, during the twelfth century, Placentinus established a school of civil law at Montpellier in France, and Vacarius was invited to England by Archbishop Theobald during the 1140s to teach Roman law.

The remainder of the twelfth century and the thirteenth century saw a growth in the legal literature of contemporary jurisdictions. This took the form of collections of laws and customs, but also the employment of dialectic reasoning in their presentation. There was also adoption of civilian approaches to solving legal problems and sometimes the adoption of civilian solutions themselves. In England, for instance, the start of the twelfth century saw the gathering of the laws of the Anglo-Saxon kings into a Latin text, the *Quadripartitus*, and the century ends with a dialectically presented account of the remedies given by the king's courts in the work known as *Glanvill*. The thirteenth century sees the first attempt to present English law according to the institutional scheme of persons, things and actions, in the *De Legibus* attributed by some to Bracton, and there is also clear awareness of both civilian terminology and solutions in that work. In France, the same period saw the production of the *Établissements de St. Louis*, as well as the first collections of local, regional customs in such works as the *Très Ancien Coutumier* of Normandy, and Phillipe de Beaumanoir's *Coutume de Beauvaisis*, which not only presents the customs of that lordship but also includes a commentary on them. In Germany, the thirteenth century saw the production of Eike von Repgow's great *Sachsenspiegel*, the mirror of Saxon law, the inspiration for which, though certainly not the substance, may have been the dignity which writing was seen to afford a legal tradition. Some of the Italian cities also reduced their laws to writing: Pisa in 1160 and Milan in 1216. These laws contained not just the enactments of the popular assemblies but also the *brevia* issued annually by the magistrates, again a reminiscence of the Roman model.

Fear may also have been a motive behind some of these compilations. There appears to have been a genuine concern lest the civil law being taught at the universities should supplant the laws of secular rulers in their own jurisdictions or even that of the Church itself. In 1219, Pope Honorius III, in his bull *Super Speculam*, banned monks and priests, but not other clergy, from studying civil law, and Roman civil law was not suffered to be taught at the university which had grown from the cathedral school of Notre Dame at Paris. Pope Innocent IV renewed the ban of his predecessor in 1254. The Church may also have been cautious lest the learning of the civilians might revive notions of the supremacy of the emperor as against all other authorities, secular or spiritual. Conflict between the claims of the Papacy and those of the Empire were still prevalent in the politics of western Christendom, and the kings and lords of western Europe were also on their guard against the claims of the emperor to have superiority over them, claims which the study of Roman law might encourage.

Questions were certainly being asked as to whether civil law was a fit subject of study for those who had chosen to serve the Christian Church, and much the same question could be asked of anyone in a Christian society. Given that Roman law had been developed in the main when Rome was a pagan society, the propriety of Christians devoting their energies to the legal works of pagans was questionable. It was true that Justinian had been a Christian emperor, but the jurists quoted in the Digest were most certainly not, and in Gratian's *Decretum*, it could now be asserted there was a more suitable, Christian compilation of laws fit for study. These criticisms mirrored those which were at the same time being directed at the students of philosophy who directed their attention to the works of pagans such as Plato and Aristotle rather than devoting their time to the Scriptures and the Church Fathers.

4 St. Thomas Aquinas and the Secular Revival

St. Thomas Aquinas met these criticisms directly. Born in the shadow of the great Benedictine abbey of Monte Cassino, he became a Dominican and spent much of his distinguished career in the north of Europe at Cologne and Paris. There, he produced his great works, the *Summa Theologica* and the *Summa contra gentiles,* which marked the zenith of systematic theology according to the dialectic method, the school called Scholasticism. He is regarded to this day as the greatest theologian of the Catholic Church, by many as the greatest philosopher of the Middle Ages. He is referred to as *Doctor Angelicus*.

St. Thomas had no doubt that the proper end of all human study was to increase in the knowledge of God's truth. That truth was revealed to man directly and infallibly in the Scriptures. The truth of the scriptural texts was beyond question. However, God had made man in his own image and given him the faculty of reason. By use of reason, man could discover truth for himself, although if reason contradicted Scripture, this was a sign of error in the use of the human faculty not in the God-given word. Revelation was the principal source of knowledge; reason the second.

However, it was not only Christians who had been made in God's image. This was true of all mankind. Likewise the faculty of reason was present as a gift of God not only in the baptized but in all people. Therefore, any human being by the use of this divine gift could discover truth. To argue that the reason of pagans such as Plato or Aristotle, who had lived before Christ, was not worthy of a Christian's contemplation was to err against Scripture which stated that all men were made in God's image, and to despise their rational discoveries was to despise the gift that God had given and thereby also the divine giver. There was nothing wrong with studying the achievements of classical antiquity provided its conclusions were mediated by the truth of Scripture. On the contrary, it was respectful to the God who had given these thinkers the gift of reason to reflect upon their use of it, and also appropriate to make full use of the talent to reason which every man possessed.

At a stroke, St. Thomas had not merely defended the study of the authors of antiquity, he had made the cultivation of their work respectable. In a whole range of disciplines, this produced a reaction which was to transform the culture of western Christendom. St. Augustine had written his great theological work *De civitate Dei*, concerning the City of God, when the western empire was collapsing in the face of the advance of the Huns, the

Goths and the Vandals. Darkness was closing in on all sides. It was clear that not even a Christian empire was going to usher in the kingdom of God on earth. Hope was to be placed in a kingdom not of this world. This world was a vale of tears, to be endured not enjoyed, to be despised not celebrated. This was the world view which the Church had by and large espoused during the Dark Ages, but St. Thomas released the Christian spirit of the west from this perspective. The world was God's creation, and should therefore be enjoyed in conformity with God's will.

The effects of this release are to be seen in the art and architecture, read in the literature and heard in the music of the succeeding centuries. No longer do artists depict saints against an other worldly background of sheer gold, they set them in a real world of towns and country landscapes, together with birds, animals, trees and flowers. The figures themselves become really human, and their humanity was to be depicted realistically through the use of perspective and attention to physical detail. Classical themes began to appear alongside Christian subjects in painting and sculpture. In architecture, designs taken from nature appear in the building work of cathedrals and buildings of a secular nature were also commissioned. Music became based on secular as well as sacred themes, and was no longer confined to religious compositions. In literature, poetry and prose began to be written in the modern vernacular spoken by the people and not exclusively in the learned Latin of the Church. St. Thomas ushered in the world of Dante, Giotto and, later, the Italian Renaissance.

For the development of legal studies, the writings of St. Thomas were also to be of profound importance. He took the idea of natural law which had featured somewhat confusedly in the writings of the Roman jurists and fashioned it into a full-blown statement of the relationship between divine law, the law given by God in Scripture, the law of the Church and the natural law, the law which God had placed in nature and which man could discover by reason. God's law was either revealed in Scripture, taught by the Church or discoverable in nature. Whatever its source, it was in accordance with the divine will and was just. Human laws, regardless of their provenance, could not offend against divine law or natural law and be valid. Nor should they transgress the law of the Church, which exercised the authority that God had himself in the person of Christ bestowed upon St. Peter, the first bishop of Rome, which authority continued to be enjoyed by his successors in that office.

Thus, St. Thomas built upon the natural law theories of the ancients and the notion which had been present in their laws that human laws had to conform to a greater law in order to be just, whether the *mores maiorum* of the Roman republic or the divine law recognized by the Christian emperors. This outlook was now thoroughly Christianized. However, St. Thomas had also rendered respectable human endeavour to create just laws, whether in ancient Rome or elsewhere. The emergence of collections of native laws across Europe in the later thirteenth and fourteenth centuries can also therefore be attributed to the movement which took its impetus from his work. One thinks especially perhaps of Eike von Repgow's celebration of the Saxon laws in the *Sachsenspiegel*.

There was one further development at this time which would also appear to have resulted from the new confidence in human achievements which St. Thomas had instilled in his contemporaries. Interest began to be shown not only in the form and system of the civilian compilations, but also in their substance. It began to be essayed that the techniques of the students in the law schools might actually be serviceable in the contemporary world, or that the civil laws themselves might be fit for use even in the context of a Christian society.

5 The Commentators and the Reception of Roman Law

This step by which civil law was taken out of the classroom and into the courtroom is attributed to the jurists who followed the school of the Glossators and are known for that reason as the post-Glossators. They are more generally known in English as the Commentators, because their literary work was composed in part of commentaries upon the *Corpus Iuris Civilis*. However, in that their fame rests chiefly upon the practical element rather than the academic in their output, it is perhaps the title which they are given in German which is most appropriate, *Konsiliatoren* or counsellors.

To understand the progression which their work achieved, it is necessary to know something of the form of teaching employed at Bologna and the other Italian law schools. The main method of instruction was the lecture, *lectura*, which had by student demand come to be a comprehensive exposition of a text by the teacher, *punctatio librorum*, with no opportunity for discussion by the students. To compensate for the one-sidedness of the *lectura*, *repetitiones* were held at which students and other professors could discuss difficult questions concerning the text with the teacher. These questions were not open ended, in that they were on points which had an answer in law. The practice also developed however of discussing questions to which there was no correct answer according to the civil law. In such *disputationes*, the students would argue for and against a particular solution to the problem, *quaestio*, which they had been set, utilizing the juristic skills and knowledge they had acquired to suggest a solution. At the end of the *disputatio*, the tutor would either assent or dissent to the students' argument, often by simply saying *sic* or *non*. Nothing was decided, for there was no answer in the texts. All that was tested was the strength of the foundations of the *opinio* given.

Thus, the academic jurists took a step beyond expounding what the law of the *Corpus Iuris* provided. They began to express opinions as to what the underlying principles and system of the *Corpus Iuris* suggested should be the answer to questions for which the text itself did not provide. If the text revealed an answer, that was accepted as beyond question to be the law, but if the text did not reveal an answer, the trained reasoning of the jurists could express an opinion, which while not of the same authority as an answer revealed by the texts, was nevertheless of some persuasive value. Already in the time of the Glossators, such opinions were on occasion sought, but during the fourteenth century the frequency of such requests increased greatly.

The Reception in Italy

The need for such opinions is not difficult to appreciate. In Italy, the decline in the power of the Carolingian emperors had resulted in the cities and communes having an unrivalled opportunity to assert their independence. During the eleventh and twelfth centuries there had been struggles between those who wanted a closer relationship with the Holy Roman Emperor and those who wanted autonomy within the empire. The former were called Ghibellines, the latter Guelfs. The towns and cities of north and central Italy in particular were governed therefore according to their own statutes, being a mixture of laws ratified by the popular assemblies - often customs reduced to writing and formally agreed by them - and edicts issued by magistrates to regulate their year in office but continued by their successors, based on the model of the Roman republic. These statutes were in the main concerned with government and administration, the relationships of the inhabitants with one another continuing to be governed by their customary laws, often again being reduced to writing. In the south of Italy, these customary rules of private law were often also referred to as statutes, but in the north the statutes and customs of a city were usually distinguished.

The statutes of the cities were often based on the statutes governing the affairs of the guilds of craftsmen and merchants who lived there, and in many ways the city corporations were the trade guilds writ large. While the nobility and aristocracy of mediaeval Italy were largely descendants of the Germanic invaders of earlier centuries, who had of course been the rulers, the merchant classes and artisans tended to be the descendants of the original Roman inhabitants. The influence of their customs therefore played no small part in shaping the government and commercial organization of the Italian towns during the great revival of their prosperity. In particular, the mercantile practice of these towns, and the maritime law governing trade in the great sea ports of Italy such as Venice, Genoa, Pisa and Amalfi, was heavily dependant upon their preserved memory of Roman legal arrangements.

Nevertheless, the customs of the inhabitants generally and even of the merchants, being based on their memory of Roman law, was markedly inferior to the civil law of the *Corpus Iuris* as taught by the doctors of the laws. The magistrates and guild masters of the cities therefore were not backward in the later thirteenth century, and more particularly in the fourteenth and fifteenth centuries, when faced with problems of a juridical character to which their laws did not give an answer, in sending the questions which vexed them to the jurists at the universities for their opinion. If the *Corpus Iuris* gave an answer, it would of course be followed, but the jurists of this generation were also prepared to give their opinion as to what the law should be according to the principles of the civil law even if no definitive answer were available, in the manner in which such a question would be resolved at a *disputatio*. Thus, alongside the authority of the texts, there developed as in ancient Rome a subsidiary authority attaching to the opinions of those learned in the law, what was to be called by modern civil lawyers, *doctrine*. By the middle of the fifteenth century it was settled that if an opinion which could not be faulted was shared by the community of jurists, *communis opinio*, it was to be treated as equivalent to a law in the text. The civil law was thus extending beyond the limits of the texts once more in order to adapt itself to the needs of the contemporary world.

The jurists who provided these opinions were still primarily teachers at the universities, but increasingly they were called upon to act as counsellors to city corporations and to princely rulers. They often travelled from town to town at the invitation of the civic authorities rather than spending their whole careers in one place like the Glossators. Cities and communes rivalled one another in attracting the most famous names to advise them and, having established law schools of their own, sought the services of eminent jurists to teach at them.

Among the leading lights of this generation of jurists was Bartolus of Sassoferato (1314-1357), who taught at Perugia, and wrote extensive commentaries on the civil law and the gloss as well as monographic works on particular legal topics, another innovation of this period. His pupil Baldus (1327-1400), who ended his career at the university of Pavia,[7] was the first to specialize in the giving of *consilia*, which were collected in order that their wisdom might be preserved for posterity.

The cities were also able to enlist the services of jurists by offering them another form of occupation. The popular assemblies of the Germanic period had ceded their judicial functions to judges drawn from among the people who were able to declare the customs of the community. These popular judges were called in Italy *scabini*. Increasingly, it would be the unfortunate *scabini* who would, in disputes between the citizens, find that the custom of their community did not provide a solution to the problem. Gradually, the leading cities preferred to offer the office of judge to a trained jurist who could provide legal solutions to problems according to the civil law in situations in which the local custom failed to provide an answer. The presence of Church courts staffed by lawyers trained in canon law must have given the civic authorities an added impetus to recruit professionals in their courts so that the secular tribunals would not lose out to the expertise of their spiritual neighbours. The need for the secular judges to be acquainted with the statutes and customs of the community employing them would have increased the demand for written redactions of the local laws.

The result of these developments in Italy was to move the learning of the civil law from academe into the world of practical politics and business. The civil law became once more a living source of law. Not only its techniques and principles, but also its actual provisions, began to play a part in the life of the communities which it served. Piecemeal though the process was in Italy, a reception of civilian learning and of the civil law was taking place, and this development was not confined to the prosperous cities and communes of the Italian peninsula.

The Reception in Germany

Students from all over Europe travelled to the Italian law schools to study civil and canon law. One of the largest nations, as they were termed, at Bologna was the Germans. They came from the land which was still most directly under the control of the emperor, but nevertheless it was a land composed of many and various feudal lordships and princedoms, together with free cities and other urban communes, all of which had their respective customs as well as recognizing the titular overlordship of the emperor. In the manors and lordships of the German people, it was customary for the popular assembly to meet annually to rehearse the customs in question and answer form at what was called the *inquisitio*. This would be conducted by an official of the feudal overlord of the area. Thus the customs were proclaimed and remembered. As in Italy, the assemblies no longer acted collectively in the adjudication of disputes, but had entrusted the task of finding and declaring the law to lay judges called *Schöffen*. These attended court to declare the law from their knowledge of the customs, the court being presided over by an official of the lord called the *Richter*. The *Schöffen* however faced the same problems in Germany as their brethren in Italy, the *scabini*, had encountered, namely what to do in situations where the local customs did not provide an answer to legal questions posed. In Germany as in Italy, resort was had in such circumstances to the knowledge of those who had been abroad to learn their law and had brought back with them their expertise in the legal learning of the civilians.

In Germany, however, the princes and lords made use of this opportunity to increase the prestige of their own tribunals and jurisdictions at the expense of the older local courts. Litigants would frequently petition the lord directly for a judgement by arbitration according to the civil law rather than submit their dispute to the local forum. They would agree, as their predecessors who used the Roman formulary system had done, to accept the verdict of the lord's official. Thus, bit by bit, litigants abandoned the jurisdiction of their local courts in favour of arbitration according to the learned laws under the tutelage of their secular rulers. Appeals to the emperor for justice were always possible and, in 1495, the emperor created a new tribunal to determine disputes which came to him from among his chief vassals and also on appeal from their courts. This imperial state court, the *Reichskammergericht*, was to be composed of sixteen judges, half of whom were to be nobles and the other half jurists qualified in the learned laws. By this time, universities with law schools had been established in several of the principal cities of the empire, beginning with the Charles University at Prague in 1348. The adoption, in effect, of civil law as the proper law of the imperial state court marked the Reception of Roman law in Germany, and that in a manner so complete as to lead some scholars to deny the title of Reception to the adoption of the civil law in other parts of Europe.

The emperor had, of course, a particular claim to the civil law as his own. He was the Holy Roman Emperor and, as such, the successor of the Roman emperors of antiquity. Indeed, at the time of the foundation of the *Reichskammergericht*, the Byzantine empire in the east had fallen before the advance of the Ottoman Turks, so that the western emperor was now the only surviving claimant to the imperial title of ancient Rome. He could therefore with some justification regard the law of the *Corpus Iuris Civilis* as in a sense his own. His twelfth and thirteenth century predecessors had indeed sent their legislation to the law faculties to be incorporated into Justinian's compilation as an integral part of it or at least as a continuation of it, intending that it be taught thus. Sending the enactment to the law schools was in the thirteenth century the method of promulgation, although after Hugolino had added a tenth collation of these laws to the Novels of Justinian, no further addition was made other than a somewhat half-hearted addition of imperial laws up to 1300 added as an eleventh collation to the *Volumen parvum* by Bartolus.

The towns and cities of mediaeval Germany also received injections of civilian legal culture. This probably began with the cities which had important markets and fairs, entertaining merchants and traders from all over Europe, including those from the Italian towns. The merchants of these cities would themselves have visited the markets and fairs of northern Italy. Wherever commerce on this level was practised, recourse would be had to the custom of the mercantile classes which was heavily based on Roman law, and full advantage would be taken by the businessmen of the age of the new sophistication on commercial matters which civilian learning afforded. At home, in Germany, those learned in the civil law would again have been in demand to shape the charters and statutes of the guilds and of the cities, and it was common for lesser towns and boroughs to adopt the statutes and laws of more prosperous centres to modernize their own legal arrangements. The laws of Magdeburg were particularly favoured in this regard. Moreover, when the laws of another city were adopted, it was common for the citizens of the adopting city to reserve the right to remit difficult points of law to the courts of the 'mother' city, the *Oberhof*, for determination.

Both centres would probably employ learned civilians to declare the law in their courts. In matters of serious difficulty or dispute, town authorities and feudal lords frequently requested the advice, *consilia*, of the nearest university law faculty, which opinions would be treated as authoritative where the revered texts were themselves silent.

In both Italy and Germany, civil law would appear to have entered smoothly into the legal life of the land. This was in part due to the lack of any strong overall authority in either country and in part because of the innate sympathy of the titular overlord with the system adopted. Things were not so in all parts of western Europe. Resistance to the new legal learning was encountered in various ways for example in France and Spain.

The Reception in France

The kingdom of France had emerged out of the empire of the Franks, from whom it took its name. It had become free of imperial control when Hugh Capet, previously an adviser to the Carolingian kings, took the throne in 987. The decline of imperial control in France had resulted in the emergence of feudal lordships, which legally lived according to the custom of the territory which the lord governed. Thus had emerged a multitude of customary jurisdictions in the northern two-thirds of France, the portion known as the *pays des coutumes*. In the southern third of the kingdom, the population continued to live according to the written code of law given them when under the hegemony of the Visigothic ruler Alaric II, the *Lex Romana Visigothorum* or *Breviary of Alaric*. The inhabitants of the south regarded their memory of Roman law as recorded in this work to be their customary law.

France then was not a unified land legally, and thus it remained until the Revolution in 1789. The kings of France did not enjoy that central control within their realm which their counterparts had established in England after the Norman Conquest. Although the kings could and did legislate for the whole kingdom in the form of *ordonnances* and for individual provinces within it in the form of *édits*, these enactments dealt with governmental and administrative matters and hardly ever affected issues of private law between the king's subjects. The custom of the king's own court, the *Parlement* of Paris, only bound those who lived within the king's own domain, the Île de France, extending from the area around Paris southwestwards towards the Loire. In other parts of the kingdom, the king's subjects lived according to the local custom.

These customs were administered in local courts, where the customs were ascertained by means of inquests of people in the locality thought likely to know or remember the local law. These inquisitions were called *turba* and consisted of at least ten persons who were called upon to state the custom on a given point. The number could exceed ten, but ten had to agree for the custom to be proved. Indeed, under the influence of canon law rules of evidence, where the testimony of one witness was not treated as reliable, it became necessary for two *turbae* to prove a custom before it was permitted to be treated as binding. This control over the proving of customs marks one feature of the incursion of the learned laws into France. It was insisted that customs to be valid must not only be followed in the locality generally but also be good and approved, *bona* and *probata*. This idea, which harks back to the notion that to be valid a law of human provenance must conform to law of a higher level, enabled the Church to claim the right to approve local customs in order to ensure that they were not contrary to the law of God nor of his Church. It gave the Church not only power over the content of the law in particular areas but also influence over the direction of its development.

The problems which had beset the Germans and the Italians with regard to the inadequacy of their customs in certain departments of the law also afflicted the French, and there was clearly a desire manifested in some quarters to turn to the learned laws for assistance. Indeed, schools of law had been founded in France by scholars from Bologna, most notably at Montpellier and Orléans, the latter centre becoming very famous for developing legal principles and maxims from the civil law sources in the manner of the Commentators. The jurists of Orléans were known to their Italian brethren as the *ultramontani*.

However, the king of France was not prepared to countenance the incursion of the learning of the civil law into his realm gladly. The ban on the teaching of Roman law at the university of Paris imposed by the Pope in 1219 was specifically upheld in a royal *ordonnance* of Philip IV in 1312 in which he emphasized that France was a kingdom governed by customs and had no need of foreign legal learning. The ban remained in place until 1679.

Whenever therefore a gap appeared in the customs of a particular locality in the *pays des coutumes*, recourse was to be had not to the civil law but to the custom of the king of France as administered in the *Parlement* of Paris. To that end the customs of that court and its decisions came to be recorded in writing. Only if the custom of the *Parlement* was unable to provide a solution was recourse to the learning of the civilians allowed.

The same of course could not be true of the *pays du droit écrit*. There the custom was based on Roman law, albeit not originally upon the written texts of the Justinianic corpus. However, it was virtually inevitable that in those parts of the French kingdom, the teachings of the civilians should be seen as a continuation and explication of the customary traditions of the people, and civil law made its way into the customs of the south.

The great attraction of the civil law, even in France, was its written form, which gave it much greater certainty than the unwritten customs of the north. The stark contrast between the precision and sophistication of the canon law, administered throughout the kingdom in the Church courts and taught at the universities including Paris, and the uncertainty of the customary rules made the defects of the latter all the more difficult to bear. Unofficial compilations of the customs of the various regions had been made, but they were not authoritative and often showed considerable civilian influence in their arrangement and interpretation. Recourse in any event had to be had to the *turbae*. It was against this background that Charles VII, when he had finally freed his kingdom from the hostile incursions of the English at the end of the Hundred Years War, issued his order for the reduction of all the French customs into writing, so that for the future they could be the subject of systematic study and official citation. This was commanded in 1453 by the *Ordonnance* of Montils-les-Tours, although the task was not completed for more than a century. However, civil law had won one victory; French law had surrendered to the advantages of having its laws enshrined in written texts, and this would let in that other feature of civilian learning, the opportunity for reasoned, juristic development of legal doctrine.

The Reception in Spain

Spain was not a united kingdom until the marriage of Ferdinand of Aragon to Isabella of Castile in the fifteenth century. It was under their joint rule that the Moors were finally expelled from Granada in 1492, returning the whole of the peninsula to Christian governance. For centuries, the Christian rulers of Spain had systematically laboured to reconquer the country from its Islamic powers, a movement which gave Spain a unity of purpose despite its political and legal divisions.

Until the close of the fifteenth century, as well as the Moorish territories which were gradually diminishing in size, Spain was divided into four main political units: Castilla-León, which was the territory of the reconquest which had commenced from the kingdom of Asturias; the kingdom of Aragon, Catalonia, which extended its influence to Valencia and the Balearic Islands through reconquest, and the kingdom of Navarre and the Basque country in the north. All of these have their distinct legal histories, but each was affected by the revival of the civil law which swept through continental Europe at the end of the Middle Ages.

While living under Moorish domination, the people of the former Visigothic kingdom had continued to live according to their Christian customs, being known as the Mozarabs. The law by which they lived was therefore customary, but based on the text of the *Fuero Juzgo*. As the reconquest extended southwards from Asturias through León and into Castile, the liberated lands and towns often recorded their rules of municipal government in their own particular *fuero*. These would sometimes be confirmed by royal authority. The kings were able to legislate for their territory as a whole, firstly in councils in which they met with their nobles and the leading churchmen, later in an assembly which included representatives of the towns and country areas, called the *Cortes*. In Castile, this may have been established as early as 1188.

Such royal enactments were valid throughout the kingdom, but did not cover the whole field of legal requirements. Matters of local government and the private law governing the legal relationships of the people with one another continued to be determined according to the individual *fueros* of the towns and the local customs of the people, by and large rooted in the provisions of the *Fuero Juzgo*. It was not uncommon for problems to arise which were not solvable by recourse to any of these sources, or to which these sources did not give a satisfactory contemporary answer. It became customary in such situations to refer such issues to the judgement of arbitrators, *albedrios*, not chosen by the parties but supplied by royal authority, and their determinations were accorded the status of binding precedents, *fazañas*, for use in future cases.

As well as the municipal *fueros* given to towns, some of which were in a standard form received by several communities with but slight if any variation, certain classes of persons also enjoyed the privilege of living according to their customs or *fueros*. Principal among these were the nobility, whose privileges were to be a source of difficulty for central government in the years ahead. Mindful of the difficulties which such a diversity of laws engendered, the Castilian kings of the thirteenth century acted to inject some uniformity into their kingdom's legal arrangements. The most famous of these endeavours were those of Alfonso X, called the Wise, *El Sabio*.

Alfonso X's legislative efforts began with the production in 1254 of a *fuero* which was basically meant to govern the territory ruled directly by the king and also to be used by the royal court to determine appeals from inferior tribunals. However, it was adopted by some municipalities as their local *fuero* and even appears to have been granted to some as a *fuero* as though it was to be their special law. This *fuero* became known as the *Fuero Real*, the royal custom. Thereafter, Alfonso issued further laws as occasion demanded to deal with problems not satisfactorily resolved by the *Fuero Real* in laws which were collected as *Nuevas*, reminiscent of the Novels of late antiquity. He also had produced a legal work called the mirror of all the laws, *El Espéculo de todos los derechos*, which purported to gather together the best laws from whatever source, and was used as a reference tool by later lawyers.

Alfonso X's chief legal work, however, is without doubt that undertaken at his behest in 1256 and probably completed by 1265. It was an attempt to fuse the new learning of the canon and civil law with the royal and ancient customs of Spain. Structured in seven parts, it was called *Las Siete Partidas*, and drew on the *Fuero Real*, the *Fuero Juzgo*, the recently promulgated texts of the canonists - which had of course been in part compiled by a Spaniard, St. Raymond of Peñafort, the Roman law of the *Corpus Iuris* as glossed by the Bolognese scholars, and the commentaries of the scholars themselves upon the civil law. It is almost certain that Alfonso intended the work to become law throughout his kingdom, producing a legal unity therein. In this he was disappointed, for both the localities and the nobility were resistant to surrendering the independence of having their several customs. As a result, the *Partidas* did not replace the existing laws of Castilla-León, and did not officially become law until 1348, when by the *Ordenamiento de Alcalá*, Alfonso X's great-grandson, Alfonso XI, promulgated the *Partidas* as law throughout his kingdom, but as a supplementary source of law in a hierarchy of sources established in that year. According to that hierarchy, royal enactments made in the Cortes, such as the *Ordenamiento*, had pride of place. Next to them came the provisions of the *Fuero Real* and the local *fueros* in their respective territories, including the *Fuero Juzgo* where observed, and only as a supplement to these sources were the provisions of the *Siete Partidas* to be binding.

The *Ordenamiento de Alcalá* formally recognized that law in Spain was an amalgam of the general and the particular, an arrangement which was destined to endure and remain a feature of the Spanish legal system to the present day. However, the supplementary role of the *Partidas* was nevertheless an important one, particularly in those areas of the law which the *fueros* were not sufficiently sophisticated to cover. Hence, in the area of obligations, in the introduction of adoption and in many areas of the law of succession and inheritance, civilian influence began to take a strong hold upon the Castilian legal consciousness.

After 1348, the Castilian kings continued to legislate, and from time to time the need for ordered collections of these enactments became felt. One of the most important of these was accomplished in the reigns of Ferdinand and Isabella. It is known from the name of the jurist who compiled it as the *Ordenamiento de Doctor Montalvo*, and appeared around the year 1484.[8] It is composed of eight books, including not only royal enactments from 1348 onwards but also *cedulas*, edictal legislation by the kings, going back to the time of Alfonso X. Its official title was *Ordenanzas Reales de Castilla*.

The same resistance to legal unification was also encountered in the other parts of Spain. Aragon had a legendary custom for its nobility, which also features in the legal history of Navarre, the *Fuero de Sobrarbe*. The ordinary people however lived according to their local customs which were collected at the instigation of the king during the thirteenth century as the *Compilación de Canellas*. This work was to be added to over the next century until it was enlarged into what became the *Fueros Generales Aragoneses*. Matters not dealt with adequately by the laws contained therein were to be settled by reason and natural equity, concepts which let in a certain amount of civilian and canonist learning.

Aragon however was more resistant to such incursions that its neighbour Catalonia, which had a stronger tradition of sending its law students to the Italian universities and those of Montpellier and Toulouse. Although civil law was treated as being supplementary to the native customs of the Catalans, the *usatges*, it enjoyed considerable influence in legal development. Catalonia was a major trading area, with the great port of Barcelona, which inevitably brought the region into closer contact with parts of Italy and southern France where the civilian learning was gaining ground, particularly in maritime and mercantile affairs.

Navarre, like Aragon, was more resistant to the incursions of the civil law, but its customs were also reduced to writing in a *Fuero General* during the thirteenth century. Valencia and the Balearic Islands were likewise encouraged to reduce their customs to written form after their reconquest from the Moors, but were nevertheless permitted to live according to them by their new rulers.

The pattern of diversity which is still a feature of Spanish law can therefore clearly be seen emerging before the close of the Middle Ages. Civil law was making its mark in several parts of Spain, notably Castilla-León and Catalonia, but everywhere there was a continued loyalty to local custom. The attraction of having the law reduced to a written text was however strong, and there was also a respect for juristic learning in both systematizing the various bodies of laws and adapting them to meet the needs of social change. The particular characteristics of Spanish law were to play a significant role in the next phase of the development of civil law in Europe and further afield.

6 Conclusion

The first five centuries of the second Christian millennium are a decisive turning point in the history of civil law. They mark not only the rediscovery and exploitation of the Digest of Justinian in western Europe, but also the revival of two signal features of the civilian inheritance. The first is what can only be termed faith in a legal text. The *Corpus Iuris Civilis* was regarded as written reason, the embodiment of perfect law. Its form, as much as its content, allowed it to be regarded and studied as such. When such exaggerated reverence for Justinian's compilations gave way to critical respect, this belief in the desirability of having one's laws in a written form was destined to survive. Even in areas resistant to the advance of Romanism, the advantages of having local laws reduced to writing was perceived. It was the recognition of these advantages which had led to the great compilation of canon law which was also to prove so influential.

The second important advance was the growth of juristic reasoning based upon the text. Techniques were fashioned to allow jurists to develop the principles to be found in the written laws to suit prevailing social conditions. Again, this looks like a revival of a feature of classical Roman law. These techniques, once in place, could be used not only upon the raw materials of the ancient law of Rome, but also upon the canon law of the Church, the customs of feudal societies, the customs of localities and regions from Saxony to Seville. Moreover, the techniques of the jurists could be employed to produce results which were harmonious not only in the terms of one legal system, but in two or more. Thus, legal principles and maxims could be stated which expressed underlying notions of justice, fairness and natural equity which appeared to underlie and be common to a whole range of human legal orders.

The application to the law of rules for reasoned development was one of the great contributions of this age. In many respects, faith in this technique was destined to replace faith in the written text of the *Corpus Iuris* in the next phase of the development of civil law. What shattered that faith in the *Corpus Iuris*, and the circumstances which made for its undermining, must now be examined if the next stage in civilian development is to be properly understood.

Notes

[1] Some claim that there was a school of law also at Ravenna, and that this was the remnant of the Roman law school of Justinian's day which had been moved to Ravenna with the seat of government of the Exarchate. It is also claimed that a knowledge of the Digest had survived here which formed the basis of the Bolognese revival. See for example M. Bellomo, *The Common Legal Past of Europe* (Washington D.C., 1995), p. 60.

[2] See above, chapter 4, and J.A. Brundage, *Medieval Canon Law* (London and New York, 1995), pp. 70 ff; *Law, Sex and Christian Society in Medieval Europe* (Chicago, 1987), pp. 348 ff.

[3] These were held during the fourth century.

[4] These courts arguably could exercise jurisdiction over the faithful, clerical and lay, in all matters, and were therefore true competitors to the secular courts.

[5] Attempts were made to update Justinian's laws as well, in the belief that imperial legislation was a continuance of them. Thus, some imperial enactments were inserted into the Code under the appropriate title, and Hugolino added the learning of feuds to Justinian's Novels as a tenth *collatio*, Bartolus adding an eleventh containing the enactments of the western emperors up to 1300. These attempts were not however destined to set a precedent.

[6] The Justinianic compilation was divided into five parts for the purposes of instruction. The first three parts were divisions of the Digest: *Digestum vetus*, being the Digest as far as book 24, title 2; the *Infortiatum*, being 24.3-38; and *Digestum Novum*, being book 39 to the end. The fourth part was called the *Code*, but consisted of only the first nine of Justinian's twelve books. The remaining three followed the Institutes in the last part, called *Volumen* or *Volumen parvum*, and also contained the Novels, divided up into nine *collationes*. It was to these that Hugolino added the *Libri Feudorum* and the imperial enactments as a tenth *collatio*.

---

[7] Despite his advanced years, he is said to have died unfortunately as a result of being bitten by a mad dog. His memorial is still to be seen in one of the courtyards of the university.

[8] For details see C. Calisse et al., *General Survey of Continental Legal History* (Boston, 1912; reprinted New York, 1968), p. 626.

6 Humanism and the Age of Reason

1 The Sixteenth-Century World View

The year 1492 saw not only the final expulsion of the Moors from Spain; it was also the year in which Christopher Columbus discovered America. The latter event immediately transformed the contemporary concept of what the world was like. What had previously been the known world was now known to be not the whole world. Man's knowledge of the world had previously been incomplete and was now known to be so. Moreover, the discovery of America is generally regarded as confirming an idea which had been current for some time, namely that the world was not, as had long been believed, flat, but was instead round. The maps of the ancient cartographers were therefore shown to be if not unreliable at least incomplete and imperfect. Human knowledge had increased beyond that of the classical world, and for once, not by building on the achievements of the ancients but by challenging their opinions and correcting them.

This was truly a turning point in the history of human ideas. The inhabitants of Europe had to come to terms with a world which was very different from that which they had previously believed existed. Whether the discoveries of the great navigators were perceived as a threat or as exhibiting a brave new world depended upon the spectator's point of view, but in any event they posed a challenge to everyone's concept of the world in which they lived.

It was not just the shape of the world that had to be rethought. The idea of the universe in which the world was set had been questioned. From the ancient world, the Middle Ages had adopted the concept of a universe which was centred upon the earth, with the moon, the sun and all the known planets orbiting the still centre occupied by man. This notion was one which had been underwritten by the great astronomers of antiquity, most notably Ptolemy of Alexandria.[1] Copernicus had the temerity to challenge this orthodoxy as a result of his own observations, that is by the use of his human faculty of reason. He was not prepared to accept the revelation of the ancient texts with regard to the form and mechanics of the universe; he preferred the fruits of his own rational researches if they were in conflict with the findings revealed in the literature of an earlier age. Copernicus held that it was the earth which revolved around the sun and not *vice versa*. He laid the foundations of a new cosmology with the sun at the centre of what was to become known as the solar system, with the earth and the other planets in orbit around it. This was the view which Galileo was to uphold, and which met with the hostility and condemnation of the Catholic Church.

To understand much of what occurred during the closing decades of the fifteenth century and during the sixteenth and seventeenth centuries one must appreciate the momentous nature of these discoveries. People were required to cast aside their fundamental conceptions about the shape of the world in which they lived and the universe in which it was set. There was a great deal that was not known, but which it would be possible to discover. It was an age of radical revision with vast opportunities for adventure. It was not an age for acceptance of orthodoxies and resistance to change.

The challenge to the prevailing orthodoxies extended to other areas of life in which much had been taken for granted on the basis of the authority of the ancient writers. The most profound social and political changes in western Europe stemmed from the impact of this challenge upon the prevailing religious order. The authority of the Church had been maintained successfully in the west by the Papacy throughout the mediaeval period. Criticism of the Papacy and its style of governing the Church had however surfaced, particularly during and after the Papal Schism of the fourteenth century, which had seen the seat of the Popes moved from Rome to Avignon and the existence for some years of two claimants to the papal title. The fact that such a situation could arise, albeit that it had been resolved by the Council of Constance, gave fuel to those who found in the wealth and political power of the bishops of Rome a stark contrast to the life and example of Christ in the Gospels. The authority of the Popes was however based upon the words of Scripture and the evidence of the ancient world in the form of the Donation of Constantine.

It was against a background of such criticisms that some of the fundamentals of catholic Christianity came under challenge. In 1453, the city of Byzantium, home of the eastern empire since its foundation by Constantine over a millennium before, fell before the advancing armies of the Ottoman Turks. At roughly the same time as the forces of Islam were being expelled from Europe's western extreme, a Muslim incursion took place at the eastern end. The effect of the fall of Byzantium upon the west was considerable. Not only did many Greek-speaking, orthodox Christians[2] flee to the west, they brought with them a knowledge of the language in which the New Testament had originally been written, while in the west the Scriptures had only been known and studied in the Latin translation of St. Jerome called the Vulgate. They opened up therefore for the first time an awareness of the possibility that there might be differences between the Scriptures as they were originally written and the western Church's knowledge and perception of them.

Some of these differences had profound implications for the authority of the Papacy. Thus, for instance, the Greek word εκκλεσια was translated in the Vulgate as *ecclesia* meaning 'church', in the sense of an institution, whereas in the original Greek it was said to have meant only an assembly of the people. Likewise, the Greek επισκοπος, was given in the Vulgate as *episcopus* meaning 'bishop' in the full, ecclesiastical sense of a chief pastor with authority over the Church in his diocese, whereas in the original Greek the meaning was 'an elder', one who enjoyed and governed by respect rather than through power. Such knowledge allowed questions to be asked about the very basis of ecclesiastical government. It invited questions about what the shape of the Church was meant to be as significant as those which had been asked about the shape of the earth or of the universe.

One of the main criticisms of the Papacy and of churchmen generally during the fourteenth and fifteenth century had been on account of their use of their powers to raise money. In particular, the practice of selling indulgences, by which persons were supposedly remitted suffering in Purgatory after death in return for money paid while alive on the authority of the Pope's power to remit their penance, was severely questioned in certain quarters. Doing penance in order to have the penalty for one's sins remitted was a cornerstone of this aspect of mediaeval Catholicism. The Greek word upon which 'doing penance' was based was μετονειν. It was now said that this did not mean 'doing penance' at all; it meant 'changing one's attitude', an altogether less profitable activity from the Church's viewpoint.

While it had always been recognized during the mediaeval period that mistakes would occur in the copying of manuscripts, it was equally firmly believed that the Vulgate itself was a work of perfection. The perfect text which had underlain all study and investigation of the Scriptures was now itself under challenge. The demand was made to produce a new and better translation than that of St. Jerome. Scholars such as Erasmus strove to learn Greek and Hebrew in order that the imperfections of the previous centuries' understanding of the word of God could be removed. However, the damage to the Papacy and the catholic Church was done. It was now open for men to propose alternative understandings of the Scriptures, of the structure of the Church and of its ministry, to question the nature of the sacraments and to challenge the necessity of having bishops at all let alone a supreme pontiff in the shape of the bishop of Rome. The arrival of Greek scholarship heralded the advent of the Reformation.

Knowledge of Greek had an impact upon philosophy as well as theology. The west's understanding of the great works of Plato and Aristotle was founded upon Latin translations of their works, some of which had been translated from previous Arabic versions and not from the original Greek. Again, access to manuscripts in the original language revealed a substantial number of errors, and, as well as causing revision of previously accepted ideas about Greek philosophy, reinforced dissatisfaction with knowledge which was mediated by long processes of copying or of translation.

This gave rise to a zeal to discover the earliest possible manuscripts of a given text. This in turn led to an appreciation that to ascertain which manuscript was the earliest required some knowledge of how manuscripts from different periods could be dated. The need to find the earliest possible version of a text was increased by the invention of printing, which allowed for the mass production and wide distribution of works which previously would have had to be individually copied by hand. As searches for the most reliable texts from which to produce printed editions progressed, there arose also an awareness that not all extant texts were what they were claimed to be. Some were forgeries, masquerading as texts from an earlier age than that in which they had been produced. The unmasking of the Donation of Constantine, upon which Papal claims to supremacy in the west were based, as such a misleading manuscript drastically undermined the Pope's authority, as did the revelation that many of the decretals upon which the government of the Church was based, the collection now known as Pseudo-Isidore, were also false.

The invention of the printing press also broke the monopoly of learning previously enjoyed by the clerical classes of Europe. When knowledge and learning was communicated by means of parchment manuscripts, produced relatively slowly and in a labour intensive fashion which was inevitably expensive, there was but little incentive to acquire the skill of reading. The possibility of mass production at a far cheaper cost of the great works of theology, literature and philosophy, led to a greatly increased demand, particularly among the ambitious middle classes, for education. Learning to read was now worthwhile. This meant that there was a much larger educated class of people in Europe than was the case in previous generations, people who were able to read the Scriptures and other literature for themselves and make up their own minds about their meaning. This further challenged the authority of the Catholic Church and boosted the popularity of Protestantism with its emphasis upon the importance of individual faith. The availability of printed Bibles in the vernacular languages played an important role in elevating the position of Scripture among believers as opposed to the role of the sacraments, which had assumed a far greater role in popular belief among an illiterate population. Secular governments also felt threatened by this growth of popular information, and in many lands a censorship was imposed upon the activities of the printing and publishing houses.

The advent of printed books transformed the world of scholarship, including legal scholarship. Whereas previously, the works of a jurist might be known only to those who had access to a manuscript of his work, and there might arise confusions if different manuscript traditions provided differing readings of his opinions, it was now possible for an authoritative text to be printed in large numbers so that the works of a jurist could be widely disseminated without any variance to a very large public. This substantially increased a problem which had beset lawyers and courts during the fifteenth century, namely what to do in the face of a mass of juristic opinion upon a particular point. It was established that if the jurists were at one in their opinion, such a *communis opinio* was to be treated as binding. However, with the advent of printed books, the opinions of many more jurists, albeit of varying quality, could be cited and the chances of there being an uncontroverted view diminished. This would leave lawyers and courts with a problem not dissimilar to that which afflicted their brethren in the later centuries of the Roman empire. Indeed, the *communis opinio* solution had as little to commend it in many ways as the fifth century Law of Citations. It was against this background that some legal scholars began to kick against the accepted methods of the school of Commentators and their technique of interpretation, the so-called *mos Italicus*. It was felt that the cumulative solution of *communis opinio* should be abandoned in favour of a more qualitative approach.

Allied to dissatisfaction with this approach to the use of juristic learning in both secular and canon law was the awareness also that the text which had for so long been the lawyer's equivalent to the Bible, the *Corpus Iuris*

Civilis, was but another text from late antiquity. Although it contained excerpts from the writings of classical antiquity, the compilation had been made by the servants of a Byzantine emperor some centuries after the great jurists of ancient Rome had themselves flourished. Indeed, as much time separated the works of Justinian from the classical writers as divided St. Jerome from the authors of the New Testament. Further, Justinian's compilations themselves stated that alterations had been made in the process of excerpting. There was no doubt therefore that the *Corpus Iuris* contained material which was not classical and therefore in the eyes of the men of the Renaissance, who had developed a veneration for classical rather than late antiquity, certainly no longer worthy to be treated as written reason or some kind of legal perfection. Along with so many other revered texts, the *Corpus Iuris* had been knocked off its pedestal. Further, in that the works of the Commentators took the *Corpus Iuris* as their starting point, their work was therefore not exclusively based upon classical Roman law at all. It was against this background that the next phase in the development of civil law was set to occur, with the emergence of a new approach to civilian legal studies, that of the Humanists.

2 The Humanist School of Legal Science

The Humanist approach to civil law marked a return, in full accord with the spirit of the age, to a study of the texts rather than reliance upon the commentaries of earlier ages. The text of the *Corpus Iuris Civilis* was recognized to be the result of a selection of earlier texts made some centuries after the sources from which the selections were taken had been composed. The revival of interest in classical antiquity and the increase in scholarship relating to classical Latin and Greek, ancient literature and ancient history, meant that it was possible to bring to bear upon the legal texts preserved from the Roman world the results of scholarly advances in other fields. This allowed jurists, who were now as much historians of the law as jurists in a practical sense, to identify layers of texts within the works of Justinian representing the different periods of legal development in the preceding centuries. Legal scholars were for the first time utilizing other disciplines in order to obtain a greater understanding of the legal sources. Whereas the Glossators had focused their attention solely upon the texts and sought to discover their integrity and the Commentators had used them as a basis for reasoned deduction and argument, the humanists saw them as one source of knowledge of the past, a source which could only properly be understood and interpreted in the light of all the other available sources of knowledge concerning that time, and also maintained that the legal texts themselves had an important contribution to make to an understanding of non-legal subjects.

One of the earliest exponents of this new technique was Andrea Alciati (1492-1550), a Milanese who taught, like many of his contemporaries, at a number of universities in Italy and Southern France. He is particularly associated with the universities of Avignon, Bourges and Pavia. He rejected the style of the Commentators and the search for *communis opinio* in favour of a return to a straightforward explanation of the original texts themselves so as to uncover their true meaning in the context of what was known about the times in which they were written. As well as writing on the law, Alciati was also a student of other subjects, such as philology, history, theology, medicine and even cookery. He wrote a treatise on weights and measures in the ancient world.[3] He believed that more could be learned from studying the meaning of the texts themselves than by building up a vast knowledge of all the subtleties and intricate arguments which the followers of Bartolus had amassed around them. In this, he was at one with the Humanists of his age in other disciplines, who had taken theology back, for example, to a study of the Scriptures in their original languages and away from the accumulated interpretations of the scholastics based upon the Vulgate translation rather than the original texts. Alciati was a celebrated figure in the intellectual life of Europe in his generation, being a correspondent of Erasmus and Sir Thomas More, as well as of other jurists such as Budé in France and Zasius in Germany. Although he regarded canon law and the laws of other peoples as worthy of note and study, he nevertheless clearly upheld the supremacy of Roman law as a system and saw it as being a distillation of the divine will, and the work of the jurist in interpreting it as partaking of a priestly role in the service of justice.

The Humanist approach placed before legal scholars a choice regarding their attitude to the continued study of the civil law. They could of course ignore the new learning and soldier on according to the old methods of the *mos Italicus* as exemplified by the Commentators. This to some extent was the path pursued in many parts of Italy, with the result that the principal seats of legal learning were no longer to be found in that land. Alternatively, they could embrace the new learning, but even if they did so further choices had to be made. One avenue would be to devote one's efforts to discovering what the law of ancient Rome had actually been like. This would be to treat civil law as an object for an historical inquiry rather than anything else. Almost in recognition of this, jurists could also properly maintain that given the civil law was now known not to be a perfect system, it was no longer worthy of occupying centre stage in the activities of jurists at all, which place should be taken by native laws which should be studied so as to develop a suitable jurisprudence for the contemporary age. Somewhere between these two views, it was also possible to maintain that despite its imperfect nature, Roman law was still a valuable reservoir of legal principles and rules of proven worth, which should still be studied, albeit critically, in order to adapt its riches to the needs of the present time.

These approaches each found their champions, and each champion was connected in some way with the centre of Humanist legal learning during the sixteenth century, the university of Bourges, where Alciati had done arguably his most important work around the year 1530. Chief among those who advocated a purely historical approach to the Roman sources was Jacques Cujas (1522-1590),[4] who held a number of posts at various universities during his illustrious career. He had left his original post at Toulouse after the chair in Roman law there had been given to a rival, Forcadel, a militant Bartolist. Some would describe another eminent Bourges jurist, Hugh Doneau (1527-1591),[5] as a Bartolist, but his respect for civilian learning was not based on reverence for the work of the Commentators. He believed that the texts themselves could be used as a quarry to extract materials for the construction of modern legal systems together with suitable extractions from canon law and the native legal systems. Ultimately, his juristic judgement was not based on a belief in the perfection of any text or a single technique, but upon an openness with regard to sources and a trust in reason to select and develop what is best from the past for use in the future. Francis Hotman (1524-1590) maintained the extreme thesis that, as Roman law was not a perfect system and that contemporary knowledge of the classical law was distorted by the surviving texts, it would be better to turn juristic attention away from the ancients and rely more on the inherent suitability of the customary laws of France and the reason of living jurists rather than abdicate intellectually in favour of reverence for the ancients.

All three of these men suffered during their lives as a result of the religious turbulence of the times, and their repeated movements between universities were often motivated by the need to avoid persecution rather than academic choice. Doneau and Hotman in particular left France altogether after the St. Bartholomew's Day massacre in 1572. Doneau taught in Geneva, Heidelberg, and Leiden before ending his days at Altdorf. The freer Protestant air in those places afforded greater amenity for a man of his religious sympathies. Thus was broken that academic unity within Europe which had been such a potent factor in the intellectual development of the later Middle Ages. The unity of western Christendom ended just as the colonial expansion of its secular powers began. For the future, individual national languages would replace Latin in the communications of scholars and the nation states would become the focal areas of legal development. The Catholic Church was no longer supreme in the west, but now one Church among many, religious persuasion being a matter for the choice of the secular ruler under the principle, *cuius regio, eius religio*. The Council of Trent (1545-1548; 1551-1552; 1562-1563) saw the Roman Church undertake an internal reform in an attempt to counteract the forces of the Reformation. The recently unified kingdom of Spain was to become the champion of the Catholic cause in Europe and further afield, and it was from Spain that another major juristic development was to emerge during the sixteenth century.

3 The Spanish Scholastics and Natural Reason

The chief university in Spain was Salamanca and its chief discipline was theology. In the first half of the sixteenth century, a jurist-theologian called Francisco de Vitoria (1484-1546) taught there. Vitoria had studied the traditional scholastic philosophy of the school of St. Thomas Aquinas at Paris during the very years when Christian Europe was being shaken to its roots by the rebellion of Martin Luther against Rome. On his return to Spain, Vitoria developed ideas which were to have a profound effect upon the future of religious liberty in Europe, but at first appeared to be more concerned with the position of the native inhabitants in those newly discovered lands which Spain and other countries were colonizing.

Roman law taught that everyone should be given their due, *suum cuique tribuere*. Indeed, it conceived of Justice as being the constant and perpetual wish to give to each his due - *Iustitia est constans et perpetua voluntas suum cuique tribuens*.[6] That which was to be given to everyone, his due, was described in Latin as *ius suum*, and in modern English, as in most other modern languages, *ius suum* would be translated as his or her right. Civil law recognized that it was a duty to give another what was their due, but until the sixteenth century it had not conceptualized this situation as involving the other party as having a right to that which was due to him. He could of course require another to give to him what was his due, because there was an obligation, a duty, to do so which the law enforced, but jurists had not spoken of this in terms of anyone having rights to certain things or certain conduct. This perspective only appears with Vitoria, and in a sense marks the jurisprudential step from the mediaeval to the modern world.

According to the Second Scholastics, so-called because they were perceived to be building upon the work of St. Thomas Aquinas and his followers, God had disclosed his will for Man by making it manifest in the workings of nature. Man was able to attain knowledge of the divine will as manifested in nature by interpreting nature in consonance with the divine will according to the right use of the faculty of reason. Reason disclosed that nature, and therefore God, intended Man to live in social groups or societies, and to enjoy certain things which the existence of such groups helped guarantee and safeguard. Thus, Man needed shelter - a home - and food to survive. Therefore, when an individual had possession of land upon which to live and food to eat, tools with which to cultivate the ground in order to produce food and the like, he needed to be confident he could retain these for his well-being. Thus, he should be recognized by others as having a right to them, to be the owner of them, and it was the duty of a civil society to uphold those rights which were fundamental to a human being's survival and progressive enjoyment of life. For the first time, western jurisprudence presents the notion of people having basic human rights which societies are bound to protect.

This perspective upon human life had profound implications for the attitude of the Church and the colonial powers towards the native inhabitants of the lands they were conquering. For Vitoria, the natives were human beings, made in the divine image and endowed, like the pagans of Greece and Rome, with the faculty of reason. Therefore, they were capable of discovering from nature the divine will which gave them rights in the land they occupied and the things which they possessed. It was not therefore permissible to treat them as incapable of owning property or as being incapable of being owed obligations. Their possession of their lands and chattels ought not to be disturbed, but indeed should be upheld.

Not surprisingly, Vitoria's views were not universally accepted. Although finding support in many quarters,[7] his opinions also encountered considerable opposition. His most extreme opponent was another Spaniard, Juan de Sepúlveda, who totally denied the equality of human beings, refusing to regard non-Christians as being capable of legal personality and thus of owning property or being owed any obligations until they accepted the Christian faith through Baptism. Sepúlveda argued that if the natives refused to be baptized, it was perfectly permissible to confiscate their lands and chattels and even to put them to the sword. His views were obviously convenient to the less scrupulous elements among the colonizing forces, and also had implications for relations with Protestants who had placed themselves outside of the Roman Catholic Church.

While Sepúlveda's views were to be of importance in underwriting the legality of colonial conquest and such commerce as the trade in slaves, Vitoria's opinions were to have profound influence upon the subsequent development of western jurisprudence and the analysis of human social relationships in terms of fundamental, natural rights. In Spain, they were developed by thinkers such as Soto (1495-1560) and Suarez (1548-1617), but it was to be in the Netherlands that the next decisive step was to be taken in the formulation of the rights-based view of human law.

Hugh de Groot (1583-1645), better known as Hugo Grotius, despite being incarcerated and forced into exile for his religious beliefs, insisted upon the rationality of law, as being derived from nature through the use of right reason. Although Grotius himself believed that nature was an expression of the divine will, he admitted that his theory of law could subsist without the divine element. Therefore, his ideas support those of Vitoria with regard to the inherence of natural rights in human beings regardless of their status as Christians. They also inevitably mark the first signs of secularization in the western legal tradition.

Grotius' greatest achievement was the construction in his work *De iure belli ac pacis* of the idea of a legal order capable of governing the relationship of nation states with one another. For Grotius, reason discerned that in nature men were intended to live harmoniously together in societies, and within them this was achieved by respecting the interests of others, avoiding harmful conduct and fulfilling one's promises. In so far as states existed and were governed to achieve these ends, then reason also required that they, or their rulers, should conform to these precepts if their activities were to be just and lawful. Therefore, reason could ascertain rules not only for harmonious living among individual human beings and groups within a state but between states themselves, and such rules could be agreed amongst the states which agreements reason required should be observed and upheld.

Grotius drew on a range of sources to identify by reason what nature manifested to be the best order for a human society. Human laws to be valid had to conform to the dictates of the natural law, but within those limits, human societies were free to choose the legal policies they would pursue. Grotius drew on history, literature, Roman law, the Glossators, the Commentators, native laws and customs and a wealth of sources for illustrations of what was permissible and what among those choices might be deemed the best. Although for him human reason, rather than revelation in any one text, should determine the choices made, nevertheless in his own conclusions, the influence of the models of the civil law remains great. However, the civilian heritage is subjected to a critical evaluation and, where necessary, reconstruction. Thus, Grotius is prepared to systematize his legal provisions in what he deems to be a rational manner rather than follow the structures of earlier ages and writers. He wrote, for instance, a treatise on the laws of the United Provinces of the Netherlands[8] in which he subjected the notion of wrongs, delicts, to a novel categorization according to the nature of the fundamental right transgressed - life, freedom, the person, property, reputation, and so on. This is a simple illustration of the sort of rational development to which legal sources were now to be subjected. This introductory work laid the foundations for the juristic and rational development of the law which the Dutch people were to take to their colonies, the Roman-Dutch law, which drew on natural law, Roman law and the native customs of the people of the Low Countries for its content. While the authority of the ancient and mediaeval legal tradition was not accepted, its achievements were readily embraced and carried forward. Grotius' work forms a bridge between humanism and rationalism.

During the seventeenth century, Samuel Pufendorf (1632-1695), took this systematizing agenda further by developing a scheme for a legal order based upon the concept of rights which were fundamental to human life and society. Basing himself upon the notion of law as being derived from nature by reason, he went on to place within a systematic framework all those laws which he regarded as being necessary or desirable for harmonious, peaceful existence, ranging from laws regulating the family, succession, obligations between individuals and property, to rules of public law governing the relationship between individuals and the State, and rules of international law mediating the relationships between nations themselves. Pufendorf regarded the function of law as being to direct human conduct towards that which made for social harmony and peace and away from conduct which undermined such living. He saw criminal law as being fashioned with this end in view. The idea that the threat of punishment should be a deterrent to bad conduct and an incentive to good influenced later thinkers on penal policy to criticize harsh and cruel punishments and demand that penalties should be justifiable upon rational grounds. Foremost among these jurists and social reformers was the Italian, Beccaria.[9]

In the eighteenth century, the great German philosopher Immanuel Kant (1724-1804) postulated the view that the fundamental rights which reason disclosed that nature intended all men to enjoy were inalienable, that is they could not be surrendered by human beings or their rulers. Laws, according to Kant, could only be justified as protecting those liberties, in part from being invaded by the exercise of similar liberties by others. Kant's ideas were to influence both the Declaration of Independence of the American colonists[10] and the constitutional protection of basic rights which followed the French Revolution in 1789.

Humanism had freed the study of civil law from reverential submission to the legacy of the past. Suspicion regarding the authenticity of what had been accepted as revealed truth in earlier times led to first a loss of confidence in and then a rejection of revelation as a source of knowledge. According to the Thomist dichotomy, that left reason alone as a reliable guide to what was true and just. Rationalism and the school of natural law were the result. The idea of natural law had been known to the ancients, but their concept was not simply accepted. The Roman jurists had maintained that natural law governed all animals, but the natural law school rejected this. It was a law which governed humans only, in that its precepts were only disclosed to reason, and that faculty was unique to man. Faith in reason had replaced faith in revelation, and respect for the past had yielded pride of place to confidence in the present. It remains to consider how this manifested itself in the legal orders of the nation states which came to maturity at this time.

4 The Growth of National Laws

Humanism had undermined the authority of the Roman law texts, which gave rise to the question of whither jurists should look to find their authorities in the future. The organization of Europe into nation states resulted in the emergence of national legal traditions which were gradually to oust the civil law inherited from Rome and developed by the Commentators, which had formed the *ius commune*, common law, of continental Europe both in that it provided a common technique for juristic interpretation and a common reservoir of supplementary legal rules.

In France, there had been throughout the preceding centuries a reluctance to surrender the place of local customs to the claims of the civil law. Although Charles VII had in the *ordonnance* of Montilz-les-Tours of 1453 called for the reduction of the customs of the various parts of his kingdom into writing, very little was accomplished prior to the advent of printed books. Printing made it possible to publish the texts of local customs very widely, and also meant that the text distributed would be a standard one. Thus, at the end of the fifteenth century and throughout the sixteenth, the local customs of France appeared in written form. The effort involved in doing this was so great that some minor customs were not collected and published, giving place to the customs of larger, more significant neighbours. In all, some sixty general customs were published and some three hundred particular ones. In sum, however, they constituted the laws of the French kingdom reduced to written form for the first time, which meant that they were available for juristic analysis and comment.

Throughout the sixteenth century and later, eminent jurists such as Guy Coquille and Loysel examined the customs of the various parts of France to discover similarities of content and application. It was immediately apparent that there was a considerable amount of convergence and, perhaps more importantly, the opportunity for more. The juristic techniques which had served to extract general principles suitable for application in the present from the *Corpus Iuris* of Justinian were now called to the service of performing the same function in relation to the amassed customs of France. Certain jurists asserted the supremacy of the French laws to the exclusion of the Roman civil law, while others blatantly sought to interpret and develop the native product in a manner which brought it as close to its civilian predecessor as possible. For the first time, a general literature of French law became available, which increased further the national identity of the legal order.

During the mediaeval period, the kings of France had at times issued their ordinances with the consent of the Estates-General, which represented the estates of the realm. The lengthy wars with England had made meetings of the Estates difficult. The kings however should not be thought to have turned into absolute rulers of the kind exemplified by the Roman emperors of the Dominate. They did however regard the courts which administered justice in their name as being under their control, and therefore assumed the power to determine the procedure of those courts. Many of the *ordonnances* issued by the kings in the sixteenth and seventeenth century are administrative or procedural rather than substantive in content. Thus, the

Ordonnance of Villers-Cotteret of 1539 introduced criminal process according to the model of canon law into the royal courts; the *Ordonnance* of Moulins in 1566 substituted written evidence for oral testimony as the source of proof in civil proceedings, and the formalities of marriage were regulated by that of Blois in 1579, inspired by the decisions of the Council of Trent and the bull *Tametsi*.[11] They had the effect however of uniting the methods by which the customary laws were administered, and played a great part in uniting the laws of the nation. In the seventeenth century, Colbert, successively chief minister to Louis XIV and Louis XV, engineered the compilation of several more *Ordonnances*, which dealt with both procedural and substantive issues. In 1667, an *Ordonnance* on civil procedure was promulgated, and this was followed in 1670 by another on the criminal process. These were in effect procedural codes for the administration of justice in the royal courts. Technically, the king was not legislating on substantive matters, but providing for the enforcement of already existing laws. Similarly when further *ordonnances* were produced dealing with overland trade in 1673 and maritime commerce in 1681, they were presented as systematizations of the pre-existing customs, although in reality they amounted to new codes of law for the whole kingdom based upon the previous customs as interpreted and developed by the jurists. Indeed, many of the *ordonnances* were the work of eminent jurists, such as during the reign of Louis XIV, Lamoignon and Savary, and during the reign of Louis XV, D'Aguesseau. Louis XV's reign saw *ordonnances* on matters of private law, such as inheritance and gifts.

Several of the leading jurists of the period functioned as magistrates in the courts of France, including the *Parlement* of Paris. Decisions of the *parlements* were recorded and published during these centuries, witnessing to the role which interpretation in the courts played in harmonizing the various customs into a national law. It is clear from both the works of the jurists and the reports of the decisions of the *parlements* that, although the French customs were regarded as the chief source of law in the courts together with royal enactments, considerable use was also made of concepts and even rules derived from Roman civil law. In particular, the method of reasoning employed owed much to the style which had been developed in relation to the civilian sources in earlier times. The *Parlement* of Paris also had the right to be informed of royal legislation and to request the king to think again concerning it if it was not happy with the proposal. This power of making a *remonstrance* was specifically recognized in the *Ordonnance* of Moulins, 1566.

The composition of the *ordonnances* highlights another feature of this age in French legal history, and in that of Europe. The demotion of the *Corpus Iuris* from its lofty position as a result of the criticisms of the Humanists had left the jurists of seventeenth and eighteenth century Europe without what had been for generations the focal point of their analytic powers, namely an authoritative text. This, in some measure, the production of the written customs and then the *ordonnances* supplied. However, there began to be a yearning for a national compilation to fill the vacuum left by the *Corpus Iuris*. Towards the end of the sixteenth century, Henry III had toyed with the prospect of producing a compilation of French law to rival that of Theodosius or Justinian in the Roman sphere, but had died before the project he entrusted to the jurist Brisson had been completed, although it was published after the king's assassination in 1589 as *Code Henri III, Basilica*. The seventeenth century saw the production by Domat of *Les lois civiles dans leur ordre naturel*, which set out systematically the principles of French and Roman civil law, forming what was recognized to have been a virtual preface to the codification of private law under Napoleon. During the eighteenth century, one of the great juristic systematizers, Pothier, reworked the Digest of Justinian by re-ordering the materials under each title into a systematic presentation of each topic, which system was to provide an influential model for later codifiers. He also wrote extensive, systematic treatises on virtually every area of native French law. Colbert's *ordonnances* were also to be foundations upon which the codifiers of French law in a later age would be able to build with confidence. A distinct French national law had come into existence.

Following the Reception of Roman law in Germany in 1495, German legal education centred almost entirely on the *Corpus Iuris Civilis* of Justinian and the *Corpus Iuris Canonici*. As this development took place at roughly the same moment as the advent of printed books revolutionized the material available for education, it became of paramount importance for those wishing to preserve the particularly Germanic legal culture contained in the local laws to have them published. In Germany, much of the work of producing statements of the local laws fell into the hands of eminent jurists whose training in the civil and canon law led to them to incorporate a great deal of civilian learning into their exposition of private law and canonical procedure into their elucidation of the judicial process. Throughout the sixteenth century, local codes, *Landrechten*, were produced at the behest of the territorial rulers, many of which sought to blend the local traditions with the civil law taught at the universities. The result was the incursion into the

German states of a tremendous amount of Italian legal science, albeit that in the future this would be developed at the hands of native German jurists. A particular advance was made in the area of criminal procedure, where from the end of the fifteenth century attempts were made to produce codes of criminal procedure by territorial rulers. A very famous example was the *Bambergensis*, prepared for Bishop Georg of Bamberg in 1507 by the eminent jurist, Johann von Schwarzenberg. Basically a textbook of Italian criminal procedure, it was presented as legislative enactment of the procedure to be used in the bishop's territory, but proved influential as the basis for other such procedural enactments in the following decades. The greatest step forward in the area of criminal justice was however made in 1532 when an imperial law on criminal procedure, with some substantive criminal law secreted in its interstices, was published by the Emperor Charles V. It was entitled the *Constitutio Carolina Criminalis*, but is more generally known as the *Carolina*. Although ostensibly only to be used as a supplement to the local provisions on criminal procedure, it came to dominate criminal justice in the German lands for two centuries. It contained and made for a successful blend of the native German and imported Roman traditions, the latter providing for instance for greater attention to the element of fault in assessing criminal liability.

The territorial rulers of Germany possessed legislative power in varying degrees. While some could legislate of their own motion, others were required to submit their legislative proposals to the local assembly. In virtually all cases, however, actual legislative texts were drafted by jurists trained in civil law. The end result therefore was an increase of the Roman element in German law, and this was furthered by the growth of the natural law school. Pufendorf's ideas of systematizing the legal order were carried further by Christian Wolff (1679-1754) who held that only the fundamental legal rules were deducible from nature and that the remainder had to be deduced therefrom in a hierarchy of rules, leaving some choice to the individual legislator. Christian Thomasius (1655-1728), while accepting the need for rational system, rejected the notion that nature provided any laws for human society, seeing the basis of law rather in the will of a powerful sovereign. Both views were to prove influential in the development of German jurisprudence.

The Netherlands experienced influence from both France and Germany at this time. Possibly following the French example, but also in response to the invention of printing, collections of the customs of the various parts of the Low Countries were made. Some of these clearly exhibit a strong remnant of Frankish elements, particularly in the Frisian lands. A start was also made in the modernization of criminal justice, and the influence of natural law ideas in this field was very strong. After the establishment of the United Provinces in 1579, Amsterdam took the lead in mitigating the severity and cruelty of punishments, and the example of the Dutch is known to have inspired both the reforms of William Penn in the new world and the ideas of John Howard for penal reform in England. The Dutch also made a signal contribution to the development of techniques for dealing with commercial disputes, such as using juries of merchants to state the customs in commercial cases,[12] and their ideas would appear to have influenced Savary's commercial *ordonnance* in France.

Although in Italy, respect for the jurisprudential techniques developed by the Glossators and the Commentators remained undiminished, the impact of the new faith in reason was nevertheless felt. From the sixteenth century, it was expected that reasons would be given for judgements arrived at in disputes, a practice not followed in Germany until the eighteenth century. The reason given however would often be that the *communis opinio doctorum* pointed to a particular result. Dissatisfaction with such mechanical reasoning led to its prohibition in Savoy in 1729 and in Naples in 1774. Likewise, Portugal in 1769 liberated its judges from having to justify their decisions upon *communis opinio*, as had been required by seventeenth-century ordinances, unless that opinion conformed to right reason, *recta ratio* or *boa razão*.[13]

For the greater part of the sixteenth and seventeenth centuries, Spain was ruled by the Hapsburgs, who left virtually undisturbed the legal divisions which had emerged after the Reconquest. While the kings regularly legislated in the fields of public law, private law was barely touched, and the public law enactments were periodically collected in a work entitled the *Nueva Recopilación*, first issued in 1567 and re-issued in an updated form several times thereafter. Although legal science was intensely cultivated in the Spanish universities, little was achieved in producing a national legal tradition at home, although within each of the regional legal traditions, civilian learning made a considerable advance at the expense of the native *fueros*. This Roman element was also preponderant in the laws which were given by the Spanish rulers to their colonies in the New World, the *Leyes de Indias*, collected in 1680. However, when after the period of Napoleonic occupation, an attempt was made to state the law of the whole kingdom in the *Novissima Recopilación* in 1807, the result was no more than a confused and confusing amalgam of regional variations.

Spain did however experience the first serious attempt at unification of its public law under the Bourbon kings who ascended the Spanish throne after the War of Succession ended in 1707. Partly to punish those parts of Spain which had opposed their claim, the governmental and administrative autonomy of Aragon, Valencia, Catalonia and Majorca was abrogated, and institutions of a Castilian stamp imposed. In Aragon and Valencia, this involved at first a repudiation of their autonomy in the field of private law as well, but Aragon was allowed to retain its particular custom thereafter. When Spain regained her independence after the defeat of Napoleon, however, the legal particularities of her regional components surfaced once more, and in Catalonia especially the nineteenth century saw a revival of local jurisprudential pride. One of the distinguishing features therefore of the emerging national legal tradition of Spain was the tenacity of its local legal traditions.

5 Conclusions

The three centuries following the discovery of the New World in 1492 saw the emergence of many of the features which individuate modern law from its ancient and mediaeval predecessors. The reverential acceptance of the *Corpus Iuris Civilis* as a revelatory source of law had gone and taken with it, in most parts of Europe, the slavish adherence to accumulated juristic opinions of the previous centuries. Instead, there was substituted an immense faith in the power of human reason to identify within nature the laws by which mankind should choose to live. The notion of fundamental natural rights was to form the basis of the modern secular constitutions and bills of rights which are an important feature of modern civil law systems.

The passing of the central authority of the *Corpus Iuris* also removed from the legal scene a key unifying factor in European jurisprudence, releasing the jurists of the new nation states to develop a legal science which could be based upon the specific legal traditions of the nation in question, including, as in Spain, its diversity. Already, at this time, the *ius commune* was giving ground to the national laws which were to reach maturity in the nineteenth century.

Reason also played its part in shaping the manner in which law was now analysed. Instead of following the various divisions of the *Corpus Iuris Civilis* and the *Corpus Iuris Canonici*, the latter published in a standard printed form in 1582 after the Council of Trent, the modern classifications of law into public and private, civil and criminal, substantive and procedural, begin to be seen, and in some universities professorial appointments began to reflect this new categorization.[14] It was a redrawing of the legal map akin to the new appreciation of the world and the universe which this age had seen. Chairs in national law as opposed to civil and canon law began to be established in several European countries during the eighteenth century.[15]

However, it is equally clear that the jurists of the respective national traditions were at one with their ancient and mediaeval brethren on one very important matter; they preferred their law to be written, and their preference was for a rational, systematic code. The faith in, and need for, a text had survived the demise of the *Corpus Iuris* as written reason. The formation and study of these texts was to dominate the succeeding phase of the evolution of civil law.

Notes

[1] Claudius Ptolomaeus, a second century AD astronomer.

[2] The Christians of the Byzantine empire had rejected the authority of the Papacy in 1054. The orthodox Churches of the east were autocephalous, that is they each had their own head, and did not recognize the primacy of any one bishop, archbishop or patriarch.

[3] See Coleman Phillipson, 'Andrea Alciati and his Predecessors' in Sir John MacDonell and E. Manson, *Great Jurists of the World* (Boston, 1914; reprinted New York, 1968), pp. 58 ff.

[4] Also known as Cujacius. Most sixteenth-century academics were known by a Latin version of their names as well as their name in their native tongue.

[5] Known in Latin as Donellus.

[6] Justinian, *Institutes* I. 1. pr.; Digest I. 1. 10. The quotation is from Ulpian.

[7] Most notably Domingo Soto (1495-1560); see M. Bellomo, *The Common Legal Past of Europe 1000-1800* (Washington D.C., 1995), pp. 226 ff.

[8] The United Provinces were founded in 1579, having broken free from Hapsburg rule.

[9] Caesar Bonesana, Marquis de Beccaria (1735-1794).

[10] "We hold these truths to be self evident." The very language is indicative of the natural law orthodoxy of the age in which they were written. Law does not give the fundamental rights, it recognizes them.

[11] This required that marriages be solemnized in a church before a priest upon pain of nullity. Henceforth, marriages could be void for lack of form as well as lack of consent.

[12] A practice which may also have influenced Lord Mansfield in England; see T.F.T. Plucknett, *A Concise History of the Common Law* (5th Ed., London, 1956), pp. 248 ff.

[13] This was the *Lei de boa razão*.

[14] See C. Calisse et al., *General Survey of Continental Legal History* (Boston, 1912; reprinted New York, 1968), pp. 355 f., on the new German divisions of the curriculum, and chapter 18 below on legal education generally.

[15] See R. David and J.E.C. Brierly, *Major Legal Systems in the World Today* (2nd Ed., London, 1978) p. 40, and chapter 18 below.

7 Codification

1 Faith in the Rational

The French Revolution of 1789 was widely greeted as the dawn of a new age in human history, an age in which reason would banish superstition from any position of dominance in human affairs, and in which human beings would be able to live together as brothers, enjoying each in equal measure the benefits of freedom. The words *Liberté, Egalité, Fraternité* sum up the aspirations of the new age thought to be dawning in France, and from France across Europe and the world.

The confidence of the age, based on its faith in reason, is difficult to appreciate in an age which is more sceptical and prone to doubt the capacity of human beings and human society to achieve anything like a perfect order. That confidence is however neatly typified, as is the belief that a new age was indeed commencing, by the plan put into effect in 1792 to create a new rational calendar. September 1792 was to mark a new beginning, Year I, and the new calendar divided the year into rational divisions of equal length. The year was to be divided into four seasons, each having three months of thirty days. Each month was to be divided into three ten-day weeks. The months bore names reflecting the weather or agricultural activity typical of the time of year, and at the end of the twelve thirty-day months, the remaining five days of the year were allotted for the celebration of patriotic festivals for the new republic. Gone were the months named after Roman gods; ended the cycle of time founded upon the birth of Christ. Instead, there was a new beginning under the rule of reason. The new calendar lasted fourteen years, being abolished by Napoleon in 1806, in recognition that it had not won popular acceptance within France and was a barrier separating life in France from that in other nations.

The failure of the republican calendar should not detract from the faith in reason and the hope in a new age which was its motivating force. Other rational reforms were much more successful. Thus, it was in 1791-92 that new systems of standard weights and measures for the whole of France were introduced based upon multiples of ten. The older units of weight and measurement were abolished in favour of the metre, the litre and the gram.

The simplicity of the metric system, which was based upon rational, natural units, has led to its widespread acceptance across the world. Decimal currencies have enjoyed a similar vogue. The creation of ordered administrative divisions of the country and institutions of representative government at every tier are also rooted in the rational spirit of this age.[1]

It was not only in government and commerce that rationalism triumphed at this time. One of its most abiding legacies is in the arts. It was widely believed that certain harmonious proportions were deducible from nature and that the presence of these proportions in painting, architecture, music, poetry, drama and even in the arrangement of the landscape was conducive to the creation and appreciation of beauty. Thus, in the building of the eighteenth century, classical proportions and styles predominate, producing a symmetry which in its order and elegance was believed to exhibit the rational order and elegance of nature. Artists carried this over into their painting and sculpture. The figures in the canvases of Poussin, David and Ingres are carefully arranged, often according to geometrical formations and proportions which nature was thought to teach as being particularly pleasing to the rational gaze. Likewise, the parks and gardens of the great houses built at this time were laid out in geometrical patterns, bearing witness to the contemporary belief in the beauty and naturalness of rational arrangement.

In music, the same proportions as governed the harmonious in architecture and painting, were followed in the compositions of the age. The works of Bach, Handel, Haydn and Mozart, all express this belief in order as the key to producing pleasure to the human ear. The Aristotelian unities which were thought to provide the most pleasing structure for plays were widely observed, as for instance in the works of Molière and Racine. The measured poetic metres of the so-called Augustan poets, such as Alexander Pope in England, are also an expression of the rationalism of the age. In literature generally, this is the age of standardization in spelling and the formulation of rules of grammar and style in the use of vernacular languages, based upon the rational models of the classical tongues of the ancient world, particularly Latin.

The idea that nature revealed a rational order to the human mind contributed greatly to the scientific discoveries of the age and the advances in both agricultural and industrial techniques, advances which have become known as the agrarian and industrial revolutions. Belief in the rationality of nature prompted men to search for the motive forces within nature, and was thus productive of much scientific discovery and the achievement of many notable inventions. Great strides forward were made in many fields of human endeavour. The scholars of the age believed that all knowledge could be disclosed by the use of reason; hence, the great project in France of the Encyclopaedia, which would set out in a written text the fruit of this rational investigation. Nature was thought to operate in conformity to laws which were discoverable by the rational mind, and the laws according to which human beings should live and human societies should operate were also thought to be set by nature and discoverable by human reason. The legal achievements of past ages and the practices preserved in prevailing customs were evidence of this underlying natural order which it was the duty of the jurist to discern and the legislator to enact.

2 The First Germanic Codifications

It is against this background that the first codifications of the modern period have to be viewed. It is important to remember that the rulers of the nation states of Europe did not generally alter the private law which regulated the lives of their subjects. Their powers were exercised rather in regulating the procedure within their courts, wherein the rights and duties of their subjects were determined and enforced, together with the rules of evidence which governed the proof of the existence of those rights and duties. However, while the rulers did not seek to amend the substance of the private law by which their subjects lived, they nevertheless regarded themselves as having a perfect entitlement to control the form in which those rights were presented and recorded; indeed, in certain cases the rulers undoubtedly perceived the presentation of the private law in a rational, ordered, systematic fashion as being part of their duty as good rulers of their people. In so far as they were not innovating in producing such reasoned presentations of their people's laws, it was not necessary for them to resort to the legislative assemblies of their people to produce such codes; the work was best entrusted to those learned in the law, the jurists, who had the necessary skills of rational systematization and presentation. The people's role was only to ratify the end product of the juristic endeavour, if indeed even that was deemed necessary. Thus it was that some of the earliest comprehensive codifications were regarded as being the gift of enlightened rulers to those who lived under their government.

Plans for such codifications were a feature of the policy of the Germanic rulers of the eighteenth century. In Prussia, both Frederick William I (1714-1740) and Frederick the Great (1740-1786) sought to systematize the law administered in their dominions, the system which was known as the modern usage of the Pandects, the *usus modernus Pandectarum*. However, although drafts were produced before the death of Frederick the Great, it was not until 1794 that Frederick William II was able to promulgate the code which was called the common territorial law of the Prussian states, the *Allgemeines Landrecht für die preußischen Staaten*, the ALR. It was to remain in force in all those territories governed by the Prussian monarchy until it was supervened in 1900 by the German Civil Code. It was a comprehensive and detailed code, dealing with matters of both private and public law, and not confined to general rules and principles but descending to the regulation of very detailed matters. It began with a general introduction dealing with legal personality and was thereafter divided into two parts: the first dealing with the rights and duties of the individual person and the second with relationships within which the individual functioned in ascending order from the family to the State. Its conception mirrors the legal perspective of Pufendorf as mediated by the work of Christian Wolff. This idea of a code covering all areas of the law and not just a particular body of law, such as civil law or criminal law, had already borne fruit in the codes promulgated in Denmark in 1683 and Sweden in 1734, the Danish code being extended to Norway in 1688.

The great contribution of the natural law school of jurisprudence to codification was however to insist upon the systematization of the law upon institutional lines, that is according to the presentational scheme originated by Gaius and followed by the *Institutes* of Justinian. This mode of presentation is more evident in the codifications produced in Bavaria and Austria at this time. The Bavarian Elector, Maximilian Joseph III (1745-1777), had produced several codifications of different bodies of law for his subjects: a criminal code in 1751, a code of civil procedure in 1753, and finally a civil code, the *Codex Maximilianus Bavaricus Civilis*, divided into four parts dealing with persons, property, succession and obligations respectively. It was not however intended to replace but rather to supplement the existing law, the *usus modernus Pandectarum*, and therefore differs from most other codifications of the age.

The most influential and long-lasting Germanic codification of this period is undoubtedly the Austrian code of 1811, the *Allgemeines Burgerliches Gesetzbuch* or AGBG. Plans for a codification of civil law in the Hapsburg empire had begun in the eighteenth century under the empress Maria Theresia (1740-1780). The intention was to produce a code reflecting the order of the institutional scheme, the content of which would be based upon the *usus modernus Pandectarum* and the dictates of natural law. The end product was a code of private law, excluding both public law and commercial law, divided into three parts, the first dealing with the law of persons, the second with property, the final section being devoted to principles of greater generality. The whole content witnesses to an amalgam of Roman law and natural law ideas, and the code was very influential as a basis for the legal orders of the lands which composed first the Austrian and then the Austrio-Hungarian empire. Although the advent of socialist and communist government in many of these lands in the years after the Second World War has affected the nature of their legal orders, nevertheless in the area of private law, their experience of the ABGB during the period of Hapsburg rule has contributed greatly to their continued acceptance of civil law as a basis for their private law arrangements.

3 The French *Code Civil* of 1804

Whereas the Bavarian code of 1756 was intended solely as a supplement to the existing law of that region and both the Prussian ALR and the Austrian ABGB were specifically described as codifications for a particular territory or the subjects of a particular dynasty, the French *Code civil* of 1804 was altogether more ambitious in its scope. If nature manifested to human reason the laws by which mankind should live, it followed that those laws were immutable, the same for all societies at all times. A rational code of law, therefore, should not be limited in its application to subjects of one ruler or the inhabitants of one territory. Such notions belonged to the dark age of human history when the light of reason had not liberated mankind from the shadows of superstition. In the new age of freedom and equality, a rational system of law could and should be devised which was capable of serving any human society, regardless of place or time.

The inspiration of the jurists who framed the *Code civil* was therefore completely in harmony with the spirit of the age. They recognized that rational order in private law had been achieved by the Roman jurists, as shown in the *Institutes* of Justinian. Domat had already indicated the order in which a rational code of law should be arranged. Equally, Pothier during the eighteenth century had already begun the task of actually arranging both the substance of the Roman law of the Digest and the principles underlying the customary laws of France according to a rational, institutional scheme. The *ordonnances* had already achieved a large measure of rationality for

French law in their respective areas of operation both with regard to order and content.

One of the main differences however between the institutional structure of the ancient jurists and the form of the new codes was the omission from the latter of a section on actions. The modern codes deal solely with substantive private law, removing the law of procedure and placing it in a separate code of its own. The civil code therefore deals only with persons and things. Indeed, on the French model, the civil law deals only with those topics of private law which are of relevance to all people, and excludes matters which are of relevance to only a section of the populace, so that transactions of relevance only to men of business are dealt with separately in a specific commercial code. Again, the influence of the earlier *ordonnances* is apparent in these arrangements, there having been separate *ordonnances* governing civil and criminal procedure as well as overland and maritime commerce. The codification of French law was not therefore completely accomplished by the *Code civil* in 1804. Civil procedure was dealt with separately in a code published in 1807, and a separate commercial code was brought out in 1808. Crime was dealt with in a Criminal Code and a Code of Criminal Procedure, both inaugurated in 1811. Each is a systematic presentation of its subject, replacing all extant law in the area.

The Civil Code itself consists of three books, divided into titles and articles. The first book is concerned with the law of persons, that is to answering the question as to who may have rights. The second book deals with things or property, that is over what legal persons may enjoy rights. The third book, which is very large, then deals with the manner in which rights are acquired, that is how legal persons acquire property. This is treated sufficiently widely as to encompass not only the whole of the law of obligations, both contracts and civil wrongs being treated as means whereby persons acquire rights, together with the methods of acquiring ownership, including by lifetime transfer and by succession upon death. Later civil codes, such as those of Spain and Italy, have favoured greater subdivision than this, allocating specific books of the code to obligations and succession.[2] Nevertheless, the French codification sets the pattern for the codes of the modern civil law. Modern civilian jurisdictions share at least four main codes: the Civil Code, the Code of Civil Procedure, the Criminal Code and the Code of Criminal Procedure. Some retain a separate Commercial Code, while others have incorporated the provisions of the commercial code into their civil codes. The original French commercial code consisted of four books, dealing respectively with internal trade, maritime commerce, bankruptcy and procedure in commercial cases.

While the form of the French codes reflects the rationalism of the period and the legacy of the natural law approach to jurisprudence, the content is overwhelmingly derived from civil and canon law. The law of procedure in particular, both civil and criminal, is heavily imbued with canonical elements. The Commercial Code draws considerably upon the mercantile customs that had for so long governed the dealings of businessmen, and contains little in its first two books that were not in the earlier *ordonnances* of 1673 and 1681 which it replaced. The provisions of the civil code are drawn in part from the customary rules which had operated in the northern parts of France for centuries and which had been worked into a system by earlier writers, and in part from the accumulated learning of civil law from the time of the Glossators, through the Commentators down to the humanists and natural lawyers of the more recent centuries. Customary rules predominate on matters relating to the family, in particular family property including the community of goods between spouses, and issues of succession, again in particular the checks upon freedom of testation in favour of family members. In the area of obligations, however, particularly contractual obligations, Roman influence is very much to the fore. Throughout the Civil Code, the terminology and analysis is thoroughly civilian. Moreover, the promulgation of the codes heralded a new era in which the written text of the law was supreme, and the function of judges was restricted to applying and interpreting its provisions. As so often in the past, it was originally intended that no comment upon the code should be allowed, but juristic expositions soon followed, now confined to expounding the literal meaning of the code and harmonizing its contents in line with its aims, the intention of the legislature and the overall system of its provisions. Henceforth, legal science in France was to be the science of the national law, which was to be taught and administered on its own terms and not as a part of any larger system such as the *ius commune*.

The law of the codifications was the law made by the legislator, and it was therefore thought very wrong that the judicial power, still less unofficial juristic commentators, should influence its meaning or interpretation. In this, the civil law adopted a quite rigorous acceptance of the doctrine of the separation of powers as advocated during the eighteenth century by Montesquieu in his work, *L'Esprit des lois*. This doctrine demarcated sharply between the three state powers of the legislature, the executive and the judiciary. The legislature alone should make laws; the executive should govern and administer according to those laws, and the judiciary should apply the law according to the legislative intention as manifested by the plain meaning of the words used - the literal approach, or as deduced logically from the law's stated purpose, the materials extant concerning its introduction and passage, or by reference to its place in the code or the legal system as a whole - the logical approach according to the teleological, historical and systematic criteria respectively. Judges and jurists should not by their activities usurp the role of the legislative power. With the increase in the concept of popular sovereignty, such an usurpation would be particularly resented, as the legislature was seen as representing the people itself.

The *Code civil* itself was introduced by Napoleon while he was first consul of France, a title which signals the debt owed by the French republicans to their Roman predecessors, albeit Napoleon was to progress from the office of consul to that of emperor in a manner which also recalls the fate of the Roman republic. The legislative method by which the Code was enacted also deserves comment. Several of its components hark back to the Roman republic and the division of functions marks a continuity between those early civilian institutions and their modern counterparts. The legislative initiative lay solely with the consul, in true Roman manner. Legislative projects however would be drafted by the legislative section of the Council of State prior to agreement by the whole Council consisting of 80 members, which itself had no power to pass laws. If satisfied with their draft, the First Consul could introduce it for debate into the body called the Tribunate, consisting of one hundred members. These debated the proposal on its merits, but were not allowed to amend it in any way, having finally to vote upon it as a whole. If they agreed to pass it, it was then forwarded to the Legislative Assembly, which had the power to pass it into law but which was not allowed to debate it. Instead, it was debated in the presence of the Assembly by three members of the Council of State and three representatives of the Tribunate. If passed by this body, the proposal would become law provided that it was in accordance with the Constitution, and to ensure that this was so, it was forwarded to the Conservatory Senate, one of whose functions was to certify the propriety of such formally enacted laws. The work of the Tribunate recalls that of the Roman senate in discussing the policy of legislative proposals with the magistrates, while the Assembly recalls the voting *comitia*. The role of the Conservatory Senate is reminiscent of the part played by the *patres* in ensuring that *leges* were not contrary to the good customs of the Roman people, the *mos maiorum*.

Napoleon took his role as a law-giver very seriously, and some elements in the laws issued by him were the result of his own intervention. These include provisions for the military, refusal to concede foreigners the privileges of citizens and the introduction into the civil law of adoption and divorce by consent. His activities as a legislator are celebrated alongside his other achievements in the bas reliefs which surround his imposing tomb at Les Invalides in Paris.[3]

4 Reaction, the Historical School and the German BGB

The reaction to the French *Code civil* of 1804 was predicated upon several factors. Firstly, its rationalism tied its fate in some measure to the reaction taking place in the cultural life of Europe against what was now viewed as the over-exalted place given to reason by the philosophers and natural lawyers of the later seventeenth and eighteenth centuries. This reaction has become known as the Romantic movement, and its adherents asserted that man did not live by reason alone, but also had spiritual and emotional components to his being which also had to be nurtured alongside the intellectual. The poets and authors of the Romantic movement celebrated feeling rather than reason, and somewhat ironically, the French Revolution itself was one of the great inspirations of the Romantics albeit that it was meant to be the victory of rational forces over prejudice, superstition and blind adherence to tradition. Wordsworth's description of the event instantly strikes a Romantic rather than a rational chord: "Bliss was it in that dawn to be alive" is a description of an emotional response not the record of a reasoned reflection. Likewise, in music, composers such as most notably Beethoven were inspired to express great waves of feeling in their works, despite channelling them still in the accepted forms of the classical models. In art and architecture, subjects and styles were no longer drawn in the main from classical antiquity, but the Gothic of the mediaeval centuries, the styles of the ancient Greeks and the Egyptians, together with the traditions of the Orient, the New World and other colonial lands were all plundered in the diversification of vernacular painting, sculpture and building. Sensibility was resorted to even in philosophy, as witness the works of Nietzsche. The career of Napoleon himself was seen by many as a romantic inspiration.

Hand in hand with the growth of romantic feeling went a renewal in national and nationalist sentiment. Napoleon embodied the spirit of the new France, freed from the burdens of feudal monarchy and the divisions of local loyalties. Its new laws, like its new administrative divisions and its new weights and measures, all played their part in fashioning a new national identity. Across Europe and in the New World, the impetus to throw off the yoke of absolute rule and awaken a national consciousness was felt. Unfortunately for the *Code civil*, this militated against the reception of a French code of law which had been introduced into many parts of Europe as a result of Napoleonic conquest. The law of the conqueror was unlikely to be retained by peoples who had been liberated from the conqueror whatever the virtues of the laws themselves. Moreover, in such circumstances, its aspirations to be suitable for all peoples at all times were viewed askance as pretensions and impositions. Accordingly, in many of the lands where French laws had been introduced in the wake of the success of French arms, the law of the *Code civil* was rejected upon liberation. While the merits of the codification were recognized, the ambition to produce a code suitable to the tradition of each particular country was far greater than the readiness to accept the French compilation.

Allied to this irrational rejection of the French code were certain rational criticisms of it. Its approach to law and to legal rights was highly individualistic. Its basic assumptions were that in a state of nature, individuals had certain fundamental rights and it was they who then grouped to form social relationships of different sorts, from the family and the community to the State. It did not accept that certain social formations, such as the family, might also exist in a state of nature, and therefore be deserving of fundamental protection. This individualist viewpoint also resulted in the code as a whole failing to take adequate notice of the importance of corporate activity to human life, a feature which had in some measure demarcated the Germanic from the Roman elements in the previous legal orders of the continent. This led, according to the critics of the code, to an undervaluing of associations, in particular associations of workers. The code was thus perceived to be a bourgeois compilation in that it favoured the interests of the capitalist, entrepreneurial class against those of the workers. Likewise, it was thought that the individualist conception of ownership adopted by the code stressed the freedom of the proprietor to do as he wished with his own property regardless of the interests of others, favouring liberty above fraternity and thus in a way undermining equality as between those who were rich in goods and those who were not, the former having more power to shape the environment and social relationships than the latter through their economic superiority. To counteract this, there came into being a body of administrative law, by which the State sought to regulate the use or abuse of individual property in the collective interest. This development of administrative law, like that of labour law to protect workers against exploitation, redressed the balance between individualism and corporate solidarity. It also involved an intrusion upon private law rights by public law activity, blurring the distinction between the two basic divisions of law which modern civil law had inherited from its Roman ancestor.

Nowhere was this antipathy to the French model more keenly felt during the nineteenth century than in the emerging nation state of Germany, where the spirit of romanticism had produced some of the greatest poetry, music and art of the period. Moreover, the foundation of the German Reich, perceived by many as the refoundation of the Germanic empire, fused this feeling with the nationalist sentiments common to the age and combined them with a powerful legacy in the domain of law, namely the tradition of the *usus modernus Pandectarum*. At the very moment when the initial defeat of Napoleon was secured in 1814, the German jurist A.J.F. Thibaut called for a codification of the law of Germany, both to give the nation a focal point of unity and also to present it with a scientific and rational system of law. Thibaut's clarion call to codification met with an immediate rebuff from the greatest German jurist, probably the greatest jurist anywhere, of the age, Friedrich Carl von Savigny (1779-1861).[4] Savigny maintained that codification stifled the legal tradition of a nation, and that the three great codes of the time - the French *Code civil*, the Austrian ABGB and the Prussian ALR - were all failures. He saw law as an entity which needed space to grow organically and that space was created not by codification, which restricted growth, but by legal science, the work of the jurists. For Savigny, law was an expression of the tradition of a people and to be acceptable to its subjects had to be a manifestation of their spirit at a particular point in time. It had to be imbued with the *Volksgeist*. A system of law, however scientific, which could serve all peoples at all times was a chimera. Successful laws had to be imbued with the spirit of those they governed and allowed to develop as the life of the people developed. Savigny saw law in terms of a people rather than of individuals and saw it as being specific to their corporate needs. This was the basic tenet of the historical school of jurisprudence, which is in essence the legal component of the romantic movement.

Despite the tremendous influence of Savigny's ideas and scholarship, the notion of a codification continued to seduce the jurists and the statesmen of nineteenth-century Germany. Savigny most likely delayed the introduction of a German code but he did not succeed in preventing it. His pupil, Georg Friedrich Puchta (1798-1846), while upholding many of Savigny's theses, nevertheless engaged in attempts to reduce the laws of Germany into a scientific order. The raw material for this system was to be the Roman law of the *usus modernus Pandectarum* and the basic form the institutional structure, but Puchta believed that law could be presented in terms of a hierarchy of principles, descending from the very general to the most specific, but each having a definite place in the overall rational system. His followers, the Pandectists, believed that legal principles of general application were as discoverable as the laws of nature disclosed by science. Their highly conceptual approach to legal science was destined to have a profound influence on the shape of the German code, but it also produced a reaction. Rudolf von Jhering (1818-1892) declined to subscribe to this jurisprudence of concepts, *Begriffsjurisprudenz*, insisting instead upon a jurisprudence of interests. Jhering believed that when a judge was called upon to apply a law, he should not confine himself to elucidating the terms and system of the norms which he was called upon to employ but should also interpret them according to the interests which it was apparent that the law should serve from the intention of the legislature. While all three schools believed that law had to develop and grow, Jhering believed it should develop according to the ends which it served rather than according to an inner logic which was separate from both the intention of the legislature and the preference of the judge.

The previously disparate states which composed Germany were united into the German Reich under Bismarck in 1871. Already in 1866, a North German Confederation had been created with a bicameral legislature under the King of Prussia with authority to legislate on certain matters for all the members of the federation. A commercial code had been composed in 1861 which had at that time to be adopted by the states individually; this was now reissued as an imperial code, and was reformed and reissued in 1897.[5] An imperial Penal Code was issued in 1871.

The German civil code, the *Burgerlichesgesetzbuch* or BGB, was not promulgated until 1900. It bore the hallmarks of Pandectist influence with regard to its structure and the heritage of Roman law via the *usus modernus Pandectarum* in its content. It consists of a mixture of Roman and Germanic rules, the Germanic governing issues of family property and succession, while the Romanist elements are strongest in relation to property and obligations, a pattern which is familiar in the codifications of modern civil law. The BGB is divided into five books, following an order almost exactly the reverse of the French *Code civil*. The first book, in true Pandectist spirit, sets out the general principles which govern all departments of the law and without which much of the other areas cannot possibly be understood. Thereafter throughout the code, the laws are presented in a hierarchical fashion, preceding in each area from the general to the particular, which requires constant cross-referencing for a full appreciation of the law involved on any topic. The second book deals with obligation, the third with property, the fourth with family relationships, and the final book with succession. It is an order which has found much favour in the teaching of civil law even in countries where the structure of the civil code has not followed the German order. It is a clear departure from the traditional institutional scheme, yet one which is based upon the virtues of that scheme and is manifestly a thoughtful and thought-provoking development of it.

5 The Spread of Codification

Almost a century separates the promulgation of the French *Code civil* from that of the BGB. During that century, the codification movement progressed considerably in both Europe and the wider world. At the time of the promulgation of the French code, certain other countries were already annexed to France as a result of the Peace of Amiens of 1802, and therefore automatically became subject to the new law. These were Belgium, Luxembourg, parts of what is now Germany - namely the Palatinate and those parts of Prussia and Hesse-Darmstadt on the right bank of the Rhine, Geneva in Switzerland, and Savoy, Piedmont and the Duchies of Parma and Piacenza in what is now Italy. Napoleon's conquests after 1804 involved the territorial expansion of the *Code civil*'s jurisdiction as well, incorporating eventually the whole of Italy, Holland, the Hanseatic Departments, and the Grand Duchy of Berg. Some countries adopted the French code of their own volition, for instance the kingdom of Westphalia, including by incorporation in 1810 Hanover, the Grand Duchies of Baden, Frankfurt and Nassau, several cantons of Switzerland, Danzig - at that time a free city, the Grand Duchy of Warsaw, the kingdom of Naples and the provinces which were to become in 1819 the kingdom of Illyria.

The defeat of Napoleon and the expulsion of the French from many of these territories resulted in a reaction, at times violent, against the retention of the French laws, but in many places there was also an acceptance of the virtues of codification. Exposure to the *Code civil* acted as a catalyst to the production of native codifications in many parts of Europe.

Italy

French influence remained supreme in Naples and Sicily, now called the Kingdom of the Two Sicilies and ruled by the Bourbons. There, a Code was promulgated in 1819 covering the whole field of law in five books, dealing in turn with civil law, criminal law, civil procedure, criminal procedure and commerce. The Papal States also acted swiftly upon the French defeat to make good the deficit of codification producing a code of civil procedure in 1817 and a commercial code in 1821, with codes of criminal procedure and criminal law following in 1831 and 1832 respectively. It is also worth noting that the canon law of the Roman Catholic Church was itself to be reduced to an official code, to be called by the traditional title of the *Corpus Iuris Canonici*, and published in 1917. In the north of Italy, Lombardy and Venice returned to Austrian rule and the ABGB of 1811 was therefore brought into force there in 1816. The independent Duchy of Parma retained the French code until a civil code of its own was introduced in 1820, heavily reliant upon Roman law and the French codification, a code of civil procedure being promulgated there in the same year and codes of criminal law and criminal procedure followed in 1821. The Duchy of Modena produced a civil code and a code of civil procedure for itself in 1852 and a criminal code in 1855. 1853 saw the introduction of a remarkably progressive criminal code in the Grand Duchy of Tuscany.

From the point of view of the future history of Italy, the most important codifications were those which took place in the kingdom of Sardinia, a realm which included Genoa and Piedmont, as well as the eponymous island. It was under the auspices of this kingdom that Italy was to be gradually united by a process of incorporation into this kingdom, a process which culminated in unification in 1861, leaving only the Papal territory claiming independence until 1929.[6] Under Carlo Alberto, a civil code was published in 1837, a criminal code in 1839, a commercial code in 1842, and codes of civil and criminal procedure in 1848 and 1854 respectively. The same king conceded a constitution to his subjects also in 1848, the *statuto Albertino*. As the other territories of Italy were absorbed into the kingdom, the laws of that kingdom were extended to them, although some insisted upon independence in certain fields. Almost immediately upon unification, a plan was activated to assist the unification of the kingdom by producing a codified law for the whole territory to express its legal tradition and to assist therefore in the process of unification and finding a national identity. The influence of the historical school in this is plain. A civil code and codes of civil and criminal procedure were ready in 1865, but the commercial code of that year was replaced in 1882. 1890 saw the introduction of the first criminal code common to the whole nation of Italy.

Spain

Spain, like Italy, reacted to French domination under Napoleon by wishing to break immediately with the French code, while nevertheless recognizing the advantages of codification. The Spanish legal tradition however was not uniform, and although the Bourbon kings pursued a policy of unification in public law, this was not extended to private law with any degree of success. Throughout the nineteenth and twentieth centuries, the political history of Spain has been fraught as the result of a continual tension between liberalist and absolutist forces, the former favouring a large measure of local autonomy and the latter insisting upon centralization of government.

Several codifications were made in Spain during the nineteenth century, with successive criminal codes being promulgated in 1810, 1822 and 1848-1850; codes of criminal procedure in 1872 and 1882, and commercial codes in 1829 and 1885. It was 1889 however before a civil code was introduced, and it bore the imprint not only of French but also Italian influence. The particular legal traditions of Spain were protected in that the code did not set out to replace the foral laws of the several communities which composed the kingdom, but instead was only to operate in those areas of the law where there was no valid foral law in operation. It continued therefore in a supplementary role, together with natural reason and equity in the law of Aragon, together with Roman law and canon law in Catalonia, and together with Roman law and the *Siete Partidas* in Navarre. Today, these local laws have themselves been codified, in what are called the *Leyes Civiles Forales* of Spain, the *Codigo Civil* only operating in those areas where there is no local *ley civil foral* on the issue in question. Thus, a large measure of local autonomy still exists within the private law of Spain, which therefore manifests a remarkable blend of the advantages of codification in providing a systematic text with insistence upon the historical school's view that the law must be in accord with the spirit of the people. Even Moorish elements can be found surviving in some of the local *fueros*, for instance in the irrigation laws of Valencia and in institutions such as the partnership contracts for the sharing of land leases, the *aparcerías*, in Aragon.[7]

The Netherlands

Despite the distinct legal tradition of the country, the original codes of the Netherlands were markedly Napoleonic in inspiration. Apart from those portions of the codes dealing with the family, succession and maritime trade, the national tradition was virtually ignored in favour of the content of the *Code civil*. A civil code, a code of civil procedure, a code of criminal procedure and a commercial code were all introduced in 1838, but it was not until 1886 that a criminal code was promulgated. This last codification differed from its forerunners in that it bore the unmistakeable imprint of German influence, emphasizing the two directions from which juristic influence flowed into the Netherlands during the nineteenth century. The Dutch civil code has been revised and reissued in the last decade, in a form which is intended both to be an inspiration to other lands and to be readily adoptable by them.[8]

Switzerland

On its establishment in 1848, the Swiss Federation, as opposed to the governments of the individual cantons, had no power in the area of private law. The only method therefore of achieving any degree of legal unity in private law matters was by the agreement of the cantons on the so-called inter-cantonal compacts. In the cantons themselves, some had been influenced by the French code to the extent of adopting it, some had made codes of their own on the French model or else to reflect native juristic science, while some had continued to live in accordance with their time-honoured customary rules.

In 1874, the Federation was given powers to legislate in the private law areas of marriage and obligations, and the result was a statute on marriage of that year and another on obligations in 1881. This latter enactment was known as the Code of Obligations, and was destined to become in effect a part of the Swiss civil code. The federal power to legislate was extended in

1898 to cover the whole area of civil and criminal law, and the task of producing a civil code for Switzerland as a whole was undertaken. The *Zivilgesetzbuch*, or ZGB, was completed in 1907 and brought into force and effect in 1912. It consists of four books, arranged in true institutional order, the first dealing with persons, the second with the family, the third with succession, the fourth with property, with the 1881 code on obligations in effect forming a fifth part of the code. A criminal code had been introduced in 1799 at the time of the Helvetian Republic, but a new code was issued in 1937 which became uniformly applicable throughout Switzerland in 1942. Procedure in both civil and criminal matters remains governed by cantonal as opposed to federal regulations.

Codification in the Wider World

As well as the influence of the *Code civil*, which was after all meant to be applicable to any society in any age, the BGB, the ABGB and even the ZGB have found adherents, Turkey having adopted the Swiss civil code in 1926 as part of its programme of westernization. Perhaps the most remarkable adoption of the BGB was that of Japan in 1898, but it is also the basis of the law of Brazil as well as having proved very influential in eastern and central Europe. The ABGB formed the basis of the civil law of those countries which had been part of the Austro-Hungarian empire prior to its demise. Nations such as Poland, Czechoslovakia, Hungary, Dalamatia, Croatia and Slovenia continued to make use of its provisions. The advent of socialist systems of law into these areas after the Second World War profoundly affected their legal orders, but following the break up of Yugoslavia and the end of Russian domination in eastern Europe, the Germanic compilations - German, Austrian and Swiss - are again influencing legal development. Romania originally adopted the ABGB, but transferred its allegiance to the *Code civil* in 1865.

The codification of Napoleon has however had the most widespread impact upon the world at large. As well as its influence within Europe, in Italy, Spain, Belgium, the Netherlands, Luxembourg and Portugal, it has formed the basis of codification in those countries which were once part of the French empire in North Africa and the Middle East. Thus, Morocco, Algeria, Tunisia, Egypt, Syria and the Lebanon have codes on the French model. The former French possessions in Indo-China have been similarly affected. Through Belgium, its influence has reached the former territories of the Belgian empire, such as, in Africa, the former Belgian Congo, and through the Spanish and Portuguese imperial influence, codes on the French model serve as the basis of the private law of the greater part of Central and South America. In the United States, Louisiana is the one state to have a civilian legal system, and the *Code civil* has greatly influenced its provisions. In Canada, French law is the foundation of the private law of Quebec.

6 Conclusions

The codifications of the last two centuries brought to its conclusion that process by which, since the Renaissance, law had tended to become national in its outlook. Each nation state is thought of as having its own legal order, the development of which may be similar to, but is in fact separate from, that of any other nation state. Legal education and legal science has also become national in its orientation, national law being taught so that the jurists and practitioners educated and qualified in one system are not thereby entitled to practise in any other. Codification ended the days of the *ius commune*.

Codification also ended the life of Roman law and the mediaeval scholarship surrounding it as a living source of law. Again, the roots of this development are to be found in the soil of the Renaissance as nurtured by humanism. The national codes however mark a return to dominance of a written text at the centre of legal study and of legal science, albeit that there are now as many texts as there are national jurisdictions in the civil law world. Ideally, these texts should only need to be applied, and any interpretation of them should not be regarded as in itself creating any binding rules of precedent. The reality has however been, as was the case with earlier attempts to limit interpretation in the wake of the production of a definitive, authoritative text, that respect for the decisions of the superior courts and the writings of learned jurists upon the system have given rise to a jurisprudence and doctrine within each national legal order without which a knowledge of that system is scarcely complete.

Codification has also meant that the laws of the nations which have codes are readily adoptable by other nations seeking a systematic, ordered and text-based foundation for their law. Thus have the products of the French, German, Swiss and Austrian codifiers found themselves transplanted into jurisdictions across the globe. This globalization of civil law, as well as further extending its scope, which seems to occur regularly in each phase of its development, has also opened up an awareness that the similarities linking the several systems, both as national systems and groups of legal families following the basic codifications, could be the foundation for the development of a pan-European or even a global codification or at least be the material from which a pan-European or global legal science could be fashioned, much as French law, for instance, emerged from the reduction to writing of the old customs of France in the sixteenth century.

Finally, before leaving the topic of codification, it is worth noting that there are still parts of the world with civilian systems, in whole or in part, where codification has not taken place. This is true for instance of the mixed systems of Roman-Dutch law in South Africa and in Sri Lanka, as well as nearer home in the combination of civil law and common law which makes up the law of Scotland. The relationship between the civilian and common law elements in such mixed systems has a powerful part to play in any attempt to achieve a European or global legal order.[9]

Notes

[1] See chapter 14.

[2] Italy has six books namely: 1. Persons and Family; 2. Succession; 3. Property; 4. Obligations; 5. Labour; 6. Registration. Spain has four books: 1. Persons; 2. Property; 3. Acquisition; 4. Obligations and Contracts.

[3] Napoleon is depicted seated as a Roman emperor in all his state with the tomes containing the old French customs being crushed like a serpent under his feet. At his left hand, a figure offers him the *Corpus Iuris Civilis* of Justinian as a worthy replacement for the old French laws, but the emperor disdainfully raises his left hand to signal their rejection. In his right hand, he holds up to the gaze of his adoring nation his own *Code civil*.

[4] For a recent reassessment of this debate, see R. Zimmermann, 'Savigny's Legacy: Legal History, Comparative Law and the Emergence of a European Legal Science' in T.G. Watkin (ed.), *The Europeanisation of Law* (London, 1998), pp. 1 ff.

[5] The earlier codes differed from the French approach on how a commercial transaction is defined, emphasizing the commercial nature of the transaction rather than the mercantile status of the persons involved.

[6] In 1929, the Vatican City State was created by the Vatican Pacts, and a Concordat signed between Italy and the Vatican as independent sovereign states to govern relations between the Roman Catholic Church and the State within Italy.

[7] See E.N. Van Kleffens, *Hispanic Law until the End of the Middle Ages* (Edinburgh, 1968), p. 248; R Altamira in C. Calisse et al., *General Survey of Continental Legal History* (Boston, 1912; reprinted New York, 1968), pp. 604 ff.

[8] Hopefully making the Netherlands a centre for the marketing of legal skills.

[9] See R. Zimmermann, 'Roman Law in a Mixed System: the South African Experience' in Robin Evans-Jones (ed.), *The Civil Law Tradition in Scotland* (Edinburgh, 1995), pp. 41 ff.; 'Savigny's Legacy : Legal History, Comparative Law and the Emergence of a European Legal Science' in T.G. Watkin (ed.), *The Europeanisation of Law* (London, 1998), 1 ff; and, with D. Visser (ed.), *Southern Cross: Civil Law and Common Law in South Africa* (Oxford, 1996).

8 An Historical Overview of Modern Civil Law

The remaining parts of this book are devoted to an historical examination of private and public law within civilian jurisdictions. Before embarking upon that examination, it is worthwhile to pause and take stock of what the history of civil law presented in the foregoing chapters has prepared one to expect.

Firstly, the very distinction between private and public law is one which has been familiar to civil lawyers since Roman times.[1] Although the ambit of public law has increased considerably during the last two centuries, the basic distinction between it and private law remains unaltered, namely that private law is concerned with legal relationships between legal persons who are private individuals while public law is concerned with legal relationships between persons one or both of whom are State bodies. Thus, in a relationship such as "A owes B £50", if both A and B are private individuals, the relationship will be governed by the rules of private law, while if either A or B or both of them are State or public bodies, the relationship will be governed by the norms of public law.

If the relationship is one governed by private law, the rules which govern it will be found in the provisions of the country's civil code, its main compendium of private law rules. There, they will be presented according to the traditional civilian method of dealing in turn with the law relating to persons - those who may have rights and duties, and then with things - what those persons may own and owe. This mode of presentation goes back at least as far as the Roman jurist Gaius, and was adapted by the lawyers of the natural law school to meet the demands of rational presentation in advance of the modern codifications. The codes themselves, both the civil codes and the other modern bodies of rules, are legal texts, legislative enactments in written form, manifesting the civilian preference for having laws reduced to writing, a preference which can be traced back to the XII Tables, but which owes much in its modern guise to the authority accorded in the Middle Ages to the legal compilations of the emperor Justinian in the sixth century. From the work of the mediaeval Glossators also arose the belief that such texts should be harmonious wholes, each part blending with every other in a true systematic unity.

Gaius' systematic division of the law was threefold, into persons, things and actions. The law of actions, that dealing with how rights and duties are adjudicated upon and enforced, is today found in separate codes of civil procedure, having come to be regarded as distinct from the substantive law of persons and things during the sixteenth century. The modern law of procedure owes far more to development by the canon law of the western Church than to its Roman origins, and in its modern form also owes much to the rationalizing tendencies of the eighteenth century.

In some countries, not all of the private law is to be found in the civil code. In France and Spain, for instance, there is another code of private law, namely the commercial code. This code is concerned with the regulation of legal relationships between persons who are both businessmen or with transactions which are of a clearly mercantile character, that is more likely to be entered into by way of business rather than as part of private life. The division recognizes that when a businessman buys goods from another businessman as part of his commercial activity, his expectations and requirements must be governed by mercantile practice and are not the same as those of an ordinary citizen who buys goods as part of everyday living.

The chapters which follow will therefore deal in turn with the law of persons and the family, the law of family property and succession, the law of property and the law of obligations. These are the chapters dealing with the history of private law in civilian countries. In each case, it will be seen that the original Roman rules have had to accommodate during the course of the intervening centuries different and differing conceptions introduced as a result of contact with the practices and legal regimes of other peoples. The development of the modern law is the story of how that accommodation was made and, in particular, how the techniques of juristic analysis, reasoning and presentation, which began with the jurists of ancient Rome but which were refashioned by the Glossators and Commentators of the mediaeval period, succeeded in producing from this conflict of legal cultures, modern systems which remain recognizably the inheritors of the Roman tradition while having been considerably enriched by the absorption of previously alien juristic concepts. The role of the jurists in developing the law in civilian systems via their teaching or doctrine is another feature which has its origins in ancient Rome but has continued to serve the civilian tradition well down to the present, the jurists having continued their quest for systematic unity. In each chapter, an attempt will be made to illustrate the extent to which the Roman foundations have remained, but also to assess the contribution of succeeding ages - from the Germanic heritage, the canonical development, the humanist critique and the rationalizing tendencies of the natural lawyers - which all played their part in fashioning the laws contained in the modern civil codes.

The private law part of the volume ends with a brief look at the law of actions in Roman times as a precursor to considering the law of procedure, both civil and criminal, as part of the public law of modern times. Again, in the public law part of the volume, the modern condition of the law will be related to its Roman origins and the main forces which have shaped legal development in the intervening centuries. Thus, in the examination of the constitutions of modern civilian states, it will be seen how the Roman requirement that enacted law, *lex*, should conform to the ancestral traditions in order to be valid has, via the demands of the Church that human laws and customs should conform to the divine will and the secularization of this doctrine at the hands of the jurists of the natural law school, resulted in the constitutional distillation of natural rights as part of the fundamental law of the State which even legislation must not transgress.

The chapters on civil and criminal procedure will also relate the Roman and Germanic roots of the modern law of actions, while recognizing the immense contribution of canon law to these areas, the adoption of canonical models by secular rulers and the reaction of the eighteenth-century thinkers to some of the practices which the absolutist rulers followed, the sum total of which has resulted in a modern law which, particularly in the realm of criminal justice, seeks to discover the truth of a claim or accusation while respecting the rights of a suspected person to the utmost extent possible.

The public law part closes with a brief examination of administrative law, a body of rules which has developed in some civilian countries over the last two centuries, and an outline of the development of the legal professions which serve the needs of modern civilian systems.

Note

[1] See Justinian, *Institutes* I. 1. 4; Digest I. 1. 1. 2.

PART II

PRIVATE LAW

9 The Law of Persons

1 Introduction

The law of persons addresses the questions of who may be the subjects of rights and duties within a legal system. In other words, if a proposition of law asserts that "A is the owner of X" or that "A owes B £50", the law of persons answers the question of who or what may be A or B in those sentences. In civil codes which follow the French pattern, the law of persons accounts for the greater part of the first book, while those civil codes which follow the model of the German BGB deal with the law of persons after rather than before their discussion of obligations and property.

The Roman jurist Gaius stated that all laws appertain to persons, things and actions, and while the modern division of private law into persons, things and obligations, with actions left to a separate code of civil procedure, is manifestly based upon Gaius's distinction, it is probably wrong to believe that Gaius intended his comment in the same sense that modern systems effect the division of private law. Nevertheless, both Gaius' and Justinian's *Institutes* commence their discussion of the law with persons. Under that heading they deal with the questions of freedom, citizenship and family, the three things which the jurist Paul said were of paramount importance to the Roman. The modern civil codes reflect this in dealing with nationality, civil status and family law. Indeed, some modern civil codes reflect the importance of family law to this part of their provisions by calling it the book relating to persons and the family.[1] The principle of equality which has been of such importance to the legal orders of the last two centuries has ended that view of the family as a unit governed by one person, the father, alone, just as the topic of slavery, which was of major importance in the Roman discussion of persons has now vanished from the provisions of the modern civil codes. Instead of the virtually limitless powers of the Roman father over his family, modern law recognizes a matrix of rights and duties between husband and wife and parents and children. These family obligations have no monetary value, and therefore do not belong among the obligations of property law. Instead, civil lawyers refer to them as being obligations with a moral rather than a material content, reflecting a distinction based upon the presence or absence of pecuniary or commercial value. Moral in this sense is not used in contradistinction with legal; moral obligations in this sense are a type of legal obligation.

This use of the word *moral* to describe rights and duties which are non-material is also employed in the law of persons to describe those entities which can be the subjects of rights and duties, whether moral or material, even though they have no natural existence in the material world. Thus, a common initial distinction drawn in the treatment of the law of persons is that between natural and moral, or juristic, persons.

2 Natural and Juristic Persons

Jacques de Révigny, the thirteenth-century jurist of Orléans, distinguished persons by operation of nature from persons by operation of law.[2] Although the Roman jurists had appreciated that bodies such as the State or a municipality or, in later centuries, the Church could, for instance, own property, they had never set forth the doctrine of legal personality in such stark terms. The notion of bodies of people enjoying a corporate legal personality separate from those of the individuals composing them was a concept developed by Germanic rather than Roman law, but it has come to form a basic tenet of modern civilian systems.

Natural Persons

A natural person is a human being, who from the moment of birth until the moment of death is capable of enjoying, that is being the subject of, rights. The doctrine that all human beings have inalienable, fundamental rights which it is the duty of the law to recognize and uphold, entails that living human beings are of necessity legal persons. They do not enjoy their rights because they are given them by law; the law exists to protect the rights that they enjoy by their very nature.

This was certainly not the view of legal personality espoused by ancient Roman law. The legal subject *par excellence* for the Roman was the Roman citizen, the *civis Romanus*. Being a citizen meant that one had certain rights in public and private law. The public law rights, which pertained to males only, were the right to vote in the assemblies, *suffragium*, and the right to stand for public office, the *ius honorum*. These rights could be lost if one suffered loss of reputation, *infamia*, by for instance having a black mark for misconduct, the *nota censoria*, placed against one's name on the quinquennial census list. In private law, the citizen enjoyed three main rights: *conubium*, *testamenti factio* and *commercium*, being respectively the right to contract a Roman law marriage, the right to make, take under and witness a Roman law will, and the right to engage in contracts enforceable by Roman law. Only citizens enjoyed these rights. They were therefore rights accorded by the law, not natural rights recognized by the legal system.

This is not to say that the Romans denied to non-citizens rights of any sort, although there were for the Romans human beings who were completely rightless, that is the slaves. Slaves were not legal persons, that is they were not subjects of legal rights. Rather they were the objects of such rights. In a sentence of the *A owns X* variety, there were for the Romans some human beings who could not be *A*, the owner, in that sentence, but could be *X*, the thing owned. Such were slaves. They could not form legal marriages, make or take under wills, engage in trade or own property,[3] much less vote in the assemblies or stand for office. They were things in the ownership of their masters, and could be destroyed by him, that is put to death, in the same manner that he might put down a domestic animal of throw away an unwanted chattel. Their status, if one can call it such, arose from capture in time of war, or by being born to a slave mother.[4]

Somewhat remarkably, however, the Romans did not regard the slave as being perpetually set in that condition. It was possible for a slave to be freed and to obtain thereby not only the status of a free man but also that of a Roman citizen. This was achieved by the slave undergoing formal manumission, either by being entered by his master on the census roll as a citizen, or being freed by the decree of a magistrate, or being granted freedom as a gift in the will of his deceased master.[5] While it was not uncommon for ancient societies to permit slaves to be freed, it was exceptional for them to qualify for citizenship. The possibility of manumission testifies to the underlying Roman recognition that, although slavery was practised by all known societies and was therefore part of the *ius gentium*, nevertheless it was contrary to the law of nature, by which all men were by nature free. Therefore, each had the potential to achieve his place in the natural order. The germ of the modern idea is already present in the soil of Roman jurisprudence.

Between the rightlessness of the slave and the plenitude of rights enjoyed by the citizen, the Romans categorized human beings according to a series of gradations. Nearest to the Roman citizen were the citizens of those towns in the region of Rome with which Rome had, in the early years of the republic, entered into a treaty relationship, had become federated. These were the cities of the Latin league, and their inhabitants had, while resident in Rome, many of the rights of citizens. Such status, from its origins, was called Latin status, and it came to be used as a stage on the road to full citizenship. Thus when Rome established colonies in other parts of Italy outside of Latium, it frequently gave to the inhabitants of those colonies some, but not all, of the rights of citizens. Most frequently, they were given the right to trade using Roman law contracts, *commercium*. In the late republic, foreigners whom Rome wished to reward for loyalty or service might be given Latin status as a promotion, and later, they or their children, might receive full citizenship. Whole communities were sometimes promoted in this way.[6]

Foreigners generally did not enjoy any of the rights of citizens. Originally, as in many societies, foreigners were thought of as enemies, and the Latin word *hostis*, which came to mean *enemy*, originally designated any foreigner. Later, friendly foreigners were called *peregrini*, but were not given citizen rights, having to trade under the provisions of the *ius gentium* as developed by the peregrine praetor, not being able to use the institutions of civil law reserved to citizens. Beneath them were the *dediticii*, peoples whom Rome had conquered and who, being unable to accept Roman domination, were expelled from their lands and condemned to wander the empire under pain of enslavement if they went within a hundred miles of Rome itself.

Despite the emperor Caracalla's grant of the citizenship to all free inhabitants of the empire in 212 AD, foreigners outside of the imperial domains had no rights within it, and this discriminatory approach was continued in the legal arrangements of the tribes who occupied the lands of the former western empire. While they countenanced the distinct legal regimes of peoples resident in their midst, they accorded no privileges as a rule to those from outside their territory. Unless a foreigner placed himself under the protection of the local ruler, or accepted the protection of a subject in those lands, he was likely to be enslaved and any property he possessed confiscated.

This uncompromising approach was to continue throughout the early Middle Ages until the rise of the communes in the twelfth and thirteenth centuries. Only natives had rights under the customary legal systems, and a stranger had to place himself under the protection of a local lord in order to acquire rights, otherwise, for default of another protector, he would be within the protection of the king. Such protection however only endured while the foreigner was resident in the territory concerned, and on his departure or death, his property would be forfeit to the king. Indeed, it was not unknown for whole classes of foreigners, the Jews for instance, to be expelled from a land thereby losing all their possessions in the process. Even a person suffering shipwreck had to seek protection from the lord of the place wherein he had been washed ashore, otherwise he could be enslaved or even killed. This was the so-called *ius naufragii*, and even when his life and freedom ceased to be at risk, it remained the case that his possessions were at the mercy of the first taker.

The person born elsewhere, *alibi natus*, could own property in the State in which he was resident but upon his death such property passed to the State and not to his family. This was the so-called *aubaine* or *albinaggio*, which proved, with the *ius naufragii*, remarkably resilient against attempts to secure its abolition. Already in the ninth century, the Lombard rulers ceded their right to the escheat of an *albinaggio*'s property if he had surviving sons, but despite attempts by the communal governments and the princes of mediaeval Italy, and even by the emperor Charles V in the sixteenth century, to abolish the practice, it continued to reappear throughout the eighteenth century, when as a rule it was only when States had entered into treaties of reciprocity with regard to the treatment of their subjects that the practice ended. Even the spirit of equality which prevailed at the time of the French Revolution was not sufficient to ensure that foreigners be treated on an equal footing with citizens under the *Code civil* of 1804. The first Italian civil code of 1865 did however give foreigners equality of private law rights with citizens, and today that is generally the case, and within the European Union certain public law rights, such as the right of suffrage, are accorded resident citizens from other member states, a situation not unlike that prevailing among the cities of the Latin league at the time of the early Roman republic.

The concept of a foreigner is a negative one, standing in contrast to that of a native or citizen. In ancient Rome, a citizen was a person born of Roman law marriage whose father was a citizen. Otherwise, citizenship could only be obtained by grant. Status for the Roman was something determined by descent, and this remained the case in the barbarian kingdoms which succeeded the western empire. With feudalism, however, another principle emerged, that of nationality following upon one's place of birth, hence the foreign status of those born elsewhere - *alibi natus*. Today, most systems continue to accord nationality and citizenship to all born in their territory, but also give rights of naturalization to the children of citizens or nationals who have been born elsewhere. Spouses are generally allowed to acquire citizenship in their partner's home nation.

Disability has not however been restricted to foreigners. Although slavery has not been a marked feature of European life since the fall of the Roman empire, serfdom has, and slavery itself was widely practised in the civil law countries of the European empires.[7] Only gradually did both institutions decline. In this regard, there was a marked distinction during the mediaeval period and under the rule of absolute monarchs between rural and urban legal practices. In the country, those of servile status were tied to the lands upon which they worked. Although not slaves, and therefore free in the sense of being persons not property, they had no right to leave the estate on which they worked. Indeed, strangers who settled in some such areas and did such servile work for a year and a day might find themselves similarly restricted by the local custom. In the towns and communes on the other hand, residence for a year and a day would release a stranger of servile status from the bonds of that condition. The serfs of the feudal countryside were probably the descendants of the class of agricultural labourers present in the later Roman world who were called *coloni*, and who, though not slaves, were not free to leave the estates upon which they laboured. Serfdom survived in France, for example, until the Revolution, but has since perished in the face of the principle of equality.

Disabilities and privileges also attended social classes in Germany until the last century, and there the privileges of noble birth proved more difficult to eradicate. The higher nobility obtained their status from being the children of marriages contracted between those of high noble birth. A high noble could not marry out of his caste; if he did, the marriage was deemed morganatic and his children would not inherit his status. It was well into the nineteenth century before such distinctions of birth were eradicated within the German States, while in France they had gone with the Revolution. Likewise in Germany, individuals who did not conform to the faith of their territorial ruler suffered disabilities in public law, which were not generally removed until 1848.[8]

Inequalities of status also attend differences of age, sex and physical and mental ability. These by and large however turn upon the structure of family life rather than that of the community, and will therefore be discussed in relationship to guardianship. It is however pertinent to note that the public law disabilities of women present in the early Roman republic were mirrored in the laws of the Germanic tribes, where public law rights depended upon the capacity to bear arms. Even after the principle of equality was generally adopted after the French Revolution, equal status for women in public law has largely only been achieved during the twentieth century.

Juristic Persons

Civil law systems also recognize the legal personality, the capacity to enjoy legal rights and duties, of corporations and associations. Some juristic or moral persons are public in nature and some private, while others partake of elements of both types and are described as mixed. The juristic persons of public law are entities such as states, municipalities, regions and provinces. They are descendants of the public bodies of Roman times which Roman law itself recognized as having the capacity to acquire property and to be subject to obligations. While Roman law however recognized the juristic personality of such public bodies, it had not developed a clear notion of corporate or associate personality in the realm of private law. When individuals joined together to exercise a profession or a trade in association, Roman law regarded them as being joined together by a contract of association as between themselves, the contract of *societas*, but did not see that agreement as giving rise to a separate juristic person with which third parties could contract and enter into further legal relationships. Rather it saw such third persons dealing with the individual partner alone, leaving the partners to work out how his actions affected the others' relationship with him. The third party had no call upon the other partners or the partners as a group.

Modern civilian systems have taken this consensual contract of *societas* and developed it into a major institution of both civil and commercial law. It serves as the basis for joint ownership among ordinary citizens, as well as forming the foundation for professional and trading partnerships, the legal structures required for corporate activity and some charitable activities. In addition to the *societas*, modern civil law also recognizes the legal personality of associations formed for specific purposes and of foundations in which property is dedicated to certain ends usually of a charitable nature.

The modern civilian concept of juristic personality owes much to Germanic law and the canon law of the western Church. Its beginnings in Germanic law are probably to be found in the village communities of the early Middle Ages. These communities were often extensions of the family group or *Sippe*. In Germanic law, sons were emancipated from their father's control or *Mund* upon leaving their father's household and establishing a household of their own, an event which often occurred upon their marriage. Despite their emancipation, and capacity thereby to own their own property, it was likely that some items of property, such as grazing land, the local mill or wine-press, might still be enjoyed in common. This might even be the case if a son-in-law, who had never been in the family *Mund*, moved into the village, and also with strangers who made their homes there. Germanic law recognized that these common lands or implements were owned by the community as a whole and not by the members in individual shares. It came to regard the community as a legal person separate from the individuals who composed it, which would continue to exist after all its original members had died and been replaced by others. This is the essence of juristic personality. Roman law on the other hand regarded a *societas* as terminating upon the death or defection of any one member.

The village communities also existed in the realm of public law, but their identity with regard to the ownership and sharing of property was early distinguished from their identity as a governing body for the locality. Their corporate identity became even more apparent when, with the clearing of forests and extension of the arable land, such lands brought into cultivation were owned by the community as a whole, the so-called mark communities. These came to be governed by an assembly of the local families who appointed a *Vorman* to administer the lands, but who was accountable to the community at regular meetings. As will be seen, this foreshadowed the arrangements for communal ownership to be found in the modern civil codes.[9]

While such communities in the countryside gave rise to the corporate idea, the towns and communes of the Germanic lands were also contributing to the development. These were the context for the development of trade and craft guilds and corporations. The merchant guilds were usually associations of traders who were travelling away from their homes and therefore in need of lodging and representation in the places where they traded. In such locations, they came to own collectively inns and trading outlets which were regarded as theirs as a group which had an identity separate from that of their individual personalities. In the towns themselves, craftsmen were often required by the civic authorities to ply their trades in a particular street or area of the market and the civic authorities would also place them under the supervision of an officer to ensure that their work was of a professional standard. It came therefore to be in the interests of the craft as a group to regulate the standard of their work. This led to the practice of having to qualify in order to practise the craft in that place. The Guild became the regulatory body of the craft, and would discipline members who fell short of the required standards. The Guild often acted as a body which arranged religious services for the members, provided for their funerals and celebrated feasts of relevance to the craft. It acquired an identity separate from that of its members, and took on charitable functions. It was long believed that the corporate identities of the towns and communes of mediaeval Italy and Germany were based upon that of the guilds contained in them, and there definitely was a mutual influence in the development of their legal institutions.

As well as these rural communities and urban corporations, the Germanic lands also saw the development of what are termed communities of the collective hand. These were associations of people, sometimes relatives, who chose to live a common life together rather than to live out separate individual existences. The house in which they lived and their possessions might all be held in common, while other possessions of theirs, such as the tools with which they prosecuted their respective professions or trades, would be owned by them individually. These collectives were often based upon the determination of the descendants of one man not to split up the family property following his death, but to go on enjoying it as a household, or often upon the decision of individuals unrelated by blood to pursue a common life together in furtherance of a religious ideal. Such were the *Beguinage* of the Low Countries. Whatever their origins, the communities thus formed were recognized as having a personality in law distinct from that of their individual members, and were the forerunners of the associations formed for charitable purposes in modern law. The idea of the collectivity giving rise to a separate legal personality also influenced the development of the concept of the communion of family property.[10]

The other entity which enjoys legal personality in modern civil law is the foundation. Its history extends back to Roman times, where it was accepted that property could be dedicated to a particular purpose, often of a religious or civic nature. Thus, *collegia*, such as the College of Pontiffs, had property which was not susceptible of disposal even by the members of the college in question. Such blocks of property were not susceptible to the rules of private ownership allowing sale, transfer and inheritance, but were dedicated to the purpose concerned in perpetuity. Gifts to the gods and to their temples produced this result, as did gifts for instance to establish a theatre or a stadium. There was no human owner. With the advent of Christianity, the number of such foundations greatly increased, the ecclesiastical authorities overseeing their administration, with bishops and other prelates often acting as formal overseers, or visitors. The property was regarded as that of Christ or his saints; it was a patrimony with no earthly owner. Sometimes in the Middle Ages, it was the patrimony of a hospital, school or university. No human members needed to exist. The patrimony had a distinct identity of its own - St. Martin's Church, St. Bartholomew's Hospital, its own legal personality.

Whereas such foundations were acceptable as legal entities in canon law as a development of the Roman law *universitates*, the revived civil law of the later Middle Ages found the various corporate arrangements of Germanic law difficult to assimilate. With the Reception of the closing years of the fifteenth century, the civilians struggled to achieve a synthesis between the Roman concept of the *societas* and the Germanic *Genossenschaft*. The result in Germany and France was a perspective of corporate identity which found a place for the canon law foundation in the form of the *Stiftung*, but began to require a grant of legal personality to other entities as a condition of their achieving legal personality. In France, Loysel was to propose that the king's permission was requisite for a corporation of any sort to achieve legal personality, and in 1794 it was settled by royal *ordonnance* that only corporations which satisfied legislative preconditions could enjoy legal personality upon registration. This restrictive approach was born of the basic idea that rights and duties were the inherent legal properties of human beings and that to accord them to other entities was a fiction of the law. In 1791, revolutionary French law went so far as to abolish both corporations and foundations. In nineteenth-century Germany, State disapproval of incorporation also emerged, first in Prussia in 1810 and thereafter throughout Germany from 1869.

The refusal to recognize corporate identity as anything other than a fictitious personality accorded by law was in part the result of the stern individualism which had prevailed at the time of the drafting of the French codes and bore witness to the victory of Romanism over Germanic concepts in those compilations. However, the nineteenth century also saw a revival of support for subjunctive associations of individuals existing within the State, ranging from the family and local clubs and groups to large-scale associations such as trade unions and industrial organizations. Modern constitutions frequently assert that the State exists not only to promote the interests of individual human beings but also associations of people, thereby subscribing to the view that such entities, like people, exist prior to legal recognition and that their legal personality is therefore but the law's response to their existence and not its creation of them. Thus, in modern France legal personality in private law is accorded not only to commercial *societés*, based on the Roman contract of *societas*, but also to *associations declarées*, which are registered by the State upon satisfying certain conditions, as well as *fondations*, likewise registered, being patrimonies devoted to specific charitable purposes. In Germany, the rich diversity of corporate association to which the law of that country is the heir is manifested in the existence of *Vereinen*, *Stiftungen*, *Gemeinschaften* and *Gesellschaften*, offering a range of corporate possibilities, each enjoying legal personality.[11]

Perhaps the most basic of the associations recognized by law which modern States see it a constitutional duty to protect and promote is the family. This institution has also been influenced by Roman, Germanic and Canon law in the course of its development in Europe.

3 The Family in Civil Law

The word *family* is used in a variety of contexts, but three principal meanings are relevant to its place in civil law. Firstly, it is used to describe a household, consisting of members related by common descent from a living parent or parents. Most typically, and to a large extent the norm from which other arrangements are contrasted, it consists of parents and children living in the same house. Secondly, *family* is used to describe a wider group related by descent from a common ancestor or ancestors. This is the family as a kinship group and consists of collateral relatives who do not usually live in the same household, for instance uncles and aunts, cousins and remoter relatives. These constitute the family in the sense of those who might meet only on significant occasions, such as baptisms, marriages and funerals, but would admit kinship among themselves at all times. Finally, there is an even wider meaning to the word *family*, where it is used not only of living members but also of ancestors who are dead and generations which are yet unborn. The family in this sense can have importance in terms of religious and cultic observance.

The countries of the civil law tradition are heirs to a concept of the family which is derived in part from Roman law and in part from Germanic law, but has in both cases been shaped by the influence of the canon law of the western Church during the Middle Ages and later. The result is a concept of the family which, while by no means uniform throughout the civilian world, nevertheless has common features. Most notably it is based upon the marriage of one man and one woman to the exclusion of all others and their life-long commitment to mutual support, fidelity and the raising of their children. These children owe their parents respect and obedience, while the parents owe them support, upbringing and education. In modern law, these obligations are seen as being due to the children and last until they have reached an age at which they are able to assume independent control of their own lives. In many countries, however, the parents remain obligated to support their children and their families if serious need arises, and the children have the same obligation towards their parents. There may also be similar if less onerous obligations of support in time of need between brothers and sisters. The individuals who compose the family will, as individuals, enjoy ownership of property, but some property will be regarded as pertaining to the family as a unit rather than to the individuals separately. Accordingly, the law may recognize the existence of a separate patrimony called the family communion. Indeed, even with regard to the property enjoyed by family members as individuals, there will be no absolute freedom to dispose of it according to individual choice; instead, the surviving spouse and the children will have a definite right to receive due portions upon the death of a family member, as in some cases will surviving parents.

These features will be found in almost all modern civil law systems. They reflect a concept of the family as a corporate and continuing entity. This concept is heir to Roman, Germanic and canonical ideas. The nature of those three roots must now be examined.

The Roman Family

The Roman family, in the sense of the household, consisted of the head of the family, the *paterfamilias*, and all those within his power, or *potestas*. Those within his power were children born to him of a lawful Roman marriage, *iustae nuptiae*, whether they were male or female, grandchildren born of the lawful marriages of his sons, and even great-grandchildren born of the lawful marriages of his grandsons. While his daughters were in his *potestas*, their children would not be because, if born of lawful Roman marriages, they would be in the *potestas* of their father, the daughter's husband. Likewise, the great-grandchildren born of granddaughters rather than grandsons would be in the power of their respective fathers, the granddaughter's husbands, and not in that of the *paterfamilias*. All those descended from him through males, whether those descendants were male or female, were however in his power. Such relationship, traced through the male line only, is called agnatic.

His wife might or might not be in his power, and therefore might not be a member of the family. She would only be in his power if she had been married to him with *manus*, that is had passed into his hand. Most Roman marriages were not with *manus* but were free marriages, *liberum matrimonium*, according to which the wife retained her family membership, property and succession rights in her own family. Likewise his descendants' wives would only be in his power and in the family if they had been married with *manus*, and his female descendants would remain in his *potestas* and within the family unless they had married their husbands with *manus*, in which case only would they have passed into their husbands' families.

The *potestas* of the *paterfamilias* continued until his death. His children and other descendants within his *potestas* were in his power, *alieni iuris*, while he lived, only becoming *sui iuris* when he died. This meant that only he could be the subject of private law rights. Only he could own property; only he could have contractual obligations; only he could sue for compensation or be liable to pay damages for wrongs suffered or inflicted. Whoever was injured or caused an injury within the family, it was the *paterfamilias* who was to sue or be sued. Children did not achieve independence in private law terms by reaching a particular age, only by being freed from the *potestas* of their father, and that only occurred naturally on his death, although they could be emancipated by operation of law during his lifetime.

The power of the *paterfamilias* was considerable. Over those in his *potestas*, as over the slaves in his *dominium*, he enjoyed the right of life and death, the *ius vitae necisque*. This not only meant that he could expose unwanted children at birth, but also that he could order the death of a child at any time thereafter, although there are few recorded instances of this power being exercised and in later Roman law it required the consent of a magistrate for its exercise.[12] His consent was required for his children to marry, although again in later times appeal to a magistrate against an unreasonable refusal was possible. While within his power, children could be allowed to manage a share of the family property called the *peculium*, but in law this remained the father's, and any contractual rights obtained by them became his. Again, by degrees, sons on military service were permitted to enjoy property as their own, and this privilege was eventually extended to sons serving the State as civil servants in the provinces, and property coming to children from the mother's family or other outside sources could not be diminished by the father although he was allowed the income thereon.[13]

Although the *paterfamilias* might appear from this to have been an absolute ruler in his family, in some ways he was more of a managing director. If insane of even spendthrift, he could be removed from control, and he was expected to keep strict accounts. Moreover, on his death, he was not free to dispose as he chose of the family property, for such in reality it was although owned by him; rather his patrimony, or fixed proportions of it, had to pass to his children who were, by nature as much as by law, his rightful heirs.

Beyond the family as the household was the wider kinship group, also at first in Roman law agnatic. It consisted of all those who could trace descent from a common ancestor through males. Kinship was also reckoned through females, and blood relations, whether traced through males or females, were recognized for some purposes in law as relatives. This group was called cognatic. Kinship was reckoned by degrees, counting up to the common ancestor and then down to the other person. Thus, parent and child were related in one degree, brothers and sisters in two - one step to the parents and a second to the other person. Uncle and niece were related in three degrees, first cousins in four. Kinship was recognized to the sixth degree, and the seventh in the case of the child of a second cousin, which may reflect the farthest that the *potestas* of one man was likely to extend during his lifetime, second cousins being great-grandchildren of the common ancestor. Marriage to a relative within the sixth degree was prohibited in the early republic.[14] When a *paterfamilias* died, his children became *sui iuris*, but his grandchildren passed from his power into the power of their fathers. Only when their fathers died would they become *sui iuris*.

The Germanic Family

The Germanic family was also in its origins agnatic, with the father having power over his children. The power of the Germanic father was called his *Mund*, a word meaning, like the Latin *manus*, hand. It came to mean protection or peace. Within his *Mund*, the Germanic father had his wife, who normally passed into his *Mund* on marriage. Marriage in Germanic law was not at an early stage as essentially monogamous as in Roman law. Children born to the father of his lawful wife were within his *Mund* if he chose to retain them, but like the Roman *paterfamilias* the choice lay with him and he could choose to expose an unwanted child.

The children remained in his *Mund* until they left his household to establish their own, this usually occurring upon their marriage. The father could also drive a child from his hearth for disobedience or other good cause and a child could abscond and leave the *Mund* of his own motion, but generally Germanic children became *sui iuris* by leaving the father's home with his consent to establish their own household. The Germanic system is therefore regarded as freer with respect to the independence of the individual adult than the Roman. The Germanic family household as a result tended to consist of only two generations, parents and dependent children, although it was not uncommon for one son to remain at his father's home after marrying to look after his parents in their old age, when the father's *Mund* would cease as his faculties declined.

Beyond the household, kinship in Germanic law was also reckoned by degrees, although these degrees were reckoned differently from the Roman system. Germanic law regarded relatives as being related in whatever degree the persons were removed from their common ancestor, in the event of the relatives being of different generations, the greater degree being that attributed. Thus, children were related to their parents in one degree, but under this system, so were brothers and sisters, each being one degree from their common ancestors. Uncle and niece would be reckoned as related in two degrees, that being the greater of the two links to the common ancestor; likewise first cousins. Second cousins would be related in the third degree in Germanic law as opposed to the sixth in Roman law. This difference was to prove important in the later marriage law of the western Church.

Unlike Roman law, the Germanic system allowed for independence in the ownership of property once the children established their own homes, and this in turn permitted of greater freedom of testation. Wives however were much less independent than in Roman law, passing into the power of their husbands from that of their fathers at marriage, and generally passing into the *Mund* of their sons if widowed. Provision for the wife was therefore a greater feature of Germanic law.

The Canon Law of the Western Church

In that the western Church developed from the fourth century within and as a part of the Roman empire, it inevitably adopted many of its concepts regarding the structure of the family from Roman law. However, it was also determined to influence the development of that law in a Christian direction. Thus, under the Christian emperors emphasis was placed upon the permanence of the marriage contract, with restrictions being placed upon the freedom to divorce. Husband and wife were one flesh and therefore mutual support and fidelity were upheld, with sexual relationships outside of marriage generally discountenanced. Adopting from Roman law the concept that marriage was based upon the consent of the couple, the canon law discouraged the idea that marriages could be arranged for children by their parents, or daughters married off by their fathers regardless of their wishes. To the Christian Church, all human life was sacred and therefore the exposure of new-born children, *neonati*, was abhorrent and the right of life and death unacceptable. The former proved virtually impossible to eradicate, although the latter was reduced to a power of reasonable chastisement.

Outside of the household, canon law made no distinction between agnatic and cognatic relationship, a distinction which had already in effect passed into Roman legal history by the time of the conversion of the empire to Christianity. However, the Church also placed emphasis upon relationship with a spouse's family as a result of marriage, so-called affinity. It also insisted that marriage should only take place outside of the family, which it was eventually to define as extending to the sixth degree, like Roman law, but reckoning those degrees in the Germanic fashion, thereby greatly extending the range of prohibition.

4 Marriage and Divorce

Most modern systems of law treat of marriage in terms of the capacity of the parties to marry one another and the formalities that are required for solemnization of the contract. Capacity relates to the minimum ages which the parties must have achieved, the consents that are required and the lack of an existing close family relationship between them. The formalities are concerned with the steps which have to be taken prior to the ceremony and the manner in which the ceremony if any has to be conducted.

Capacity to Contract a Marriage

While there is general agreement among legal systems that the prospective husband and wife must have achieved a certain level of both physical and intellectual maturity in order to contract a marriage, there has not been much consensus with regard to the age at which such maturity can be presumed. It would appear that in early law, both Roman and Germanic, the physical maturity of the parties was determined by inspection to establish whether they had reached puberty and were therefore capable of consummating the union. In Roman law, this was early equated with achieving certain ages, namely fourteen for boys and twelve for girls, ages which were also of importance in their mental and intellectual development.[15] These ages were retained by the Romans and found their way from their law into that of the western Church, where fourteen and twelve remain the minimum ages for canonical matrimony, although the Church accepts the propriety of individual societies setting higher minimum ages in their territories.

Lombard law regarded the respective ages as being thirteen and twelve, while the emperor Charlemagne increased the minimum ages in his realms to eighteen and fourteen respectively. This marks a move away from physical towards mental maturity as the indicator of readiness to undertake matrimonial obligations, and is also indicative of a society in which the spouses would have greater responsibility for their own welfare upon marriage.

Although the law fixed the minimum age for marriage in these societies, it must be remembered that the spouses were not free to marry as they wished on attaining these ages. Their freedom was also constrained by parental consent. The parents could still decide on the readiness of the particular person even if he or she had reached the minimum age. One would therefore expect there to be a raising of the minimum ages as the necessity for parental consent gave way to the concept of the consent of the parties being paramount, as their capacity to consent would have become as, if not more, important than their capacity to consummate the union.

In Roman law, the consent of the *paterfamilias* was always required for the marriage of a son or daughter in power. The consent of the parties was also necessary. By the late republic, it had been established that it was the parties' consents that were paramount and an unreasonable withholding of consent by a father could be overruled by the magistrate. Marriage was recognized as being a matter primarily for the parties.

Germanic law on the other hand regarded marriage as being a matter for the prospective husband and the father of the bride. The bride's consent at first would appear to have been unnecessary. Moreover, to take a daughter in marriage without the consent of her father was regarded as abduction and a legitimate cause for the pursuit of the blood feud. The canon law of the Church upheld the freedom of the parties to marry against the view that marriages could be arranged by the parents, and the consent of the parties, through canon law, came to be the consent which was essential to the contract. If it could be shown that the parties had not in truth consented to the marriage, then it was a nullity in the same manner as if they had not reached the necessary minimum age, while the absence of parental consent was not necessarily fatal to the validity of a marriage in canon law. This view has also found its way into the modern codes.

Parental consent came therefore to be seen by the law as a safeguard to ensure that, in the case of youthful couples, they were regarded by their families as sufficiently mature to undertake such an important step in life. Nevertheless, parents themselves often acted from different motives, such as ensuring their child married an acceptable partner - acceptable perhaps to the parent as much as, if not more than, to the child. Thus, parental consent came to be required in some systems for as long as civil law decreed that a young person needed assistance in making important decisions The tension between the freedom to marry and the need for parental consent is clearly shown by the development of French law upon this issue. In the sixteenth century, to marry without parental consent under twenty-five was deemed to merit disherison, while for Pothier in the seventeenth century, such marriages were completely void and disherison was merited by any who married without consent under thirty years of age. By the *ordonnance* of Blois of 1579, to marry a woman without her father's consent was deemed to be abduction, and abduction in these terms had been punished as a crime in the Netherlands during the later Middle Ages. Even after the Revolution, with its emphasis upon freedom and equality, the *Code civil* required that males achieve the age of twenty-five and females twenty-one before they were able to marry without parental consent, and thereafter maintained that proper respect for one's parents required that they be asked to consent before a marriage was solemnized. Throughout the nineteenth century, young Frenchmen and women were required to seek parental consent formally by notarial letter on three occasions before contracting their matrimony. This was reduced to one written request in 1896 and in 1907 was converted into a duty of notifying the parents with a month's grace for them to object before the marriage was solemnized.

Generally today, the age at which couples may marry without consent is that of majority, commonly eighteen, and provided that the minimum age for marriage has been reached, lack of consent beyond that age renders the marriage voidable upon the objection of the parents rather than void in itself.

Couples must also have capacity to marry one another. In Roman law, the capacity to form a lawful Roman-law marriage was termed *conubium*, and was only enjoyed by citizens. Thus, a Roman law marriage could not be contracted with a foreigner. The Germanic laws also treated capacity to marry as something which was internal to the tribe, and only in 895 at the Diet of Treves was the principle established that a marriage should be valid wherever contracted provided the parties were capable of marrying according to their personal laws. Throughout the mediaeval period, marriages between Christians and non-Christians were not recognized as valid, and marriages between persons of different status were not generally accepted either, a position which was retained by the high nobility of Germany until very recent times.

The greatest bar to capacity to marry, however, was the rules relating to the prohibited degrees. In Roman law, it would appear that originally marriage was not permitted within the sixth or seventh degree, measured in the Roman manner, nor in the direct line of descent to any degree.[16] The canon law adopted this rule, but adopted the Germanic method of calculating the degrees, thus considerably widening the range of the impediment. Eventually, the Church accepted that marriage should only be barred within the fourth degree and that dispensation could be obtained to marry within the third and fourth degrees. The Church therefore developed the doctrine that some impediments were absolute while others were dispensable, a view which contributed to the distinction between marriages which were void in themselves and those which were only voidable on the complaint of an affected party. The latter were not sinful, but merely irregular. The Church also developed the concept that the invalidity of marriages should not affect related questions such as the legitimacy of offspring and property matters. A marriage which had been undertaken in good faith by at least one of the parties and had been duly solemnized would therefore be treated as putative, that is believed to be valid, for adjacent purposes.

Formalities of Marriage

Today, it is generally the case that marriages have to be solemnized formally. Many civil law countries insist that the ceremony take place in a civil registry, and that no religious service may precede the secular registration. Some countries, however, permit the religious service to be the context in which the secular formalities take place, and accept the ecclesiastical ceremony as sufficient for civil purposes.

Marriage has become in modern civil law very much a formal contract, that is one in which the consent of the parties has to be manifested in a formal manner if their contract is to be valid. This in no way reflects the history of the institution. In Roman law, marriage was seen as a consensual matter, the parties common intention to live together as husband and wife being sufficient to render them married. It was common at Rome for promises to marry, the *sponsalia*, to be exchanged, and for the groom to escort his wife ceremoniously to his house and carry her over the threshold, but these were not legal requirements. Only if the wife were to pass from the power of her father into that of her husband, that is a marriage with *manus*, were formalities required. Patricians could contract such marriages by the ceremony of *confarreatio*, conducted at the temple of Jupiter Farreus and involving the eating of a cake made with special flour, called spelt or *far*. Plebeians could contract *manus* marriages by *coemptio*, a ritual selling of the bride by her *paterfamilias* to her husband. Generally, however, as has been said, *manus* marriages were very much the exception rather than the rule. Most marriages were free marriages, *liberum matrimonium*, leaving the wife independent of her husband's power.

The Germanic marriage tradition was very different. There, marriage was in effect the transfer of the wife from her father's to her husband's *Mund*. The wife's consent was unimportant compared with her father's. To marry her without his consent was abduction and a cause of the blood feud, which would have to be bought off by a compensation payment. This payment if offered in advance, before obtaining consent, appears to have been the bride-price, although it was later the property by which the husband indicated he was able to support his wife. On payment of the price, promises to marry were exchanged and the parties were betrothed. If the man defaulted, he lost the bride-price; if the wife's family defaulted, they had to return the bride-price two-fold. In later times, the earnest offered by the husband took the form of a staff or a ring.

The promises made at the betrothal had to be repeated at the marriage, which was also a formal ceremony. At the marriage, the bride's father solemnly handed her over to the husband. When her independent consent was perceived to be necessary to the validity of the transaction, it became customary for the father to hand her over into the custody of a third party, the *Salman* or *Treuhand*, thus making her free to declare her own will. He it was who then transferred her into the power of her husband. The husband would then lead her to their matrimonial home where a feast for their families would be enjoyed, after which witnesses would accompany them to the bridal chamber where the union was to be consummated.

The canon law of the Church emphasized that marriage should be consensual and struggled to eradicate the power of the father to give a child in marriage against his or her wishes. In this, it followed Roman law but confronted the Germanic tradition. In the eyes of the Church, lack of consent invalidated the marriage. Therefore it encouraged the declaration of those consents before independent witnesses. The Church sought therefore to have one of its priests perform the role of the third-party who received the daughter from her father and gave her to the groom, while two witnesses were to be present to testify to these events. This procedure can be seen in the thirteenth-century marriage ritual of Cardeña in Spain. It illustrates the intrusion of canonical substance into the Germanic forms.

The Church however faced a problem. It was difficult to be sure that a daughter was consenting freely if she married in the presence of her father. The canon law therefore refused to insist upon the necessity of a solemn ceremony before witnesses for the contracting of a valid marriage. While it encouraged marriage *in facie ecclesiae*, it did not require it. During the twelfth century, canonists disputed what were the essential requirements for a valid marriage. Eventually, they adopted the view that either the parties must exchange promises to marry in the present tense, in which case they were married forthwith, or else if they exchanged promises in the future tense, the marriage would take effect when it was consummated. No formalities were required.[17]

The solution to the problem of ensuring consent gave rise to a further problem, that of clandestine marriages. If marriages could be solemnized in secret with only the parties present, it was difficult to prove who was and who was not married. That a clandestine marriage had taken place might not be discovered until a father tried to force his daughter into a match not of her choosing. Even if the second wedding went ahead *in facie ecclesiae*, it would be a nullity if there had been an earlier secret exchange of vows. There was also a serious risk of the union being within the prohibited degrees given that they had been extended so far by the Church. In an attempt to prevent void marriages being contracted, the Fourth Lateran Council in 1215 required that parish priests should ask whether there were any impediments to a forthcoming marriage on at least three Sundays prior to the ceremony. This formality was the calling of banns, and had already been introduced into England by Archbishop Hubert Walter.[18] Another solution was to require the clergy to register all the marriages which they solemnized. This had been attempted in the early years of the Church, during the fifth century, and the practice was revived in some of the Italian republics of the fifteenth century. It was not until after the Reformation, however, that registration became a general requirement.

The Council of Trent, which met at Trento on several occasions during the middle years of the sixteenth century, decreed a major change in the canon law of the Roman Catholic Church relating to the solemnization of matrimony. For the future, it was to be a requirement of a valid marriage that it be solemnized by a priest in the presence of witnesses. Without these formalities, the marriage was void. Moreover, the priest was obliged to register the marriage with the names of the witnesses. The modern form of marriage ceremony was in effect born at Trent.

Throughout the Middle Ages, the Church courts had successfully upheld their claim to jurisdiction over matrimonial causes. With the rise of nation states in the sixteenth century in the same period as catholic Christendom fragmented as a result of the Reformation, the new polities sought, even if catholic, to control the legal affairs of their people. Thus, the French kings adopted the policies of the Council of Trent as law in their realm not by virtue of their ecclesiastical promulgation but by incorporating similar provisions into the *Ordonnance* of Blois of 1579. Moreover, the priest, it was decreed in France in 1679, was not just a witness at the ceremony; he it was who declared the union to be made. A similar role was given to Protestant ministers in the German states during the eighteenth century, and in effect the ecclesiastical model served for the construction of the secular rites of marriage which were adopted after the French Revolution. Marriages had now to be solemnized not *in facie ecclesiae* but before a

State official who would declare the parties married and register the ceremony. Germany followed the same pattern from 1875, and Spain for a while sought the same solution.[19] Today, however in some countries, including Spain and Italy, couples may choose to have their marriages solemnized in an ecclesiastical ceremony, the priest registering the marriage and forwarding the registration to the civic authorities, a practice which had been followed in some places, such as the duchies of Parma and Modena in Italy, since the early nineteenth century.

Obligations of the Spouses

The obligations of the spouses are set out in positive terms in the civil codes. They are basically to be faithful to one another, to live together and to provide one another with support and assistance. Support is regarded as maintenance and mutual co-operation, while assistance relates to what may be termed cherishing the other at times of illness, disease or even insanity.[20]

Breaches of these obligations are recognizable as matrimonial offences which sometimes serve as grounds for separation and divorce. Infidelity is adultery; failure to cohabit, desertion; and wanton failure to support and assist can amount to cruelty. As well as being matrimonial offences, these wrongs have at times been treated as delicts, punishable by the criminal law. Adultery, for instance, has been a criminal offence in several nations; in Italy it has only ceased to be so in the second half of the twentieth century. Indeed, its criminality was deemed unconstitutional in that only the adultery of the wife produced penal consequences, this creating an inequality between the spouses.

In modern law, the equality of the spouses is now generally accepted, although this is of recent provenance. Traditionally, the husband was viewed as the head of the household. Although outside of *manus* marriages in ancient Rome, the husband had no legal authority over his wife, in Germanic law, she was very definitely within his *Mund*. The husband's authority was similarly accepted in the customary jurisdictions of northern France, while in the land of the written customs in the South, wives enjoyed their traditional Roman freedoms. Even after the French Revolution removed many of the previously existing inequalities of status, that of wives remained, and it has in reality been only in the last half century that equality between the spouses has been embraced by the codes of civil law.

Separation and Divorce

The development of the law relating to separation and divorce has been heavily influenced by the canon law of the western Church and its relationship with the secular jurisdictions of the states alongside which it has coexisted.

Roman law, as has been seen, emphasized the consensual nature of marriage. It followed therefore that if either of the spouses withdrew their consent for the union, thus ending the *affectio maritalis*, the marriage was at an end. This was also the case if both spouses agreed to end their marriage. Although the State disapproved of unjustified repudiation by one spouse of the other and of divorce, that is an agreed end to the union, and sometimes visited its disapproval upon the parties with the *nota censoria*, it did not seek to restrict their freedom to repudiate each other or to divorce by consent. As wives were independent of their husbands in most Roman marriages and the children were always in their father's power, there were no attendant property or custody problems. Hence, divorce was not legally regulated.

The emperor Augustus, however, reacted against the lax sexual morality of his age and in particular against the widespread adulteries of the time. In a series of *leges Iuliae* relating to marriage, he criminalized adultery, and sought to encourage high matrimonial standards and the procreation of children. However, the great change in the Roman law relating to the dissolution of marriage came with the conversion of the empire to Christianity.

The Christian Church taught that marriage was not just a union of the husband and wife for the procreation of children and their mutual support and comfort, but also a sign of the mystical union between Christ and His Church. This sacramental view of matrimony, which made it holy, rendered the concept of divorce unacceptable. Successive Christian emperors therefore sought to regulate the availability of divorce. While none attempted to regulate divorce by mutual agreement until Justinian, from Constantine onwards the emperors sought to limit the availability of repudiation by penalizing its abuse. Constantine regarded as good cause for a wife repudiating her husband the fact that he was a killer, a poisoner or a tomb-robber, while a husband might lawfully repudiate a wife who was an adulteress, a poisoner or a procuress. Unlawful repudiations incurred penalties, but were nevertheless valid. Justinian's attempt to regulate consensual divorce survived the emperor by less than a year. The Church and the Christian emperors found the problem of divorce as intractable as that of the exposure of the newly born.[21]

It was Charlemagne who incorporated Christian teaching on this matter most thoroughly into his laws. While he was prepared to allow spouses to separate, he banned remarriage after such separation. In some ways, this step was easier in an empire which had in part a Germanic legal heritage. In Germanic law, unlike the Roman, the wife was transferred into her husband's *Mund* and repudiation by the husband involved her expulsion from his *Mund* and return to her own family. This inevitably brought shame upon them and could lead to retaliation if they did not accept there was good cause. While the husband was entitled to drive his wife out of the community for adultery, and even to kill her and her paramour if they were caught in the act, unreasonable repudiation would lead to a feud with her relatives. Only when the German tribes came into contact with the traditions of Rome did they begin to adopt divorce by mutual consent and allow the wife in certain circumstances to repudiate her husband.

The Church sought to equate the adultery of the husband with that of the wife, making either a legitimate ground for separation from table and hearth, but not ending the marriage bond itself. The Church insisted, somewhat unsuccessfully, that an adulterous husband could not complain of his wife's infidelity. From the twelfth century onwards, the Church courts successfully gained control over matrimonial causes and the indissoluble view of marriage was upheld. While separation for a just cause such as adultery was upheld, divorce *a vinculo matrimonio* was not possible. Marriage was for life.

With the Reformation came diversity. In the lands of the Protestant Reformation, marriage was regarded as a contract and not as a sacrament, so that divorce again became possible, although there had to be a just cause such as adultery or some other moral delinquency. In the territories governed by Catholic rulers, however, only separation was available for a just cause. Thus things stood until the rationalists of the French Revolution introduced their secular conception of marriage into the French State and with it, in 1792, divorce. The influence of Roman law on this move was considerable for the *Code civil* recognized divorce for incompatibility without the need for other just cause. By 1816, the number of divorces produced a legislative panic, and divorce was abolished in France, not to be restored into the law until 1884, when again it was based on the just cause of a matrimonial offence. In Germany, meanwhile, the Prussian *Landrecht* accepted divorce, basing the institution upon some cause of insurmountable aversion, such as childlessness. In 1875, legislation on personal status for the whole *Reich* introduced a completely secular divorce law, but the BGB in 1900 allowed the parties to choose between separation and divorce, although a separation was always to be convertible into a divorce at a later date if required. In both Germany and Switzerland, divorce was to be based on matrimonial offences but also on the breakdown of the marriage. Divorce was not allowed in Italy until 1975. Today, with the requisite periods of separation, the parties may in effect consent to a divorce, and after a lengthy separation, either may in fact demand it. The Roman element appears to have triumphed in this fluctuating area of the law - at least for the moment.

5 Parents and Children

As with the relation of husband and wife, modern civil law has gradually replaced the power of the father over his children with that of both parents acting in concert. Paternal power has become parental power, with the father and the mother having an equal say in the upbringing of their children. The civil codes articulate the duties of the parents as being to bring up, maintain and educate their progeny, while children owe their parents duties of respect, obedience and assistance.[22] Children remain subject to their parents' authority until they come of age. The usual age of majority in civil law countries today is eighteen. The authority of parents over their children is meant to be exercised for the child's benefit, and not that of the parent, although the interests of the family as a whole must be taken into account.

The modern law has again resulted from the interplay of Roman and Germanic elements. In Roman law, as has been seen, the children born of a lawful Roman marriage, *iustae nuptiae*, were within the *potestas* of their father for as long as he lived and were incapable of enjoying any rights in private law. It was possible for a father to emancipate a child from his paternal power during his lifetime. Originally, this may have been a form of punishment, driving out a delinquent child from the family, but the method employed, which involved selling a son three times into bondage and then having him released, was adapted to permit of emancipation during the father's lifetime. If due attention was paid to the manner of the final release, the father would become the emancipated child's patron, so that respect and services would remain due from the emancipated child and the child could continue to expect moral and material support from the father. The patron/client relationship between parent and emancipated child foreshadowed the continued alimentary obligation between parents and adult children in modern civil law systems.

While Roman law therefore did not recognize an age at which children were freed from parental power, Germanic law regarded sons as free of the authority of their fathers once they were capable of bearing arms themselves. This would be indicated by the father investing his son with weapons before the popular assembly. The father could also free himself of responsibility for the wrongs of a delinquent child by driving them from the community, and children could free themselves from paternal power by flight. The most common method of emancipation for sons was to bear arms or to leave the father's house to establish their own home, usually upon marriage.

In Germanic law, no distinction was drawn between coming of age for different purposes - attendance at the popular assembly, bearing arms, getting married. In Roman law, on the other hand, distinctions were drawn partly because public law rights were acquired by sons in power and partly because reaching maturity was regarded as a gradual process rather than a sudden event when children were left fatherless and therefore *sui iuris* at a tender age. The Romans distinguished between infants, under seven years of age, who lacked understanding, *intellectus*, regarding the conduct of affairs, *impuberes*, under fourteen if male, under twelve if female, who while capable of understanding business and other transactions lacked the necessary judgement to undertake such matters without guidance, and minors, between the age of fourteen and twenty-five who while both understanding the nature of transactions and capable of conducting them for themselves were still at risk of being overreached by persons of greater skill and experience. These ages were to be influential in the development of rules relating to the reaching of majority in later centuries. These ages were also of significance for the Roman male within power with regard to his capacity in public law; he could vote in the assembly at fourteen but not stand for office until twenty-five. Such distinctions as these have also endured in civil law countries.[23]

In the regions of the Germanic customs, therefore, including Germany and the *pays des coutumes* of northern France, paternal power of the *patriapotestas* variety was not known. Children were capable of independence, owning property and conducting their own affairs even while their father was living. This is what Loysel meant when, commenting on the customs of Senlis in 1539, he wrote that parental power was unknown in customary France. In the lands of Roman law, however, including the *pays de droit écrit* of southern France, paternal power endured for life. Children were not independent while their fathers lived, could not own property in their own right as distinct from enjoying a *peculium* at their father's sufferance and could not enter into contracts on their own account, unless emancipated. The Germanic customs however adopted ages for the reaching of majority which were clearly influenced by the Roman ages used for categorizing the gradual growth to maturity of young people. Thus, the Lombards allowed men to come of age at eighteen, while girls became marriageable at twelve. The Carolingian Franks equalized the coming of ages of the sexes at fourteen, which was also the age of majority for royal children during the Middle Ages. The Ripuarian Franks also regarded fourteen as the age of majority, while the Salic Franks opted for twelve.

Distinctions were also made on the grounds of status as well as sex. Thus, young noblemen in France achieved majority at the start of their twenty-first year, while their plebeian counterparts came of age on the completion of their fourteenth year. Young noblewomen could marry at fourteen, while plebeian girls could wed at twelve.

During the eighteenth century, greater emphasis came to be placed upon parental power existing for the benefit of the child's upbringing rather than in the interests of the parents or the father. This mirrored the view that monarchical power was meant to be exercised in the interests of the people not the prince. Paternal authority of the *patriapotestas* variety was therefore abolished in France in 1792 and an age of majority of twenty-one for all young persons substituted therefore. Twenty-five had been the chosen age in 1789, and the completion of the twenty-fourth year was the age chosen for majority in both Prussia and Austria. The protection of the rights of the child came to be accepted as the basis of parental power, and during the nineteenth century, in the first Italian civil code in 1865 and also in the first codifications in Spain and Portugal, the State as the guardian of all its subjects reserved the right to intervene to protect children even as against their parents.[24] This marked a major departure from the previous powers of the father as head of the household in both Germanic and Roman law, and a vindication of the canon law's struggle against infant exposure and exploitation.

The employment of exact ages for achieving majority required that a precise record of births be kept. This was not done until the nineteenth century. Instead, the only reasonably reliable records were those of baptism, and the French *Ordonnance* of Villers Cotteret of 1539 had enjoined the keeping of baptismal registers by all clergy.[25]

Children of the Family

The Constitutions of modern civil law countries recognize the rights of the family as a natural association founded upon marriage.[26] The children of the family are therefore as a rule those who have been born to a married couple. Children born within a lawful union are regarded as legitimate, but it is also possible for children who have not been born to parents who are married to be legitimated. This is achieved by and large by one of two methods, both with a substantial history rooted in Roman and canon law, namely legitimation by subsequent marriage of the parents and legitimation by rescript, that is by decree of an authorized person.

Legitimation *per subsequens matrimonium* was introduced into Roman law by the emperor Constantine who wished to encourage lawful marriage among his subjects, particularly the military. It had been the rule in Roman military law that legionaries could not marry while on service and such duty could last for twenty years. Soldiers tended to form unions which, while monogamous, were not lawful Roman marriages, with the result that the issue of such concubinage were not within their *potestas*. Constantine decreed that if there were no impediment to marriage of the parents at the time of such an illegitimate child's birth, the parents' subsequent marriage would legitimate the offspring. This was in effect an encouragement for those in a long-term permanent relationship to marry. The privilege did not extend to children born of casual affairs or adulterous liaisons. The later emperors were however prepared to legitimate by imperial rescript children born to concubines when it was no longer possible for the parents to marry, as for instance when one or both were dead.

Germanic law permitted illegitimate children to be legitimated, generally by a public act within the popular assembly. The father might take such children under his cloak, thus demonstrating his acceptance of them. The canon law however took over the two methods of legitimation practised by the later Roman law and extended them quite significantly. Thus, the canon law did not insist upon the children having to be born within a stable relationship, and was prepared to legitimate by subsequent marriage the issue of casual, but non-adulterous, affairs. The Church also utilized legitimation by rescript, the Pope having power to grant legitimation to anyone and allowing limited rights of legitimation to be granted by secular rulers, communes and even selected jurists. Bartolus exercised such powers. Legitimation by rescript found its way into Germany in the time of the emperor Frederick I, probably via his Sicilian domains, but it was not until the Reception of Roman law that legitimation *per subsequens matrimonium* came to be accepted generally in Germany, it having previously been resisted.[27] Both forms of legitimation continue to exist in modern civil law, with the power to legitimate by rescript now being exercised by the judiciary.

The other method by which children might be incorporated into a family even if not born to the parents at all is by adoption. The nature of adoption has changed greatly from the ancient to the modern world, and reflects a change of emphasis from the needs of the parents to those of the child. In Roman law, for a *paterfamilias* to have no children to continue his line was a disaster, as one of the duties of the children after his death was to continue the family cult which involved ritual ministrations to the needs of deceased ancestors. To be childless was therefore disastrous. A *pater* without natural children of his own could however adopt a person as his heir. Such adoptions were not undertaken to provide a home for an orphan child, but in order to provide an heir for a childless person. Accordingly, it was usually adults who were adopted and only adult males. A female could not continue the family line which was reckoned agnatically. Two forms of adoption were available: *adrogatio*, which was the adoption of a person in his own power, and which therefore required the consent of the popular assembly, the *comitia curiata*, and *adoptio*, the adoption of a person in the power of another, which was a private law transaction by which the adoptee was transferred from the power of one *paterfamilias* to that of another. The emperor Justinian also allowed adoption to be accomplished by imperial rescript.

Germanic law also enabled persons without descendants to adopt in order to obtain an heir. The popular assembly was the venue for Germanic adoptions, this ensuring publicity for the transaction. The adopting parent would perform some act *vis-à-vis* the adoptee to manifest his acceptance of him into his *Mund* or power. Thus, the child might be taken under the adopting father's cloak or the father might cut his hair. An older adoptee might be invested with weapons by his new father before the assembly.

Adoption declined as a legal institution throughout Europe during the Middle Ages, although orphaned children were often brought up by parents who 'adopted' them.[28] It was not until 1792 that the institution was revived in France, and in the nineteenth and twentieth centuries it has been practised no longer to obtain an heir but to provide orphaned children with homes and children for childless couples. Traces of its earlier concerns can still however be found in some of the provisions of the relevant laws, not all of which are contained in the civil codes. State authorization is now however generally required for legal adoptions.

6 Guardianship

If it was a disaster for a Roman *paterfamilias* to have no children to continue his line, it was also a disaster for the children if he died and they became *sui iuris* at so young an age that they were not able to manage their affairs and those of the family. Even in modern societies where there is a fixed age of majority and parents share responsibility for the upbringing of their children, it remains a disaster for children to be orphaned while they are still minors. As with adoption, modern civil law looks primarily to the welfare of the children and the safeguarding of their interests in such a situation. As with so much of the law of persons, the rules applying to this problem are an amalgam of Roman, Germanic and canonical elements.

Roman law dealt with the guardianship of children left fatherless by the institution of *tutela*. It identified a *tutor* to secure the ward or pupil's estate. Originally, the tutor would be the ward's nearest male agnatic relative, usually an elder brother or an uncle on the father's side of the family. The agnatic or legitimate tutor was the person who would succeed to the ward's inheritance if the ward died while still under age. The tutor's primary concern therefore was protecting the family property rather than the person of the ward, who would probably be brought up by his mother.[29] It was not long before the conflict of interest between ward and legitimate tutor led to fathers seeking to choose tutors for their children by nominating trusted friends in their wills. Such testamentary tutors would not normally have a right to succeed to the property and thus would be managing it in the ward's interests and not their own. In the absence of such agnatic or testamentary tutors, the praetor had the power to appoint a tutor for the ward, the so-called dative tutor. Any tutor could be removed from office for defrauding the ward's estate, and in the later republic tutors were expected to give security for their good management of the property and to furnish the ward with an account at the end, themselves only being entitled to remuneration of expenses by way of payment. Tutorship had become a trustee function.

The duties of the tutor varied according to the age of the ward. While the ward was under seven, the tutor had to administer the estate. When the ward was between the ages of seven and fourteen - or seven and twelve in the case of a girl, the tutor was expected to involve the ward in the conduct of business but to interpose his authority for the ward's acts. Children were freed from the need of such a tutor at marriageable age, although females continued to need a tutor while independent throughout their lives subject to certain exceptions.[30] In the later republic, it was recognized that teenagers were liable to be overreached by more experienced persons when managing their own affairs, and it became customary for them to obtain the advice of an independent third party to guarantee that any transaction they were making was not to their disadvantage. Thus was born the institution of the *curator minorum*.[31] Minors needed the services of such a curator until they were twenty-five, although they could be freed from the requirement upon proof of maturity at a slightly earlier age.[32] Burdensome transactions undertaken without the assent of a curator were voidable at the suit of the minor on reaching mature years.[33] A special magistrate was appointed at Rome to oversee guardianships; he was the *praetor tutelarius*.

While one tutor was sufficient in Roman law, although they could act in plurality, Germanic law preferred to place its faith in a family council, the 'born' guardians of the *Sippe*, consisting of relatives of the fatherless child. These would supervise the transactions carried out during the ward's incapacity and decide upon questions relating to his or her upbringing, marriage and coming of age. The Lombard laws testify to this institution and state supervision of the work of such guardians can be found in the legal arrangements of the Carolingians. This preference for a group of guardians rather than a sole guardian can also be found in the laws of the Italian communes of the Middle Ages, who revived, under the influence of civilian learning, the institution of the testamentary tutor, which was unknown to Germanic law, and also adopted the dative tutor who had featured in the Lombard arrangements and in canon law. The mediaeval jurists saw tutorship however as a form of representation of the ward rather than the discharge of a public duty.

In the feudal lordships, guardianship took a very different form. While the children of the middle classes had guardians who managed their lands on their behalf until they came of age and were accountable to them, the children of the nobility if left fatherless found themselves and their lands in the wardship of their lord who had both the right to give them in marriage and to manage their lands for his own benefit until they came of age. In

Germany and northern France, this led to the lands of the minor being leased, often to his relatives to manage for their benefit until he came of age with a payment of rent to the lord. From the thirteenth century, however, testamentary guardianship and the appointment of relatives as guardians crept into the northern arrangements from the customs of the south.

In Italy during the later Middle ages, the renewed influence of Roman law led to the appointment in the communes of a special magistrate, along the lines of the Roman *praetor tutelarius*, to supervise the work of guardians. Guardians again had to provide security for their tutelage and render accounts, being removable for default or bad management. Special bodies existed at Venice, Florence and Siena to oversee the work of guardians, and such boards also appeared in some of the German cities, such as Basel, Leipzig, Vienna and Görlitz. In the *pays des coutumes*, it became customary to appoint a second guardian, the *tuteur subrogé*, to supervise the work of the first, an institution which survives to this day in French law. This institution was later taken up by Prussia and has became the *Gegenvormund* of the BGB.

By the time of the nineteenth-century codifications, the principle that the guardian was to act in the interests of the ward and not his own was firmly established, as was the State's right to intervene on the ward's behalf. In the modern regimes of guardianship, various elements drawn from the different legal traditions of Europe can be identified. Modern French law provides an excellent example with its special magistrate, the *juge de tutelles* appointing a family council, who in turn appoint the *tuteur* and the *tuteur subrogé*. The fusion of the Roman and the Germanic in this arrangement is patent.

Finally, it is worth noting that the influence of the Roman concepts of guardianship are also evident in the constitutional provisions for a regency in the restored monarchy of modern Spain.[34]

Other Forms of Guardianship

The capacity of human beings to manage their own affairs can be affected adversely by factors other than youth. Some reflect the vicissitudes of life, while others are inflicted by the social order. Illness and insanity are of the former kind; the disabilities suffered by women in previous generations of the latter.

It is only since the doctrine of equality has taken hold upon the western consciousness that women have been regarded as being as capable of managing their own affairs as men, and even after the proclamation of equality by the French Revolution, equality for women in private and public law has been obtained but slowly, indeed only very recently in some countries within western Europe itself.

In Roman law, as has been said, women enjoyed perhaps greater freedom and independence than possibly at any time in western history before the last years of the nineteenth century. They never enjoyed the public law rights of voting in the assemblies or standing for public office, but in private law they were remarkably free. While males and females remained in the *potestas* of their *paterfamilias* while he lived, once he died both became *sui iuris*. However, women always needed the services of a tutor; they were subject to perpetual tutelage. This however was not a burden generally speaking. Given that daughters inherited an equal share of the family property along with sons, and that, if married, they would be living with their husbands away from their own family's estate, the need for them to have someone to manage their assets for them is manifest. Originally, as with children, this duty fell to the nearest male agnates, but eventually fathers could appoint tutors for their daughters by will from outside of the family. Moreover, by the late republic, it was accepted that, although women needed the authority of their tutors for their acts in law, if that authority was not forthcoming, the woman was able to change her tutor with ease. The tutor was a representative not a controller. Under the empire, agnatic tutelage of women was abolished and some women were allowed to manage their own affairs without the need of a tutor.[35]

In Germanic law, the position of women was very different. While unmarried, a woman was within her father's *Mund*. Upon marriage, she was transferred to her husband's *Mund*. If widowed, she either became subject to her sons' protection or reverted to that of her brothers. Women enjoyed but little independence. The feudal preference for males over females also meant that women had little opportunity to enjoy property in their own right, and upon marriage, the wife's property became subject to the control of her husband. Married women had virtually no independence until the reforms of the late nineteenth and twentieth centuries. The law of family property will be considered in more depth in the next chapter.

Roman law permitted the appointment of a curator to look after the affairs of a family when the *paterfamilias* was insane. Germanic law allowed the family council to act in such circumstances, but also permitted a son to take over the running of the family affairs when the father became incapacitated by reason of old age. Modern systems continue to make provision in such circumstances. One very interesting form of curatorship which existed in ancient Rome and which continues and has indeed been developed by modern legal systems is the curatorship of prodigals, that is of those whose spendthrift ways are dissipating the family property. This institution clearly recognizes that ownership can be a family rather than an individual matter. Roman law allowed a curator to be appointed if the *paterfamilias* was squandering the family patrimony, and this institution continues to exist in modern civil law. The BGB requires that the prodigality must endanger the family's security, whereas the Prussian *Landrecht* had been content that squandering was occurring. Swiss law regards bad management as sufficient cause for intervention without need of any moral stigma, and also provides for the appointment of guardians for those in prison. Dipsomaniacs and drug addicts can also be subjected to guardianship, and guardians can be appointed for those who are missing or absent from home.[36]

7 Conclusion

The law of persons and of the family in modern civil law is a rich amalgam of elements drawn from the Roman, Germanic and canonist traditions. Whereas the Roman element, as will be seen, tends to dominate the law of property and obligations, the Germanic contribution to the law of persons has been considerable. This department of the law is therefore an example of the convergence of distinct legal traditions.

In dealing with the family so far, however, the emphasis has been upon the family as the household and to a lesser extent the kindred, but little has been said of the family as a continuing entity over several generations. This aspect of the law relating to the family will now be considered as its importance is manifested in the law relating to family property and succession.

Notes

[1] In Italy, Book I of the Civil Code is entitled 'The Law of Persons and the Family'.

[2] Following the teachings of his master, Jean de Monchy: see O.F. Robinson, T.D. Fergus and W.M. Gordon, *European Legal History* (2nd Ed.; London, 1994), p. 61 f.

[3] Slaves did however form marital unions, referred to as *contubernium*, which were not classified as lawful marriages but which were respected so that, for instance, the partners to such unions were not sold separately. Slaves could be instituted heir to a citizen's will, in which case they were freed; this was *manumissio testamento*. Any contracts they entered into benefited or burdened their masters, and the property which they were allowed to manage on his behalf, their *peculium*, remained in law the master's property.
[4] There were exceptions to this rule; see J.A.C. Thomas, *Textbook of Roman Law* (Amsterdam, 1976), p. 390.
[5] These were respectively, *manumissio censu, vindicta* and *testamento*. For details, see J.A.C. Thomas, *Textbook*, pp. 397 ff.
[6] For details of such pacts, see A.N. Sherwin-White, *The Roman Citizenship* (2nd Ed.; Oxford, 1973).
[7] See Alan Watson, *Slave Law in the Americas* (Athens, Georgia & London, 1989).
[8] See R. Huebner, *A History of Germanic Private Law* (Boston, 1918; reprinted New York, 1968), pp. 79 ff.
[9] See chapter 11.
[10] See chapter 10.
[11] *Vereinen* are associations of members, while *Stiftungen* are foundations based on property rather than membership. *Gemeinschaften* are communities, while *Gesellschaften* are partnerships or companies. See also chapter 11.
[12] See R.M. Ogilvie, *Early Rome and the Etruscans* (Glasgow, 1976), pp. 47, 123, 145 f.
[13] The different kinds of *peculia* were classified as: *peculium castrense* for military service, *peculium quasi-castrense* for civil servants, and *bona adventicia* for property descended from the maternal line. The *peculium* allowed by the father became known as *peculium profecticium*. For details, see J.A.C. Thomas, *Textbook*, pp. 416 f.
[14] See R.W. Leage, *Roman Private Law* (3rd Ed., by A.M. Prichard; London, 1961), p. 106; Susan Treggiari, *Roman Marriage* (Oxford, 1991), pp. 37 ff.
[15] See below on guardianship, pp. 201 ff.
[16] This was later narrowed considerably in Roman law but re-extended under the influence of the Church; see Susan Treggiari, *Roman Marriage*, pp. 37 ff.; J.A. Brundage, *Law, Sex and Christian Society in Medieval Europe* (Chicago, 1987) for subsequent development.
[17] For the history of this problem, see J.A. Brundage, *Law, Sex and Christian Society in Medieval Europe*, pp. 262 ff.
[18] For the background to this development, see J.A. Brundage, *Law, Sex and Christian Society in Medieval Europe*, p. 362, and Richard Hanford, 'The Medieval Foundations of the Banns of Marriage' (unpublished University of Wales, Cardiff LL.M in Canon Law dissertation, 1995).

[19] Namely, between the years 1870 and 1875; see R. Altamira in C. Calisse et al., *General Survey of Continental Legal History* (Boston, 1912; reprinted New York, 1968), pp. 693 ff.
[20] See for instance France *Code civil*, art. 143-148; Germany BGB art. 1353-1362; Italy *Codice civile* art. 212-226; Spain *Codigo civil* art. 66-72.
[21] See A.H.M. Jones, *The Later Roman Empire 284-602* (Oxford, 1964), pp. 974 f., and J.A.C. Thomas, *Textbook*, pp. 425 ff.
[22] See for instance France *Code civil*, art. 371-387; Germany BGB art. 1616-1625; Italy *Codice civile* art. 315-342; Spain *Codigo civil* art.154-161.
[23] In Italy today for instance, one may vote for the Chamber of Deputies at 18, but not be a candidate until one is 25, the minimum age for voting in elections to the Senate, for which one may not stand until one is 40.
[24] See A. Alvarez et al., *The Progress of Continental Law in the Nineteenth Century* (Boston, 1918; reprinted New York, 1967), pp. 237 ff.
[25] Article 50 of the *Ordonnance*.
[26] For instance, article 29 of the Italian Constitution. In Spain, no such provision is to be found in the Constitution nor in the Civil Code, but the juristic doctrine so treats of marriage: see E. Ruiz Vadillo, *Derecho Civil* (18th Ed., Logroño, 1991-92), pp. 715 ff.
[27] As in England, when the barons refused to accept the institution as part of the Statute of Merton in 1235 - *nolumus leges Angliae mutare*, so that it was not until the Legitimation Act of 1926 that it entered English law.
[28] The same was true of England and Wales, where adoption was not legally regulated until the Adoption of Children Act 1926.
[29] Hence, the stories of wicked uncles, starting with Romulus and Remus.
[30] For instance, women who had produced three children (four if they were freedwomen) were exempted from needing a tutor under Augustus' legislation, the *lex Iulia et Papia Poppaea*; see J.A.C. Thomas, *Textbook*, p. 464.
[31] See J.A.C. Thomas, *Textbook*, pp. 467 f.
[32] Constantine insisted that a young man was at least 21 and a young woman at least 18.
[33] In mediaeval France, Beaumanoir in his *Coutumes de Beauvaisis* 16.4 states that the minor was allowed to annul acts for a year and a day after coming of age, while the *Ordonnance* of August, 1539 art. 134 allowed the minor ten years from coming of age to do this, the period of prescription relating to such rights of action being borrowed from Roman law.
[34] See the Spanish Constitution of 1978, art. 59-61.
[35] Agnatic tutelage of women was abolished by Claudius (41-54 AD); see generally, J.A.C. Thomas, *Textbook*, pp. 463 ff.
[36] BGB art. 1896-1908.

10 Family Property and Succession

1 The Concept of the Family Communion

One of the most striking features of modern civil law systems is the institution of the family communion, that is a patrimony containing property owned jointly by a husband and wife which is separate from the patrimonies which they own severally as individual persons. It will be recalled that in the constitutions of many civil law countries the rights of the family are protected as those of a natural association, *societas*, founded upon marriage. The family communion is the patrimony of that association.

In Roman law, a *societas* was a contractual arrangement among partners. It had no distinct legal personality of its own apart from those of the private individuals who composed it. Only in modern civilian systems have commercial associations been accorded the status of legal persons. The Roman *societas* was formed by agreement among the partners and they, as private persons, had rights and duties against one another. A third person contracting with the partnership contracted in law only with the partner with whom he was dealing. He would have no rights or duties as against the other partners, nor they against him. The *societas* had no corporate personality. It had begun however in a family setting, when a deceased *paterfamilias* had more than one heir and those heirs decided not to divide their inheritance amongst themselves but to own and enjoy it as a single mass of property, as one patrimony. This was the *consortium*, for they had thrown in their lots, *sortes*, together. The arrangement was founded upon their agreement and continued only as long as their consents endured.

This Roman understanding of the shared family arrangement as being contractually based differed from the Germanic perspective of such family arrangements. For the Germanic peoples, such a sharing of property led, as has been seen, to the property being owned collectively, in a community of the collective hand. Such a community was regarded by the law as having a separate identity from the individuals who composed it. Accordingly, it came to enjoy a distinct legal personality from that of its members. One form of such collective-hand community was the *Eheliche Gesamthand*, the family community based upon marriage. The modern civilian institution of the family communion is a development of this Germanic arrangement, but it has undergone profound influence as a result of the contact of the Germanic concept with that of the civil law *societas*.

The Roman concept was in short individualistic rather than collective in approach. When one partner died or resigned, the partnership was over. The German community on the other hand endured despite the demise of its members and could go on from generation to generation. The individualism of the French laws following the Revolution was unsympathetic to such an approach, and the *Code civil* virtually outlawed the idea of group legal identity. The nineteenth-century reaction to this perspective, particularly in Germany, restored the legal personality of communities and corporations to a place in western Europe's legal systems, and the family communion is one such institution.

The basic problem to which the family communion provides an answer is how does one analyse in law the ownership of property which is devoted to the purposes of, or is shared by, a married couple and possibly their children. Modern civilian systems generally provide the spouses with a choice. If the couple so wish, they may continue to own property entirely separately with no common patrimony coming into existence upon their marriage. Alternatively, they may wish to create a common patrimony, the family communion, as a result of their union. This common patrimony may consist of all their property whether acquired before or after their marriage, but such a universal community of goods is rare. A more usual arrangement is for the spouses to adopt a regime by which property acquired from the time of their marriage, whether by acquisition or by increment upon their existing separate patrimonies, falls into the common pool. They may opt to pool all their moveable property in this common patrimony as well as their acquisitions, but exclude both previously acquired immoveables and such property acquired after marriage. Again, they may opt not to have a communal patrimony during marriage but to equalize their acquisitions when the marriage finally ends by the death of one or upon its dissolution by divorce or separation.

Although the spouses are generally free to choose one of these arrangements or even to devise a specific regime for themselves, most civilian systems provide a standard regime which couples are presumed to adopt in the absence of a personal election on their behalf. Thus in contemporary France, Italy and Spain, a universal communion of after-acquired property is presumed to be the couple's choice in the absence of an alternative being chosen at the time of the marriage and registered with a notary or annotated upon their wedding certificate. In Germany on the other hand the regime imposed in the absence of an alternative being chosen is the equalization of acquisitions. Whichever regime is adopted, other than separate property, it will bring into existence a third patrimony alongside that of the husband and wife. One patrimony will be his, one hers, and one theirs. *His* or *her* creditors cannot proceed against *their* property until *his* or *her* assets have been exhausted; nor can creditors of the family patrimony proceed against that of the spouses as individuals until the family communion has been exhausted. If the marriage ends by death or divorce leaving children below the age of majority, then the communion can remain in existence if necessary until the youngest has come of age. Thus, the family patrimony is truly that, and not just that of the spouses. The interest of the children in the patrimony connects with their rights both in the succession of their parents and their alimentary rights and obligations.

The principle of equality which has extended to the relationship of husband and wife in modern law entails that the family communion is the property of both spouses. They are both equally owners of the whole patrimony. This degree of equality is of fairly recent provenance in many civil law countries. It was only really achieved in Italy for instance in 1975 and in Spain from the introduction of the democratic constitution in 1978. In Germany, it dates from 1957. Today, this equality allows both spouses not only to own and enjoy, but also to manage, the family property. Previously, even in those countries which allowed the wife rights of ownership and enjoyment in the patrimony, control was usually firmly in the hands of the husband. Under some systems, ownership was also the prerogative of the male as head of the household. If the Germanic contribution has been the growth of the corporate concept of family property, then the establishment of the wife's independent ownership and control can be fairly claimed to be an inheritance from the Roman approach.

2 The Development of the Law of Family Property

There are many similarities between the Roman and Germanic approaches to the property arrangements attendant upon a marriage, but there is also one fundamental difference. That difference consists in the independence of the Roman wife, married without *manus*, from her husband's power. The Germanic wife on the other hand was always within her husband's *Mund*.

The Roman Marriage Portions

The Roman law marriage, as has been seen, was based squarely upon consent and did not need any formalities for its creation. There was therefore little to distinguish it from concubinage. The distinguishing factor was usually the endowment of the wife by her father or some other male relative. This would be the transfer of a sum of money or of some property from the wife's father to the husband in order to provide for the wife during her marriage. This block of property was called the dowry, or *dos*. It would be promised to the husband at the time of the betrothal and the property would be his while the marriage subsisted, although he would be expected to use it for the maintenance and benefit of his wife. In the event of his dying first, the property would pass back from whence it came: to her father if he was still living, or to whoever had provided it. If she were by that time *sui iuris*, it would be part of her inheritance from her father. Even if she had been married with *manus*, a *dos* would have been given, and this would be part of her inheritance upon her husband's demise.

In later Roman law, probably as an oriental innovation, it also became customary for the husband to endow his wife with property upon the occasion of their marriage. This property was meant to support her, particularly in the event of her widowhood. This block of property was called the *donatio propter nuptias*, and might only be promised by the husband at that time. In later mediaeval law, it was promised at the church door and often consisted of a third of the husband's estate. It was then referred to as the dower of the bride. Both the dower and the dowry were forms of endowment for her, but the dower came from her husband, the dowry to her husband from her father. Under the Christian emperors, a spouse who repudiated the other without good cause forfeited their right to recover the marriage portion advanced from their side of the family, while a spouse who was repudiated for good cause suffered the same penalty. If the wife predeceased her husband, he retained the *donatio* but the *dos* went to her heirs, while if he died first, she retained the *donatio* and recovered the *dos*. It should also be remembered that a wife who was *sui iuris* and married without *manus* was capable during marriage of owning property in her own right and managing it herself with the aid of her tutor.

The system of marriage portions was to remain the matrimonial property regime of those inhabitants of southern Europe who lived according to their remembered Roman customs after the invasions of the Gothic tribes from the North. In the *pays de droit écrit*, the system of endowment was to last until the French Revolution as the matrimonial property regime of the people of southern France. In the northern parts of France, however, and in much of Germany and Italy, customs of Germanic origin were to play a significant part in the shaping of the laws of family property.

The Germanic Marriage Portions

Unlike Roman law, the laws of the Germanic people did not allow women independence in the ownership of property. Before marriage, a woman would be in the *Mund* of her father; at marriage, she would pass into that of her husband; if widowed, she would pass into the *Mund* of her sons or, in default of issue, back into that of her male kindred.

On betrothal, the Germanic husband paid a bride price to the wife's father, and it became customary for this to be returned to the husband as a dowry when the wedding took place. In due course, the husband retained the bride price on betrothal and gave it to the bride as her *mefio*[1] at the time of the marriage. Although he remained in control of this property, it had in fact become the endowment by which she would be supported if she were widowed. Her father, on the other hand, also gave her a portion of property on her marriage, called the *faderfio*.[2] This was property which was to be enjoyed by her, not like the Roman *dos* property with which she should be supported by her husband. The wife would also receive from her husband on the morning following the first night of her marriage the *morgengabe*[3] or morning gift, being an acknowledgement of her virginity at the time of consummation. The wife would retain all three portions on the death of the husband; as she had no other property of her own, they would support her in widowhood. Some Germanic systems allowed her enjoyment of the portions while she lived if she had children, but required the property to revert to them thereafter.

According to this system, the wife acquired no other property during her marriage, being dependent upon her husband. However, perhaps through contact with the Roman law and the canonical doctrine of the spouses being one flesh, there developed the idea that acquisitions made by the spouses during their marriage were as much the wife's as the husband's. Here began the concept of the family communion.

The Family Communion of Germanic Law

Acquisitions made after the marriage of the spouses were perceived to arise as a result of the endeavours of both spouses, albeit that their contributions to those endeavours were of different kinds. Nevertheless, it was thought to be unfair that the husband should retain the title of such acquisitions for himself alone. Accordingly, the community of acquisitions was recognized whereby property acquired by either spouse once married was deemed to accrue for the benefit of both.

This gave rise to another problem almost immediately. This was the difficulty with regard to moveable property of distinguishing what had been acquired before and after marriage. Very soon, therefore, a second sort of community came into existence, that of the community of moveables and acquisitions, which comprised all of the spouses' moveable property in addition to property acquired after their marriage. From this, it was but a short step to recognizing a third kind of communion, comprising all of the spouses' property whether acquired before or after marriage, whether moveable or immoveable. Such an universal communion was regarded as the arrangement typical of the mercantile classes in the towns of the thirteenth century onwards, where immoveable property was not the primary source of the family wealth. In rural areas, it was associated particularly with the serfs, whose property again would be formed in the main of moveables. However, in Italy, the urban populace tended not to employ the universal community as their matrimonial regime, preferring what was called the community of use, whereby during marriage the property was capable of being enjoyed by both spouses but was not regarded as being owned jointly by them.

The universal community of property became typical of the urban areas of what is now Belgium, Holland, Switzerland and Denmark, as well as in Sicily and Portugal, and parts of Germany, where in some areas the wife's rights in communion were dependant upon her having produced children of the marriage. In customary France, the community of moveables and acquisitions was more common. In the south of France, the institution of the communion confronted the Roman system of marriage portions and the wife's independent property rights. In the south-west, around Bordeaux and into northern Spain, the community of acquisitions operated from the thirteenth century in tandem with the institution of the *dos*, a situation which King John of England, as Duke of Aquitaine, found intolerable so that he abolished the community in Bordeaux itself in 1206. The marriage portions he thought should be enough. His regulation did not however prohibit spouses from agreeing at the time of their marriage to have the community as well, so that they were free to institute a community of acquests alongside the dotal regime by express stipulation. During the thirteenth century, it was gradually accepted in France that the spouses should be free to create for themselves a matrimonial communion of their choice, and this freedom developed steadily during the fourteenth and fifteenth centuries. It had however to be expressly chosen by the spouses, else the local custom determined the regime under which their property would be held. It also came to be established that once chosen the regime was thereafter immutably binding the couple throughout their married life, a position upheld for France as a whole by decision of the Paris *Parlement* in 1584-85. In the north of France, the existence of the community of moveables and acquisitions rendered gifts between spouses inadmissible, while in the south, following the Roman rule, gifts were banned during the lifetimes of the spouses but were permitted upon death, a gift *mortis causa* remaining revocable until the donor's demise.

The dotal regime made some headway in parts of Germany, particularly in Bavaria and Austria following the Reception of Roman law at the end of the fifteenth century. The Reception also led to juristic attempts to express the Germanic notion of the community in terms of the Roman *societas*, attempts which while often ingenious were ultimately unsuccessful. By the late eighteenth and the nineteenth century, the family communion was seen as being peculiarly Germanic and allowed to exist on its own terms without being forced into a straitjacket of Roman concepts. It was also recognized, in the Prussian *Landrecht* for instance, that each region should have the right to its own prevailing arrangement in this regard while allowing spouses the right to choose a communion of their choice. In Spain also, the Visigothic institution of the communion came up against the revived Romanism of the *Siete Partidas* in the thirteenth century, but although this increased the popularity of dotal arrangements in certain regions, the prevalence of Germanic community arrangements as mediated by canon law ideas of the spousal partnership remained typical of Spain when considered as a whole.

Upon the death of one of the spouses, the communion ended and had to be split between the successors of the deceased and the surviving spouse. The manner in which such division was effected varied according to the locality and other factors such as the presence or absence of children. While it was argued in some places that the surviving spouse should succeed to the whole of the communion on the death of the other, the general solution was to effect a division. Among the Visigoths, the communion was divided in accordance with the proportion of property brought to the communion by each spouse at the time of the marriage. In Westphalia and according to the Saxon law, the communion was to be divided equally between the surviving spouse and the deceased's estate. Among the Franks however, a surviving husband had been deemed entitled to two-thirds of the communion on division, while a surviving wife obtained one-third. The share of the wife in some places depended upon whether the deceased was succeeded by children, parents or collateral relatives. Sometimes for instance where there were children of the marriage, the spouse would take the chattels but the land would all go to the children subject to a usufruct in the wife's favour. During the later Middle Ages, it was also accepted that, if there were children not yet of age, the communion could remain in existence until the youngest attained majority,

In those parts where the Germanic system of marriage portions had remained in force or been assimilated under the influence of Romanism into a dotal regime,[4] there would be no proper communion to divide. Nevertheless during marriage there would have been an administrative communion, in the sense that the husband would have been in control of managing the entire property of the family, including that of the wife. It could therefore be very difficult upon the death of one of the spouses to attribute ownership of the various items of property enjoyed by the family to each of the spouses. There therefore developed the custom in some parts of Germany of allowing the wife to take a fixed portion of the entire estate in satisfaction of her property rights in the patrimony enjoyed by the family. Again, this fraction would vary according to the presence or absence of children. This fraction replaced her claim to recover her marriage portion and anything else to which she might be entitled. Modern German law allows a spouse to accept an extra quarter of the deceased's estate in satisfaction of their interest in the community of acquisitions.

The family communion is one of the greatest contributions made by Germanic law to the legal heritage of the civilian countries. It has withstood the attempts to Romanize the institution and has gained a place in most modern civil codes. It is also a victory for the Germanic recognition of collectivity over the individualistic ideals of the French Revolution.

3 The Property of Children

In the same manner as the nineteenth and twentieth centuries have seen a shift in the concept of parental power from its exercise in the interest of the parent to its exercise in the interests of the child, so also there has been during the same period a change in the law's perspective upon property ownership by children. No longer are parents thought to have the right to use and enjoy the property of their children; instead they are restricted to its management and control, the income on the property being devoted to the benefit of the child rather than to that of the parent. This marks a considerable difference from the position with regard to children's property in both Roman and Germanic law.

In Roman law, a child in the power of a *paterfamilias* could not own anything. All property rights were vested in the head of the family. The *pater* might give an adult son a small portion of the family property to manage under his supervision, as a way of educating the son in the running of a household. Such a share, which had no legal status, was called the son's *peculium*. A change however came about with the growth of empire, when sons serving in the legions would be away from the family home for long periods on military service. It was in these circumstances impractical not to allow them some sort of legal control over the property at their disposal, at least while they were on military service. Thus came to be recognized by law a patrimony which a son in power could enjoy as his own property, at first while on military service but ultimately thereafter as well. This was called the *peculium castrense*. Under Constantine, sons in power serving in the imperial civil service, which was organized upon military lines from the time of Diocletian, were allowed a similar *peculium quasi-castrense*. Although fathers would be allowed to use and enjoy such property after the son returned, that is have a usufruct in it, they could not dispose of its capital value and had to manage it according to the standard of a *bonus paterfamilias*, a good head of household. By Justinian's time, the same rule applied to property which came to a child from the mother or her relatives, *bona adventicia*. These rules continued to influence the property arrangements on behalf of children in the lands in which Roman law survived after the collapse of the western empire, and were also of influence after the revival of Roman law studies in the twelfth century.

Children did rather better under the Germanic family arrangements. There, as has been seen, children only remained subject to paternal power until they reached majority by leaving home with the father's consent to establish their own household. At that point, they were entitled to ask for their share in the family property with which to establish themselves. Until that time, they were seen as having an interest in the family property, but only then did they acquire the legal capacity to own it themselves. Property acquired from outside of the household before then would be controlled by the father who could apply it for family purposes until the child gained emancipation. Thereafter, a son was responsible for his own property, a daughter's husband for hers.

The concept of a child having property of his or her own to enjoy free of parental use only appears in the law codes of the modern period, when the child's independent rights were acknowledged. Thus, the Prussian *Landrecht*, the French *Code civil* and the German BGB all limit parental interest to use and enjoyment and allow children to be the owners of their own goods. The modern system derived from those compilations follows that tradition. It marks in this area of the law an increase in individualism at the expense perhaps of the corporate view of the family, although children's power to dispose of their property is strictly curtailed and under the control of the parents or guardians.

4 Intestate Succession

When a person dies, the whole of the property which he or she owned at the time of death ceases to have an owner. It forms a vacant patrimony. If the deceased person was married, the family communion will come to an end at that moment and the deceased's share will pass into his or her patrimony, the remainder going to the surviving spouse. If the deceased person has made a valid will, called in civil law jurisdictions a testament, the patrimony will devolve in accordance with that will subject to certain limitations imposed by law in defence of the family's interests. If there is no will, the deceased is said to have died intestate and the patrimony will devolve in accordance with the rules laid down by law. Those same rules will apply to any portion of the patrimony which has not been disposed of by the will when the deceased has made one.

In any legal system there is therefore a certain tension between the power of an individual to determine what shall happen to his property after his death and the interests, if any, of the family in that property. Freedom of testation is an individualist concept which stresses the rights of the owner as an individual against all the world including his nearest relatives. While in common law countries, freedom of testation is regarded as an important right, in civil law nations it is generally looked upon as less important than the obligations owed to and the interests of the immediate family. This is very much a feature determined by the history of those systems, and both the Germanic and Roman elements have combined to produce this result, with canon law stressing the right of a person to make a will.

The development of the law of intestate succession has much to say about the changing notion of what constitutes the family and the closeness of relationships within it. The modern law of intestate succession in civil law countries displays by and large a family in the sense of a kindred group which encompasses all living descendants and ancestors of an individual, together with collateral relatives to the sixth or seventh degree calculated according to the Roman system.[5] Within this framework, descendants are preferred to others, the nearer being preferred to the more remote. In the absence of descendants, the parents are regarded as the next nearest relatives and then brothers and sisters and their progeny. In the absence of such near relatives, the succession falls to the relatives of the nearest degree of relationship as far as the sixth or seventh, and in the absence of any such, the State will take the property of the deceased as goods without an owner, *bona vacantia*.

In the above, nothing has been said of the surviving spouse, if indeed there is one. A spouse is not of course a blood relative. The spouse's place in the succession varies considerably from country to country and can depend upon what other relatives the deceased leaves. In most countries today, though not all, the surviving spouse will inherit the whole of the deceased's patrimony in the absence of descendants and parents. If such survive however, and depending upon their number in the case of children, the share of the spouse will be reduced and may even be converted from an absolute interest in a share of the estate to a usufruct in a part of it. This is sometimes justified on the basis that the surviving spouse will already have received a share of the divided family communion or, in the absence of such, will have opted at marriage for independence in property matters. Nevertheless, the end result appears strange to those from common law countries where the surviving spouse is usually the first beneficiary of a deceased's estate upon an intestacy.

The Roman Contribution

In many ways, the exclusion of the spouse from any prominent place in the succession to the deceased's patrimony is a result of the independence enjoyed by the Roman woman. As it was rare for a Roman wife to pass into the power of her husband, and his family were those who were either in his power, the household, or who were descended from men who had been in the same power, his kindred, the Roman wife was not a member of her husband's family in either sense. Thus, she originally had no interest in his succession, other than recovering her *dos*. In Roman law, succession was primarily concerned with identifying the deceased's heir or heirs, who not only succeeded to his property but also had religious duties to perform relating to the family *sacra*. The original order of intestate succession, which was always regarded as that of the civil law, was set out in the Twelve Tables.

Upon the death of a Roman *paterfamilias*, his heirs were all those who became *sui iuris* as a result of his passing. Thus, all of his children in power, whether born to him or adopted by him, together with a wife who was in *manus*, would qualify to be his heirs. Emancipated children and daughters married with *manus* did not qualify. Grandchildren would only qualify if their father had predeceased his *paterfamilias*, and they would not take equally with the other children but only take the share their deceased father would have received had he lived.

In the absence of descendants, the next person to be called to the succession were the nearest agnates, that is the nearest blood relatives of the deceased related to him through males, for instance his brothers and sisters, nephews and nieces through his brothers, uncles and aunts, cousins through uncles, and so on. Only the nearest could take, and deceased persons of that degree were not represented by their offspring. Beyond the third degree, males were preferred to females. Unlike descendants, the nearest agnates could refuse the succession. If there were no agnates to succeed, the property went to the *gens*, that group larger than the family containing all those who shared the common gentile name, the *nomen*. It is unclear how this group enjoyed the succession; some believe they put it to charitable or religious uses.

A wife with *manus* counted as a child in this scheme of succession, otherwise she had no place in it.

This agnatic family model was gradually replaced by praetorian activity with an alternative family structure more closely connected with blood relationship. Through his edict, the praetor could not alter the civil law, but he could control its application. He therefore called to the succession persons who were not heirs in civil law but whom it was felt should have a share in the succession. These he placed in possession of the deceased's goods, *bonorum possessio*, which possession would with the passage of time convert itself into full civil law ownership, *dominium*. The first persons that the praetor called to the succession were the children of the deceased, but he did not exclude those emancipated. In default of such claimants, he would summon the nearest agnates following the civil law, but if they did not claim he would next allow the property to be taken by the nearest blood relatives within six or seven degrees regardless of whether they were blood relatives in the male or female line, that is he would call cognates as well as agnates. Finally, for want of claimants in any of these categories, he would give the succession to the surviving spouse, the first time that this relationship enters into the Roman order of succession.

During the second century AD, further adjustments were made to the order of succession by *senatusconsulta* to allow mothers to inherit more readily from their children and children from their mothers, and it is the system thus modified that found its way into the Theodosian Code and thence was preserved in many parts of southern Europe after the fall of the western Empire and was even retained in Toulouse after the greater part of the *pays de droit écrit* had adopted the revised order of succession enacted by Justinian in 537 in his Novel 118. According to this order, descendants once again came first, the share of deceased descendants being allowed to pass to their children. In the absence of descendants, ascendants were preferred, the nearer excluding the more remote. Parents took equally; but remoter ancestors had to share with any surviving brothers and sisters. If both paternal and maternal grandparents or remoter ancestors were the successors, the succession was divided equally between the paternal and maternal lines. In the absence of ascendants, brothers and sisters took equally with the shares of deceased brothers and sisters passing to their children; brothers and sisters of the half-blood only took for want of brothers and sisters of the whole-blood. For want of siblings, the nearest collateral relatives shared equally without representation, nearness of relationship being calculated by degrees through the connecting ancestor, that is the Roman method. Finally, in the absence of blood relatives, the surviving spouse inherited. If there was no spouse, the property went to the imperial treasury, the *Fiscus*, as *bona vacantia*. With the revival of Roman law in western Europe from the eleventh century, this system was adopted in the lands of Roman law and also constituted the order of succession utilized by the western Church in its canon law, the Church courts acquiring a considerable influence in some countries in succession issues during the Middle Ages.[6]

The heir or heirs in Roman law succeeded to the whole of the deceased's patrimony in equal but undivided shares, they were each equally owner of it all. This is what is known in civil law as universal succession. Moreover, upon the death of the deceased, his former patrimony and that of the heir merged to become one, all of which was available to satisfy creditors of the deceased. If the deceased's or the heir's creditors feared they might be prejudiced by this merger of patrimonies, they could request a separation of the patrimonies, *separatio bonorum*, but it was not until Justinian that the heir could protect his property from the deceased's debts by asking that he be allowed to succeed with benefit of inventory. The patrimonies thereafter remained distinct. Heirs by descent could not refuse the succession; they were *sui et necessarii heredes*, necessary heirs to themselves. The term *sui*, which is what they were usually called, emphasizes the underlying family element in Roman ownership. The heirs already had an interest not just an expectation while the *pater* lived. Separation of goods and benefit of inventory continue to play a part in civilian systems of succession. Although modified, universal succession also remains a recognizable feature of modern civil law systems.

The Germanic Contribution

The inheritance system of the Germanic laws had some things in common with the Roman, but was at other points very divergent. Like the Roman, it regarded succession as being grounded in the rights of the family rather than the preference of the deceased, but unlike the Roman it did not accord such equal treatment to male and female descendants and, owing to its view of marriage bringing the wife into her husband's *Mund*, gave increased rights in the succession to the spouses.

The Germanic family structure, as has been seen, placed children under the power of the father only until they were emancipated, usually by leaving the paternal home on marriage. At this point, males took with them a share of the family property in order to set themselves up in life; daughters took their marriage portion and passed into the *Mund* of their husbands. On the subsequent death of a family member, the question which the Germanic laws sought to answer was in what manner the property of the deceased should pass back to the family. If the deceased had children, the succession was shared by them, but they had to bring into account the shares in the family property they had received upon emancipation. Married daughters could not expect to inherit. Generally, only children of the deceased were called to the inheritance; if a child had predeceased his parent, the deceased child's issue did not originally represent him in the succession, although the Lombard laws did allow this in the case of children. In the absence of children, the parents succeeded and if they were dead those relatives of the deceased descended from them to the seventh degree. Only if there were no relatives in this line to take was recourse had to the grandparents and their descendants, and when that line was exhausted to the great-grandparents and their issue. This system is described as lineal or parentelic, because it moves back one generation at a time, regarding all the issue of that generation as being more nearly related to the deceased than any descendant from a more remote generation.

Within each generation, a distinction was also drawn between property which the deceased had acquired from the father's and the mother's side of the family. The rule described as *paterna paternis, materna maternis* split the property in accordance with the source from which it had come to the deceased. This could lead to difficult inquiries concerning whether items had come from, for example, the paternal or maternal grandfather or grandmother's side of the family. In the customary regions of France this was known as the *fente*. Closeness of relationship was reckoned by the line and not by degree as in Roman law. Descendants were the first line, the issue of parents the second, of grandparents the third and of great-grandparents the fourth. Within each step of descent from a common ancestor, the nearest generation excluded the more remote, so that if there were brothers and sisters living, nephews and nieces would not succeed. Representation allowing a child to take a deceased parent's share was not permitted to collaterals until the Lombard rule relating to the issue of descendants was extended to them by the Italian communes, probably under the influence of Roman law. Representation was established in Germany by the emperor Otto I in 942.

The transfer of the wife into her husband's *Mund* meant that the question of inheritance from her was also of importance in Germanic law. The Lombards allowed the husband to succeed to his deceased wife's property, whereas the Franks preferred the children to the surviving spouse, allowing him only the use of the property while he lived, title passing to the children. In the absence of children, the husband inherited. The emperor Henry I in 1019 provided that the children should always succeed, the husband only having a right if there were no surviving issue. The laws of the mediaeval communes witness to various permutations of these rules.

The wife who survived her husband was provided for by the marriage portions she had either received or been promised. However, it also came to be recognized that in the absence of such provision, the widow should receive a third part of her deceased husband's estate or a portion related to the number of children alongside whom she succeeded. The communes followed this pattern, but generally gave the widow a quarter, whether she took it absolutely or only by use depending at times upon the presence of children. Otherwise, the Roman rule prevailed that only in the absence of blood relatives did the wife inherit. This was also the case in the customary areas of France. The Reception of Roman law in Germany increased the emphasis upon blood relatives succeeding rather than the spouse, but before considering the importance of the Reception, something must be said of feudalism.

The Feudal Contribution

The feudal compact between lord and vassal required the vassal to provide services, most typically of a military nature, on behalf of the lord. It was therefore important that the lord's tenant should be able to provide such services and that the land given in return should be sufficient to support the fighting man's needs. Two things followed from this. Firstly, the tenant should ideally be male, and secondly the land of the tenant should not be divided into ever-decreasing portions by succession. Although feudal land was granted to tenants on terms which allowed their issue to inherit, the needs of feudalism militated in favour of there being one rather than several heirs, and also in favour of that heir being the male, preference being accorded to the eldest. Thus developed the rule of primogeniture by which feudal land passed to the eldest son. It was also established that the line of that son was to be preferred to younger sons, for instance by Konrad II in

1037 in an enactment which passed very influentially into the *Libri Feudorum*.

The importance of the feudal compact in the development of mediaeval land law resulted in different rules of succession applying to immoveable property as opposed to moveables, thus further complicating the rules of inheritance. Throughout France, for instance, inheritance of land was governed by different rules from the customs already described, whether Roman or Germanic, relating to chattels. Even in the *pays de droit écrit*, fiefs were inherited according to the feudal rules. This further division in the law of succession remained in France until the Revolution. Although D'Aguesseau's *ordonnances* on gifts and settlements created a unified law for France in the eighteenth century, and his *ordonnance* on testaments unified systems for each of the *pays des coutumes* and the *pays de droit écrit*,[7] feudal fiefs were unaffected. The first unified system of succession for the whole country had to wait until 1804 for the *Code civil*. Succession to land in the communes was largely unaffected by the influence of feudalism.

The Reception and the Modern Law

The Reception challenged the Germanic parentelic order with the alternative system of Justinian. During the sixteenth and seventeenth centuries, many of the territories of Germany altered their orders of succession under the influence of revived Roman law and the Church. In Saxony and Magdeburg, for instance, a system was introduced by which descendants, ascendants, brothers and sisters and then remoter collaterals were called in that order. More generally, as in Hamburg, Lübeck and Breslau, brothers and sisters were allowed to take before remoter ascendants, but it was in the Prussian *Landrecht* that the basis of the modern Germanic compromise was first achieved. Five classes of successors were identified: descendants, then parents, then brothers and sisters of the whole-blood, then brothers and sisters of the half-blood alongside remoter ascendants, and then finally all other collateral relatives according to the degree of their relationship regardless of the parentelic line. The Prussian *Landrecht* also abolished the *ius recandantiae* of *paterna paternis, materna maternis*. Although Austrian law, following the succession law of Joseph II in 1786 has adopted a more strict parentelic approach, modern German law has stuck with the idea of classes of successors based on the parentelic lines, but adopting the Roman preference for the relatives nearest in degree once beyond the descendants of the grandparents. Indeed, Swiss law refuses to trace successors beyond this point. The French *Code civil* called descendants first, parents and their issue second, remoter ascendants third, and finally remoter collaterals according to nearness of degree.

In all of these systems, however, emphasis upon blood relationship all but eclipses the rights of a surviving spouse. While the development of the family communion of property is sometimes used to justify this, it was also recognized that the result flew in the face of what was now regarded as natural affection. In France, under the *Code civil* for instance, the claim of the spouse was not admitted until after remote collaterals of the twelfth degree had been eliminated. The position of the surviving spouse in modern French law has been gradually, but only gradually, improved. Given rights of usufruct in the estate in 1891 and 1925, in 1930 the spouse was allowed to succeed to the inheritance of a line which failed, for instance if there were paternal but no maternal collaterals, the spouse would take the maternal half, thus utilizing the old rules of the *fente*. Only in the 1950s,[8] was the spouse finally allowed to take a specific portion of the inheritance: in usufruct, if there were successors among the children, parents or siblings; absolutely, in their absence. In Italy, the spouse now has a definite share in the succession, not just in usufruct, alongside children and parents, and ousts remoter relatives. In Germany, the spouse inherits alongside children, parents and siblings, and takes entirely in their absence.

Although Germanic law had at first not made successors liable for the debts of the deceased, this was gradually introduced, first being limited to the assets received and eventually to include the heirs' own property, but modern law recognizes both the Roman *separatio bonorum* and the benefit of inventory. In the absence of heirs, property passes to the State, or in Germany the *Land*, which takes free of debts beyond the value of the estate. Such succession is deemed irregular. At one time, in the absence of family, an estate was passed to a charitable body with which the deceased had shown some association, or even in some places to some other body connected with him. The University of Vienna for instance succeeded to the estates of its deceased staff if they had no families. Land once escheated to the lord for want of heirs.

Today, illegitimate children are generally accorded equal inheritance rights with their legitimate brothers and sisters. Such developments are however relatively recent. Their claims, if recognized at all, were more usually postponed to those of sometimes quite remote collaterals.[9] In France they were allowed a half share alongside their legitimate brothers and sisters from 1896; in Germany, they achieved equal rights in 1969.

5 Testamentary Succession

The law of intestate succession has illustrated that inheritance in civil law countries is viewed from the perspective of the family interest in the deceased's property rather than from the perspective of what the deceased might have wished to occur. In England, by contrast, the order of succession on intestacy is based upon what the law perceives is done by testators generally. In civilian jurisdictions, the right of testation is jealously supervised to ensure that it does not defeat the family's legitimate expectations.

The Roman Testament

In this, there was no difference in underlying policy between Roman and Germanic law. Both proceeded from a family-based perspective. In early Roman law, some believe that the word *familia* referred to property which belonged to the family and over which the *paterfamilias* had no power of alienation. Early law it is argued gave the *pater* no power of testation. Only if he had no legitimate heirs by descent could he turn to the *comitia* to allow him to adopt an heir, either during his lifetime by adrogation or upon death by means of appointing an heir. Thus, the hallmark of the Roman will was established. It existed not to make gifts of property but to appoint an heir. A will which failed to do this was invalid. Indeed, the only functions that the *comitia curiata* performed in historical times were adrogations and the making of wills. Undoubtedly, at an early date, the approval of the assembly had really to be obtained.

As the *comitia* only met at fixed times in the year, if a *pater* without a legitimate heir was taken seriously ill and was likely to die before the next session, he would be unable to appoint an heir by this method. Thus, some believe, the other method of making a will mentioned in the Twelve Tables first developed, namely that by the bronze and the scales, the *testamentum per aes et libram*. This involved the *pater* transferring the whole of his patrimony, the *familia*, to another person for a nominal payment as a sign of the transfer. That other person was called the *familiae emptor*, the purchaser of the family, and the transfer was effected by the solemn ceremony of *mancipatio* before five witnesses and a sixth person who held the bronze scales which the *familae emptor* struck with a bronze bar when declaring that the property of the testator was being bought into his mandate in order that the testator could make a will.[10] The testator would then tell the *emptor* his choice of heir or hand him his wishes in writing. The *emptor* was in effect a sort of executor of the will who could prove it with witnesses before the assembly.

This later form opened the door to some measure of freedom of testation in Roman law, and became used in situations other than emergencies. It was early settled however that testators were not permitted to disinherit their legitimate heirs, the *sui et necessarii heredes*, unless for good cause. These had to be expressly disinherited in the will, individually and by name if they were sons in power. Moreover, *sui* might be disinherited for their own convenience, because it was not practical for them all to perform the religious duties attaching to an heir. Accordingly, although disinherited, they would still expect to receive provision under the will which disinherited them, legacies to effect that purpose being imposed upon the heir under the will. The heir of course was the universal successor charged with paying the deceased's debts and providing the legacies, if necessary out of his own patrimony. *Sui* who were not provided for or not provided for adequately under the will, either by being instituted heirs or being given legacies, could complain that the will was unduteous and therefore void. The procedure for accomplishing this was the *querela inofficiosi testamenti*, the complaint of the unduteous will. It was eventually established that each *sui* had cause for complaint if he or she did not receive a quarter of what they would have done on intestacy.

The freedom of the testator to leave his money to strangers, in the sense of persons other than his rightful heirs, was very early circumscribed. Nor could he impose so many or so substantial legacies upon his estate so as to leave his testamentary heir without provision. The heir was also entitled to be left with a quarter of the patrimony, called the Falcidian quarter after the *lex Falcidia* by which it was established in 40 BC. If the shares of the heirs were less than this, they could have legacies and gifts made by the testator reduced in value proportionately until they were left with their just portion.

By this time, and subject to these safeguards, other methods of making wills had been developed. The praetor would grant *bonorum possessio* in accordance with a will written on wax tablets and sealed by seven witnesses, carrying the testation of the bronze and scales to its practical conclusion. In the imperial period, the tripartite will was allowed which combined the features of the earlier varieties, in that it had to be written, sealed by seven witnesses and signed by the testator. The later emperors allowed wills to be registered in the imperial registry or in the courts, thus granting them validity by public authentication. Constantine allowed property to be shared amongst descendants by means of a document written entirely in the testator's own hand, the holograph will. In addition, soldiers on military service were allowed to make wills in very informal ways, hardly any of the normal rules applying. Such military wills, which foreshadow the emergency wills of modern civilian systems, were valid for a year after the military service ended.

The German Institution of an Heir

Germanic law, like Roman law, appears to have known no power of testation in its earliest stages, other than the right of the popular assembly to allow a man without legitimate heirs to adopt one. This was done by allowing him to vest a stranger, that is a person other than a legitimate heir, with arms before the assembly. This adopting of an heir became, as at Rome, a means of appointing an heir. This stage can be seen in the *thinx* or *gairethinx* of Lombard law and the *affatomie* of the Salic Franks. Both involved a symbolic weapon or *festuca* being given to a person in the assembly, which person would return to the house of the testator and stay there for a period as a sign of lawful possession and leave having been charged with the identity of the person to whom the property should be given on the owner's death. Among the Lombards, Liutprand in his laws permitted a charter to be used for the same purpose. The *festuca* could also be handed over to the middle man, again a sort of executor as at Rome, but here called the *Treuhand*, in a private ceremony at the testator's house in the case of his illness, which may again have been the underlying cause of this development outside of the assembly.

Apart from the provision of an heir for a person with no descendants to inherit, Germanic law was unwilling to defeat the expectations of the family in order to accommodate the wishes of the deceased. Freedom of testation was not recognized.

The Influence of the Church

It was customary among the Germanic peoples to bury a certain proportion of the deceased's property with him for enjoyment in the afterlife. This part of his patrimony was called the share of the dead. With the conversion of the Germanic peoples to Christianity, such burial was perceived to be a superstitious practice, and the Church sought to adapt it to a Christian purpose. Accordingly, the Church encouraged those nearing death to donate this part of their property either to the Church or to charitable purposes. Instead of being the share of the dead, it would be a gift made by the dying man for the benefit of his soul, *pro anima*.

Such gifts would often be made at the same time as the dying made his last confession and received the last rites of the Church. They were therefore often made before a priest. This influenced the development of the rules relating to the validity of such gifts. Canon law normally required two credible witnesses as proof of a transaction. As the priest might be receiving property for his parish, he was not always eligible. Accordingly, it was required that the priest be present together with two independent witnesses. This rule, which was originally devised for the making of wills by ecclesiastical persons, came to be extended to the laity, although it was disapproved of from the fifteenth century.

That gifts *pro anima* might be made to the Church was recognized among the Carolingians from 818 by capitulary. The amount that might be disposed of in this fashion was however subject to limitations. Among the Visigoths it was a fifth; among the Salic Franks a third; among the Burgundians, a half. It became known as the disposable part or quota of the deceased's patrimony, the residue, which had to go to the family, forming the reserve. This was the terminology of the *pays des coutumes*, while in the *pays de droit écrit*, the Roman heir's Falcidian quarter continued to limit the dispositive powers of southern French testators and the rights of the family to a quarter of what they would have had on intestacy continued to operate. This was known as the *legitim*. By the thirteenth century, it was established in the *pays des coutumes* that four-fifths of the deceased's separate patrimony, his *propres*, were reserved for his family, while he could dispose of three-quarters of his whole patrimony, being his share of the moveables and acquisitions as well as the *propres*, subject to the *légitime* of the other quarter. The combination of both elements protected the family of testators with little in the way of *propres* to be reserved.

The distinction between the inheritance of *propres* and moveables and acquisitions was one of many that could apply to freedom of testation. In the Italian communes, it was also usual to distinguish between a person's right to dispose freely of acquired property and the lack of such right with regard to property which had been inherited. This appears to hark back to the distinction believed by some to have existed in ancient Rome concerning inherited property, the *familia*, and acquisitions, *pecunia*, although this may also have turned upon the importance of some types of property.[11] Feudal land was generally not available for disposition by will, and often could not be alienated during a tenant's lifetime either. This was often the result of the land having been subjected to what in English law is called an entail, but was described in mediaeval and modern civil law as a *fideicommissum*, whereby the land was destined to pass in perpetuity from father to eldest son or the other nearest heir with a reversion to another branch of the family when the line expired. These *fideicommissa* were most unpopular, as land subjected to them was permanently withdrawn from the market. They were gradually abolished, starting in Tuscany in the late eighteenth century, and throughout France after the Revolution, although they reappeared there under the Empire. They play no part in modern civilian systems. Their existence is worth noting however if only to observe the difference between them and the ancient Roman *fideicommissa* which were gifts outside of the will which were nevertheless binding upon the heir or legatee, and which were also not allowed to diminish either the heir's Falcidian quarter or the *legitim* of the close family.

If it was ecclesiastical influence which freed a portion of a person's property for free disposal upon death, the Church also influenced the form which a testament should take. The Germanic peoples were originally unhappy with testaments being made other than in the assembly. The Church however insisted that it was intention not form that was important. Nevertheless, intention had to be proved, and the canon law refined the Roman formalities for wills. The Italian communes favoured registration before the courts or in the communal archives, but often followed the death-bed precedent of asking for witnesses to be present as well as the officer of the commune who effected the registration. The number of these witnesses varied, as they did in southern France where the registration of testaments was also practised. As well as the notary, five or seven witnesses had to be present. Seven was the number drawn from Roman law, but five had been the number that that system required if the testamentary document was a codicil disposing of property but not appointing an heir. The *pays de droit écrit* also developed the secret or mystic will, whereby the testator could hand the notary a sealed document in the presence of the appropriate number of witnesses, which the notary endorsed but did not open until the testator's death. The will by deed was normally dictated to the notary. In the North of France, the canonical rules prevailed; the will had either to be registered by the notary in the presence of two witnesses, or alternatively by two notaries. The holograph will was also recognized, which had to be written throughout in the testator's own hand, signed by him and dated, with the place of execution sometimes also being required. Finally, the nuncupative will was also generally known, that is a will declared orally before five or seven witnesses, as the local law required, who were usually required to commit what the testator said to writing as soon as possible in the interests of certainty.

Although the canon law courts did much to unify the ground rules of the law of testamentary succession during the later Middle Ages, they did not always succeed in securing a monopoly of this jurisdiction. In parts of Germany, such as Magdeburg, the secular courts insisted during the thirteenth and fourteenth century upon wills being registered with them, and the Church courts never obtained jurisdiction over testate succession in Spain. France during the sixteenth century required notarial registration of gifts[12] as well as increasing secular control over inheritance, and it was finally the royal *ordonnance* of 1735 which unified the succession customs of the north and the south respectively, although it was not until the *Code civil* that France as a whole had a unified law of succession.

Testamentary Executors

It was noticed earlier how both the Roman *familae emptor* and the Germanic *Treuhand* were harbingers of the ecclesiastical testamentary executor, one who is not necessarily the heir but who manages the payment of the deceased's debts out of the estate, sees that the legacies are paid and that the family get their share. The executor is not present in all systems; indeed, in Roman law, it was the heir who performed these functions. However, the Lombards made use of the services of a *dispensator* and executors appear by that name in the mediaeval Italian communes and in the *pays des coutumes* in France. They are not however found in the Romanist *pays de droit écrit*. Where found, they are normally allowed a year to complete their work. They can be appointed in several modern civilian systems.

6 The Modern Law and Forced Inheritance

While Roman law gave the deceased a free hand in the disposal of his estate upon death subject to protecting the family's interests, Germanic law was jealous of the latter and limited freedom of testation severely. Modern civilian systems generally do much to safeguard the rights of children, the spouse and parents, but are prepared to allow freedom of testation as against remoter relatives. The right of the immediate family to be protected results in the existence of a distinction between a disposable quota and a reserve, the size of which as a fraction of the deceased's estate varies according to the number and identity of the privileged successors. It is often also related to the fraction of the estate which the relative would have received upon intestacy. The task of a modern will is therefore usually to make legacies and not to appoint an heir, for if there are privileged relatives, their share is in a sense the heir's share, although the deceased's debts are payable out of the whole estate and not just their part, although they may still need to protect their own assets against an insolvent estate by taking with benefit of inventory. Gifts in excess of the disposable quota, whether legacies or gifts made during the deceased's lifetime, can be reduced so as to restore the reserve of one or more relatives.

The methods of making wills are still various. Holograph wills are allowed, but more generally wills are made before notaries or handed in sealed envelopes to notaries for registration. Witnesses are still sometimes required, but this is steadily becoming less frequent.[13] Most systems still allow the making of privileged wills in emergencies, following the Roman military will, although these are no longer confined to soldiers or time of war, but can be made in times of earthquake, disaster, pestilence or even on board ship or an aircraft. Their validity however expires within a short while after the cessation of the emergency in question.

Germany continues to allow inheritance contracts, a form developed in the mediaeval period. It also allows mutual wills, in a form commonly called the 'Berlin will'.

Executors when used are regarded as acting under an unpaid mandate. Wills are not usually revoked automatically upon marriage or the birth of children, as the existence of the reserve already protects family interests. In some systems, brothers and sisters may qualify in certain circumstances for a share in the reserve and that of the spouse may be limited to a usufruct. Although formal disinheritance for cause has been abolished, privileged relatives can nevertheless lose their shares if they are unworthy as can legatees. Unworthiness is generally connected with unlawfully killing the testator or having committed a serious act of violence against him or having seriously traduced his reputation.

7 The Alimentary Obligation

Finally, before leaving the law of the family, it is worth mentioning the alimentary obligation, which is an important feature of modern civilian systems of family law and which constitutes in effect the reverse side of the coin from forced inheritance, both illustrating the concept of the family as a continuing entity over several generations. Whereas in Roman law, children remained in their father's power throughout his life and had protected interests in the family property when he died, in Germanic law the children, although they retained rights of succession to the family property, became independent upon leaving the family household, but were required to take their parents into their *Mund* when they became old or disabled.

Modern civilian systems, as has been seen, reserve a portion of the parent's property to the children and, in the absence of offspring, the parents retain an interest in their children's estate. While all are living, they remain obligated by law to provide for one another if they become necessitous. The spouses owe this obligation to each other, parents owe it to their children - regardless of age - and children owe it to their parents. In some systems it extends to in-laws where there are children whose parents have become needy - in other words grandparents cannot assist their grandchildren and ignore the needs of a surviving parent who is not a blood relative of the grandparents. Brothers and sisters are also sometimes liable, but usually only to provide the basic necessities.

The alimentary obligation as a legal obligation can be traced back in Roman law to a rescript of the emperor Antoninus Pius in the second century AD, and has come to influence modern systems through inclusion in the Digest and its obvious affinity with Christian concepts of family duty.[14]

Notes

[1] This is the Lombard term. It is also called *Wittum* and *meta*; see C. Calisse, *A History of Italian Law* (Boston, 1928; reprinted New York, 1969), pp. 572 ff.
[2] Again the Lombard term; it is also called *maritagium*, *Austeuer*, *Heimsteuer*, *Heisteuer*, *huistüre* and *Heiratsteuer*; see R. Huebner, *A History of Germanic Private Law* (Boston, 1918; reprinted New York, 1968), p. 624; Calisse, *History*, pp. 573 ff.
[3] A more generally-used term than *mefio* and *faderfio*, but also called *morgive*; see Huebner, *History*, p. 625; Calisse, *History*, p. 574 ff.
[4] For instance, in Electoral Hesse, parts of Westphalia, Pomerania and Hannover, in Lanenburg and parts of Bavaria, and in Hesse-Darmstadt, parts of Mecklenburg and Brunswick.
[5] See chapter 9 for a description of this system and the Germanic.
[6] England surprisingly is an example.
[7] *Ordonnance sur les donations* (1731); *Ordonnance sur les testaments* (1735); *Ordonnance sur les substitutions fidéicommissaires* (1747). See R.C. Van Caenegem, *An Historical Introduction to Private Law* (Cambridge, 1992), p. 92.
[8] Being preferred to ordinary collaterals in 1957 (Loi 26. 3. 1957) and being given *saisine* in 1958 (O. 23. 12. 1958); see Amos and Walton, *Introduction to French Law* (3rd. Ed.; Oxford, 1967), pp. 299 ff.
[9] Sometimes as in Spain, distinctions were drawn between natural children and those of corrupt or criminal connection; see C. Calisse et al., *General Survey of Continental Legal History* (Boston, 1912; reprinted New York, 1968), p. 635 ff.
[10] *Mancipatio* is dealt with in chapter 11 below; mandate in chapter 12.
[11] Some regard *familia* as an early term for *res mancipi*. See below chapter 11.
[12] *Ordonnance* of Villers-Cotteret 1539, art. 132.
[13] Spain for instance has recently abolished the need for witnesses to a *testamento abierto*.
[14] See Justinian, Digest. XXV. 3. 5. 5 and 7; and see H.F. Jolowicz and B. Nicholas, *An Historical Introduction to the Study of Roman Law* (3rd. Ed.; Cambridge, 1972), p. 396 and n. 2.

11 The Law of Property

1 The Concept of Property in Civil Law

When Gaius divided his treatment of the Roman civil law into the three categories of persons, things and actions, the law of property was with obligations part of the law relating to things. In terms of legal propositions, the law of property is concerned with propositions of the sort "A owns X", while the law of obligations is concerned with propositions of the sort "A owes X to B". The assertion that A owns X proposes that A's right to X is good against all comers, good, as lawyers sometimes say, against all the world, whilst to say that A owes X to B merely proposes that A is under a duty to render B whatever X is, that is B's right to X is only good as against A. The latter situation is therefore sometimes expressed by saying that B's right is *in personam*, against a particular person, while A's right in the former utterance is true about his relationship to the thing X without reference to any other person, it is a right *in rem*.

The law of property is concerned with propositions of the first type, the law of obligations with the latter. The law of property therefore provides the legal answers to questions such as what things may be owned by A, what ownership means, how it is acquired, transferred and lost, what rights persons other than the owner may have in a thing, the relationship between ownership and possession of a thing, and whether an owner who has lost possession or custody of his property can recover it, although how an owner may do this is a subject more properly explored as part of the law of actions. The question who may own property is answered as part of the law of persons which has already been considered.[1]

It will be seen in the course of the discussion which follows that the modern civil law of property has been heavily influenced by the principles and categories invented by the ancient Roman jurists. The same will be true of the law of obligations. However, in both cases this has been in part the result of the adoption of the Roman categories and principles by the legal rationalists of the seventeenth and eighteenth century and of their use in the codifications of the nineteenth and twentieth centuries more than their survival from the ancient world into the modern as living concepts. Indeed, it will be seen that competing Germanic and feudal conceptions of ownership for long withstood the revival of Romanism, and that both made significant contributions to the development of the modern civil law of things in both of its two departments of property and obligations.

2 The Classification of Things

One of the most significant distinctions wrought by the Roman jurists with regard to things was that between those which could be owned by a private individual and those which could not. Those which were susceptible of ownership in private law were classed as being *res in patrimonio*, they were capable of forming part of the patrimony of a legal person. Those things which could not form part of a private individual's patrimony were dubbed *res extra patrimonium*.

Res extra patrimonium were then subdivided into those which were subject to divine law and those subject to human law, *divini iuris* and *humani iuris* respectively.[2] Both of these categories were further subdivided into three sub-categories. *Res divini iuris* consisted of things which were sacred, *res sacrae*, things which were religious, *res religiosae*, and things which were specially protected or sanctioned, *res sanctae*. *Res sacrae* were things dedicated to the gods above, such as temples, shrines and altars, while *res religiosae* were those dedicated to the gods below, the rulers of the world of the spirits of departed ancestors, the *di manes*, and included such things as graves, tombs and funerary monuments. *Res sanctae* consisted of boundary zones which were placed under special protection because of their peculiar role in dividing what was mine from yours or ours from theirs; they included the walls and gates of cities, and other such liminal areas. They were not dedicated to the gods, but were nevertheless under their special protection.

Such things could not be owned by a private individual, a legal person in private law. One could not buy a temple in the way one bought a house, or acquire legal ownership of a sacred grove by possession for the length of time it would take to acquire title to an ordinary field. Such things were not susceptible to such ownership; they were dedicated to a particular purpose in perpetuity.

The other category of things *extra patrimonium humani iuris* consisted of those things which could not be the property of any particular person because they were the general property of all mankind, *res communes*, or of all the citizens of a particular state, *res publicae*, or of all the inhabitants of a particular town, city or other community, *res universitatis*. *Res communes* consisted of the air which one breathed, running water, the sea and the sea shore between high and low tide. These were common to all mankind and could not be denied to citizens of other states. *Res publicae* consisted of rivers, public roads, bridges, market places, public meeting places, the theatres, baths and ports. No citizen could be denied access to their use; non-citizens could not expect equal access. *Res universitatis* were things belonging to a municipality, colony or other community, which were to be enjoyed freely by its inhabitants.

The subject matter of the Roman law of things consisted of those things which were *in patrimonio* and therefore capable of ownership by individuals. However, the category of things *extra patrimonium* continues to be of importance. With the change to imperial government, a distinction had to be made between property which the emperor controlled because he was in charge of the State, and property which constituted his own personal patrimony. The distinction was sometimes easier to state in theory than to make in practice. Originally, the emperor's private property was referred to simply as his *patrimonium*, but from the time of Septimius Severus (193-211) onwards it became known as the imperial *res privatae*, and the income therefrom was often applied for state purposes, the emperors not making much of a distinction between their private patrimony and the public domain. Indeed, with the invasion of Italy by the Ostrogoths in the fifth century, both Odoacer and Theodoric created a personal treasury for which they revived the Roman title of *patrimonium*, the term *res privatae* being applied to the old imperial lands which were now under their control.

Whatever the difficulties of terminology, the distinction between a ruler's private and public property was to be adopted by both the Gothic and the Frankish laws; the eighth Council of Toledo in 653, for instance, so demarcated the property of the king.

Feudalism played a further role in confusing the Roman distinction. Feudal rulers were accepted as protectors of their domains; their lands were within their protection or peace. Thus, as well as the lands held of them by their vassals, those items which the Roman jurists had described as being *extra patrimonium* were also under the ruler's protection. Indeed, they were under his special protection inasmuch as there was no other owner to protect them. While the original intention was doubtless that this protection was meant to be for the benefit of all the ruler's subjects, the reality quickly became that they were thought to be the special property of the ruler, from which he could exclude his subjects or set strict conditions with regard to their access to or enjoyment of them.

Already under the Lombards and the Franks, it was established that lakes, rivers, ports, roads, bridges and market places - things which had been *res publicae* to the Romans - were State property from which the ruler was entitled to exact duties from those who wished to use them.[3] With feudalism, such property came under the protection of the ruler and became confused with his own property in such a way that no one was allowed to hunt in a forest or fish in a river without the lord's permission. At the Diet of Roncaglia in 1158, the emperor set out the rights which he claimed were exclusively his. These *regalia* included mints, tolls and customs, markets and castles, grants of safe conduct and protection to merchants, Jews and foreigners, goods confiscated from convicts and the goods of those who died without heirs, lordless estates, the sea-shore, rivers, roads, hunting and fishing, mines, salt beds, treasure trove, the right to practise certain trades and the right to administer justice.[4] This list found its way into the *Libri feudorum* and thus into the corpus of civil law which was to form the *ius commune*, thus ensuring its continued influence in many parts of western Europe, particularly Germany, until the eighteenth century.

In Italy, however, the communes were not prepared to relinquish their claim to communal ownership of many of these rights at all easily. After their victory over the emperor at the Battle of Legnano in 1176 they were able to force concessions from him at the Peace of Constance in 1183. Under its terms, woods, pastures and rivers were restored to common ownership, and during the succeeding centuries the communes were able to recover their rights over activities, such as hunting and fishing. Under the communal regimes, irrigation, milling, mining and hunting were open to all, subject only to the State's right to police them in the interests of good order. Common lands however remained the property of the ruler, withdrawn from cultivation and requiring an easement from the ruler to allow their use for pasture, the collection of wood, seeds, and so on. By the end of the Middle Ages, jurists were learning to distinguish between a ruler's private domain and the property in his control for the benefit of the State, although in the Renaissance states of Italy, the concept of *regalia* was once again broadened. It was as a result of the reaction against such encroachments that the idea of every person having a natural right to use waterways, highways, woods and forests developed, together with the notion that activities such as hunting, fishing and so on were freely exercisable by all. While these ideas gained ground during the eighteenth century, there was also a widespread wish to free privately-owned land from subservience to the uses of others in the interests of preserving its marketability, and this led to the abolition of various common rights - in Tuscany in 1778, in Naples in 1806 and later throughout Italy. In France, the rights which the kings had enjoyed over major roads and rivers, and to extract tolls for their use, were abolished at the Revolution, and the natural right to their use for hunting and fishing recognized. To this day, these pastimes are engaged in with a fervour more attributable to the exercise of hard-won constitutional rights than simply as leisure pursuits. The modern codifications distinguish between property which by its nature belongs to the State and cannot be susceptible to private ownership, property which happens to belong to the State but could be privately owned and property which can be and is privately owned. Specific police laws regulate activities such as mining, hunting and fishing.

Ancient Roman law also recognized a classification of things according to their nature as being moveable or immoveable. Although not much turned on this distinction in Roman civil law, although a longer period of acquisitive prescription was required for land, the distinction has become important in modern civil law. Immoveable property is primarily land, but also includes whatever is built upon or planted in it. All other forms of property are moveable. This at least was the Roman distinction, and it is the one most commonly adopted by modern systems, but mediaeval Germanic law, while recognizing the distinction, did not apply it in the same manner. Germanic law regarded wooden structures as moveable, and was also prepared to accord the status of immoveables to wild animals and fish which lived in a particular place and had not been reduced into anyone's ownership. Although the Roman classification was generally adopted at the Reception, the Germanic distinction has nevertheless proved influential, allowing the ownership of things built upon land to be distinguished from that of the land itself, and thus allowing distinct ownerships to exist in different floors in a block of flats. Modern civilian systems, unlike Roman law, follow Germanic law in having different regimes relating to the transfer of moveables and immoveables, although modern Swiss law has attempted a unified treatment.

The question of the transfer of property rights raises two further sources of classification. Firstly, it is recognized that some things over which property rights are exercised have a physical existence, while others do not. Thus was born the distinction between corporeal things, such as lands and chattels, and incorporeal things, such as easements over land, securities over lands and chattels, and the like. Whereas corporeal things can be transferred by the transfer of physical possession of them, the same is not possible with regard to incorporeal things. Thus, different forms of transfer may be required. This connects with, but does not entirely coincide with, the distinction between those things which require formal transfer and those which do not. In virtually every society, such a distinction exists, connected as it is with the fact that some forms of property are regarded as being of greater importance within the community than others, so that their transfer requires greater certainty and this is usually achieved by according such transfers greater publicity. In ancient Rome, a distinction was drawn between *res mancipi* and *res nec mancipi*. The former, which consisted of slaves, beasts of draught and burden, certain servitudes and lands in Italy - the economically most important forms of property in the early Roman economy, had to be formally transferred before witnesses or before a magistrate; the latter could be transferred by simple delivery from one person to another. Although the distinction between *res mancipi* and *res nec mancipi* was abolished by Justinian, the later legal systems of western Europe continued to distinguish between property which required formal transfer of ownership and that which did not. Land normally required formal transfer, so the distinction between moveables and immoveables came to approximate to that between things requiring and not requiring formalities for transfer. In modern civil law, immoveables generally require formal transfer while moveables do not, and incorporeal things by their nature require some formal act for their creation, transfer and destruction. Most modern civilian systems also require formalities for the transfer of very valuable or important kinds of moveable property such as boats, aeroplanes and motor vehicles. The usual formality required for the transfer of such objects in modern civil law is registration, and therefore they have become known as registrable moveables.

Transfer of property rights by delivery necessarily connects ownership of a thing with its physical possession. The relationship between ownership and possession is one which has exercised the minds of jurists since Roman times, as has the meaning of the two concepts in themselves. Something must now be said of the concepts of ownership and possession in civil law and the relation that they bear to one another.

3 The Concepts of Ownership and Possession

Ownership

The concept of ownership in modern civil law is complicated by a number of historical factors. The chief of these is the difference between the Roman and Germanic conceptions of ownership, together with further differences injected into the concept by the notions of feudalism. In that the modern civil law is the result of all these influences, it was bound to be something of an amalgam.

One of the hallmarks of ownership, *dominium,* in Roman law was that it was exclusive. Only one person or group of persons could be owner of an item of property at any one time. If other persons had rights to that thing, their rights were of necessity less than ownership. This did not exclude the possibility of shared ownership. Roman law recognized, for instance, that the heirs of a deceased person became owners together of his patrimony, which remained undivided until they took the initiative to divide by means of the *actio familiae erciscundae*, but other associations in Roman law, lacking legal personality, shared property by contractual arrangement rather than by common ownership. Although it is highly likely that, in very early Roman law, all property belonged to the family or the *gens* rather than to single individuals, individual ownership had clearly become the norm by the time of the Twelve Tables, the first solid evidence available for Roman legal arrangements.[5] In that the Romans did not develop any concept of corporate legal personality, individual ownership of an exclusive nature was the norm in Roman civil law.

Germanic law on the other hand presents at its earliest stages a clear picture of common or corporate ownership. The clan or the family was an entity to which property rights attached. Germanic law had a much greater sense of common ownership which gave rise to a clearer concept of corporate personality. Groups, as opposed to their members, could be owners of things, and the group's ownership was not dependent upon agreement among the members, that is it was not fundamentally contractual. Although there were serious attempts to reconcile this strand of Germanic legal development with the Roman view in the centuries following the Reception, it did not prove wholly possible and it was far from satisfying to force the Germanic tradition of corporate ownership into a Roman straitjacket based on contractual structures. Accordingly, many modern civilian systems have incorporated into their law of ownership elements of joint and common ownership, such as the *condominium* by which blocks of flats are owned and governed, which owe their genesis to Germanic rather than Roman civil law ideas.

Feudalism also introduced into the law an element which was wholly foreign to Roman arrangements. A tenant who gave his land to a lord in return for the lord's protection and received it back in return for a promise of allegiance was setting up a relationship between himself and the lord which, though based upon contract, affected the legal title to the land. Within the structures of feudalism, it was possible for there to be many hierarchical relationships of lord and tenant, each of whom had an ownership of a sort in the land. Only one person would actually be in possession of the land, but his ownership was derived from the grant of his lord, and this might in turn be traced through several other layers of seigniorial interest until the highest lord, possibly the king or the emperor, was reached. The feudal concept of land tenure was concerned with the right to hold land from a superior lord and not with an abstract concept of individual ownership. It was therefore at stark variance with the Roman approach. It was also primarily concerned with title to one form of property only, that is land, and rights appurtenant to it. A division between the rules relating to land tenure and the title to goods was therefore inevitable under this system. Feudalism and Germanic group ownership both contributed to the idea that when individual ownership of a thing ended, by for instance death without heirs, the interest of the group revived, and in certain circumstances the underlying or overriding feudal or group interest was sufficient to check the right of the existing owner or tenant to encumber or alienate the property. It could also prevent the possibility of the current owner disposing of the property freely at the time of his death.

Such restrictions were generally reckoned to be contrary to the Roman concept of *dominium* as an exclusive or indeed absolute form of ownership. Already however it has been seen that even in ancient Roman law an owner was not free to dispose of his property freely at the time of his death, having to recognize what could be viewed either as his obligations to his family or their continued interest in the property.[6] The civil law and praetorian rules of succession upon intestacy also witness the continuing recognition of family and *gens* interests in a person's property. It would appear therefore somewhat at odds with the evidence to suggest that Roman ownership was absolute in the sense that no one could interfere with an owner's right to do as he wished with his own goods.

Such an absolute conception of ownership was however adopted by the French *Code civil*, and that in the belief that it was restoring the Roman conception of *dominium*. Indeed, the provisions of the *Code civil* reflected the prevailing orthodoxy among writers of the natural law school concerning the nature of ownership as an unlimited and absolute power. This view was in many respects a reaction against the feudal restrictions which had hampered free commerce in land in pre-Revolutionary France and also against the hierarchical and therefore inegalitarian basis of the feudal order. The Revolution saw the abolition in France of those feudal fiefs which had not fallen into desuetude in the preceding centuries, when they had been superseded by the central authority of the monarchy.[7] Much the same had occurred in the lands of the German princes during the eighteenth century, and the nineteenth century saw its continuance until all feudal landholding was abolished, this being one of the demands of the revolutionaries of 1848.[8]

The feudal centuries had however been productive of serious juristic attempts to marry the structures of feudal landholding with the Roman conception of ownership. Thus, Pothier had during the eighteenth century maintained that only the tenant who held the land in demesne, that is in actual possession, was legal owner of it. The lord from whom he held the land was according to this view also an owner, but his ownership was a sort of servitude over the land by which he was entitled to certain dues and might restrict certain of the tenant's activities. Earlier jurists had also sought to accommodate feudalism and Roman *dominium*. The Glossators and Commentators had noted how in Roman law, the praetor had given the owner of property direct actions to defend his rights, *actiones directae*. Certain other persons with interests in the thing, though not owners, were sometimes given actions to defend their interests on analogy with those of the owner, *actiones utiles*. Although the distinction between what was *directa* and *utilis* was one relating to actions in Roman law, the mediaeval jurists developed it into a classification of kinds of ownership, *dominium directum* and *dominium utile*, according to whether a person had full ownership or merely a limited use of the property. Thus, for instance, the emphyteuta with his virtual right to farm an estate in perpetuity in return for a fixed rent or *canon*, was classified as having *dominium utile* while the corporation or municipality from whom he rented the land had *dominium directum*. This classification found its way into Germanic discussions of ownership in the later Middle Ages and thence into both the Prussian

Landrecht, which adopted an absolutist concept of ownership, and into the Austrian Civil Code. It was not however adopted by the BGB.

Another conundrum facing the mediaeval jurists as a result of the need to reconcile the Roman and feudal perspectives was what to make of the rights of a vassal to land of which he had never been placed in possession. Once the land had been delivered into his possession, he would be seised of it and have what the Romans would have termed a *ius in rem*, a right to the thing. However, if he had only a claim to be put into seisin by the lord, was this anything more than a personal due, a *ius in personam*? The latter did not square with the facts in that the prospective tenant in many feudal societies and according to canon law had remedies by which he could claim the land itself even though it was not yet his. The right of the prospective tenant was described by Jacques de Révigny, the famous jurist of the Orléans school, as a *ius ad rem* as opposed to a *ius in rem*, and this creation entered into the common currency of mediaeval jurisprudence and thence into the Prussian *Landrecht*. It is an interesting example both of juristic ingenuity and of the fruitful outcome of the interaction of one legal perspective with another.

The civilian concept of ownership which the French *Code civil* embodied was one of absolute right, sometimes described as the right to use, take the fruits of and abuse property, *ius utendi fruendi abutendi*. It did not require that an owner conduct himself in relation to his property according to any standard of reasonableness nor with consideration for others. All that was required was that he did not use his property in such a manner as to injure his neighbours, *alterum non laedere*. It is doubtful whether ancient Roman law ever allowed so wide an ambit for the owner's discretion, and modern civil law has found that it is not possible to concede such powers either. The *Code civil* embodies them in part because it marks the culmination both of the reaction against ownership being constrained by seigniorial power and also the realization of a legal order which approaches legal relationships in a rights-based rather than a duty-based manner. Hence, ownership was described as an unrestricted right and as freedom from obligations to others. The markedly individualistic stance of the *Code civil* contributed to this new emphasis.

Not surprisingly, such an absolute concession of unrestricted power to individuals did not make for comfortable social relations. It is interesting that in the century which followed the publication of the *Code civil* French law saw the growth of a body of administrative law, *droit administratif*, which had as part of its goal the regulation of the powers of owners with regard to their landed property. Far from being free to do as they wished with their own, owners found themselves constrained by public law obligations to obtain permissions before indulging in certain developments of their property. The fact that they were not injuring their neighbours by their activities was not enough to ensure that they could do as they wished. The social interest in property use, particularly industrial use, was reasserted through public law. In more recent times, environmental concerns have also involved public law restrictions being placed upon owners. The absolute concept of ownership given by private law has had to be checked by public authority. The overriding rights of lords over their tenants in the feudal hierarchy has been replaced by the overarching supervision of the modern State, seeking to ensure that the activities of its equal citizens do not adversely affect the collective interest of the community as a whole. Nor may owners indulge their property rights for the sole purpose of annoying their neighbours. French law has developed a concept of abuse of rights, and refuses to permit otherwise lawful conduct if it is directed to a spiteful end. A Roman law concept has been borrowed by civilian systems to describe this phenomenon; it is called *aemulatio vicini.*[9] The doctrine of abuse of rights is further reminiscent of the refusal of the praetor to grant actions to plaintiffs in Roman law if their cause was not just despite being superficially lawful, and of his readiness to insert a defence, the *exceptio doli*, for the benefit of a defendant who was technically liable in an action but in fairness ought to be excused. Modern administrative restrictions upon the free exercise of rights of ownership is a feature which links civilian systems with those in other traditions. Society is recognized to be more than an aggregation of individuals, and the legal expression of that recognition is a Germanic contribution to modern civilian thinking.

Possession

If ownership is an abstract concept, describing the legal relation of a person to a thing, possession on the other hand appears to be a straightforward description of a factual situation in the everyday physical world. Whether or not A owns X may be a legal question requiring knowledge of the rules of a particular legal system for its answer, but whether or not A is in possession of X would appear to be a factual question requiring no legal expertise for a response. The issue is not however so simple.

The issue is complicated because the law treats possession as being of significance in answering the question of who is the owner of a thing.

Possession is regarded as being relevant to ownership in that in order to have full enjoyment of one's property, one usually needs to be in possession of it. An owner is therefore expected to be in possession of his goods, and as a result one in possession may well be assumed to be the owner.

The presumption that one in possession is the owner leads to the legal recognition of the possessor as owner after that possession has endured for a certain length of time. Such acquisition of ownership by long possession is called acquisitive prescription. It requires however that there be other factors present, such as good faith, that no one else has a better title and that one came by the property in a manner suitable to acquire ownership. This for instance would not be the case if one had borrowed a thing or taken it by stealth or force. In such circumstances it would not be right to allow possession to mature automatically into ownership.

Classical Roman law allowed property to be acquired by prescription through the process called *usucapio*. For possession to mature into ownership by *usucapio*, it was necessary that the thing should be one capable of being owned in private law, *res habilis*, that it should have been acquired in good faith, *bona fides*, by a method suitable to transfer ownership, *iustus titulus*, and that it should have been in the possession of the acquirer for a sufficient length of time, which was one year in the case of moveables and two years in the case of land. Whereas a person who had found a thing which he genuinely believed to have been abandoned, or a person who had purchased a thing from its owner but not had it conveyed to him by the formal method required for that thing, could acquire title by *usucapio* against the true owner, the person who had taken by stealth, force or with the owner's permission could not. While such persons had physical or natural possession of the thing, their possession was not of a kind that would mature into ownership. Accordingly, such physical or natural possession came to be distinguished from juristic possession, sometimes described as being possession as an owner.

Roman law thus created a juristic concept of possession alongside the physical fact of possessing goods. This meant that mere physical possession was not always juristic possession, and was for that reason described by the jurists as detention of the thing. Juristic possession came to be protected from wrongful interference by various remedies, whereas these remedies were not available to one who had mere detention of the thing. Possession of moveables and immoveables was not differentiated.

Germanic law took a very different line. Firstly, it did not make any distinction between juristic and natural possession. When the owner allowed a thing to pass into the control of another, that other became possessed of it. While the owner retained his rights, these could only be enforced by virtue of the other's obligation to return the thing. The other's possession was subject to the condition that the thing be returned at the end of a certain period or upon request. If however possession passed into the hands of a third person, the third person had no obligation to return the thing, nor had the original owner any claim against him. Where possession of a moveable had been voluntarily surrendered, only the person who had agreed to return it was bound to do so; hand must warrant hand, *Hand mussen Hand wahren*. Where however a thing was lost or stolen a different rule was applied, illogically but in the interests of good order. A person who had involuntarily lost possession to another could reclaim from whomsoever came to possess it. This was the same rule as applied to land, where bare possession was not regarded as being indicative of ownership, but hierarchies of possession or seisin were possible. Hence, German law did not segregate ownership and possession so markedly as Roman law, but as a result, possession of land and chattels was treated differently, and there was no room for a law of acquisitive prescription.

While these principles may be taken as typical of Germanic law in the mediaeval period, it would be wrong to conclude that they were of general application. While they were widespread in both Germany and northern France, local variations were considerable. With the Reception of Roman law, various German states began to absorb the civilian subtleties regarding different types of possession. The Prussian *Landrecht* for instance regarded the possession of the borrower as being imperfect. Canon law had attempted to clothe the feudal customs in Roman garb, and therefore referred to the seisin of the lord as opposed to that of the tenant as quasi-possession. The BGB restricts the concept of juristic possession to dealings with land, preferring to retain the equivalence of possession and control with regard to chattels, thus reverting to its Germanic roots.

In Italy, the jurists were prepared to recognize that juristic possession of a thing could be transferred without transfer of the thing itself. This occurred where for instance a verbal exchange was sufficient for juristic possession to pass, what the jurists called *traditio ficta*. *Traditio vera* on the other hand involved some form of physical delivery, even if that delivery was symbolic, such as a twig or a clod of earth to represent land. The Roman jurists only recognized the latter. Although developed from Roman principles, only in mediaeval law was transfer of possession by juristic act, an act of will rather than a physical action, accepted as sufficient. It found its way from the writings of the Italian jurists into German legal thinking from the Reception onwards.

Modern civilian systems therefore differ in their approach to possession. Most have adopted via the natural law school the Roman distinction between juristic and natural possession, but in some instances those which have been influenced by the BGB have remained aloof from this subtlety in all but land transactions and in dealing with involuntary loss of goods. All however have abandoned the hierarchical gradations of ownership involved in the feudal ownership of land in favour of the simpler Roman notion that only own *dominium* in a thing can exist at any one time.

4 The Acquisition of Ownership

The portions of the modern codes of civil law dealing with the acquisition of ownership bear a marked affinity to the discussions of the Roman jurists.[10] Whether the latter would recognize the kinship to the same extent as a modern reader who looks upon them with the benefit of hindsight is a different matter. The categories, which acquired their specific names during the mediaeval period, are based on the Roman discussions, although the solutions provided to the problems raised bear the stamp of the rationalizing tendencies of the natural law school, whose subservience to the Roman solutions had been broken through the work of the humanist scholars of the Renaissance. The expression of the modes in terms of general principles rather than as solutions to specific problems is modern rather than Roman.

The Roman jurists distinguished methods of acquisition which were peculiar to Roman law in that they were juristic constructions from those which were based simply upon the juristic recognition of factual events. The former were the means of acquisition by civil law, *iure civile*; the latter, the means of acquisition by natural law, *iure naturali*. The former involved formal transfer, while the latter in the main were independent of formal mechanisms. As well as distinguishing between civil law and natural law methods of acquisition, modes of acquiring can also be categorized as either original, in the sense of being based solely upon the acts of the acquirer, or derivative, when the property rights are obtained by transfer from a previous owner. The natural law methods are predominantly original, while the civil law means are in the main derivative. The natural law methods will be considered first.

Occupatio

Occupatio is the acquisition of ownership in a thing by taking possession of it, it being a thing capable of being owned in private law and currently having no owner. The acquirer becomes owner immediately by reason of occupying it, *occupationis causa*.

One of the earliest instances of *occupatio* concerns the acquisition of wild animals by capture. The typical scenario is that of the hunter capturing game. It has been suggested that in early societies, where land would not have been individually owned, hunting and fishing would have been group activities giving rise to communal ownership of whatever was caught. In Roman law, it is widely held that chattels became capable of individual ownership at an earlier date than land, so that whoever caught a wild animal would be entitled to it regardless of where it was caught. With the advent of individual ownership of land, the question was bound to arise whether the landowner had any property in the wild animals which dwelt on his land. The Roman jurists denied this, always upholding the rule that wild animals belonged to no one until captured, and then only remained the property of their captor while in his control. If they escaped, they regained their freedom and became the property of no one once again.[11]

The question of what animals were wild and what amounted to capture and escape were therefore of importance and discussed by the Roman jurists at some length. Animals were wild according to the nature of the species to which they belonged, not according to the characteristics of the individual creature. Wild animals bred in captivity remained wild, and became free if they escaped despite their value. Wild animals, such as bees and pigeons, which while in captivity had the habit of leaving and returning, were not regarded as having escaped until they lost the habit of coming back, *animus revertendi*.

The Lombard laws extended this principle by insisting that a wild animal that bore any sign of ownership upon it or in its circumstances was not available for taking by capture.[12] Many of the Germanic laws also permitted wild animals to be pursued by their former owners in the aftermath of escape without immediate loss of ownership.[13] However, the biggest inroads upon the principle of *occupatio* came with feudalism, for the right to hunt and fish became a regalian right of the ruler, so that strict laws preventing the general populace from pursuing these activities were introduced. These restrictions were much resented, and in the wake of the French Revolution, equal rights to hunt and fish were reintroduced in the modern codes, and are generally freely exercisable on one's own lands and even over the lands of others, unless there is some sensitive activity being prosecuted there which precludes such intrusion and provided no damage is done.

The Roman jurists also awarded to the first taker the ownership of a new island which arose in the sea. Being an uncommon occurrence, the principle is not one that has exercised modern jurists overmuch, but has been very influential in the field of international law, where scholars such as Grotius adapted it to provide that unoccupied territories, or territories not in the occupation of Christian people, discovered by the subjects of a particular country became subject to the sovereignty of that State.[14] Much of the empires of the European nations were acquired under colour of this principle.

Whereas *occupatio* of moveable property is accepted in modern law, the Roman extension of the principle to land has not met with general acceptance. This partly reflects the unlikelihood in modern times of any land being ownerless. The Romans began to allow public lands to be occupied as private property in the later republic, and the Gracchan redistribution of land between 133 and 121 BC led to problems concerning certainty of title. In times of civil unrest or economic decline, agricultural estates were frequently abandoned by their owners, thus allowing for their occupation as ownerless property. The fall of the western empire also led to the abandonment of much land, which formed a recurrent theme of imperial legislation from the time of Diocletian to that of Justinian.[15] In Germanic law as well, waste land which had been cleared for cultivation was allowed to be acquired by the clearer, this being termed *aprisio* or *Neubruch*, and may have been one of the earliest forms of individual as opposed to communal or family property among the Germanic peoples.[16] Feudalism however left no room for such an approach, the lord or the king having an inherent right, eventually a *regalium*, to occupy any land which was ownerless. As with regalian rights over rivers and highways, this began as an extension of seigniorial or royal protection over such areas, but developed into a privilege. Land without an owner passed to the lord. Thus was born the right of the lord to succeed to lands when a deceased tenant had no heirs, as well as the right to take the lands of convicted criminals. Today, the State has succeeded to this regality in the case of property left ownerless, so called *bona vacantia*.[17]

In the case of moveables, however, the Roman approach has been successfully reintroduced against the claims of rulers and public authorities.[18] Germanic law had insisted that property found had to be proclaimed at the assembly or before a judge. This allowed a previous owner to claim it; otherwise it passed to the new owner. Mere finding was insufficient. Feudalism had again here substituted a regalian right in the lord or king, sometimes allowing the finder a claim for the expenses he incurred while looking after the thing while its legal condition was established. The mediaeval communes in Italy took a similar line, that articles found had to be proclaimed and in the absence of their owner being found passed to the State. Since the French Revolution however, the finder's claim has been preferred, the State having only a police function of receiving notice that property has been found. If the property is unclaimed after a certain period has elapsed, the finder may take it as his own.[19]

Accessio

If *occupatio* involves the acquisition of ownership through the activity of the acquirer, *accessio* is a passive method of acquisition. It is the principle according to which a person who already owns a thing acquires title to any lesser thing which is incorporated into it whether by the owner himself, nature or the actions of others. The principle can apply to the incorporation of moveables to moveables, moveables to immoveables, or immoveables to immoveables. In each case, ownership of the lesser thing is merged in that of the greater within which it is incorporated.

The Roman jurists discussed several examples of such accession. Many of the situations they discussed are still rehearsed in the modern codes. These include, for instance, the building or planting of things on another's land (*inaedificatio*, *plantatio*, *satio*), the tearing of land from the river bank by the force of a stream and its deposit farther downstream adjacent to the land of another (*avulsio*), the gradual accretion of deposits against a river bank or the formation of a new island in midstream (*alluvio*). While these instances of accession to immoveables are still discussed individually in the codes, accession to moveables is generally dealt with according to general principles. Gone are the Roman jurists' treatment of writing acceding to parchment but panels acceding to paintings, and purple thread being incorporated into the garment into which it is woven. The general principle today remains that the lesser is incorporated into the greater thing and becomes the property of the owner of that greater thing, but questions of good and bad faith have also appeared upon the scene. Thus, in modern civil law, the owner acquiring by *accessio* is required to indemnify the owner of the lesser thing if it cannot be separated from the greater if the owner of the lesser performed the incorporation in good faith or if he, the owner of the greater thing, had incorporated it in bad faith. Which is the greater and which the lesser also these days turns in part on respective economic value. In Roman law, the praetor had to some extent anticipated this approach by granting the owner of the lesser thing an *exceptio doli*, a defence of fraud, against the owner of the greater thing if he attempted to reclaim it without indemnifying the other. The situation described suggests that the incorporation might have taken place at the request of the owner who was obligated to pay for the service performed and the material used.[20]

Some of the examples discussed by the Roman jurists reflected the concerns of the age in which they wrote. Purple dye was extremely expensive, so that thread coloured purple might have a value greater than the garment into which it was woven. Nevertheless, the purple thread acceded to the tunic, and one wonders whether such incorporation was connected with the weaving of the purple hem, the *latus clavus*, into the toga of one who had achieved senatorial rank. The Roman jurists themselves commented on the irreconcilability of the rule which stated that writing acceded to the paper on which it was written while a panel upon which a picture had been painted acceded to the painting. The rule may however have been based upon the production of family portraits connected with the cult of deceased ancestors.[21]

Whatever was built or planted upon the land of another acceded to that land, the maxim being *superficies solo cedit*. The situations addressed are those in which one person builds a house on land belonging to another, or builds on his own land with materials belonging to another, or builds on another's land with materials belonging to a third. The background to these problems may lie in the crisis of the last century of the republic. At that time, the legal title to much land became obscure as a result of the reforms undertaken by the Gracchi in the second half of the second century BC. Cicero in the next century wrote of expulsions taking place from land, which again could cause confusion with regard to title. Further, considerable speculative building ventures took place around the year 100 BC,[22] and speculative builders may have obtained materials on credit to build houses on their clients' land or land bought on credit. Problems would then arise if they were unable to sell the properties. The Roman rules anticipate the modern approach by providing that if the building was done in bad faith, the landowner could treat the structure as a gift, whereas if done in good faith, he might not claim the structure as his without indemnifying the builder. There was however no chance of separating the materials from the land as the Twelve Tables forbade the pulling down of houses, but the materials could be reclaimed if at a future date the house collapsed, for instance in an earthquake. Some of these disputes may again have involved the inability of clients to pay builders for houses they had built for them; the property rules emphasize that their remedies lay in contract and not in claims relating to ownership.

The similarity of the modern provisions to the Roman texts belies the history of the intervening centuries, for the development of these principles has not been uninterrupted. The Germanic approach to these building problems was markedly at variance. Unless there was bad faith on the part of the builder, the structure built, like crops planted, on land belonging to another remained the property of the builder or planter. Germanic law saw no reason why what was built on land or planted in it could not be in separate ownership from the land itself.[23] The German territories upheld this approach throughout the Middle Ages and the Italian communes did likewise, although they allowed the owner of the land to purchase structures built thereon for value if he so wished.[24] Only with the Reception did the Germanic viewpoint begin to lose ground to the Roman, and the end result has been that the modern codes generally attempt to strike a balance between the rights of the landowner and those of the owner of the materials. Moreover, the readiness of many modern civilian systems to recognize the individual ownership of horizontal layers in blocks of flats exhibits a clear indebtedness to the Germanic heritage.

With *alluvio* also, the similarity of the modern discussions to the Roman texts is misleading, for it conceals the vacillations of principle caused by feudalism. Germanic law had nothing to say about accretions in the course of a river, but feudal law, having firstly placed waterways under the protection of the ruler as things not in private ownership, then assumed regalian rights therein in the same manner as fishing in rivers and using them for navigation became subject to the ruler's pleasure and a source of revenue for him. Islands formed in a stream therefore were asserted to be the property of the lord by regalian right. Only with the revival of the Roman rules in the modern codifications did the rights of the riparian landowners again supersede those of the territorial lord.

Fructum perceptio

In the same way as things which are incorporated into greater things become the property of the owner of the greater thing, so things produced by an item of property are acquired by its owner. The classic example is that of natural fruits produced by the soil or on plants, but the young of animals and even the rent or income produced by investment property falls under the same principle. A distinction is sometimes made between natural fruits requiring no contribution from the owner for their production, industrial fruits which require human labour, and civil or commercial fruits which are incremental to ownership but only fruits in an artificial sense. These last comprise such things as rents, dividends, and so on.

Both in Roman law and in the modern codes, fruits usually accrue to the person who owns the thing which produces them. The correspondence of the Roman and modern rules belies the history of the subject which is instructive with regard to the issues involved. Germanic law was wont to award the fruits to the person whose labour had produced them. Thus, if for instance land was sold before harvest, the previous owner could claim the fruits which he had planted and nurtured. In some localities, and in the Italian communes in particular, the rule became fixed that if land were sold after March 1st in any year, the fruits throughout that year should accrue to the previous owner. Some communities, Modena for instance, drew a distinction between natural fruits and civil fruits, the former going to him whose labour had produced them, the latter always to the current owner.[25]

Although the Reception brought the Roman rule into contact with the Germanic tradition, it did not oust it immediately. The Prussian *Landrecht* continued to recognize the possibility of a separate ownership in natural fruits from that of the parent property although the BGB has adopted the Roman principle. Swiss law however allows the person who has laboured to produce the fruits to seek an indemnity from the current owner.[26]

The underlying conflict of principle between the Roman and the German approaches is that between the rights of the owner of property and those of the person who has laboured to produce the goods. This tension is one which has been identified as existing within Roman law itself; for instance, some hold that *occupatio* favours the claims of the active hunter against those of the passive landowner upon whose land the game is taken, while *accessio* generally favours the passive owner against the active labourer, as in *inaedificatio*. The modern law comes down in favour of the owner in cases of the separation of fruits, but in a modern market economy the price of property can rise and fall to reflect the benefit of a harvest which is approaching or one which has been gathered. Much is therefore left to the parties to make their own wise or foolish bargain.

Thesauri inventio

The same tension between the landowner and he whose efforts bring some thing to light has affected the development of the law relating to the finding of treasure, treasure being precious metals concealed in the ground the ownership of which is no longer traceable. Roman law vacillated as to who should be the owner of such treasure when it was found. The contenders were the owner of the land upon which the treasure was discovered, the finder and the State. Justinian's compilations followed a rule attributed to the emperor Hadrian in the second century AD to the effect that treasure found by the landowner on his own land belonged to him; treasure found by chance by another was to be shared equally between the finder and the landowner; treasure found by deliberate search by another was to go to the landowner alone.[27] Only if the land upon which the treasure was found belonged to the State would the State get a share, being entitled to what otherwise would have gone to the landowner according to the principles aforementioned. It would appear that in earlier times, treasure had once been the property of the landowner and in the later republic that of the fisc; Hadrian appears to have struck a compromise between the interests of the finder and those of the landowner. It is interesting that during the proscriptions which occurred during the dictatorship of Sulla in the 80s and 70s BC, it is recorded that those proscribed frequently buried hoards of coins which otherwise would have been confiscated. The rediscovery of these hoards may have necessitated Hadrian's legislation.

Germanic law treated treasure in the same way as minerals excavated or mined from the ground; it belonged to the State as a *regalium*.[28] The same rule applied in the French kingdom during the thirteenth century as witnessed by the *Établissements de St. Louis*, but as Roman influence infiltrated throughout France it was provided that the finder should be allowed a quarter share, leaving the king with the other three-quarters. By the sixteenth century, Loysel was able to adumbrate a true compromise solution between the native and civilian approaches, awarding one third each to the king, the landowner and the finder.[29]

Although in Italy, the Germanic regalian right formed the basis for Lombard development, the Carolingians allowed monastic landowners a third share. The *Libri Feudorum* allowed finders a portion, employing a distinction in Roman fashion between deliberate search and chance finding. A finder would only benefit from a chance discovery, otherwise the landowner was to take alone.[30] The Roman approach of dividing between the finder and the landowner made progress even in Germany after the Reception, with equal division becoming the general rule provided there had not been a deliberate search. This approach is witnessed by the Prussian *Landrecht*, the Austrian and Saxon codes, and the BGB. The Swiss civil code gives treasure to the owner of the thing in which it is found, allowing the finder an indemnity for his trouble. Some parts of Germany, such as Schleswig, had held on to the regalian approach until unification.[31]

The Roman division between finder and landowner, which for some encapsulates the tension between labour and landownership as a source of acquisition, has been adopted by the vast majority of modern civilian systems.

Specificatio

The tension between labour and property ownership in the acquisition of title is particularly well illustrated in the natural law mode of acquisition which has become known as *specificatio*.[32] *Specificatio* concerns the manufacture of a new thing, a *nova species*, by one who was not the owner of the raw materials out of which it was created. Although the modern codes state the problem and its solution as one of general principle, the Roman jurists cited instances of the problem. These included making wine out of another's grapes, flour out of another's corn, olive oil out of another's olives, a statue out of another's gold or silver, and so on. The question was who should own the end product, the owner of the raw materials or the manufacturer. The tension between the labour principle and the property principle resulted in a division of opinion among the Roman jurists, those of the Sabinian school preferring the claims of the property owners while their Proculian brethren sided with the manufacturers. Some see in the clash a difference of underlying philosophy between the schools, while others emphasize that to favour the manufacturer is to treat him as taking the new thing, previously ownerless, by *occupatio*, whilst to align oneself with the owner of the raw materials is to view the occurrence as a type of *accessio* in which a new form accedes to the pre-existing substance of the materials.[33]

Whatever the underlying nature of the dispute, it proved difficult to reconcile. A middle opinion, the *media sententia*, argued that the outcome should depend upon whether the new thing could be reduced to the materials from which it had been made. If it could, as with a gold or silver statue, the new thing should belong to the owner of the raw materials; if it could not, as with wine and grapes, oil and olives, flour and corn, it should belong to the manufacturer. This *media sententia* was approved by Justinian and promulgated as the solution to the problem in his compilations.[34] There was however general agreement that if the manufacturer had used partly his own materials in the process of manufacture and partly the materials of another, the end product was always the manufacturer's.[35] Whoever owned the end product was however under a duty to indemnify the other either for the value of their materials or the value of their work. The claims of the owner to the new thing could be resisted by the defence of fraud, *exceptio doli*, if such indemnity was not forthcoming.

Ancient Germanic law would appear to have had no doubts with regard to the solution. According to the *Schwabenspiegel*, the new thing belonged to the owner of the materials. Indeed, the manufacturer was liable to pay damages to the owner for any loss of value incurred by his work. The Reception however brought the Roman rule into operation in the German territories, by which time it had passed through the hands of the Glossators and Commentators. Although these did not question Justinian's solution, they had by their *communis opinio* extended the principle to other factual situations and thereby had facilitated the articulation of the underlying principle. The Humanists challenged Justinian's solution, arguing that the question should be settled according to the relative value of the materials as opposed to the new thing, allowing an appropriate indemnity to the losing party. Hugo Grotius and the natural law school rejected more than just the solutions offered by previous generations; they refused to address the dispute in terms of awarding ownership to one party or the other, preferring to impose common ownership of the new thing upon the parties.[36]

The modern civil codes all address the problem in terms of which of the parties should be the owner, but there is no more consistency in the solutions they provide than among the Roman jurists. Some such as France and Spain allow the owner of the raw materials to be owner of the new thing, while Germany and Italy award it to the manufacturer. All however temper their solutions by the introduction of such elements as the need for good faith and by insisting that a marked disparity of value between the raw materials and the end product should always upset a contrary solution provided by their general rule, whichever party it favoured.[37] *Specificatio* provides a signal instance of a wealth of juristic discussion achieving very little progress after two millenia in terms of a generally acceptable solution, although the problem itself has been marvellously clarified, and in some ways the different legislative approaches of the modern codes do not produce significantly different results in practice.

Commixtio and Confusio

Where significant amounts of solids, such as corn, or liquids belonging to different persons became mixed or confused in such a manner that they could not be separated, Roman law allowed the resulting mass to be owned jointly by the parties in proportion to the contributions their property had made to the mass. Either could then demand the division of the mass in order to obtain his share by means of the *actio communi dividundo*. The same solution of regarding the resultant mass as being in common ownership, with the parties having shares therein proportional to their contributions, is to be found in the modern codes. Bad faith can vitiate a claim to common ownership.

It is worth noting that the natural law school's solution to the problem of *specificatio* treated the new thing as the result of the mixing or confusing of materials and labour.

Usucapio and Prescription

Usucapio and prescription are both original modes of acquisition, but are not natural modes in that they rely upon legal rules rather than factual events for their validity. They resemble *occupatio* in that they are both based upon the acquirer's taking possession of a thing, but differ from *occupatio* in that the thing is not a *res nullius*, belonging to no one, but is the property of someone else. Nevertheless, provided the acquirer is in good faith, his possession of the thing for a certain length of time will convert his possession into ownership. In the modern codes, this period of time will vary according to the nature of the property involved and the degree of good or bad faith involved on the part of the acquirer.

Usucapio has its roots in Roman law and is a method of acquisitive prescription, that is it acts so as to raise a title in the acquirer and not to extinguish the title of the previous owner. In ancient Rome, to acquire by *usucapio*, five criteria had to be satisfied. The thing had to be capable of private ownership, it had to be acquired by the taker in a manner susceptible of raising a title - that is by buying for instance but not by hiring, the acquirer had to take possession in good faith, the possession had to be as owner, that is not by force, stealth or permission, and he had to have the thing in his juristic possession for the required length of time. In classical Roman law, the period of time required was one year in the case of moveables or two years in the case of land. The periods may reflect the fact that in an early agricultural community, whereas moveables would be used publicly every year, land lay fallow in alternate years, so that an adverse possession might not be noticed. This also points to the likelihood that *usucapio* was originally, as its name suggests, a taking by use rather than by long possession, which it had become in classical law.[38] Good faith was only required at the time of taking possession; it was not material that the acquirer later discovered the existence of another's claim, provided the thing was not stolen. Stolen property could not be acquired by *usucapio*.

Only Italic land, that is land in Italy, was capable of being privately owned. Land in the Roman provinces belonged to the State.[39] Title to provincial land was therefore not Roman civil law ownership, *dominium*. Nevertheless, its occupiers were treated as having title and acquisitive prescription of such title was possible. It was called *longi temporis praescriptio*. Unlike *usucapio*, however, this method of prescription was originally extinctive rather than acquisitive, that is the passage of time extinguished the title of the previous owner who had taken no steps to recover the land. If both parties were resident in the same province, the period of time required was ten years, but if they were not, the period was twenty. In both cases, the new owner's adverse possession had to have a good commencement, *bonum initium*, basically good faith and just *causa*. It was however later accepted that by *longissimi temporis praescriptio* even an unjust possession or one undertaken in bad faith would be sufficient to ground a title after thirty or forty years. Justinian fused the institutions of *usucapio* and prescription and reformed them so that both became methods of acquisitive prescription, *usucapio* applying to moveables and requiring possession for three years, while *longi temporis praescriptio* was to apply to land everywhere, the periods being ten years *inter praesentes* and twenty years *inter absentes*. *Longissimi temporis praescriptio* remained extinctive, destroying claims to either moveables or immoveables not pursued within thirty or forty years and that regardless of whether there was just cause or good faith present.

In that the German tribes who succeeded to the lands of the western empire had followed a nomadic existence, they had no system for prescription of land, although in some parts claims for chattels could not be pursued after a year and a day had elapsed. The Roman rules however had their influence, so that Rothari provided that a person who had been in possession for five years was entitled to assert his ownership thereafter by oath, and by judicial duel if the oath were challenged. Grimwald later provided that possession for thirty years entitled the possessor to prove his ownership by oath alone, and Liutprand finalised the conversion to Roman ideas by providing that possession for thirty years of itself conferred ownership. The Church however developed the Roman concepts rather differently in that, although it followed the Roman time-scales, it required that the possessor be in good faith not only at the time of taking the property but throughout the period of prescription.[40]

Acquisitive prescription made its way into Germany and northern France with the Reception, the Roman periods of ten, twenty and thirty years being generally adopted, although not without considerable local variation. In France, the customs recorded in the sixteenth century witness to the periods of ten and twenty years requiring good faith and just title, while thirty years possession would ground ownership even without those elements. In some parts of Germany, the practice had arisen of recording title in land books, a practice which left no room for the possibility of prescription although it was established, again on analogy with the civilian approach, that registration for thirty years amounted to conclusive proof of title.[41]

The provisions of the modern codes display the influence of these successive phases of development. Acquisitive prescription is widely known as *usucapio*, the period of possession varying according to whether there is good faith and just title or not, and also according to the nature of the property concerned, whether it is land, a moveable or a registered moveable. Thirty years remains in many systems the period for final extinction of a claim of any sort.

Transfer

Property can also be acquired by transfer from a previous owner. Such acquisition is not original but derivative. It may be regulated by formal requirements imposed by a particular legal system or simply involve the giving of physical possession by the former owner to the new owner without the need of any legal formalities. Most legal systems demand that formalities of some sort be employed for certain types of property or upon certain occasions. Thus, whereas transfers between living persons, *inter vivos* transfers, are often informal, transfers intended to take effect upon death normally require some formalities in order to ensure the existence of proof regarding the deceased's wishes. Informal transfer *inter vivos* by handing over the thing from one person to the other has been categorized as a natural law method of acquisition known as *traditio*. Formal methods of transfer were classified by the Roman jurists, together with *usucapio*, as methods of acquisition *iure civili*.

Whenever property rights are acquired by transfer, they are lost by the transferee. Such loss may be voluntary, as with *inter vivos* gifts, or involuntary, when factors independent of the owner's wishes determine the cessation of his rights. Most obviously this occurs upon the owner's death, but can also occur for instance if confiscation of all or some property follows upon a criminal conviction, where creditors force the owner into bankruptcy or where the State expropriates a person's property. An owner may conversely be restricted from alienating his property against the wishes of others. These issues will be considered in the following and succeeding sections.

5 Transfer of Ownership

Traditio and Formal Transfers

Both Roman and Germanic law agreed that ownership could not pass from one person to another without a transfer of possession. Mere agreement to transfer ownership was not sufficient; delivery of the thing had to follow. This was in stark contrast to the Greek approach which allowed ownership to pass to the purchaser upon payment of the purchase price.[42] The only significance which the Romans attached to payment was that, according to some sources, even if delivery of possession had been effected, ownership would not pass to a purchaser until payment was made, that is unless a sale on credit had been agreed.[43]

That ownership should pass was a matter for agreement between the parties. Such an agreement might be, for instance, one of sale or one that a gift should be made. In either case, the intention that ownership should be transferred would be clear. In Roman law, however, intention to transfer was not enough; physical transfer had to take place as well. In respect of things which were not *res mancipi*, delivery of the possession, *traditio*, was all that was required. This was most obviously effected by actual physical transfer of the thing, but could be achieved by other means. Thus, if the thing were already in the control of the new owner, as where it had been lent to him and was now being given, his being told to keep it as owner was sufficient with no need to give back and retransfer. This was called *traditio brevi manu*. In the converse case, called *constitutio possessorium*, the present owner gave title to the acquirer while retaining the thing, for instance on loan or on hire. Property which did not allow of convenient physical delivery might be transferred by indication from a distance, *traditio longa manu*, suitable for example in the case of land or a ship in dock. Finally, transfer could be effected symbolically by giving the transferee some token representative of ownership of the thing, such as a twig or clod of earth in the case of land, or the keys to a building and so forth.

Res mancipi were economically the most important forms of property in early Rome, being slaves, beasts of draught and burden, land and rights of way and of carrying water over land. *Dominium* in these could only be transferred by formal methods of which there were two, *mancipatio* and *in iure cessio*. Both involved the presence of a witness or witnesses to bear record of the transfer. In the case of *mancipatio*, these were the five witnesses and the person who held the bronze scales which the transferee struck with a bronze rod when making his declaration that the thing was his by Quiritary right. *Mancipatio* was a formal, almost ritualistic, ceremony. In *in iure cessio*, the witness was the magistrate who heard the transferee assert that the thing was his by Quiritary right and who, in the absence of a counterclaim from the transferor who was also present, awarded the thing to the transferee. *In iure cessio* therefore made use of the trappings of litigation to effect a conveyance, a device which had a considerable future before it.

Relatively simple as these devices were, they could involve the parties to the conveyance in inconvenience. They had to go before the magistrate for *cessio in iure* and a cast of characters had to be assembled for *mancipatio*. The practice therefore developed of conveying *res mancipi* by simple *traditio*, which allowed the transferee to subsequently acquire *dominium* by *usucapio*, having taken possession in good faith and for a just cause. The praetor even protected the interim possession of the transferee, who became known as the bonitary owner as distinct from the transferor who remained owner in civil law until the period of *usucapio* was completed.

The other device which was frequently used in later Roman law to either supplement or circumvent the need for formal ceremonies was the use of a written instrument to bear witness to the transfer.[44] A deed could be drawn up recording that the *mancipatio* had taken place, and this could indeed be done even if the ceremony had not in fact occurred. The same number of witnesses would be employed, but it would not be necessary to have the property present at the signing, thus avoiding the need either to travel to a farm or other estate or to bring large numbers of animals or quantities of goods to a particular location. Greek influence within the Byzantine empire encouraged the use of writing both to record and effect legal transactions.[45] Justinian abolished the distinction between *res mancipi* and *res nec mancipi*, leaving *traditio* as the sole method of transferring property in Roman civil law. The informality of this method assisted in establishing the use of the written instrument as a means of proving the intention to transfer ownership, replacing the oral enunciations and formal ceremonies of the earlier law.

It is possible that both *mancipatio* and *in iure cessio* had their roots in formal transfers effected before the *comitia* in very early times.[46] If this were so, then it marks a correspondence with early Germanic law. There too transfer had originally to take place before the assembly of the people and later before witnesses. The Germanic law like Roman law was not prepared to accept that ownership could pass by agreement alone, but required a transfer of possession. In Lombard times, three phases were distinguished: firstly, the agreement to transfer, which was sometimes witnessed by the exchange of a token such as a glove, a stick or, later, a handshake; secondly, the actual or symbolic transfer of the thing itself, and thirdly, particularly in the case of land, acts by the acquirer which publicised the fact that he was now owner. The first gave the acquirer a good title to the thing; the second marked the transferor's release of his interest and the third the acquisition of ownership by the transferee. The second and third stages were eventually conflated into one conveyance. The Lombards provided for the acquisition of title to be witnessed by a solemn question and answer, while *traditio* was accomplished by the handing over of a written instrument which recorded the transfer. This might be signed by a notary and witnessed. Whereas the Roman approach was to see the document as a proof of the transfer - *traditio cartae*, the Germanic view was that the transfer was effected symbolically by the handing over of the deed itself - *traditio per cartam*. Other symbols could be used, some natural such as twigs or clods of earth, some conventional such as a rod, *festuca*, or a lance, *gaira*. The Lombard transfer became known as *gairathinx*, because the *gaira* was transferred in the assembly or *thinx*.

Traditio per cartam was widely employed by the Franks, among whom it was customary for the charter to be placed with other symbols upon the ground by the transferor to be raised, levied, by the transferee. This was often done in court as a record of the transaction made. Such transfers of land came to be registered in the court as proof of their occurrence. The Italian communes of the Middle Ages were keen that such transfers should take place publicly, before magistrates or the town council, or else that they should be preceded by the calling of banns to inquire whether there was any objection to the transfer. Registration of transfers eventually became necessary in Italy as well, as for instance in Naples and Venice from the sixteenth century.[47]

The calling of *bannies* was also a feature of land transfers in Brittany, where, as with the banns of marriage, they had to be called on three Sundays. The absence of objection would then be reported to the tribunal where the formalities would be effected. In northern France generally, transfers of land had to take place before the lord, preserving the feudal requirement that seisin of the land, that is possession as owner, required investiture at the lord's hands. His court could record the transfer. In southern France, the *pays de droit écrit*, *traditio per cartam* was the rule.

It was in Germany however that registration of transfer made the greatest progress. The churches kept books of land transactions for their own purposes and from the eleventh century so did certain towns and parishes within towns. From the thirteenth century in northern Germany, it became customary for all land transactions to be recorded, particularly in those towns which took their laws from those of Magdeburg and Lübeck, while in the fourteenth century the widespread practice of surrendering title in court in southern Germany gave way to registration of the transaction. In Bohemia and other Slavic lands, land tablets recording such transfers came to be employed and there developed throughout Germany the concept of the land register or *Grundbuch*, as sole evidence of title to land. Although the

Reception of Roman law emphasized afresh the consensual nature of property transfer, the need for formal authentication of such agreements prevailed and public registration of all land transactions was demanded by the Prussian *Landrecht* from 1783 until 1831, and this requirement remained in force in Bavaria until the BGB was promulgated in 1900. Modern German law bases title to land upon registration in land books or *Grundbücher*.[48]

Whereas registration of title developed from mediaeval times in Germany, Italy has continued to require transfer to be effected by deed and that those deeds of transfer be registered by notaries, who were originally court officials transcribing documents which recorded what had been effected by judicial decision. In France, where *traditio per cartam* was general in the South and deeds utilized to recite fictitious record of surrender and regrant of seisin in the North, the sixteenth century saw the adoption of writing as essential evidence of gifts in the *ordonnance* of Villers-Cotteret of 1539. Contracts involving property over 100 *livres* in value also had to be registered to be effective from 1626. Transcription of deeds was introduced as a requirement for validity throughout the country following the Revolution, but the *Code civil*, in a remarkable return to pure Romanist principles, opted to make transfer of title dependent upon consent alone, a point of view that had been upheld by certain of the natural lawyers, such as Grotius and Pufendorf, and by institutional writers such as Pothier. However, the inconveniences of such a position led to transcription of deeds in notarial registers being reintroduced as a general requirement in France in 1855.[49] Thus, notarial registration of land transfers became necessary.

The idea that delivery is essential to pass title in chattels was abandoned in French law on the basis of natural law teaching, so that agreement to convey is today sufficient in itself to pass title to chattels in those systems which follow the French *Code civil*. Formal transfer had been abandoned in mediaeval German law in relation to moveable property, so that simple *traditio* was generally accepted as sufficient to pass title. It was however also accepted that a deed could be used to transfer title to a moveable thing symbolically, but German law and the systems which have followed it continue to require delivery and not mere agreement to pass title even in chattels, other than in exceptional cases, such as ships, where the French approach has been followed.[50] Ships, cars and aeroplanes are however classified as registrable moveables, transfer of which requires registration. Thus, the Roman rules on transfer of property have been overtaken by the need for transfers of immoveables and certain moveables to be effected by writing, a step anticipated by the later Roman law, and although delivery remains a feature of chattel transfers in the German branch of the civilian tradition, the natural lawyers' emphasis upon the sufficiency of consent has displaced it in the systems which have followed the French *Code civil*.

Restrictions upon Alienation

The concept of individual ownership espoused by the French *Code civil*, whereby the owner is free to do as he wishes with his own property, may today appear commonplace. At the time, it was revolutionary. For centuries, there had been restrictions upon the right of an owner to do as he wished with his own; indeed, the question of whether ownership in the sense of *dominium* rested with a single private individual was not beyond challenge.[51] In particular, owners of land in previous centuries had not been free to dispose of such property without reference to the interests of their family, their neighbours and their lords.

The roots of these restrictions lie both in the circumstances of the later Roman empire and the development of the Germanic laws of landholding. In the later empire, neighbours were responsible for the payment of taxes to the State on each other's lands. Thus, if land was left unoccupied, the neighbouring owners found their liability increased. It was therefore of interest to them that, if one of their number sought to dispose of his property, it was acquired by someone able to fulfil his fiscal obligations to the State, otherwise the burden would pass to the neighbouring landowners. Their consent therefore became necessary for an effective transfer.

The Germanic tribes, being nomadic, did not at first have laws concerning land ownership, but as they began to settle and establish themselves in specific territories, so land was recognized as being the property of certain communities or family groups. Individual ownership was not recognized, the head of the household, *Hausherr*, having management and control, but not being free to do as he wished with the property. In Lombard Italy, such family lands were called *fara*, and had to descend from the father to the children. Although he might divide his lands in equal parts between his children during his lifetime, he had no power of alienation outside the family nor of testamentary disposition upon death. This lack of freedom was opposed by the Church, in part because it prevented gifts of land being made to it.

In the Frankish empire, a distinction was made between land which was inherited and could not be alienated, the *propres*, and land which had been acquired by other means. Rights of free alienation began to be recognized over the latter. Likewise, the advance of feudalism introduced a further distinction, between lands which pertained to the family, allods, and those which were held of a lord, benefices. The former needed the consent of the family for alienation, the latter of the feudal superior. Feudalism also undermined the rights of the family generally in the inheritance of land, preferring the claims of the eldest son according to the system of primogeniture. This meant that increasingly it was his consent that was required for a transfer by his father, and in parts of Germany this led to the practice of his having a year and a day to invalidate such a transfer made without his agreement.

The total ban on alienation without consent gradually became replaced by the right of the neighbours, the community, the family or the lord to reclaim the land if it was alienated without their consent. If the alienation had been for value, so that the family patrimony was not diminished by the transaction, such a claim might not be permitted, or the heir might be expected to indemnify the purchaser in the event of his deciding to reclaim the land. This was not always required, as purchasers should be aware of the need for consent and therefore would be aware of the risk they were taking. Between consent for the sale and redemption of property sold lay a third possibility, namely the right of certain persons - neighbours or relatives - to have first refusal of property which it was intended to sell, that is a right of pre-emption. This is also widely encountered.[52] In Italy, the right to redeem property sold outside of the family became limited to certain types of transaction only, namely sales and equivalent alienations, such as grants in *emphyteusis* or the creation of hypothecs.[53] In France, it was also accepted that an owner might sell family property in situations of emergency, such as hardship caused by poverty, although relatives retained a right of pre-emption and redemption upon payment of an indemnity remained possible.[54]

By the thirteenth century, ecclesiastical pressure and the growth of trade and commerce combined to encourage freedom of alienation. There was however resistance. The *Sachsenspiegel* continued to demand the consent of the heirs given in the communal assembly for inherited land to be alienated. The German higher nobility devised ways of entailing their lands so as to keep them permanently within their families and attached to their titles of nobility. The lesser nobles could not make use of these devices, called *stemmatica*, *bona aviatica* or *Stammgüter* which were given the higher nobility by special dynastic statutes called *Hausgesetze*. Instead, they developed from the Roman *fideicommissa quod familiae relinquitur* an entirely different institution allowing entails to be created by agreement, which were termed family *fideicommissa* or *Stammgutsstiftungen*. These became part of the *ius commune* regarding property ownership in Germany.[55]

It was not until the French Revolution that these devices began to be swept away in the face of the assertion of the rights of the individual owner. The rights of lords to restrict alienations by their tenants were abolished with the hierarchy of feudal tenures, and those of neighbours and the family were abolished in 1790. The imposition of the *Code civil* by Napoleonic conquest led to the termination of rights of pre-emption and redemption in many parts of Italy and of *fideicommissa* and noble entails in parts of Germany, but they were restored in many places when the yoke of foreign conquest was removed. Nevertheless, the individualistic and egalitarian spirit of legal development during the nineteenth century militated against their maintaining a place in the national codifications.[56] Today, the rights of relatives are safeguarded only by the rules of forced inheritance which safeguard their interests against those of the owner, while the interests of neighbours are largely protected in public rather than private law by the growth of regulations relating to the use to which property is put and the activities which may take place on it.

Restrictions upon the alienation of land were also imposed during the Middle Ages to prevent land passing to owners in whose hands it would be inalienable. Such institutions were known as mortmain corporations, bodies with a dead hand in that they could not pass on their property. The Church which had so supported freedom of alienation by individuals was one such dead hand, and during the thirteenth century many rulers acted to prevent land becoming inalienable in perpetuity through acquisition by the Church. In 1231, a constitution of Frederick II supplied the principle which was to become general throughout southern Italy and in the following two centuries was to spread to the communes of the north, namely that land given to the Church had to be resold by it within a year. Other rulers demanded that the Church pay a tax upon lands which were given to it in mortmain so as to compensate for its removal from the market.[57]

In Germany, moveable property was also treated as becoming part of a special ecclesiastical patrimony when given to a church and from this there developed the concept of group ownership of certain things attendant to, for instance, a partnership. Although this perspective was adopted into the *ius commune*, it was attacked as being contrary to the individualistic notions of ownership current in the nineteenth century, but it has survived into modern German law as a form of property ownership and not just as a contractual relation between persons which affects property.[58] The development of corporate personality in law has in large measure overcome the problems of mortmain experienced in the Middle Ages.

Expropriation and Forced Alienation

The mediaeval requirement that religious orders sell land acquired by them within a year was in effect a form of forced alienation. Unlike the requirement that purchasers of lands without family or seigniorial consent return it to the heir or the lord, such compulsion was not based upon the other party having a greater right which had been overridden by the transfer. Resale by mortmain corporations was required to satisfy social policy not justice.

Just so in modern civilian systems, the need of the State for items of property is sometimes allowed to override the rights of its private law owners. Such compulsory purchase or requisition by the State is known as expropriation, but is sometimes justified by the claim that the State has a superior title, its eminent domain. Such a view belongs more to the hierarchical world of feudalism than to that of modern civil law, where the State is viewed as existing in order to uphold private rights such as ownership. It marks a direct conflict between Roman ideas of justice and Germanic and feudal concepts of regalian right.

Unknown in the ancient and early mediaeval world, it was in the Italian communes and the German cities that this concept first made its presence felt. Communal life occasionally required that the rights of private owners be sacrificed for the benefit of the community as a whole, as for instance in the taking of land to provide defences or to install drains and other public amenities. The Glossators and their successors struggled manfully to limit such incursions upon private right or else to attempt to find a justification for its breach. In general, this found issue in the principle that compensation be provided. It was the Natural lawyers and Grotius who first provided a clear rationale for the practice, arguing that the State had an eminent domain, the *ius eminens*, in all property, but under the influence of Montesquieu and the concept of fundamental rights, it was settled that this right to expropriate could only be exercised for a good reason, *iusta causa*, and upon provision of full compensation. In France, it was settled by 1810 that the existence of cause and the adequacy of the recompense should both be settled by judicial determination if necessary.[59] The natural law principles were incorporated in the Prussian *Landrecht*, and the laws of both Bavaria and Austria, while during the nineteenth century, the French approach influenced the many statutes passed on the subject as land had to be purchased for the coming of the railways.[60] Romano-canonical ideas of justice thus came to control the assertion of Germanic feudal regalian right as manifested in the powers of the modern State.

The mediaeval Italian communes also gave private owners certain powers of compulsory purchase as against their neighbours. These could only be used in certain circumstances, basically where there was a just cause. Such circumstances included where for instance a person's property was too small to be viable while a neighbour's property was more than sufficient for his needs. A compulsory purchase of an enlargement was possible. Land might also be acquired to facilitate passage to a highway, and in modern law there remains a right to claim an easement of necessity to provide access to a landlocked property.[61]

One of the disadvantages of dividing property equally among a deceased person's children is that it can lead to inheritances becoming smaller and smaller in succeeding generations so that they are no longer viable estates. German law has evolved two devices, one to prevent this occurring, the other to remedy it. Under the *Hofrecht*, a father is allowed to choose which of his heirs shall inherit a small farm to the exclusion of the others, while a municipal authority is allowed to regroup small parcels of land in the ownership of inhabitants so that each retains land of the same value but in more convenient blocks. This is called *Arrondirung*.[62] Modern Italian law also prevents smallholdings being divided upon inheritance to such an extent that they become non-viable. In such circumstances, they must be sold as viable units.[63]

Finally, the rights of a private owner can of course be overridden by the claims of his creditors if he is insolvent. The history of the law relating to security and the execution of judgement debts will be treated hereafter.[64] It is however worth noting that modern French law has created since 1909 the concept of family land, whereby a small portion of a person's property can be notarially designated family land and thus be unavailable for the satisfaction of subsequent creditors in the event of bankruptcy, remaining instead as a means of support for the family.[65]

6 Rights over the Property of Others

The absolute conception of ownership adopted by modern civil law in the French *Code civil* militates against the notion that other persons can restrict an owner's rights with regard to his property. Yet all civil law systems recognize the existence of such rights. Firstly, an owner is not permitted to use his property or conduct activities upon it which injure the legal rights of his neighbours. If he does so, he will be liable for the wrongs he has caused. Such liability will arise under the law relating to civil wrongs which is a part of the law of obligations. Nevertheless, it does amount to a restriction upon the rights of an owner, in that it places owners under a legal duty to respect the interests of their neighbours.

Owners may also restrict their rights through agreements made with their neighbours. Therefore, if an owner of one property enters into a binding contract with one or more of his neighbours the terms of which limit his right to use his property in certain ways or to perform certain activities on it, even if they would not apart from the contract amount to unlawful interference with the neighbours' interests, the owner will be bound by the terms of the agreement he has made. Again, his liability arises from obligation and does not give his neighbour a property right.

If an owner's activity is lawful and he has not agreed to limit it by contract, then his neighbours have no right in law to prevent him in that behaviour. However, modern civil law has developed a concept by which an otherwise perfectly lawful activity is rendered unlawful because the owner's only motive in prosecuting it is to annoy or damage his neighbour's enjoyment, even though the annoyance or damage does not amount to a legal injury. This can take one of two forms. Firstly, an owner will not be allowed to succeed in an action enforcing his own rights against a neighbour if the only motive for pursuing it is spite, there being no genuine interference with the comfort and enjoyment of the owner by the neighbour's activities although technically they invade the owner's rights. To bring an action in such circumstances is deemed by modern French law, for example, as an abuse of rights, and the action will be disallowed. This is reminiscent of the Roman praetor's discretion not to grant an action if the circumstances were not meritorious. Secondly, an owner who prosecutes otherwise perfectly lawful activities on his own property will be liable for damage caused to a neighbour if his only reason for indulging in that behaviour is to annoy or harm his neighbour. This is known in modern civil law as *aemulatio vicini*, and is an interesting concept in that it derives from a Roman law ban upon public building which was inspired solely by the wish to emulate neighbouring towns - *aemulatio alterius civitatis*. Transferred to private law by the natural law school and the institutional writers of the seventeenth and eighteenth centuries, *aemulatio* has acquired the technical meaning of 'spite', so that *aemulatio vicini* is conduct whose sole aim is to spite one's neighbour, and having thus no merit is rendered unlawful.[66] This suggests that an owner's right to do as he wishes on his own property regardless of the effect on his neighbours is limited if the effect is deleterious and he was inspired by an unjust cause.

None of the above gives the neighbour any property right over the other's things. Obligations only exist between the parties. They are nevertheless rights over the property of others, but rights *in personam*. Civil law has however from Roman times recognized that rights *in rem* may also exist, *iura in re aliena*. In Roman law such rights were called servitudes, and according to Justinian's classification, which may not reflect the views of the classical jurists, servitudes were of two sorts, praedial and personal. Praedial servitudes, which some modern civilian systems consider to be the only kind of servitude, are those which burden one piece of land called the servient tenement for the benefit of another estate called the dominant tenement. Such servitudes are capable of existing in perpetuity but can only confer rights and impose duties upon persons who own the respective tenements. They are rights which have to be appurtenant to land. They cannot exist for the benefit of persons other than the landowners. Personal servitudes on the other hand, as their name suggests, exist for the benefit of particular persons who do not have to be owners of a dominant tenement. They operate over the property of another person, but that property need not be an immoveable as in the case of praedial servitudes. Personal servitudes are of limited duration, normally being confined to the lifetime of the beneficiary or a maximum period set by law in the case of juristic persons. The modern civilian systems which confine the title of servitude to those which the Romans called praedial categorize personal servitudes as rights in property less than ownership or as limited forms of ownership.

Praedial Servitudes

The Roman jurists subdivided praedial servitudes into two categories - rustic and urban. Rustic praedial servitudes were *res mancipi*, being essential features of the early agricultural economy of Rome. They were four in number: *iter*, a right of way over another's land on foot; *actus*, a right of way over another's land driving cattle; *via*, a right of way over another's land in a vehicle, such as a cart, so that the way had to be properly metalled and at least eight-feet wide generally and sixteen-feet wide at bends; and *aquaeductus*, the right to draw or carry water across another's land. All involved activity by the owner of the dominant tenement on the servient tenement. The Sabinians recognized other such positive agricultural uses as rustic servitudes, such as burning lime, *calcis coquendi*, and pasturing cattle, *pecoris pascendi*, and some believe these also to have been *res mancipi*.[67]

The four original rustic praedial servitudes are thought to have been capable of private ownership before land itself. This envisages an early Rome in which land was communally owned and periodically shared among the citizens who were given rights of way and of irrigation over one another's parcels. They were rights originally and primarily enjoyed in the fields and were thus called rustic. Urban praedial servitudes on the other hand are primarily, though not exclusively, concerned with rights over town houses, hence their title of urban. They were not *res mancipi*, and included such items as rights to light over a neighbour's property, rights to drain water onto a neighbour's plot (*stillicidium*), a right that one's neighbour should not build higher on his land (*ius altius non tollendi*), a right to build as high as one liked on one's own land (*ius altius tollendi*), a right to an unimpeded view. In the main, they were aimed at stopping a neighbour doing things on his own property which adversely affected the enjoyment of one's own. Occasionally, as with the right to build higher and to drain one's land they involved the right to affect adversely a neighbour's enjoyment of his estate.

Servitudes, whether rustic or urban, could be created by agreement, but rustic servitudes had also to be conveyed by either *mancipatio* or *in iure cessio*. Urban servitudes could be created by pacts and stipulations, but however created all servitudes endured until the owners of the dominant and servient tenements extinguished them by agreement or they were extinguished by the two properties becoming owned by the same person. Being property rights and not personal obligations, they survived change of ownership without difficulty.

For most of their history in ancient Roman law, servitudes could be created and extinguished by prescription. Although a *lex Scribonia* of the late republic attempted to outlaw their creation by *usucapio*, its provisions were circumvented and the usual periods of ten and twenty years for *longi temporis praescriptio* operated *inter praesentes* and *inter absentes* respectively for their creation, with thirty years for their extinction. Prescription required use which was neither by force nor by stealth nor with permission, *nec vi nec clam nec precario*.

Whereas rustic servitudes may once have been created by the community of necessity to ensure that all land communally owned had fair access to the highway and to water, in historical times all servitudes seem to have been created in private law. Moreover, it must be remembered that Roman houses, even blocks of flats, stood in isolation from one another, which is why they were called *insulae*, so that rights of mutual support were not general, although such a servitude did exist, the *ius oneris ferendi*. In northern Europe, it was usual in the towns and cities for buildings to be contiguous, and rights of mutual support in a party wall were imposed upon contiguous properties by law. Moreover, as there was no ban upon building up to a boundary as there had been in ancient Rome, it was permitted to build right up against a neighbour's property and forcibly acquire a servitude of support provided an indemnity was given.[68]

The Roman law relating to praedial servitudes has been immensely influential in shaping the modern law of servitudes in civilian countries and even the law of easements in the common law world.[69] Modern systems classify servitudes as being created either by nature, the law or human act. The right to allow one's water to drain by gravity on to a neighbour's land is deemed natural, while the law allows the owner of a landlocked property to purchase from his neighbour the right to a means of access to and from the highway regardless of consent. Mediaeval German law knew a range of necessary servitudes imposed by law, *Legalservituten*.[70] Most servitudes however were and are created by grant or agreement, that is by consensual human conduct. German law requires registration of servitudes in the *Grundbucher*.[71]

French law also allows for servitudes to be created by prescription and by *destination du père de la famille*. During the Middle Ages, the custom of the *Parlement* of Paris set its face very much against the acquisition of servitudes by prescription. Emphasis was placed upon the need for some written evidence, a deed, to verify a servitude's existence. This has been somewhat tempered in modern law by a further fourfold classification of servitudes according as to whether they are continuous or discontinuous, apparent or unapparent. The *Code civil* allows prescription of a servitude which is both continuous and apparent over a period of thirty years, as it is always clear that the right is being exercised and the opportunity to challenge it is therefore provided. In that the same cannot be said of those which are discontinuous or unapparent, prescription of them is not permitted.[72]

It was also in the custom of the Paris *Parlement* that creation *per destinationem* was recognized. This contradicts the Roman principle that one cannot have a servitude over one's own land and the consequential rule that once the dominant and servient tenements pass into the ownership of one person, any servitudes are automatically extinguished by *confusio*. *Destination* recognizes that if the same person owns two properties and uses them in such a way that if they were in separate ownership one would enjoy a servitude over the other, if and when the properties become separately owned, such a servitude will be brought into existence. Likewise, where the owner of a dominant tenement acquires title to the servient tenement, modern civil law does not insist that the servitude is extinguished, but allows it to survive until the properties are again partitioned.

The list of servitudes is also far from closed, each age finding new burdens to place upon neighbours. Although the territories of Italy during the Middle Ages were strongly influenced by the Roman rules, they nevertheless took the opportunity to increase the items in the catalogue of servitudes. Travellers were allowed to pasture their horses on land contiguous to the road and, as common lands were enclosed, the rights of the commoners were often preserved in the form of servitudes over the enclosure. In Germany also, the rights which the men of the Mark had once enjoyed in common were reinterpreted by the jurists of the Reception in terms of Roman servitudes. In the nineteenth century, statutes imposed fresh burdens on many landowners whose premises adjoined the railways then being built.[73] Coupled with the German attachment to registration of land rights, the Roman categories have introduced into this area of the law considerable clarity and simplicity. Allowing for modern additions of *destination*, private expropriation of necessity and the abandonment of extinction by *confusio*, the inheritance of the civil law of Rome is particularly marked in this area of the modern law.

Personal Servitudes

Unlike praedial servitudes which burden an immoveable with a particular obligation as against another property in the vicinity, personal servitudes are a sharing of the essential incidents of ownership among different persons so that the titular owner lacks the full complement of ownership rights, some being enjoyed by another. The most typical personal servitude is *usufruct*, the right to use and enjoy the property of another, enjoyment signifying taking the fruits or income which the land or capital produces. The usufructuary therefore has two of the three rights of ownership, *ius utendi fruendi*, but must not damage or diminish the substance of the thing, that is he does not have the *ius abutendi*.[74]

In that the usufructuary is not allowed to diminish the substance of the thing, it followed that there could not be a usufruct over property which necessarily was diminished by use and enjoyment. Such property was known as fungible, and included such things as food and money. With regard to property such as a herd of cattle or a flock of sheep which would both decrease and increase as individual animals died and were born, the rule was that the usufructuary had to replace those which perished from the increase, keeping only the balance of the increase for himself. This process was called *summissio*. It provided the principle which allowed later ages to permit a quasi-usufruct over fungibles such as money which allowed of set off between increase and decrease, thus protecting the capital while allowing a profit to be made from the balance of the income.

The usufructuary was sometimes required to provide a sum of money called a *cautio* to protect the *dominus* against the possibility of bad management of the thing. This would be forfeit if the thing were diminished upon return. The usufructuary was expected to look after the thing as would a conscientious family head, the standard of diligence of a *bonus paterfamilias*. He was liable for failure to do so. The *cautio* provided evidence of the usufruct's existence and was often expressed in writing, a general feature of usufructs in the later empire.

The usufructuary did not pay for use and enjoyment of the property; if he did, it would not be usufruct but the consensual contract of hire, *locatio/conductio*. This points to its origins being in family arrangements rather than in commercial contexts. It has been argued that it began as a means of providing support for a widow who had married without *manus* without diminishing the capital inherited by the heirs. Such usufructs would be created by legacy, and it is claimed that the first usufructs created in the late republican period were definitely connected with such gifts.[75] This would also explain why usufructs could not last beyond the lifetime of the usufructuary. They would also have been useful as a means of providing support for sons emancipated during their father's lifetime and to whom the father might not wish to advance capital ahead of the other heirs or until the emancipated son had established himself. In effect, the usufruct could then be over the property which had previously been the son's *peculium*. The usufruct was also imposed by law, for instance on property which came to children other than from the father, thus limiting his interest in it to income.

The usufruct remains a most important method of dividing the rights of ownership between different people in modern civilian systems. It corresponds in many respects to the creation of a life interest under a trust in English law, the *dominus* being equivalent to the remainderman. In the Frankish empire, the life tenancies which were created bear strong resemblance to usufructs, but already the tenants were pressing for them to be heritable which usufructs were not. During the course of the intervening centuries, it provided both an explanatory device and an inspiration to successive generations of jurists. It was used for instance by the Glossators and Commentators to explain the rights of vassals in the land given them by their lords. In the fourteenth and fifteenth centuries, it was described as being a *ius ad rem* rather than a *ius in rem*, adapting the term which Jacques de Révigny had earlier used to describe the interest of a tenant in land of which he had not yet been invested. By the seventeenth and eighteenth centuries, the term *ius ad rem*, had come to be understood as referring to a claim rather a property right.[76] In Germany, the native concept of the *Nießbrauch* was with the Reception fashioned to conform with the Roman institution.

Although German law still has a concept of personal servitudes, usufruct is not among them, for it prefers to treat this institution, as do those systems which follow the French model, as a division of ownership between several persons. Usufruct still however bears many of the hallmarks of its Roman origins, being available only for a limited period which must never exceed the lifetime of the usufructuary.[77] Although a usufruct of certain fungibles is now possible, it remains a method of allowing one person to enjoy the income of property while another retains rights to the undiminished capital. It is widely used by modern civilian systems, in the same manner as the trust in English law, as a device to serve competing family interests, including for instance in France and Spain the means by which surviving spouses receive their share in succession to the deceased partner.

Of much less importance than usufruct are the personal servitudes which the Roman jurists called *usus* and *habitatio*. *Usus*, as the name suggests, was the right to use property, but not to take its fruits or diminish it. Thus, for instance, a person with the *ius utendi* of a horse would have a right to ride it for his own purposes but not to hire it to another at a profit; a person with *usus* of a field might pasture his animals in it, but not cultivate and take the crops for consumption or sale.

The Roman jurists agonized as to whether a person who was allowed to live in a dwelling house with his family had the use or usufruct of it. It had been common for freed slaves to be given a house for life by their erstwhile masters, but there would have been no objection for instance to their letting a room in it but they would not have been permitted to let the whole dwelling permanently for profit. Justinian resolved the problem by classifying such a grant as a separate personal servitude called *habitatio* and thus it has remained, being the right to use a dwelling oneself and with one's family and to take incidental profits from it which do not amount to its commercial exploitation. Justinian did the same with the grant of the services of slaves and animals, over which there had been a similar controversy, but unlike use and habitation, *opera servorum vel animalium* has not survived as a personal servitude into modern civil law.

Leases, Emphyteusis and Superficies

In the development of most western legal systems, there arrives a time when large landowners seek to utilize their property so as to produce a steady and reliable income in preference to large and unpredictable profits. This frequently takes the form of a letting of their land to others in return for either a share of the produce which is the fruit of the others' labour or else a fixed monetary payment or rent in return for allowing the others to work the land exclusively for their own profit. Even in early Rome, it would appear that the patricians let their lands to plebeian clients in return for agreed renders and political support.[78] Such a grant became known as a *precarium*. The comfortably-off Roman landowners of the second century AD often let their lands for money rents to tenants who were even allowed to postpone their payments in years when the harvest was poor. The normal length for such an agricultural lease was five years.[79]

Arrangements of this kind were classified as contractual, a form of the consensual contract of hire called *locatio/conductio*, and therefore gave rise to rights which were *in personam* only and not *in rem*. Being contractual not property rights, they offered no protection against third parties. Although leases of land are recognized in modern civil law as a special instance of the contract *locatio/conductio rei*, they are still treated as primarily contractual. Even in the centuries of hierarchical feudal landholding, the essentially commercial nature of leases was maintained so that the leaseholder was not readily conceded a property right good against third parties unconnected with the landowner. Today, however, registration of a leasehold interest does afford a greater degree of protection for what is still considered primarily from the standpoint of contractual obligations.

Emphyteusis was originally concerned with lands held by the State or municipalities in the Roman empire and which they let out on very long leases to tenants who were charged with improving the land agriculturally and paying an annual rent, called the *vectigal*, but who were entitled to keep the produce. Originally a public law concept, during the fourth and fifth centuries, it became common for the large-scale proprietors of land from the emperor in the provinces to sublet their lands on such terms, so that it became a private law arrangement as well. This led to questions about its juristic nature. In that it was based on agreement or gift, and did not require conveyance, it appeared to be contractual rather than proprietorial, but in that it could be perpetual it savoured of sale while in that a rent was payable, called now the *canon*, it was similar to hire. The emperor Zeno decreed it to be *sui generis*, and Justinian determined that it conferred a right *in rem*. Hence, a new property right was born, but one which did not make the *emphyteuta* owner.

In the centuries following the fall of the western empire, the Church made use of *emphyteusis* as a means of granting improvement leases of its lands. The institution was also much affected by feudalism, with arguably both the fief and the manor being modelled on it.[80] The grant became inalienable, thus losing a key feature of ownership. Grants in perpetuity were ended, and twenty-nine years became a common length for such a lease. Although money rents remained in use, it became more usual to reserve a rent in produce, either of a fixed amount or of a fixed proportion. Sometimes the fraction was a half, and thus came into existence the *metayer* tenancies of southern France and the *mezzadria* of Italy which endured for centuries. The rendering of fixed amounts of produce resembles feudal tenancies in socage, as did the arrangements whereby the *emphyteuta* did fixed amounts of work for the lord. Where the tenant was liable to work on the lord's land at the lord's pleasure in return for his grant, the similarity was to villein tenure. Feudalism had few problems in treating the *emphyteuta* as an owner because of its hierarchical view of ownership, which did not demand that there be one and only one *dominus* of an area of land.

Within the communes of mediaeval Italy, *emphyteusis* reverted to being heritable, and there was a distinct tendency to forget about renders if the worthwhile work of improvement of the land was undertaken. The Church sometimes followed the same approach, but tended to insist on some nominal render being made as an acknowledgement of its reversionary interest. In the eighteenth century, it became common to allow the *emphyteuta* the right to enfranchise his land to become full owner. At the Revolution, France abolished the institution only to reintroduce it as a property right under the *Code rural*, which since 1955 has a maximum duration of 99 years.[81] Italy regards it as a form of ownership which is anomalously subject to the obligation of paying rent.[82]

Very similar to *emphyteusis* in its development is the institution of *superficies*, which concerns the right to a building, or more rarely a plantation, upon land. The Roman rule was that whatever was built or planted upon land acceded to it, *superficies solo cedit*, so that the owner of the land became the owner of the building or the plants.[83] Roman law had however recognized that, in return for a rent called in this case *salarium*, land could be let for improvement by building work, allowing the improver to stay and live on the property. As with *emphyteusis*, Justinian decreed that the right thus created was a right *in rem*.

Largely forgotten in the mediaeval period and thus less affected by feudalism than *emphyteusis*, the concept of *superficies* accorded with the Germanic view that structures could be separately owned from the land on which they stood. Thus, *superficies* was easily accommodated by both German imperial and territorial law at the Reception, the only question being what sort of right was it in civilian parlance. The Bavarian *Landrecht* classified it as a form of common ownership, the Prussian as a praedial servitude, Saxon law as a personal servitude and the Austrian code as a kind of usufruct. The BGB treats it as a distinct form of property right, returning to its basis in the *ius commune*.[84] French law treats it as an immoveable interest, which determines however on the expiry of the building lease on which it relies, such leases remaining contractual and of limited duration.[85]

7 Special Forms of Ownership

Certain forms of property are subjected to special regimes of ownership in the modern civil codes. Indeed, some classify usufruct, use, habitation, *emphyteusis* and *superficies* in this manner. Such special provisions are made in relation to, for instance, mines, hydraulic energy, homesteads, flats, copyright, offices, letters and businesses.[86] The homestead has already been discussed,[87] but some attention is due to the law concerning mines, flats, copyright and businesses.

Mines

The civilian principle that whatever is built or grows upon land belongs to the owner of the soil extends downwards also, so that whatever there is under the surface belongs to the owner. While this outlook was maintained in Roman law, the feudal point of view was very different. Precious metals were regarded as being the special property of the ruler, a regalian right. Therefore it did not matter upon whose land they were discovered, they belonged to the lord or the king. They could not be exploited for private profit, and the same principle was applied to other things of value, such as mineral deposits found underground. The same was true as has been shown of buried treasure.[88]

Although the modern civil codes enshrine the Roman principle, each State regulates the right of individual owners to exploit ore and mineral deposits on their land. State concessions are usually required and these are governed by public law. In France, this derogation from the rights of landowners began as early as 1810, only six years after the promulgation of the *Code civil*. Mining concessions are not usually vested in the landowner and are not freely transferable. Environmental concerns also influence State policy on mining rights very considerably.[89]

Flats

The principle of *superficies solo cedit* causes problems for those who live in blocks of flats or have offices in such buildings. In ancient Rome, the vast majority of people lived in such *insulae*, only the very rich being able to afford complete houses of their own. The Romans however did not develop any concept of separate ownership of each horizontal level. Either the flat was rented from the owner of the building, that is the person who owned the land on which it was built, or the inhabitants owned the whole thing themselves in common, regulating their relationship one with another through the consensual contract of *societas*.

Germanic law was far readier to recognize corporate ownership, allowing the March lands of the villages to be communally owned by the Markmen, whose joint interests were expressed by their government of the Mark in the assembly, which also appointed officers to represent them in the performance of certain duties.[90] From the twelfth century in the towns, systems of ownership were devised whereby the inhabitants of different floors or rooms in buildings were allowed to own the site and the communal areas in common while individual floors or sections of the building were owned by the residents severally. Such arrangements were wholly foreign to the Roman approach and could not be accommodated within it, so that after the Reception no trace of such concepts was to be found in the *ius commune*, nor in the Prussian *Landrecht*, the Saxon laws or the Austrian code. Nevertheless the local laws clung tenaciously to the native institution so that in 1900, although the BGB did not recognize the principle of *condominium*, it permitted those already in existence to continue according to the provisions of the pre-existing laws.[91] German law has since had to make statutory provision for the reintroduction of the institution, which has been accepted into the laws, indeed into the codes, of other civil law countries including France and Italy.[92] The inhabitants jointly own the main parts of the buildings, the stairs, elevators, entrances and so on, but enjoy separate ownership of their respective dwellings subject to rights of support and the like in favour of their neighbours. Depending upon the size of the block, they either govern the *condominium* themselves through an assembly or elect a board of management and an administrator who is responsible for the day to day running of the property. The *condominium* is a signal Germanic contribution to modern civil law, and is connected with that other major Germanic contribution, corporate personality. Both have their roots in the common ownership known to early German agricultural communities.

Copyright

The problem of the copyright in published work was not one which presented itself very forcibly prior to the invention of the printing press at the end of the fifteenth century. Governmental control of printing and publishing in most lands meant that authors were no longer free to publish their work without some royal, ecclesiastical or other permission. Such permissions usually gave the author the sole right to publish his work and profit from its publication during his lifetime and likewise his estate for a certain period after his death. Although such strict control of publication has vanished by and large from secular law, it can still be found in the canon law of the Roman Catholic Church,[93] and the concept of copyright which it incidentally created has survived into modern legal systems.

Business Interests

Germanic law has also contributed the idea of blocks of property rights existing as separate patrimonies distinct from the individuals who own them. The family communion is one such property block. Businesses also have such interests, and those who seek to buy or sell a business as a going concern identify with it its name, trade marks, patents, premises, the custom of its clients and its goodwill. Whereas ancient Roman law did not recognize the identity of such a business or *fonds de commerce*, mercantile practice and Germanic jurisprudence did, and from them it has found its way into most modern systems of civil law. The sale of a business does not therefore require these elements to be individuated. Instead, dealings by way of sale or charge in relation to a business can be taken to include many or all of these items according to the provisions established by the operative legal regime.[94]

8 Use of Property as Security

The history of using a thing, *res*, as security in ancient Roman law begins with the institution of *fiducia*. This was recognized as being of two sorts. *Fiducia cum amico* was the transfer of a thing, including *dominium* of it, to another person by way of loan, which could be a loan for use or a loan for safe keeping. Either way, there would be an agreement that it should be returned in due course. Eventually, as a result of praetorian development, loan for use became the real contract of *commodatum* and loan for safe keeping the real contract of *depositum*, in both cases the lender retaining ownership and the borrower receiving only natural possession or detention of the thing. *Fiducia cum creditore* on the other hand was a transfer of ownership as security for a debt incurred with an agreement to retransfer when the debt was satisfied. If it were not satisfied, the transferee could keep or sell the thing because it was his property. Indeed, if he wrongfully sold it before the debt was paid, the debtor had only a personal remedy against him and had no way of recovering the thing from the new owner. As *commodatum* and *depositum* developed out of *fiducia cum amico*, so what was to the Romans the real contract of *pignus* developed from *fiducia cum creditore*. Again, the debtor retained *dominium*, but the natural possession of the thing passed to the creditor, it being at first expressly agreed that if the debtor defaulted, the creditor could sell the thing to satisfy the debt. In later classical law, such a term was always implicit in the arrangement, the right of the creditor to sell being known as the *lex commissoria*.

Thus far, the pledge was always a private arrangement, a sort of distress levied in advance of the wrong of non-payment being committed, a security against it occurring. In the third century AD, however, it was felt that it was preferable for the creditor to obtain judicial endorsement of non-payment and his right to sell, the *impetratio domini*. This became essential after Constantine abolished the *lex commissoria*. Henceforth, the creditor had to seek judgement against the debtor, after which, if the debt was not satisfied within a fixed period, he acquired ownership of the thing and the right to sell it in order to satisfy his debt, but having to return any surplus to the debtor.

Pignus always involved physical transfer of the thing which was pledged, which could be very inconvenient if the thing was an immoveable or a very valuable moveable, in that it was lost to the use and enjoyment of the debtor. In relation to certain things therefore a different practice developed. To begin with, the things were usually a dwelling house or a farm which had been hired by the contract of *locatio/conductio*. The hirer would agree that his furniture and possessions in the house or the crops he grew on the land should be security for the rent due on the property. He remained however in possession of the things which provided the security, an arrangement which became known by the Greek word *hypotheca*. If the hirer defaulted in paying his rent, the lessor was allowed to sue for possession of the goods, and by the end of the republic he could even recover them from third parties to whom the debtor had sold or given them. By the second century AD, the hypothec was being used to secure any kind of debt and the law began to imply hypothecs to protect the interests of the State over the property of taxpayers, of wives to secure their dowries over their husband's property and of wards to secure their rights against their guardians. As an item of property could be the subject of more then one hypothec simultaneously, registration with the authorities and the use of witnesses were introduced to ensure that the correct order of priority could be established, the earlier having priority over the later - *qui prior est tempore potior est iure*.

Justinian differentiated hypothec from pledge, *pignus*, on the basis of the latter involving actual transfer of the thing, but the nature of the property did not determine the type of real security involved as a matter of law. In practice however hypothecs were used over immoveables and valuable moveables while pledge was more common with chattels of smaller value. Thus was planted the seed of the modern civilian distinction between pledge and hypothec, although in Roman law they were regarded as contractual rather than property-based rights.

Germanic law likewise made no distinction between the two situations. Among the Lombards the pledge appears as a sort of advance distress, the creditor having possession of an item of the debtor's property which becomes forfeited to him if the debtor does not make satisfaction. Germanic custom however allowed the creditor to keep the profits arising from the thing while he possessed it, unlike the Roman *fiducia* under which an express agreement to that effect was necessary for such *antichresis* to arise. The Church frowned on this element of the German pledge as being usurious and helped suppress it, and also disapproved for similar reasons of the creditor being allowed to forfeit a thing which was of greater value than the debt he was owed. The rule therefore became that he must sell the thing and return any surplus to the debtor once his debt had been recouped from the proceeds. Both developments furthered the use of the hypothec rather than the pledge, as there was no advantage in having possession of the thing as long as the creditor's interest was safe if the debtor defaulted. The Italian communes therefore for the first time distinguished hypothec from pledge and allowed the former to be registered by the public authorities to secure the interests of the creditor against third parties. A property interest was therefore emerging from the contract for security.[95]

In northern Europe, institutions similar to the hypothec had developed which, in France, took the name of *gage*. As the name suggests, such engagements were based on agreement. Initially, they were live gages, *vifs gages*, by the terms of which the land passed to the creditor and he recouped the debt from the fruits he gathered. If the fruits remained his without the debt being reduced, the gage was described as dead, *mort gage*. These institutions were also known in Germany,[96] where in the mediaeval cities two variants emerged. Both allowed the debtor to retain the land or dwelling, but one permitted the creditor to forfeit the property of his own motion upon the debtor's default while the other required the creditor to have his interest registered by the town authorities in such a way that he could apply for an automatic judicial execution of the property to satisfy his debt if the debtor defaulted. In Magdeburg, it was recognized that this gave the creditor a real right, so that if the debtor conveyed the property to a third party, the creditor could have the conveyance set aside. In other towns, the creditor was sometimes given a year and a day to reclaim a real security that had been wrongfully alienated.[97]

Although this registered real security was often described as a hypothec, it differed from the Roman institution in several important respects. Firstly, it always related to a specific thing and did not attach to a debtor's property in general. Secondly, the amount of the debt which was secured had also to be certain. In Germanic law, this was described as the specialty of the hypothec. These typical German features came under attack at the Reception in that they did not conform to the Roman model. While this threw the German forms of land security into confusion for some two centuries, eventually, from the eighteenth century onwards, the Germanic features prevailed and have found a place in most modern civil law provisions on the issue. While Roman law emphasized the contractual nature of hypothecs, many German towns retained the registration system for publicity, some such as Munich, Bremen and Lübeck insisting upon it for validity. Today, registration is essential to the validity of hypothecs in most civilian systems. German law even refuses preferential privilege and the right to follow the property to hypothecs imposed by law unless registered, seeing the wife's hypothec over her husband's property and that of the ward over the guardian's, for instance, as rights to register hypothecs and no more. French law has in the last half century followed Germany in this. Hypothecs must relate to specific items of property, which must be immoveables or registrable moveables as a rule, and must be for fixed debts. The German system, in that each hypothec is dependent upon a registered entry in the landbook allows for the vacation of space when a hypothecated debt is satisfied and the creation of a new debt in its place, rather than all the other rights moving up one rank. The German approach has also facilitated ease of transfer of rights in hypothecs.[98] While Germany requires all hypothecs to be registered in the *Grundbuch*, other civil law countries including France require them to be authenticated by a notary, French law requiring two notaries or one notary and two witnesses. While French law still regards the hypothec as a contract, only registration affords the creditor the privilege of a real security against other creditors, the *droit de préférence*, and the right to follow the property into the hands of third parties, the *droit de suite*.[99]

Security over non-registrable moveables in modern civil law has developed in the meanwhile from the Roman *pignus*. Although mediaeval German law saw the emergence of a chattel hypothec, often under the influence of mercantile and maritime practices in towns of the north such as Lübeck, this concept did not fare as well after the onslaught of Romanism at the Reception. Apart from the possibility of creating a hypothec of particular kinds of chattel, basically ships, aircraft and such registrable moveables, the creation of a real security over moveables still requires delivery of the thing to the creditor or some act which is equivalent to delivery in terms of publicizing the creation of the pledge. Registration is one option, and Germany saw the creation of a pledge register in 1881. Such formality alone allows the creditor to follow and recover the property from the hands of third parties, a need that does not arise when delivery has taken place. Otherwise, the only security the creditor enjoys is being able to proceed against the debtor's property generally if the pledged thing does not satisfy his debt in full or if it is no longer available for that purpose. This reduces the pledge from being a specific real security to a general one.[100]

9 Proprietary and Possessory Remedies

Both in modern civil law and in the civil law of ancient Rome, remedies were provided for owners to enable them to recover their property from others, together with remedies which allowed those in possession of things, including owners, to complain of their possession being violated by ouster, disturbance or the activities of others which threatened to interfere with it.

Proprietary Remedies

In Roman law, the owner was allowed to claim his property from whomsoever had it in their possession. His claim would originally have been framed by means of the *legis actio per sacramentum in rem*, a highly ritual and formal proceeding.[101] When the *legis actio* procedure was replaced by the formulary system, the praetor would grant the owner a *vindicatio* to claim his thing, in which he simply asserted that it was his by Quiritary right. His right *in rem* alone was mentioned, not that he had greater right to the thing than the current possessor. The defendant was free to defend the action himself, even if he had obtained the thing from a third party, his right to proceed against the third party if he lost to the claimant being unaffected. The owner's right to reclaim his property would endure until it was extinguished by lapse of time or an adverse possession which matured into *dominium* by acquisitive prescription. There were circumstances in which the defendant could resist an owner's claim if he were in bad faith, or had sold and delivered a thing to him informally, or was refusing to meet expenses due to the defendant. Ownership was also lost if the thing had acceded to a greater or been transformed into a *nova species*. Likewise, ownership of a wild animal was lost when it escaped or, if it had the *animus revertendi*, when it lost the habit of returning.

Germanic law on the other hand did not originally allow ownership to endure if the owner voluntarily parted with possession of a moveable thing. His only remedy was upon the obligation to return the thing. If however property was lost involuntarily, then the owner could proceed against any person in whose possession it was found. That person would have to vouch a third party from whom he had acquired the thing to appear in his stead or else defend the action himself with no further right to proceed against a third party. When 'hand had warranted hand' the claimant's dispute against the ultimate defendant would be tried. If he succeeded, he would recover his thing and a fine would be payable by the vanquished defendant unless he could show he had come to the thing in good faith. If the claimant lost, he would be liable to a fine.

The emperor Otto I restricted the vouching of third parties to three degrees and also to within a certain geographical range. This in effect limited the right of an owner to recover his property. Once the Lombard law school at Pavia began to study the Roman rules, a return began to be made to allowing the owner to bring a straightforward *vindicatio*. The Germanic approach has however borne fruit to the extent that in modern law, provided the possessor acquired the thing in good faith, he immediately obtains ownership of non-registrable moveables, leaving the former owner to a personal remedy against an interim possessor who wronged him.

Although Roman law made no distinction between the remedy for moveables and land, Germanic law did. The Lombards for instance allowed an owner out of possession to recover by claiming the land from the current possessor. In the case of land, the defendant to such a claim could plead that he had been in possession for five years, in which case according to Rothari's laws, he could defend his title by oath and judicial duel. Once thirty years had elapsed, the oath alone was sufficient according to Grimwald, and Liutprand made thirty years possession equivalent to ownership. Within the five year period, and thereafter if the defendant wished to avoid the oath and duel, the defendant could vouch a warrantor in the usual Germanic fashion, but he was also allowed to use written evidence to prove that he had good title. The increased use of documents as evidence helped stabilize the security of land ownership.

In the mediaeval communes, owners often formed corporations called *regole* to defend their interests from interference. These would employ *gastaldi* to watch over their lands and alert them to any problems.[102] The growth of Romanist legal learning saw the gradual reintroduction of the Roman *rei vindicatio*, which is still referred to in modern Italian law as *rivendicazione*. It is still the principal remedy in modern civil law to recover immoveables and registrable moveables, as well as non-registrable moveables which the current possessor has not acquired in good faith or for a just title.

Possessory Remedies

One of the greatest contributions which the Roman praetor made to civilian jurisprudence was the development of protection for possessors of property who were not necessarily owners by means of interdicts. These interdicts were available to protect the possession of anyone who had acquired possession without force, stealth or the leave of the party against whom complaint was made, *nec vi nec clam nec precario*. Originally, they only lay to protect those who had juristic possession of the thing, but not those who had only natural possession, such as usufructuaries, and those who received under contracts such as *commodatum* and *depositum*. Eventually, this latter group also came to be protected by the praetor, being recognized as having a quasi-possession in the thing sufficient to sustain the award of the interdict. Wrongful possession was also protected against anyone other than the person to whom the wrong was done.

Originally there were interdicts to protect immoveables and moveables against disturbance of possession and ouster. Those to protect against disturbance were termed *retinendae possessionis causa* and were two in number, *uti possidetis* to secure possession of land against an intruder and *utrubi* which secured the possession in a moveable of him who had enjoyed it for the greater part of the last year. *Utrubi* could also be used to recover possession, *recuperandae possessionis causa*, in relation to moveables, but for land a separate interdict to recover existed called *unde vi*, to get back land taken by force during the previous year. There was also a version *unde vi armata* which allowed land taken by an armed force to be recovered at any time. With the demise of the formulary system, these interdicts became possessory actions, and Justinian made *uti possidetis* applicable to moveables and immoveables, always protecting the actual possessor, although it continued to be called *utrubi* when applied to moveables.

Utrubi in its original form had not only been used to protect the disturbance of actual possession; it had been used to recover property from which a possessor had been ousted. There can be discerned in this a recognition of a right to possess, *ius possessionis*, which is separate from possession itself. Germanic law was to develop a concept of a right to possess which was to influence the possessory remedies when they re-emerged into the legal systems of mediaeval Europe. In the ninth century, the Germanic popular assemblies allowed a claimant of property to establish his rightful possession by making his claim three times before the assembly. Thereafter, if no one objected to his keeping within a year and a day, the so-called *rechte Gewere*, his possession was lawful and would be protected until it matured into ownership by prescription. Possession for a year was later to be adopted as a requirement for use of the possessory remedies in both Italy and France.[103]

Canon law made a very significant contribution to the development of modern possessory protection. The decretals contained in Pseudo-Isidore, later to be proved forgeries, maintained that if a bishop was ousted from his diocese, no criminal charge could be brought against him until he had been reinstated. In canon law, this gave him a defence against such a criminal charge, the *exceptio spolii*, which developed into an action for the recovery of his see. The *actio spolii* lay not only for the return of the lands but also the moveables from which he had been ousted, did not require that the ouster be violent as long as it was without judgement, and it could even be used to recover property from third parties into whose hands it had come, even those unaware of the offence until Innocent III provided by his decretal *Saepe contingit* in 1215 that *bona fide* acquirers without notice should not be liable.[104] The *actio spolii* or *condictio ex canone Redintegranda* passed into the civilian tradition as the reintegratory remedy against ouster, a successor to *unde vi*, but one with a much wider ambit.

Meanwhile, the revived Romanist learning was also assimilating Germanic concepts of possession into the remedy to maintain possession in the face of disturbance. Provided the claimant had been possessed for a year, it was from the thirteenth century no longer deemed necessary that he should still be in actual possession provided he had not been out of possession for a year. This allowed a year to intervene while the action could be brought, so that it lay on a right to possess rather than actual possession. This allowed it to be brought for interference or ouster, thus destroying the boundary between the Roman retentory and recuperatory actions. Moreover, as physical possession was no longer required, the remedies became available for disturbance or ouster from incorporeal rights of property as well, which could be possessed in Germanic law although they had not been in Roman law.[105] The Reception led to the non-Roman necessity for a year's possession being removed from the *ius commune*, despite its inclusion in the local laws of many Italian states, but the rule was resurrected in the modern French provisions.

The Roman distinction between disturbance and ouster has thus disappeared from modern civil law. The same possessory remedies will now issue, and the Germanic requirement of a year's lawful possession is widely recognized, as is the need to bring the action within a year of the interference. The term *réintegration* is now used, in French law for instance, to designate a violent dispossession in which the need for a year's lawful possession and the year's limitation period are both dropped. The Germanic and canonical contributions to the modern possessory actions are as considerable as the Roman if not more so. Nevertheless, the Roman basis is still apparent, for it was the praetor who invented possessory remedies as an additional protection of property alongside the petitory remedies of the owner which are not excluded by their use.

The modern possessory actions only lie in defence of immoveable property. There also exist, drawn from Roman roots, two other actions based upon possession connected with interests in land. These are the denunciation for feared damage and the denunciation of new work. Both are based on praetorian remedies in Roman law. The former stems from the *cautio damni infecti* which a proprietor might require if the condition of his neighbour's premises threatened the integrity or enjoyment of his own. If the neighbour would not repair the defect, the praetor would place the plaintiff in possession of the area from which the threat emanated and if the neighbour would still not oblige, then the praetor could grant the plaintiff interdictally-protected possession which would mature into full ownership by *usucapio*, thus enabling him to acquire the dangerous area and set it right. The *operis novi nuntiatio* arose when a neighbour was carrying out or planning to carry out work on his premises which the plaintiff argued would interfere with his property or the enjoyment of it. The neighbour could be required to give security that he would not continue with the work until his right to do so had been established, and if he refused to enter into such an undertaking, any work executed thereafter could be demolished by obtaining the interdict *ex operis novi nuntiatione*.

Both these concepts survived in the vulgar Roman law of Italy and southern France and were revived in the customary law of northern France in the fourteenth century through civilian influence. They were transformed however into suits for injunctions to prevent new work and to remove or repair dangerous features, usually in conjunction with an ongoing action concerning the parties' respective property rights. Although they did not feature in the 1667 *ordonnance* on civil procedure, they reappeared in the *Code civil* and from there have found their way into most modern civil codes.[106]

10 Conclusion

The modern civil law of property is presented according to the institutional scheme devised in ancient Rome. Its categories of modes of acquisition, the names of the various property rights and the importance of ownership, juristic possession and natural possession all recall Roman law. However familiar that ground plan and terminology may be, it is nevertheless important to remember that between the age of classical Roman law and that of the modern codes lay the centuries of Byzantine and Germanic development, of canonical and feudal influence, before the Roman categories were again employed and loyalty to Roman concepts of ownership embraced by the natural law scholars and institutional writers who worked in the aftermath of humanism to supply the juristic foundations for modern codification. What emerged at the end of that process still bears the hallmarks of its Roman provenance, but it is a civilian learning which has drunk deep at the fount of Germanic jurisprudence. The notions of corporate personality, ownership of horizontal strata in blocks of flats and offices, a concept of possession that embraces incorporeal rights, the development of real security over land and the modern possessory actions all testify to the profound influence that Germanic, feudal and canonist legal concepts have exercised upon the civil law during the intervening centuries. Many native concepts were forced to fit into the Roman moulds in the centuries following the Reception. While Roman law appears to have dominated the modern civil law of property, it has also assimilated along the way a wealth of content from other European legal traditions.

Notes

[1] See chapter 9.
[2] According to Justinian but not Gaius.
[3] See C. Calisse, *A History of Italian Law* (Boston, 1928; reprinted New York, 1969), pp. 107; 675.
[4] See *Monumenta Germaniae Historica*, constitutiones I. 244; see R. Huebner, *A History of Germanic Private Law* (Boston, 1918; reprinted New York, 1968), p. 269, and J.-B. Brissaud, *A History of French Private Law* (Boston, 1912; reprinted New York, 1968), pp. 279 ff.
[5] See pp. 14, 20 ff.
[6] See chapter 10.
[7] See J.-B. Brissaud, *A History of French Public Law* (Boston, 1915; reprinted New York, 1969), p. 282.
[8] Huebner, *History*, pp. 347 ff.
[9] See further below, pp. 255 ff., and David Johnston, 'Owners and Neighbours: From Rome to Scotland' in R. Evans-Jones (Ed.), *The Civil Law Tradition in Scotland* (Edinburgh, 1995), pp. 176 ff.
[10] For the Roman Sources, see Gaius, *Institutes*, II. 65 ff; Justinian, *Institutes*, II. 1. 11 ff; Digest, XLI. 1. 1. pr. ff. For examples of the modern sources, see for instance, France *Code civil*, art. 544-577; Germany BGB, art. 925-984; Italy *Codice civile*, art. 922-947; and Spain *Código civil*, art. 348-391.
[11] Even if bred for commercial purposes: see T.G. Watkin, '*Occupatio* and the *Pastio Villatica*', (1990) 11 *Journal of Legal History* 5 ff.
[12] Laws of Rothari, 309-321, in *Monumenta Germaniae Historica*. See Calisse, *History*, p. 693.
[13] The legal position relating to bees is dealt with in the *Schwabenspiegel*, 315; see Huebner, *History*, pp. 427 ff.
[14] See H. Grotius, *De iure belli ac pacis* (1625).
[15] See A.H.M. Jones, *The Later Roman Empire 284-602* (Oxford, 1964), pp. 812 ff.
[16] Brissaud, *French Private Law*, p. 351.
[17] Huebner, *History*, p. 254.
[18] Brissaud, *French Private Law*, p. 353.
[19] Brissaud, *French Private Law*, pp. 284 ff.; Calisse, *History*, p. 695; Huebner, *History*, pp. 428 ff.

[20] This would involve the consensual contract of hire, *locatio/conductio*, for the services of the other and possibly of sale, *emptio/venditio*, for the materials used.

[21] See T.G. Watkin, '*Tabula Picta* - Images and Icons', (1984) 50 *Studia et documenta historiae et iuris* 383 ff.; F. Lucrezi, *La Tabula Picta: tra creatore e fruitore* (Naples, 1984).

[22] M. Crawford, *The Roman Republic* (Glasgow, 1978), pp. 117, 172 and 134 respectively.

[23] Huebner, *History*, p. 172; Calisse, *History*, pp. 699 ff.

[24] Calisse, *History*, ibid.

[25] Calisse, *History*, p. 697; Huebner, *History*, p. 175.

[26] Huebner, *History*, p. 436; Germany BGB art. 953-957; Switzerland ZGB art. 756.

[27] See Justinian, *Institutes*, II. 1. 39; J.A.C. Thomas, *Textbook of Roman Law* (Amsterdam, 1976), pp. 178 ff.

[28] Huebner, *History*, p. 431.

[29] Loysel, *Institutes Coutumières* 280.

[30] *Libri Feudorum* II. 56.

[31] Huebner, *History*, p. 431; see BGB art. 984 and ZGB art. 723.

[32] This was not a Roman term. It was first found in the *Brachylogus*.

[33] Some have seen in the division of opinion between the Sabinians and the Proculians on this issue a reflection of the two schools' adherence to different philosophical perspectives upon the world. Thus it has been argued that the Sabinians' preference for the owner of the raw materials over the manufacturer indicates their adoption of a Stoic world view, while the Proculians on the other hand adopted a Peripatetic standpoint, following the teaching of Aristotle. See P. Sokolowski, *Philosophie im Privatrecht* (Halle, 1907), I. 69ff; also, H. Hägerström, *Der römische Obligationsbegriff* (Uppsala and Leipzig, 1927), I. 236ff; P. Bonfante, *Corso di diritto romano*, I. (Rome, 1925; rep., Milan, 1963) 1, 10ff; II. (Rome, 1926; rep., Milan, 1968) 2, 74ff, 116ff; J.G. Wolf, *Error in römischen Vertragsrecht* (Köln and Graz, 1961), 139ff. Some modern writers believe that the division of juristic opinion was based initially upon divergent views regarding the mode of acquisition rather than the divergent philosophical perspectives, the Proculians seeing the manufacturer as acquiring the new thing by *occupatio* of a *res nullius* while the Sabinians saw it as a matter of a pre-existing substance adopting a new form by *accessio*. Some modern writers have gone further by suggesting that the Proculian view was based on the same principle but upon a different appreciation of the relative importance of form and substance. For this debate, see C. Ferrini, *Opere*, IV. (Milan, 1930) 43, 103ff; S. Perozzi, *Scritti giuridici*, I. (Milan, 1948) 227, 255ff. Their debate was castigated as being too rarefied by Bonfante, *Corso*, II. 116ff, at 118. Some scholars have discerned in the juristic disputes of the Sabinian and Proculian schools perspectives based upon the traditional conflict of landed wealth and labour or between landed wealth and trade, but J.A.C. Thomas

argued that the basis of the juristic dispute turned not upon allegiance to Stoicism or Aristotelianism, let alone some latent Whig or Tory view of property, but rather upon the context of the formulary system. The question for Professor Thomas was which of the rival claims, that of the owner of the raw materials or that of the manufacturer, made sense in the context of a *vindicatio*. See J.A.C. Thomas, 'Form and Substance in Roman Law', (1966) 19 *Current Legal Problems* 145ff. F. Wieacker had also believed that the *formula* of the *vindicatio* had led to the Proculian approach: see F. Wieacker, *Festschrift Rabel* (Tübingen, 1954), II. 263ff.

[34] See Justinian, *Institutes*, II. 1. 25; Digest XLI. 1. 7. 7. Many believe that the *media sententia* predated Justinian, some attributing it to the jurist Paul; see W. Osuchowski in *Studi Arangio-Ruiz*, (Naples, 1953), III. 37 ff.

[35] This points to the dispute being about sale or hire; see T.G. Watkin, 'Concrete Cases that Could Occur' in *Studi in onore di Giuseppe Gandolfi* (Pavia, forthcoming).

[36] Franciscus Conanus (1508-1551) favoured awarding ownership according to the relative value of the raw materials and the end-product; see generally D.J. Osler, '*Specificatio* in Scots Law' in R. Evans-Jones (Ed.), *The Civil Law Tradition in Scotland*, pp. 100 ff.

[37] See for instance France *Code civil*, art. 572; Germany BGB, art. 950; Italy *Codice civile*, art. 940; and Spain *Código civil*, art. 383..

[38] See A.M. Prichard, 'Early *Usucapio*', (1974) 90 *Law Quarterly Review* 235 ff.

[39] Originally, either to the Senate and People of Rome in the senatorial provinces or to the emperor in the imperial provinces. This distinction was swept away by the territorial reforms of Diocletian.

[40] Calisse, *History*, pp. 702 ff.

[41] Brissaud, *French Private Law*, pp. 363 f; Huebner, *History*, pp. 254 ff, 439 ff.

[42] See H.F. Jolowicz, *An Historical Introduction to Roman Law* (2nd Ed.; Cambridge, 1952), p. 525.

[43] Justinian, *Institutes* II. 1. 41, attributed the rule to the XII Tables, but this has been doubted: see W.W. Buckland, *Manual of Roman Private Law* (2nd Ed.; 1939).

[44] Cf. the *Testamentum per aes et libram*.

[45] Cf. Written evidence in sale; see Jolowicz and Nicholas, *Historical Introduction*, pp. 509 ff., and the references given there.

[46] This would link with the *comitia curiata*'s residual jurisdiction over adrogations and the making of wills, and would also a furnish a putative common root for the *mancipatio*, the *cessio in iure* and the *legis actiones*.

[47] See Calisse, *History*, pp. 704 ff; Huebner, *History*, pp. 244, 246; Brissaud, *French Private Law*, p. 374.

[48] See Huebner, *History*, pp. 209, 220 ff., 244, 249, 253; Brissaud, *French Private Law*, pp. 390 ff.

[49] Loi 23 mars 1855; and see Brissaud, *French Private Law*, pp. 385, 399.

[50] See Huebner, *History*, pp. 436 ff.
[51] For Germany, see Huebner, *History*, p. 306 ff.
[52] See Huebner, *History*, pp. 306 ff.; Brissaud, *French Private Law*, pp. 426 ff.
[53] See Calisse, *History*, p. 685.
[54] See Brissaud, *French Private Law*, pp. 436 ff.
[55] See Huebner, *History*, pp. 306 ff.
[56] See Huebner, *History*, p. 313; Brissaud, *French Private Law*, pp. 426 ff.
[57] See Calisse, *History*, p. 688.
[58] See Huebner, *History*, pp. 181 ff.
[59] See Calisse, *History*, pp. 690 ff; Huebner, *History*, pp. 256 ff.; Brissaud, *French Private Law*, p. 282.
[60] See Huebner, *History*, p. 257.
[61] See Calisse, *History*, p. 691.
[62] See A. Alvarez et al., *The Progress of Continental Law in the Nineteenth Century* (Boston, 1918; reprinted New York 1969), pp. 162 ff.
[63] See T.G. Watkin, *The Italian Legal Tradition* (London, 1997), p. 207.
[64] See below, section 8, pp. 267 ff., and chapter 12, section 4, pp. 297 ff.
[65] Loi 12 July 1909; see Alvarez, *Nineteenth Century*, p. 162.
[66] See David Johnston, 'Owners and Neighbours: From Rome to Scotland' in R. Evans-Jones (Ed.), *The Civil Law Tradition in Scotland*, pp. 176 ff.
[67] See J.A.C. Thomas, *Textbook*, p. 197.
[68] See Brissaud, *French Private Law*, pp. 422 ff.
[69] Largely because the leading text, *Gale on Easements* (1st Ed. With T.D. Whately, 1839) made extensive use of Roman and continental authorities.
[70] See Huebner, *History*, p. 262.
[71] BGB art. 1018 ff.
[72] *Code civil*, art. 690.
[73] See Huebner, *History*, p. 263.
[74] See for instance Justinian, *Institutes* II. 4. pr., following Digest. VII. 1.1: 'Usus fructus est ius alienis rebus utendi fruendi salua rerum substantia'.
[75] See W.W. Buckland, *A Textbook of Roman Law from Augustus to Justinian* (3rd Ed., by P.G. Stein; Cambridge, 1963), p. 268.
[76] See Brissaud, *French Private Law*, p. 308.
[77] Corporations were allowed to enjoy a usufruct for 100 years in Roman law, which was believed the longest that a human being might live.
[78] See O. Tellegen-Couperus, *A Short History of Roman Law* (English Ed., London, 1993), p. 71.
[79] See W. Kunkel, *An Introduction to Roman Legal and Constitutional History* (2nd English Ed., by J.M. Kelly: Oxford, 1973), p. 6.
[80] See Brissaud, *French Private Law*, p. 54.
[81] See Amos and Walton, *Introduction to French Law*, p. 130.
[82] See Calisse, *History*, pp. 727 ff.

[83] See above pp. 250 ff. for discussion on *accessio*, *inaedificatio*, etc.
[84] For details see Huebner, *History*, p. 334.
[85] See Amos and Walton, *Introduction to French Law* (3rd Ed.; Oxford, 1967), pp. 95, 130.
[86] Ibid., pp. 93 ff.
[87] See above, pp. 254, for *Hofrecht*, etc.
[88] See above, pp. 239 ff.
[89] For further details see Amos and Walton, *Introduction to French Law*, p. 93.
[90] See Brissaud, *French Private Law*, p. 37.
[91] See Huebner, *History*, pp. 174 ff.
[92] For Germany, see *Wohnungseigentumgesetz* 15 March 1951 and N.G. Foster, *German Legal System and Law* (2nd Ed.; London, 1993), p. 293; for Italy, *Codice civile* art. 1117-1139 and T.G. Watkin, *The Italian Legal Tradition*, pp. 217 f.; for France, Loi 10 July 1965 and Amos & Walton, *Introduction to French Law*, p. 95 ff.
[93] The modern Roman Catholic canon law on this subject originated in the decisions of the reforming sixteenth-century Council of Trent. Permission to publish is indicated by the words *imprimatur*, *nihil obstat*, etc. to be seen at the beginning of a book.
[94] For further details see Amos and Walton, *Introduction to French Law*, p. 98.
[95] See Calisse, *History*, pp. 738 ff.
[96] Where confusingly the dead gage was that which killed off the debt, i.e. the French live-gage, see Huebner, *History*, pp. 379 ff.
[97] See Huebner, *History*, pp. 380 ff.
[98] See Huebner, *History*, pp. 387 ff.
[99] See Amos & Walton, *Introduction to French Law*, pp. 123 ff.
[100] For further details of the German development, see Huebner, *History*, pp. 440 ff.
[101] See chapter 13.
[102] See Calisse, *History*, p. 716
[103] See Brissaud, *French Private Law*, pp. 328 ff., 356.
[104] See Brissaud, *French Private Law*, pp. 318 ff.
[105] See Huebner, *History*, pp. 215 ff; Calisse, *History*, pp. 744 ff.
[106] See Brissaud, *French Private Law*, p. 349; A. Engelmann et al., *A History of Continental Civil Procedure* (Boston, 1927; reprinted New York, 1969), pp. 827 ff.

12 The Law of Obligations

1 The Concept of an Obligation

The law of obligations, together with the law of property, makes up what Gaius referred to as the law of things. Modern civil lawyers also regard obligations as a kind of thing in that obligations have a monetary value. However, unlike property rights, which are good against all the world, that is the owner asserts his right to the thing owned against all comers and not just against specific persons, obligations are rights which are claimed against specific persons, they are rights *in personam* as opposed to rights *in rem*. They are also rights which exist because there are actions to enforce them rather than because they are physically possessed by a person. Therefore, they are sometimes referred to as *choses* in action as opposed to *choses* in possession. Some therefore see obligations as linking the law of things with the law of actions. This may well be true of the Roman view, but the modern codes of civil law deal with obligations as a definite part of the law of things.

If the law of property is concerned with answering the legal questions concerning propositions of the "A owns X" variety, then the law of obligations is concerned with answering the legal questions which arise in relation to propositions of the kind "A owes X to B". A and B have to be legal persons for the proposition to be valid, and X has to be something which can be owed, a question for the law of things, but the main thrust of the law of obligations relates to the question of the circumstances in which A becomes obligated to B, how A comes to owe. Throughout most of the history of civil law, this question was seen as being concerned with the circumstances in which something is due to B from A. Since the advent of the natural law school of jurists, it has tended to be characterized as B having a right to something from A, which A is therefore under a duty to render to him. According to both perspectives, A is obligated to B.

Modern codes of civil law categorize the circumstances in which A owes something to B as being either contractual, delictual or quasi-contractual. This categorization reflects the Roman law approach to obligations as presented by the emperor Justinian, although Justinian included a fourth category, quasi-delictual obligations, which is not generally preserved today.[1] Contractual obligations are those which arise out of the agreement of the parties, and constitute the most important and numerous categories of obligations in modern civil law. Delictual obligations on the other hand result from a wrong suffered by one party which entitles that party to compensation from the other. That an obligation arises in such circumstances has nothing to do with the wishes of the parties but is rather a matter of law. If the party obligated to compensate is not personally to blame for the harm suffered, then his liability may rest upon responsibility for another, vicarious liability, or upon the fact that the harm in question is one for which the perpetrator is strictly liable, that is liable even in the absence of fault. These are the types of liability which Justinian categorized as quasi-delictual, because the person liable was not guilty of any wrongdoing. Finally, quasi-contractual obligations are those which arise as a result of one party having conferred a benefit upon another in circumstances in which it would be unjust for the beneficiary not to make good any loss suffered by the benefactor as a consequence. Like delicts, these are not based upon agreement but arise by operation of law.

The fourfold classification of types of obligations in the compilations of the emperor Justinian reflects the emphasis placed upon the number four in this department of the law by the Roman jurists. As there were four types of obligation, so also contractual and delictual obligations were each divided into four main categories. In delict, these were *furtum* - theft, *rapina* - robbery, *damnum iniuria datum* - damage to property, and *iniuria* - unjust harm. Contractual obligations were divided according as to whether the obligation arose by virtue of some thing having been transferred between the parties - contracts *re* or real contracts, its having been entered into by solemn verbal promise in question and answer form, the contract *verbis* or verbal contract, it having been reduced to writing, the contract *litteris* or literal contract, or its being sufficient that the parties had reached agreement, consensus, on certain key issues, the contracts *consensu* or consensual contracts. The jurists moreover identified four kinds of real contract and four types of consensual contract. Four was regarded as a natural number, corresponding to the number of seasons, for instance, and the points of the compass.

Modern civilian systems do not conform to this unyielding and somewhat artificial symmetry. They tend instead to categorize delicts according to the degree of blame attaching to the wrongdoer, rather than the type of harm suffered by the victim. As will be seen, this reflects the contribution of canon law to the subject during the mediaeval period, the Church insisting that without fault there could be no wrong, which view was taken up and endorsed by the jurists of the Natural law school and thereby found its way into the modern codes. In the realm of contract too, the modern classification is the result of the analysis achieved by the jurists of the Enlightenment, solemn words and writing now being seen as formal requirements for contracts which are in reality based upon consent, the words or documents merely manifesting that agreement. Real contracts are still however generally recognized, there being no enforceable agreement between the parties until the object of the agreement has been transferred from one to the other. In the realm of contract, general rules have also been worked out which apply to all contracts, and there are also some general rules which apply across the board to all obligations. The modern civil law of contracts consists therefore of general rules which apply to all contractual obligations and specific rules which apply to specific named contracts. The modern civil law of delict has tended to abandon specific wrongs in favour of general principles of tortious liability, with specific rules applying solely to situations of vicarious and strict liability. Despite these developments however the modern civil law of obligations remains remarkably Roman in its outline and in much of its substance. It is generally agreed that Roman law is the main contributor to the modern civil law of obligations, although Germanic elements and canonical contributions have also played an important if less obvious role in its formation.

There is a sense in which the civil law of obligations has developed twice, first under the Romans and then again from Germanic roots in the wake of the fall of the western empire. In truth, however, the developments of the mediaeval and modern periods were activated by the rebirth of trade and commerce, a renaissance which occurred at the same time as the sophisticated Roman rules relating to obligations were being rediscovered and which gave their recovery an added impetus. The rise of State power and the influence of the Christian religion likewise assisted in tailoring the emerging concepts to suit the social context within which they were to operate. To understand the modern civil law of obligations, it is therefore necessary to know something of that initial development in ancient Rome as well as the Germanic source from which the mediaeval laws sprang or at least upon which the Roman cuttings were grafted. From there, their development to suit the needs of trade in a Christian society need to be traced to understand the manner in which their current shape in the modern codes came to be achieved.

2 The Origins of Obligation

The evidence for the earliest stages of the development of the law of obligations is clearer with regard to Germanic than Roman law. It would appear however that in both societies the origins of obligations were broadly similar, and therefore a brief account of the Germanic origins can properly be given in advance of the earliest evidence for Roman developments.

The word *obligation* is derived from the Latin *ligatum* meaning a bond, a physical restraint, and obligations originally could and did involve physical limitations upon the person. Although in modern law, obligations are primarily viewed as being contractual and therefore entered into voluntarily by the parties, the earliest obligations in both systems would appear to have been delictual. Societies were composed of extended family groups and there was no individual ownership of property. Accordingly, the possibility of property transactions being determined by individual acts of will such as contractual agreements was not recognized. Property only changed hands between family groups when such an exchange was necessary to avoid a blood feud as a result of a wrong suffered by one family group at the hands of another. In such circumstances it was the duty of the kinship group to pursue the feud against the kin of the wrongdoer and the duty of the wrongdoer's kin to make reparation to the victim's family. The first situations in which therefore payment was due from one group to another would appear to have been when a wrong had been committed which justified the prosecution of the blood feud. Vengeance could be bought off by the payment of a composition. This is the stage encountered for instance in the Roman law of the XII Tables and in many of the Edicts of the Germanic rulers of the Dark Ages.

Whereas originally the amount of such a composition would have had to have been negotiated between the parties, the law codes testify to how these amounts came to be settled by custom according to the nature of the harm suffered. This allowed for the injured party to resort to self help if the composition was not forthcoming from the wrongdoers. Such self help took the form of confiscating all or some of the wrongdoer's property so as to coerce the wrongdoer into making good the harm. It might even be permissible to capture a member of the wrongdoer's family as a hostage in order to force a settlement. Such a human hostage or animal taken in distraint would be kept prisoner, that is bound, until the obligation was satisfied. Hence, the earliest meaning of obligation.

The wrongs which gave rise to such a response were primarily concerned with injury to the person or damage to property, but could include the wrongful taking of family property or the abduction of a family member. The latter situation has already been considered with regard to the development of the bride-price.[2] As family property could not lawfully be alienated, it followed that if a person from outside of the family were in possession of property belonging to the family, such possession was virtually of necessity wrongful, that is tantamount to theft, and many early societies had stringent rules against thieves. The thief caught in the act was liable to summary execution, and on discovery of a theft it was the duty of a group member to raise the hue and cry, and the duty of the group generally, or at least its adult male members, to pursue the thief. If caught in possession of the stolen property, the thief faced the same fate as one caught in the act, whereas a person discovered later in possession of property claimed by another family would have to establish how it came to be in his possession by calling on the person from whom he received it to warrant his title. If he was not able to do this, then his group would have to make composition for being in possession of stolen property, although the severe punishment of the hand-having thief would be avoided.

Prima facie, therefore, it was dangerous to be in possession of property belonging to another group. The sale and purchase of property between groups was therefore a matter for publicity, so that clear proof existed for the transfer so as to obviate any difficulties regarding title. Likewise, borrowing and lending required some form of security to ensure both that the borrower was not wrongly taken to be a thief and that the lender could be sure of being able to reclaim the thing lent. The early law of contractual obligations is almost entirely concerned with security for such transactions. Loans would involve the borrower giving either a member of his family or an item of similar value to that borrowed to the lender. Sales would be immediate transfers of both the merchandise and the purchase price. If there was to be a delay in payment or delivery, security would be required. In other words, to adopt the Roman legal terminology, early contracts were all real contracts, that is they involved the transfer of some thing between the parties. Originally, this would have been a thing of value as a pledge for future performance. With time, it became a symbol that performance was due, thus marking a transition from a pure real contract to one which is symbolic and therefore a formal as well as a real contract. The symbol would also be evidence that something was due from the debtor to the creditor, a sign upon which the people's judicial assembly, court or magistrate could legitimately act.

In such circumstances, breach of contract was clearly treated as a wrong, one kind of delict.[3] Only with the coming of an increase in trade and with it greater individualism with regard to the ownership of property did these arrangements gradually develop into rules of contractual engagement which were meant to facilitate commerce and not just provide security against wrongdoing. A facultative law had to replace one founded upon fear.

3 The Roman Law of Obligations

The law of obligations in the early Roman republic displays many of the features mentioned above, particularly with regard to theft. Theft, *furtum*, was a serious delict. The thief caught in the act, or the manifest thief, *fur manifestus*, as Roman law described him, was enslaved if a free man and put to death if a slave. A thief who was not caught in the act but whose guilt had to be proved by evidence was treated less harshly, which is indicative of the comparative lack of confidence which Roman law placed in such indirect proof. The *fur non manifestus* was liable to return the thing stolen and pay twice the value of the victim's interest in it. In the later republic, the praetor replaced the capital penalties of the early law for manifest theft with an action for fourfold the value of the thing, as well as giving an action for twofold in the case of non-manifest theft. He also gave an action for fourfold against a person who refused to allow his premises to be ritually searched in pursuit of stolen goods,[4] as well as an action for threefold against a person upon whose premises stolen goods were discovered. Such a person was also given an action for threefold against the person whom he could prove had placed the stolen goods there.[5] There was also in the late republic an action for fourfold the value of the thing if it had been stolen with violence, the delict of *rapina*, provided the action was brought within a year of the wrong being committed. Thereafter it lay for the single value of the thing only.

The XII Tables also gave remedies in the form of composition payments for unjust harms, *iniuriae*, that is harms which were not due to the victim and were for that reason unjust.[6] A person who cast a spell on another's crops, *carmen malum*, was to be beaten with clubs, and a person who maimed another, that is caused him a crippling physical injury, *membrum ruptum*, was to be liable to retaliation if the parties or their families could not agree upon a suitable composition. This latter rule encapsulates and fossilizes a particular stage in legal development, namely the moment when a society endeavours to replace self help, retaliation and the blood feud with acceptance of a pecuniary compensation. It is clear that for very serious injuries, Roman law in the mid fifth century BC was still striving to achieve that. For lesser injuries, it would appear to have already succeeded, for the XII Tables give fixed penalties for the breaking of a bone, *os fractum*, namely 300 *asses* in the case of a free man, 150 *asses* in the case of a slave. For all lesser injuries, there was a fixed composition of 25 *asses*.

This area of the law underwent development both by statute and the praetor's edict during the late republic. In 287 BC, the *lex Aquilia* introduced a new delict of causing unjust damage to property, *damnum iniuria datum*. Chapter I of the *lex* concerned the killing of a grazing animal, that is a *pecus*, or a slave, while chapter III dealt with lesser harms to slaves and *pecora*, as well as with the burning, breaking or destruction of other kinds of property. Although the *lex* laid down the level of compensation payable in each case, namely the highest value of a dead slave or *pecus* in the previous year or otherwise the highest value of the property in the previous month, the praetor also allowed the recovery of consequential damage, *damnum emergens*, and loss of profits, *lucrum cessans*. Moreover, in true Roman style, the delict had its penal element in that a defendant who denied liability would be liable twofold for the loss he had caused. The praetor further extended the action so that it became available for harms caused indirectly as well as directly, and even became available for injuries suffered by children in power as well as slaves, and even for injuries suffered by a *paterfamilias*.

These last developments encroached upon the territory of *iniuria* itself, which provided remedies for personal injuries. Once physical injuries to slaves and free persons were accommodated under the *lex Aquilia*, only non-physical wrongs to the person remained under *iniuria*. Thus, *iniuria* became increasingly associated with *convicium*, insult, rather than physical harm, and became an action for hurt feelings following abuse or defamation. The praetor again took a hand in its development, giving an action under his Edict whereby the judge was allowed to award damages up to a maximum contained in the *formula* unless the insult was atrocious, *atrox iniuria*, in which case he had to award the full amount. The praetor also developed remedies at the end of the republic for those who suffered as a result of fraud or were induced to suffer loss as a result of being put in fear by threats. These were the so-called praetorian delicts of *dolus* and *metus*. It can be seen however that Roman law, like the English common law, approached delictual harm from the standpoint of what the victim had suffered, and classified its delicts accordingly.

Contractual obligations were another matter. The evidence for the early state of Roman law is scant, but it appears that originally such obligations were entirely concerned with the avoidance of harm by the taking of security, either in form of human bondage, *nexum*, or a pledge of property, *fiducia*. In both cases, the security would be released or redeemed upon performance of the obligation. Thus, in common with many early societies, the first contractual obligations in Roman law would appear to have been real in nature, that is achieved by the transfer of a thing rather than by consent or agreement alone.

The transfer of a person into the civil bondage of another, *mancipium*, was probably at first intended as a form of security and coercion, but became a means whereby a child in power or a slave who had wronged another could be transferred into the power of that other to work off the debt. It could also be employed to surrender a child or slave as security in a transaction. In either event, the transfers represent the background to the rule in the XII Tables that a son who had been transferred into *mancipium* three times should not return into his *paterfamilias*' power, thus protecting the *paterfamilias* from continued liability for a delinquent child and protecting children against being constantly pledged by their fathers. Likewise, property pledged as security for a loan or future performance of a promise could be reclaimed on completion by *mancipatio* or *cessio in iure*, performance indicating that return was now due to the original owner.

The earliest Roman contracts would therefore have been formal. *Nexum* and *fiducia* are both real in that they involve the transfer of a person or a thing. They form however the security for an agreement not the agreement itself. Agreement between the parties was achieved by unilateral promises, made in solemn form by question and answer. "Do you promise? I promise" - *Spondes-ne? Spondeo*. Only certain words could be used and there had to be correspondence of question and answer. Only in post-classical law were these rigid rules relaxed. The formality served to draw attention to the making of the promise and thus to ensure either human or even divine witnesses. The verbal contract, *stipulatio*, while highly formal was nevertheless very flexible; money, things or services could be the subject-matter of the promising.

Stipulatio was the most important type of contract in republican Rome. Failure to perform could result in the praetor granting an action for the money owed, *actio certae pecuniae creditae*, the thing due, *condictio certae rei*, or even the performance of a service, *actio ex stipulatu*. The last-mentioned remedy is obviously specific to the stipulation, whereas the other two remedies could be used in other contexts. Thus, the *condictio certae rei* could be used to recover a thing which had been lent or deposited for safe keeping as well as for one to be delivered, and the *actio certae pecuniae creditae* would lie for recovering money lent or owing as well as for money promised by *stipulatio*. Indeed, the early Roman literal contract was achieved by entering and thus renewing, novating, a money debt in the creditor's ledger, which entry itself made the sum recoverable by *actio certae pecuniae creditae*.

Whereas obligations arose from formal promising, transfer of goods and ledger entries, the actions which enforced the obligations were not confined to those areas. The actions reflected the nature of the claim - for goods, for money, for a service. It was only with juristic analysis of these situations that the categories of contractual obligation emerged, and is in all probability the work of Quintus Mucius Scaevola at the start of the first century BC. Juristic analysis concerned itself with why a thing had been transferred from one person to another, whether it was for consumption as with a foodstuff, or for safe-keeping, or for use, or as security. This could be expressed by stating the loan was for safe keeping, *depositi causa*, or for the use of the borrower, *commodati gratia*, and it may be that records of such loans were kept in those terms.[7] From the reason, or *causa*, for the transfer, the jurists adopted names for the different types of transaction involved. Thus, real contracts, all involving the transfer of a thing were distinguished under the headings of *mutuum* - loan for consumption, *commodatum* - loan for use, *depositum* - loan for safe-keeping, and *pignus* - pledge. As real contracts, these were as a group distinguished from verbal contracts, such as the *stipulatio*, and the literal contract based on the ledger entry.

The jurists were able to distinguish these contracts further by their typical incidents as well as their typical cause. A loan for consumption did not require the return of the exact thing lent; thus, ownership in the thing passed from lender to borrower, and therefore, as the lender had no more interest in that particular thing, the borrower was under no duty to exercise any degree of care in his dealings with the thing in the lender's interest. His obligation was to return a thing or things of equivalent quality and quantity regardless of what happened to the original. The loan for use, *commodatum*, on the other hand, required that the self-same thing lent be returned, so that ownership did not pass. The Roman lawyers also denied that possession in the legal sense passed, for possession could ripen into ownership by *usucapio*, and that should not occur here as the transfer had not been for a reason which would ground a just title. Therefore, the jurists reckoned that the borrower for use obtained but detention of the thing, not legal possession. As the lender expected the same thing back as he had lent, it was incumbent upon the borrower to take good care of it. He was required to look after it as a good *paterfamilias* would take care of his own property, the standard of care called due diligence, *exacta diligentia*, and failure to achieve this standard amounted to negligence. The borrower for use was liable to the lender not only for the thing's safe return but also for any loss or deterioration caused by his negligence.

Whereas the borrower for use received the thing for his own purposes, the person who received a thing for safe-keeping took it to assist the lender rather than himself. Therefore, it was recognized that, while there was, equally with *commodatum*, a duty to return the thing so that ownership did not pass, it would not be fair to expect the same standard of care as from a borrower for use. Accordingly, the depositee was only liable for damage caused to thing by his deliberate fault, *dolus*, or for damage caused by gross lack of care on his part, *culpa lata*, that is recklessness bordering on deliberate fault. However, the advent of the *lex Aquilia* upset this neat distinction in that under the *lex* anyone who caused damage to another's property was liable for that harm if the damage had been caused by his fault, *culpa*, in the sense of being negligent. It would appear absurd to excuse a depositee from such liability if perfect strangers would have been liable for the same acts. Accordingly, depositees became liable for *culpa levis*, ordinary negligence, although a distinction was still made between them and borrowers for use. In that a depositee was specifically selected by the lender, it was regarded as sufficient if the depositee had exercised the same degree of care with regard to the thing deposited as he exercised with regard to his own property. Breach of that standard was termed *culpa levis in concreto* to distinguish it from the breach of the standard of care expected of the *bonus paterfamilias* in his activities, *culpa levis in abstracto*. *Culpa* generally was sometimes distinguished from negligence in that it always required some act by the guilty party, whereas negligence in the sense of a lapse from due diligence could be constituted by an omission.

Mutuum, *depositum* and *commodatum*, with their distinct purposes and the above distinctions, are still to be found in the modern codes of civil law under the heading of contractual obligations. They testify to the tenacity of the Roman achievement in this area of the law. The fourth real contract, *pignus*, a development from *fiducia* but not involving transfer of ownership, has become in modern law a form of real security, although it is still necessary for the pledgee to exercise due diligence in his custody of the thing, and whereas with early forms of chattel security the thing could be sold by the pledgee in both satisfaction of the debt and punishment of the debtor, so that there was no question of the pledgee having to account for the sale price, in *pignus* the pledgee must account to the debtor for the proceeds of sale and hand over any excess once the debt has been satisfied.

Pledge is a contract which can have a commercial dimension. The early law of *fiducia* had recognized this by distinguishing commercial pledges from the security that might be asked of a friend for a loan. *Pignus* developed from *fiducia cum creditore* whereas the other real contracts arose from *fiducia cum amico*. No interest was due on a loan by *mutuum*; no charge was made for a loan for use by *commodatum* or for the safe-keeping of the chattel in *depositum*. Payment would have made them commercial contracts of hire rather than arrangements between friends.

The growth of trade in the later republic required a freeing of the law of contracts from the straitjacket of formalism, and it is during the last two centuries of the republic that the fourth category of contracts developed in Roman law, the consensual contracts. These were also four in number: sale - *emptio/venditio*; hire - *locatio/conductio*; partnership - *societas*, and mandate - *mandatum*. These differed from the other three categories of contracts in that they required no formal words, writing or the transfer of a thing for their perfection; they were binding and enforceable as a direct result of the parties reaching agreement, consensus, upon the key elements of the contract. Thus, in sale, which was by far the most important, agreement on the thing to be sold and the price made the contract binding. Thereafter the parties were bound to perform their respective obligations, the seller to deliver the thing to the buyer, the buyer to pay the purchase price.

Although no formalities were required for the validity of a contract of sale, it was usual for the agreement to be evidenced either by writing or by one party giving the other an earnest of his good faith. This earnest or *arra* was generally a small coin as a token of the promise. However, in later Roman law, as a result of Greek influence, the *arra* often took on a new character, that of *arra poenitentialis*, the payment by the buyer of one-half of the purchase price on the understanding that if he did not go through with the purchase, this sum would be forfeit, and if the vendor did not go through with the sale, he had to return the *arra* twofold.

Sale in Roman law was a bilateral contract in that the parties had distinct obligations, one to buy, the other to sell. Hence, its double name in Roman law - *emptio/venditio*. The buyer's duty was to pay the purchase price in money; a juristic dispute between the Sabinians and the Proculians as to whether the price could be some other thing ended with victory for the latter. Where one thing was transferred in consideration for another, this was deemed to be a different contract with different duties, that of exchange, *permutatio*.[8] In sale, the seller's duty was to deliver the thing to the buyer or allow him to take possession; there was no duty to make him owner. The seller's promise was to transfer quiet possession not *dominium*. In this the Roman version of sale differs from that in many modern civil law systems, and some explanation should be sought.

If a person who received property as the result of a *mancipatio* was disturbed in his enjoyment of it within the period requisite for *usucapio*, then he had a remedy against the transferor for twofold the value of the thing if he was evicted. This was the *actio auctoritatis*. With regard to other transfers, transferees emulated their rights under the *mancipatio* by exacting a *stipulatio duplae* from the transferor to the effect that he would pay double the value of the thing if the transferee were evicted by one with better title. There was therefore every expectation generally that the transferee was receiving good title.[9]

The explanation cannot be avoided that the contract of sale, which did not of its own motion transfer the thing from vendor to purchaser, did not originate in the context of a sale by the owner. If that had been the case, it is more likely that transfer of *dominium* would have been the vendor's obligation as in modern law. That the vendor's obligation was limited to transferring quiet possession suggests that the vendor was not the *dominus* but was believed to be selling in circumstances which would not cause the true owner to contest the sale.

This explanation connects the development of sale with that of another consensual contract, mandate. Mandate was an agreement by which one person, the *mandator*, commissioned another, the *mandatarius*, to perform some office, usually involving the establishment of legal relations, on his behalf. Roman law never developed any clear concept of agency, therefore although the mandatarius acted for the mandator, his actions did not bind the mandator as against third parties. Third parties obtained legal rights and duties against the mandatarius only. Mandatarii did not generally have the power to dispose of their mandators' property, but they could be given such power. Indeed, initially mandates were concerned with the accomplishment of a single commission, general managerial roles being given to procurators, but these eventually came to be treated as long-term general mandates. The need for such general managers of large estates became prevalent in the second century BC when service abroad became common among the Roman landed classes at the same time as land became available for occupation by them in areas of Italy and further afield which they could not manage conveniently from Rome. Senators had an added reason for using managers in that their rank precluded their participation in trade. Much farming in Africa was accomplished by *procuratores*, and in the south of Italy during the reign of Augustus most of the large estates were owned by absentee landlords.[10]

Given that only the owners could transfer the produce of these estates with *dominium*, the managers who ran them on their behalf could promise no more than that the transactions they concluded would be honoured by their employers. Thus, the most they could promise a purchaser of produce from the estate was quiet possession which would mature into ownership after a year by means of *usucapio*. If the owner reclaimed within the year, the purchaser had his action on the purchase, the *actio empti*, against the vendor, who would be able to claim any expenses occurred by reason of the mandate against the mandator. If the year had elapsed, the purchaser was secure, but the mandatarius would be liable to the owner in an action on the mandate, the *actio mandati directa*, if he had exceeded his authority by selling. There is no conceptual integrity to this juristic achievement, but, in the fashion of Roman engineering as well as jurisprudence, it works.

Sale was a *bona fide* contract, which meant that the vendor would be acting unlawfully if he failed to disclose to the purchaser any defects in the thing of which he was aware. However, originally, sales, whether by owner or another, were at the buyer's risk with regard to hidden defects in the merchandise. Gradually, regulations were introduced to protect purchasers against hidden defects as well. These regulations were introduced by means of the Edict of the Curule Aediles, which governed amongst other things trade at markets and in the *forum*. Purchasers were given an action to rescind the purchase if they discovered a material or moral defect in a slave or animal bought within six months of the purchase, and an action to recover the difference between the actual value of the thing and the purchase price at any time within a year of buying it. These were respectively the *actio redhibitoria* and the *actio quanti minoris*. By the end of the classical period, these remedies had been extended to sales in any context and were therefore implied terms in any contract of sale.

Locatio/conductio, the contract of hire was not as highly-developed as sale in Roman law. It could be used to hire a thing, to hire the skill of an artisan or the labour of an unskilled workman. In each case, there had to be agreement about the subject-matter of the hire and with regard to the cost, the *merces*. It was therefore a bilateral contract which was instantly enforceable upon agreement proved. Hire of free labour was relatively rare in republican Rome, with its slave economy, but under the empire, as many free persons sank to an abject standard of living, many were forced to put their labour on the market by this method. In the time of Augustus, the large estates of southern Italy frequently found it necessary to hire free labour at harvest time to supplement that provided by the slave gangs. Hire of skilled labour was common, as craftsmen generally worked on materials supplied by their employers rather than selling their own wares.[11]

The last of the four consensual contracts was *societas*, partnership. This began as an arrangement by which the heirs of a deceased person agreed that they would continue to run their inheritance as a joint venture rather than splitting it among them. This was the original *consortium*, and involved the pooling of all their property. Those who had not acquired such an inheritance jointly but wished to live with all things in common were able to emulate the *consortium* by agreeing to establish a *societas omnium bonorum*, of all their goods. Those wishing to establish merely a partnership of their business property and endeavours were also able to do so by means of this contract, the *societas omnium quae ex quaestu veniunt*. Partnerships also developed to enable persons to pool their resources for single business ventures, the *societas alicuius negotiationis*, of which the partnerships set up by tax-gatherers, the *publicani*, were an important sub-category, the *societas vectigalis*. Finally, an agreement to own something jointly or legal imposition of joint ownership of a thing, such as a party wall, led to the *societas unius rei*. The *societas* was capable in other words of serving the purposes of family property, business concerns and joint ownership between neighbours. Its flexibility cannot fail to remind the common lawyer of the adaptability of the trust.

The *societas* however was not a legal person in Roman law, and when one of the partners contracted on its behalf, the third party established obligations only with the partner with whom he had contracted.[12] The affairs of the partnership were regulated solely by the agreement of the partners. The death or resignation of one of them ended the partnership, although the survivors could immediately agree to enter into a new agreement.[13] Outsiders used the usual remedies against individual partners as though they were dealing with an isolated individual, while to regulate the contractual relationship existing amongst themselves the partners had the *actio pro socii*.

Agreements which did not fit into the specific contractual categories mentioned above were not of themselves legal contracts. In the eyes of the Roman jurists they were bare pacts which did not give rise to legal claims, *ex nudo pacto non oritur actio*. To support legal claims, such pacts had to be part of one of the above types of contract, *pacta adiecta*, or else have been made actionable by praetorian or imperial provision, *pacta praetoria* or *pacta legitima* respectively. Otherwise, although pacts could give rise to defences to an action, they could not give rise to claims in themselves.

This narrow view, however, was not destined to prevail. The jurists of the later classical period developed a concept of what were termed innominate contracts, that is contracts which did not fit into one of the named, nominate, categories mentioned above, albeit that some of them were known by particular names. Such agreements, it came to be held, were actionable provided that one party had performed his side of the bargain. Mere agreement did not make them actionable, but performance by one party allowed him thereafter to sue.[14] Thus wherever one person had given or done something in the context of an agreement that the other should do or give something, the former could sue on the agreement performed on his part. Four situations were delineated: I give that you should give - *do ut des*; I give that you should do - *do ut facias*; I do that you should give - *facio ut des*, and I do that you should do - *facio ut facias*. At least four of these innominate contracts came to be identified by name; these were the contracts of exchange - *permutatio*, sale or return - *aestimatum*, compromise of a legal action - *transactio*, and letting at will - *precarium*. While the last mentioned tends in modern law to be treated within the law of property, the first three are today classified as nominate consensual contracts in their own right in the civil codes.

The legacy of the Roman law of contractual obligations is patent upon the pages of the modern civil codes. Contracts are still dealt with according to type, and the real contracts of *mutuum*, *depositum* and *commodatum*, and the consensual contracts of sale, hire, partnership and mandate, enlarged by the addition of further contracts known to the Romans, such as exchange, *aestimatum* and *transactio*, are readily familiar in modern civil law. Although the rules governing these specific contracts continue to be dealt with individually, the big difference between the modern civil law of contracts and its Roman predecessor is that the former unlike the latter has developed certain concepts which are generally applicable across the contractual area. Many of these notions, such as those relating to delay, error and risk, are based upon Roman ideas, but the Roman jurists never generalized them in order to achieve anything like a unified law of contract as opposed to a law of separate contracts.

4 The Germanic Contribution and the Middle Ages

In many ways, the arrival of the Germanic tribes within the borders of the western Roman empire marked a return to the level of the XII Tables in terms of the law of obligations in western Europe. The Germanic tribes, as testified in the laws of the Goths, the Lombards and the Franks, still saw the breaking of a promise as a kind of wrong, that is a form of delict, and emphasized the necessity of taking real security against the possibility of such a disappointment. It was however the case that the form of this security had become in many instances symbolic, it being sufficient for the debtor to hand the creditor a stick or *festuca* as a sign, or indeed an earnest, of his indebtedness. The production of this *festuca* was then sufficient for the popular assembly to know that something was owing from the debtor to the creditor, and this could put his freedom or the security of his entire estate in jeopardy.

The symbolic use of the *festuca* did not however completely oust the role of real security among the German tribes. The chattel given as security for future performance, the *wadium*, was widely known and could be disposed of by the creditor to satisfy the debt without any form of judicial or popular intervention or need to account to the debtor for the proceeds. Self-help was a key factor in the Germanic system of enforcement, and it took until the thirteenth century to eradicate customs allowing seizure of goods or even of persons with the aim of coercing a defaulting debtor into submission.

The most important advance made by Germanic jurisprudence during the Dark Ages as a result of its contact with the Roman system was probably in the use of written instruments in relation to contractual obligations. The terms of a Roman *stipulatio* had for some time been routinely reduced to writing in order to evidence the promise, although the validity of the contract continued to rest upon its supposedly verbal completion.

Gradually, however, under Greek and Byzantine influence, the writing in effect became the form, rather than the spoken words. This practice was adopted by the Germanic peoples, who adapted it to suit their own needs, the Roman evidentiary *cautio* becoming the Frankish obligation *per cartam*. The debtor would hand the creditor a written acknowledgement of his obligation, and this instrument was for the Franks both of two things. Firstly, as for the Romans, it was evidence of the agreement or promise that had been made, recording the terms of the contract. However, it was also more; it took over from the *festuca* and the *wadium* the role of the symbolic real security, whereby its possession by the creditor was a sign to the community that the debtor was obligated to him, the production of which proved the obligation as much as its terms, and which indicated that the creditor was entitled to execution, first of all by means of self-help and at a later time by intervention of judicial power.

The use of the *carta* as both a symbol of indebtedness and evidence of the terms of an obligation enabled the Germanic laws to take a further step which had never been essayed by Roman jurisprudence despite its commercial sophistication. If the debtor gave the creditor a written instrument acknowledging his indebtedness in a certain sum, it would be open for the creditor by adding further writing to indicate that this credit was transferred to a third party as satisfaction of a debt owed that third party by the creditor. This could be done for instance by writing the terms of this transaction on the back of the original, called endorsing it. This was a tremendous step forward along the road to the development of commercial instruments such as bills of exchange, and it was eventually realized that by making the instrument payable to bearer, it could be used as a ready means of transferring, or assigning, rights of credit. The assignment of such rights had not been possible in Roman law; the development of this important commercial institution was a significant Germanic contribution.

The notion of debts being assignable by transfer of the *carta* was not new to Germanic law; in earlier times, the transfer of the *wadium* or the *festuca* had accomplished the same result. Such assignments differed from the production of bearer bills in that the latter from the outset anticipated that the obligation could be assigned. Bearer bills emerged in Italy during the ninth and tenth centuries, at the same period when the *carta* was enjoying its heyday in the Frankish realm. Although the use of the *carta* underwent something of a decline in the post-Frankish period, bearer bills retained their popularity and infiltrated into the laws of France in the thirteenth century and Germany in the fourteenth. They represented an amalgam of Germanic, Roman and Byzantine legal elements, infused with mercantile practice from the Italian mediaeval communes. Indeed, much of commercial law developed as a result of the contact between merchants in the German towns and fairs of the later Middle Ages, where Germanic customs mingled with the legal practices of Lombard and Roman origin as traders from the Italian communes met their northern European counterparts.

The notion of assignment of an obligation involved of necessity the benefit of an agreement accruing to a person who was not an original party to it. It opened up the possibility therefore and provided a method whereby agreements could be made to benefit persons other than the contracting parties. Roman law had not recognized the possibility of an agreement being enforced by a third-party beneficiary, but such contracts became relatively common during the Frankish period in France, Germany and Italy, where the Germanic freedom to assign obligations made the notion acceptable. Roman learning nevertheless made third-party contracts controversial until the modern civil codes accepted them.

If the use of written forms assisted the growth of mercantile law, assignment of contracts and contracts for the benefit of third parties, it also transformed the law relating to the execution of contractual claims. In this, the Germanic tradition of self-help played a significant part. Germanic law began from the principle that a disappointed creditor was entitled to proceed without judgement against both the person and the goods of the debtor. Under the Lombards, certain classes of property became exempt from this liability, and under the Franks it was established that no goods were to be thus taken unless there was an agreement demarcating the property which was to be so vulnerable. From these roots, the modern law of bankruptcy was to develop in thirteenth-century Italy, from where French merchants were to transplant it north of the Alps.

Germanic law had regarded breach of contract as a wrong, amounting in effect to a delict. The person responsible for the wrong was therefore outside of the law's protection, an outlaw, allowing his person and property to be at the mercy of the wronged party. In the same manner as resort to self-help in the taking of the wrongdoer's property came to be restricted, so also seizure of the debtor by the creditor was prevented. Instead, the family of the debtor or later any person who voluntarily acted thus was allowed to stand surety for the debt. This originally involved the surety's passing into the custody of the creditor as a hostage, but by the thirteenth century this too had changed into the surety acting as a guarantor of the debt with his property rather than his person. Eventually, the surety became a secondary debtor against whom the creditor could proceed in the absence of satisfaction from the primary debtor.

In much the same way, the right of the creditor to seize property belonging to either was diminished, although in the case of delictual wrongs, the resort to self-help by confiscation remained a reality. However, the creditor was no longer allowed to sell the property taken by himself to satisfy the debt; instead, it had to be sold by public authority, often after judicial order, and in the Italian communes the sale had to be by public auction to ensure a fair price. Salic law required that the taking of such a distress must also be a public act, carried out by the *grafio* in the presence of seven *rachimbourgs*. Eventually, the levying of such distress came to be limited to those instances in which the victim levied the thing which caused the damage as a distress damage feasant to assure compensation for the wrong suffered, and to those situations in which an innkeeper was allowed to detain the goods of a guest for failure to settle his account or a landlord to levy distress for rent due. In other words, it was confined to certain specific situations. It is important to note also that land was originally exempt from such confiscation in that it was not, in Germanic custom, capable of individual, as opposed to family or group, ownership. Even when land became capable of being owned by individuals in the feudal period, so that it could be used as security for an obligation if it was so agreed, there were nevertheless considerable formalities with regard to such use, and it was generally only available for distraint, for example in France, at the hands of the king.[15] It was during the thirteenth century that land became available as security more generally through formal agreement in court.

The thirteenth century saw a distinct turning point in the development of the law of obligations across Europe. This was in part the result of the growth in trade, in State power, in the influence of the Church and the revival of Roman law. The use of writing in contractual arrangements was transformed through the registration of written agreements in the courts. As is witnessed by the *Sachsenspiegel* and the town laws of many German cities, the registration of agreements not only enabled their ready proof but also their swift execution by judicial means. It had come to be realised that obtaining the judgement of a court that an obligation was due enabled the efficient executive machinery at the disposal of the judiciary to be used for the execution of the judgement debt. If the agreement itself were therefore initially recorded by the court in its records or made in a form which rendered further proof of it superfluous, this efficient machinery could instantly be called into play upon the debtor's default. The thirteenth century saw agreements being drawn up before judges in the manner of a judgement. Philippe de Beaumanoir presents three scenarios for such a transaction: in the court of the lord or the king; in the local court of the parties, or through the use of a seal by a gentleman as irrefutable evidence of his agreement. Gradually, the notaries who were employed to keep the written records of the courts took over from the judges this non-judicial function, and there developed the institution of the notarially authenticated document as conclusive evidence of the agreement or transaction described therein, and which could only be challenged on the grounds of forgery. The production of a sealed writing of any of these sorts entitled the creditor forthwith to execution, as the seal gave the document both authenticity and binding force.[16] Such writings commonly became an essential feature of mercantile agreements, the Frankish *carta* becoming the less formal *notitia*, beginning as a form of evidence but transforming into the sealed instruments used frequently in Italy after 1100.[17]

Another Germanic legal feature which declined as the influence of commerce, the Church and the revived Roman law was felt was its insistence upon strict liability for breach of contract and for wrongs. Germanic law knew nothing of Roman law's distinctions between *dolus*, *culpa*, and degrees of fault. It was particularly strict with regard to the obligation of those who were possessed of the property of another to return it. Any harm that came to the property while in their possession made them liable to the lender. Even when the Roman distinctions between the liability of the depositee and borrower for use entered into the Germanic legal consciousness, responsibility for safe-keeping of another's property remained severe, and the new category of *culpa levissima* was invented, very slight fault, to render the depositee or borrower liable for virtually any harm or mischance that befell the thing provided its source was not outside of his control. External misfortunes, such as the death of an animal or the destruction of a thing by storm or flood, were thus excused, but not an internal mischance, such as an accident that the borrower suffered. The property was at his risk.

Likewise, Germanic law, unlike Roman law, had no qualms about visiting liability for the wrongs of family members upon the head of the household or Sib, nor for that member the wrongs of an apprentice upon his master or that of a vassal upon his lord. The wrongdoer was in each case under the other's control and he was therefore answerable. Roman law had required some element of fault on the part of the superior; Germanic law was less fastidious. True vicarious liability therefore is a Germanic contribution, as are some vestiges of strict liability which have survived into modern law.

Germanic law also knew the concept of the pledge of faith, *fides facta*, as a form capable of rendering an agreement actionable. This was often expressed in Germanic law by a handshake or a clash of palms, *palmatio*. In any event, it attracted attention to the agreement and created enforceable obligations. The pledge of faith, however, was to be taken up by the canon law in its treatment of obligations, and the influence of the Church must next be assessed.

5 Canon Law and the Early Modern Period

The Germanic pledge of faith presented the Church with an excellent opportunity to Christianize the law relating to contractual obligations, an opportunity which it did not miss. From Carolingian times onwards, the Church encouraged the parties to swear their faith by oath, either on the Bible, or upon the cross or the relics of a local saint. This meant that their agreement was made in the context of a solemn promise to God that it would be honoured, so that breach became a threat to their eternal salvation. The Church therefore had jurisdiction over promises made in this manner if they were in any way broken. The taking of such solemn oaths was encouraged by the laws of the Lombards and the Franks, and the same was true of the laws of the emperor Frederick I. The Glossators, however, finding the institution foreign to Roman law, were very much against them.

Technically, the use of the oath to effect an obligation amounted to a formal contract if not indeed a real one, real in that the promisor had pledged his hope of salvation as security for the performance of his duty. Unlike the material pledges of the *wadium*, the *festuca*, the *carta* or the payment of earnest, this pledge was moral rather than material, if none the less real to the parties for that.

The Church however progressed its view of promises and agreements still further. To break an oath was a sin and one's very Christianity, one's hope of salvation attained at baptism, forfeit as a result. However, even without a solemn oath and the pledge of faith, it was sinful to break a promise. The manner in which the promise had been made, whether formal or informal, was not important from the Church's perspective; to break a promise was a sin and required a remedy. The Church's attitude therefore moved the law of contractual obligations from its formal, Germanic roots back towards a Roman, consensual basis, but the Church emphasized consent to a degree which had not been present in Roman law, although it could appeal to the consensual basis of important contracts such as sale under that system.

Canon law's acceptance of informality in the making of contracts was completely in accordance with the needs of the mercantile classes of the mediaeval towns and cities, who needed as much flexibility as possible in their commercial dealings. Canon law stressed that provided certain requisites were present within an agreement, then it was a valid contract which could give rise to legal obligations. Contracts being voluntary arrangements, that is made by acts of free will on the part of the parties, it was necessary that the parties should have entered into them freely and have had the intention of creating legal relations between themselves. Thus, the canon law accepted fraud or coercion as vitiating the essential consent required, following the pattern of the Roman law. It was also necessary that the parties should actually have reached agreement on the essential objects of their contract, much as had been the case in the Roman law of sale and hire, so that, for instance, both the price and the merchandise had to be certain for there to be a valid contract of sale. However, the Church also stressed the need for there to be a good motive for the agreement, and that the contract should have been entered into for a good cause or *causa*. This element had been present in Roman law, but the canonists were to develop it in a manner which has changed the meaning of the concept and arguably been the occasion of some confusion regarding its purport in subsequent law.

The manner in which the canonists developed the concept of *causa* confused it somewhat with both the motive of the contract and the object to which it related. The *causa* of a contract might be considered to be its purpose or objective. In Roman law, hire differed from sale in that the money was paid not to acquire quiet possession of the thing but to obtain its use for a fixed period. *Depositum* differed from *commodatum* because the reason why the thing was placed in the detention of another was in the former case for its safe keeping and in the latter for the borrower's use. The canonists however went further than this. They looked not only to the purpose of the type of contract employed but also the objective of the actual contract under consideration. Thus, if A lent B a dagger with which to assassinate a third person, C, the Romans would have said the purpose of this contract was loan for use but the canonists would have said its objective was to enable B to murder C. The canonists would therefore deem the contract to be void for an unlawful cause. Likewise, if an agreement were made, the objective of which was contrary to public morals or was foolish, it would be deemed by the canonists void for contravening public order or for having a worthless cause. If the objective of the contract was impossible of performance, then it would again be void for lack of a just cause. Contracts were however nevertheless identified according to their typical cause, as the Romans had identified their nominate contracts. This inevitably was a source of some confusion, which has prevailed to the present day in those systems which have adopted the doctrine from the mediaeval canonists.

In some measure, the doctrine of *causa* was developed in order to honour the Roman maxim that a bare pact was not a lawful contract. The canonists founded upon this maxim an elaborate jurisprudential conceit. If bare pacts could not appear in court, then they must be suitably clothed for such an appearance. What clothed them so as to make their appearance in court possible were certain vestments, *vestimenta*. Here the canonists resurrected the Roman categories of contract - *re, litteris, verbis, consensu*, but made them types of vestment which could clothe a contract. Thus, to be actionable, a pact had to be clothed either by the transfer of a thing, the use of solemn words, the reduction of the agreement to writing or by the meeting of the minds of the parties regarding the essential elements of the agreement. Contracts by oath fitted the verbal category, pledge contracts the real, and the increasing number of registered contracts the written, but consensual contracts were the most numerous and flexible variety. A bare pact had become acceptable in the commercial practice of Italy in the fourteenth century as the basis of an action at canon law, and by the end of the fifteenth century, a two-sided pact, that is one based on the mutual promises of the parties was actionable in both Italy and France. In Germany also, by the end of the Middle Ages, canon law had succeeded in introducing informal, consensual contracts onto the legal scene. Many of the contracts which the Roman law had only regarded as actionable upon performance by one party were now deemed actionable upon proof of consent.

This emphasis upon consent as an essential element in all contracts necessarily affected the perception of the role of writing and earnest in the formation of agreements. Contracts were now seen as binding agreements or promises and not as scenarios for the commission of wrongs for which pledges were security. Accordingly, earnest returned to its later Roman role of *arra poenitentialis* or *Wandelspön*, a payment of a forfeitable deposit rather than a symbol of agreement having been reached. Writing also was seen as a form which manifested consent rather than as itself being the foundation of the contract. Some contracts, because of their nature or value, might be required to be in writing as this was now regarded as a formal requirement for their validity, which did not affect the underlying need for consent and the other prerequisites of all contracts, and the need for writing to evidence other types of contract was seen as going to evidential certainty and not to the existence of the contract itself. Thus, for instance, the French *Ordonnance* of Moulins of 1566 required contracts with a value of over 100 *livres* to be in writing,[18] and the Prussian *Landrecht* was later to insist upon the same formality for contracts of over 50 *thalers*. Contracts concerning the transfer or creation of interests in land were generally required to be in writing or at least evidenced by a written document; increasing use was also made of judicial registration of certain agreements or of notarial authentication of certain transactions. Generally, however, the requirement of form was giving way to that of *causa* under Italian influence in the early modern period. Even in Germany, where the concept has been rejected in the modern BGB, the sixteenth century saw the importation of *causa* into the native law with the Reception of the doctrines of the Italian jurists. In Italy itself, the importance of the concept had been stressed as early as 1188 by the Glossator Huguccio in his *Summa*.

The Reception also brought into Germany the concepts of fault and degrees of fault which had begun with the Roman jurists and been further developed by the canonists. In that the canonists saw breach of promise as a sin committed by the party who reneged, rather than as a wrong suffered by the party disappointed, for them the breach was only wrong if it was in some way culpable, otherwise there was no sin. This applied not only to broken promises and agreements but to the canonists' approach to wrongs generally. Accordingly, for a remedy to be given in canon law, the victim of the wrong had to establish some blame on the defendant's part, otherwise the Church had no interest in the matter. Unlike the civil authorities, which intervened to facilitate a settlement and avoid the peace of the community being violated by a feud, the Church intervened for the good of the wrongdoer's soul, so that, if there were no blame attaching to his act and therefore no peril to his salvation, the Church claimed no jurisdiction.

The Canon lawyers played a key role therefore in developing the notion of no liability without some degree of fault and in exorcizing the Germanic preference for strict liability from the European legal scene. The learned law, the *ius commune*, came to require either *dolus* or *culpa* for liability for both delicts and breach of contracts, and introduced and developed the gradations of *culpa* - *culpa lata, culpa levis in abstracto* and *culpa levis in concreto* - as general principles of the civil law of obligations. Although the regional customs of Germany resisted this intrusion, it was nevertheless ultimately successful, even if in Germany the concept of *culpa levissima*, liability for a very slight degree of fault was invented to preserve in certain areas, such as loans for use and safe-keeping, a substantial measure of almost strict liability, excusing only harm suffered by chance or acts of God. The canonists revival of the degrees of fault related to both delicts and contracts, leaving a permanent mark upon the subsequent civilian approach to obligations in general and adding considerably to the perception of obligations as being an integral whole according to the civil law approach.

While the development of fault liability is generally deemed a progressive step taken under canon law influence, the same is not usually felt about the canonists' attitude to usury, that is the lending of money for interest. Taking a very strict view of certain Biblical texts against lending money for gain rather than return,[19] the Church placed a complete ban upon the taking of usury by Christians. The ban was introduced into secular law by the Carolingians, but was of little importance until the revival of trade and commercial prosperity in the cities and communes of the twelfth and thirteenth centuries. Thereupon the Church and the mercantile classes were at odds, but the Papacy remained obdurate on the issue, Alexander III imposing excommunication and refusal of Christian burial upon recalcitrants at the Lateran Council of 1179. Gregory X in 1274 and Clement V in 1311 repeated the prohibition. Even the Protestant reformers in the sixteenth century were in the main supporters of the ban.

Roman law had not prohibited the taking of interest, achieving that result by adding stipulations for interest payments to gratuitous contracts of *mutuum*. Justinian sought to regulate rates of interest but not to ban its taking. Ultimately, this was the solution which the modern legislators also came to adopt. The final Recess of the Imperial Diet in 1654 allowed loans at interest, and the Prussian *Landrecht* sought only to regulate rates. In 1745, the Papacy itself revised its position, with Benedict XIV allowing moderate interest as not being usury, provided that it was stipulated for alongside rather than as part of the loan itself. Thereafter, usury was regarded as the taking of excessive interest, and in effect became synonymous with overreaching the borrower.

While the Church's prohibition of usury did not appeal to the adherents of the School of Natural law, the canonists' development of fault and their analysis of contractual obligations did. The Natural law school emphasized consent as the key factor in contracts and adopted the Roman law classification of contracts but according to the canon law approach. This accorded with mercantile practice and convenience. Both Domat and Pothier were highly influential in assimilating the canon law concepts into the civil law which formed the basis of the later French codifications. Domat in particular had introduced the moral ideas of the canonists relating to motive and *causa* into his treatment of obligations, and Pothier insisted that promises generally had to be kept, regardless of form, and that compensation was due for their breach if that breach were attended by fault. With the achievements of these writers, the scene was set for the emergence of the modern civil law of obligations.

6 The Modern Civil Law of Contracts

The French *Code civil* was a product of the natural law school of jurisprudence associated with the eighteenth-century Enlightenment. The view of society upheld by the thinkers of that school was based upon the concept of the social contract, which regarded society as based upon an agreement made by individuals. Contract therefore was seen as central to human social existence and the individual freedom to enter into contractual arrangements as a basic social good.

For that reason, contractual obligations are regarded in modern civil law systems as the typical sort of obligation. Gone is the earlier notion that the law concerns itself with contracts in that broken promises or agreements amount to wrongs which require legal redress in the same manner as delicts. Instead, the role of the law in such arrangements is seen as being facilitative, enabling individuals to achieve by acts of free will legal arrangements which suit their personal requirements and tastes. This view of the role of contract permeated into German society and law as a result of the work of the Pandectists in the nineteenth century.

The basis of contractual obligations being individual acts of will, what was necessary therefore to create a contract was the meeting of minds of the parties to it, namely their consent. Consent was the essence of contractual agreements. While that consent might be manifested by some specific form, such as writing or registration or the use of solemn words, it was the consent that was important. This feature of modern contract law was clearly derived from the views of the mediaeval canonists. In that each party was viewed as acting individually in achieving consent, the existence of consent was viewed as arising from the offer of one party being accepted by the other; offer and acceptance were the means by which consent was achieved. Coincidence of offer and acceptance manifested consent; it was the *Willenserklärung* of German law. Problems with regard to the moment at which consent was achieved if acceptance was not communicated directly to the offeror were answered by theories which have become known as those of emission - when the acceptance is articulated; expedition - when it is sent; information - when the offeror becomes aware of it; and reception - when the offeror receives it. The last mentioned is the general solution of modern civilian systems.

Contractual obligations in modern civil law are therefore those which are founded upon the consent of the parties and, if that consent is vitiated in some way, the contract is a nullity. This is in stark contrast to earlier systems of law, in which the form of the agreement was paramount and it was lack of form which nullified an agreement. It was during the thirteenth century that the canonists and the Roman law scholars introduced a distinction between those agreements which were completely void and those which were merely voidable, that is vulnerable to nullification. A void contract was one which was an absolute nullity because the parties had not really consented or because the agreement lacked an object or had no lawful *causa*. An agreement lacks an object if what it purports to concern does not exist, or cannot be determined or is incapable of private ownership. Thus, for instance, an agreement to purchase a unicorn is void for lack of an object because no such animal exists, but so is one for an animal which cannot be identified, as is one for the purchase of property which by its nature cannot be the subject of private ownership, such as a national monument or shrine. An agreement is void for want of *causa* if it has no purpose, or one which the law regards as too trivial to be worthy of legal protection, or if its purpose is unlawful or contrary to public order. An agreement is void for lack of consent if consent has been obtained by threats of violence, or by fraud or due to an error relating to the substance of thing or the nature of the transaction, but not generally with regard to the identity of the parties, unless that is of significance, for example as when one believes one is contracting with an artist to produce a portrait and one is not.

A contract may also be void for what is termed in civil law lesion, that is a serious disparity between the values of the prestations made by the parties, for example as where property is sold for but a fraction of its true value. Later Roman law had recognized the concept of *laesio enormis*, when land had been sold for less than half its value, but did not extend the rule to the sale of other forms of property nor apparently to the converse case when more than twice the value of the land had been paid for it. Again, the mediaeval jurists extended the rule to all property and indeed to other contracts than sale, allowing an agreement to be nullified if too much had been paid.[20] The rule continues to apply in many, but by no means all, civil law jurisdictions, and some civil codes, for instance the Spanish, specifically state that it does not apply, thus acknowledging its existence as a principle within the law of obligations while rejecting it from the national system.

Factors which completely vitiated the consent of the parties had been contrasted by the mediaeval jurists with factors which undermined the reliability of a consent which had been achieved. Thus, where a minor had entered into an agreement without the authority of his guardian, or likewise a prodigal without the proper permission, then, despite the consent obtained, it remained open to the weaker party to have the agreement set aside. Such contracts were classed by the canonists as voidable rather than void, and their nullity classed as relative rather than as absolute. The French kings of the Middle Ages and early modern period also granted letters rescinding contracts which were in some way unenforceable according to the rules of Roman law. These included factors for which the praetor would have withheld a remedy, as well as the provisions of the *senatusconsultum Velleianum*, which annulled contracts which wives had made pledging their husband's credit, and the *senatusconsultum Macedonianum*, which avoided contracts made by sons in power tying up their future inheritance. Both laws had always been part of the system of obligations in the *pays de droit écrit*.

Roman law had also observed a distinction between those contracts which were *stricti iuris*, that is always enforceable if made according to the legal requirements, and those which were *bona fide*, requiring good faith on the part of those wishing to enforce them in addition to being legally valid. In such contracts, the praetor would always withhold a remedy if the person seeking it was not in good faith, with no need for the other party to raise a specific defence of bad faith. The mediaeval canonists had stressed this requirement for all contracts, beginning from the impropriety of allowing someone who was in bad faith to enforce a contract made by oath and advancing the principle to every agreement however made. This was to contribute to another doctrine which came to be developed quite significantly in nineteenth-century law, that of the abuse of rights, wherein it was recognized that remedies, lawfully due to a person, should be withheld if the purpose of the suit was to harm the other party rather than to obtain redress for oneself. The principle of allowing third-party beneficiaries to enforce agreements was also allowed.

Although the modern law therefore by and large rejected the *stricti iuris/bona fide* categorization of the Romans in favour of a general requirement of good faith, which looms particularly large in German law by virtue of article 242 of the BGB, other categories of contract are still enumerated. Thus, modern civil law still distinguishes between unilateral and bilateral contracts according to whether the parties' obligations differ, and also observes a distinction between gratuitous contracts and those which are onerous, rather as Roman law distinguished between those based on friendship, *amicitia*, which were not undertaken for reward and those based on commercial considerations. The latter are subdivided into commutative and aleatory contracts depending upon whether the consideration is fixed or uncertain at the time of contracting. Finally, modern law continues to distinguish those contracts which have a typical cause and are dealt with individually in the code, the nominate contracts, from those which are valid solely because they are agreements which fit the general rules of contracting but do not fall within one of the typical categories, innominate contracts.

As well as having to comply with the general rules relating to contractual obligations, the nominate contracts have specific rules which are set out in the civil code as applying to each. The number of nominate contracts has been considerably increased since the time of the Roman jurists, and many of the contracts they regarded as innominate are now nominate - *permutatio*, *aestimatum* and *transactio* being examples. The nominate contracts of Roman law are still to be found in the modern codes, although some, such as pledge, are now often classified as forms of securing property rights rather than as obligations arising through agreement, recognizing that their significance now extends beyond the parties who create them, requiring respect from third parties who may have claims against the property. *Mutuum*, *depositum* and *commodatum* still have a place in the codes, and are still classified as real contracts, dependant upon the transfer of a thing or the performance of some conduct for their validity, although they are now contrasted solely with consensual contracts, the categories of literal and verbal contracts having been dropped. It is important to stress that consent still has a part to play in the real contracts, but consent alone does not make them actionable without the transfer of the *res*; hence, their continued classification as real contracts.

The modern real contracts are typically gratuitous, although it is now perfectly acceptable to agree for interest to be payable upon a *mutuum* of money or for a fee to be paid for a *depositum*. It is also now generally the case that the depositee has to avoid *culpa* and not just *dolus* in his custody of the thing. The German approach of strict liability has been abandoned.

The number of consensual contracts has increased well beyond the original Roman four, and *societas* has become an important legal entity in its own right requiring separate discussion, and a division exists in some modern civilian systems between civil and commercial law. Sale, hire and mandate are still present, sale continuing to be the most important and indeed being recognized as the normative contract in German private law. The most important difference between modern and ancient sale is that the agreement is now to transfer ownership and not just quiet possession, and, in those countries which follow the French *Code civil*, acceptance of the natural lawyers insistence that legal transactions are acts of will means that property passes by virtue of the agreement, delivery not being essential for title to pass. The BGB and its followers retain the necessity for delivery. The Greek approach of having ownership pass upon payment of the purchase price has not been preferred. The vendor remains liable for defects in title which could or do lead to eviction and also for hidden defects in the thing, in accordance with the developments made in Roman times under the aedilician edict. Sale remains bilateral and *bona fide*. Certain contracts of sale, such as those of land or interests therein, are required to be made in writing.

Whereas the law of sale had been highly developed in Roman law, the same was not true of hire, but the mediaeval jurists gave it more attention. They it was who distinguished the three kinds of *locatio/conductio*, namely of a thing - *rei*, or of service - *operarum*, or of the doing of a skilled task - *operis faciendi*. Under Germanic influence a further distinction developed between the hire of moveables and immoveables, respectively known as *Miete* and *Pacht*, the latter of which included the right to fruits and profits, whereas the former did not. The mediaeval civilians' distinction between hire of service and hire of a skill became in early modern German law that between *Werkmiete* and *Dienstmiete*, according to the latter of which the employer, in true Roman fashion, continued to supply the materials for the work, unless the contract was with an artist, and retained the risk for the materials. These classifications were adopted by the natural law school which influenced their adoption in the Prussian *Allgemeines Landrecht* and from there into most of the modern civil codes. The hire of service has in some modern codes become a part of special rules relating to labour relations. Italian law provides an example of this development.

Mandate continues to hold a place in the modern civil law, although today it is permissible for the mandatory to be paid for his services and not just to receive an honorarium. It is still however seen as a personal service, connected with entering into legal obligations on another's behalf. Modern civil law has however developed contracts of agency which were unknown to the Roman jurists and which owe their existence to the work of the mediaeval lawyers as they responded to the commercial needs of their time. Perhaps the most significant development of a consensual contract to meet the needs of commerce is that of partnership or *societas*, which is now often dealt with apart from the other consensual contracts.

The contract of *societas* in Roman law developed from a family arrangement into an institution of considerable commercial use and flexibility, and was further developed by the mediaeval jurists and by the *ius commune*. In the Middle Ages, *societates* ceased to depend upon the continuing consent of the *socii* for their existence and could be entered into for fixed terms. Such arrangements were the first *compagnia* in the Italian communes. These companies began to acquire a personality of their own, so that outsiders trading with them acquired rights and duties against the partners as a whole and not just as against the partner with whom they had dealt, a step which had not been taken by the Roman law. This required some public knowledge of who the partners were, so that from the fourteenth century, the partners within such companies had to be registered. In France during the thirteenth century, Beaumanoir knew of partnerships which were entered into for a year and a day, and companies of serfs were common as were those entered into for the establishment of a communal life. Eventually French law, in the shape of the *ordonnance* of Moulins required that partnerships should be entered into by means of a written deed.[21]

During the Middle Ages, such partnerships presented an avenue by which money could be lent at interest despite the laws prohibiting usury. For instance, a shipowner might need money to purchase a cargo to take to another port to sell at a profit. He would therefore approach another person, in effect a moneylender, who would advance him the money necessary to buy the cargo not in return for a promise to repay with interest but as a partner who would take a share in the profit of the voyage, thus in effect as a partner. Thus became established what the French laws called the *société en commandité*, which made the partners running the business liable without limit for the losses of the concern, but limited the liability of those who only advanced money to the extent of their investment. Thus, the *societas* began to develop into a company with limited liability, a process which was completed with the development of the *société anonyme*, which required a government licence for their establishment in France prior to 1867, and since then can be freely formed subject to registration. They are regulated under the French commercial code. The *ordonnance* of 1673 required the articles of partnerships involving limited liability to be published. The advent of *sociétés anonymes* facilitated the rise of joint-stock companies which provided the capital for colonial expansion from Europe into the New World and in the Far East and Africa.

The commercial partnerships which these developments have facilitated have enabled the property of the partnership and its creditors to be separate from that and those of the individual partners as private individuals. It has resulted in the recognition of the *societas* as a legal person in its own right. Although the great mediaeval jurist, Bartolus, recognized this, the Romanists of the Reception were resistant to acknowledging the legal personality of such partnerships, while Germanic legal tradition, with its concept of ownership by the collective hand, common property and corporate personality pressed for its acceptance. The influence of the nineteenth-century German jurisprudence of the historical school has ensured that the native Germanic contribution has in this regard been appreciated so that today the *societas* can indeed constitute a legal person in its own right, its creation requiring formalities of writing and registration, but nevertheless allowing it full rein as a major institution of commercial and corporate activity. Moreover, the concept of ownership in collective hand has influenced the development not only of the family communion in property matters, but has also supplied the basis for other forms of common ownership such as the *condominium* of apartment blocks, with their assembly of owners and executive committee and administrator.

While some of the Roman innominate contracts are now consensual contracts in their own right in the modern codes and others are enforceable as consensual contracts under the general contractual provisions of the civil codes, the Roman rules on innominate contracts have nevertheless maintained an influence. Although the contracts themselves, being now consensual, do not require performance by one party to render them judiciable, performance by one party can still be significant in depriving the other of the right to rescind. If one party to a consensual contract generally fails to perform through some fault of his own, then the other may rescind that contract. Bartolus invented a somewhat subtle distinction between failure to perform for an old and necessary cause, that is one which was not the responsibility of the defaulter or one which antedated the agreement, and failure through a new and voluntary cause, that is one which arose because of the free act of the defaulter since the agreement had been made. For this latter type of default, rescission was available to the other party. Loysel supported this distinction in French law, and it has proved of influence in the modern codes.

Whereas rescission is allowed in such circumstances, there is considerable variation between modern civilian jurisdictions with regard to the provision of specific enforcement of agreements. While generally, contracts requiring personal performance will not be specifically enforced, those systems deriving from the German BGB regard specific enforcement as a standard response to breach while those deriving from the French *Code civil* do not. This in part is the result of German law regarding contractual rules generally as being based on the contract of sale, in which specific enforcement is a more suitable and convenient remedy.

7 The Modern Civil Law of Delicts

The Roman law of delicts was as concerned with punishing the wrongdoer as with compensating the victim, and approached the question of delictual liability from the standpoint of the harm which the victim had suffered rather than that of the degree of blame attaching to the wrongdoer. During the mediaeval period, a clearer demarcation came to be made between criminal proceedings leading to the punishment of the wrongdoer and civil proceedings leading to the compensation of the victim. Under the influence of the Church and canon law, it became accepted that absence of blame made it unjust to punish someone who had caused a harm, and eventually this perspective infiltrated civil law also suggesting that fault was a necessary ingredient in making an action for civil compensation sustainable.

The French jurist of the humanist school, Domat, was particularly insistent upon the necessity of fault to civil liability. This was related to the Roman precept of law that one should not injure another, *alterum non laedere*, seeing this precept broken only if the infliction of harm was blameworthy in some way. Others believed that an act was wrongful if it injured the interests of another regardless of whether blame attached to the perpetrator.[22] This reflects the traditional Germanic view that liability for harms caused is strict.

Modern civil law reflects the former rather than the latter approach. Delictual liability is no longer defined in terms of particular types of harm suffered by the victim, but rather liability attaches to the person who causes harm to another's lawful interests as a result of deliberate or negligent conduct. *Dolus* is still used to describe deliberate or reckless conduct; *culpa* for blameworthy conduct which falls short of intentional or reckless conduct but involves fault in the sense of failure to act prudently to prevent harm to another. Although *culpa* was originally thought of as applying to positive acts rather than to omissions, failure to act in a manner which harms another when it is reasonable to expect assistance to be forthcoming is now regarded as blameworthy. In France, this is partly as the result of the incorporation of this principle into article 63 of the French Penal Code. In some civil law countries, Italy being an example, the concepts of *dolus* and *culpa* as defined in the penal code are utilized in the calculation of civil liability.

German law emphasizes that to be unlawful so as to lead to civil liability an act or omission must be both unlawful and culpable. By unlawful is meant that it must harm a legal interest of the victim which is protected by the law, that is one of the enumerated legal rights which the law exists to protect. This reflects the connection between this department of the law and the fundamental law of the State, the constitution, most admirably. If the constitution protects personal integrity, for instance, the infliction of physical injury is unlawful and if done culpably will result in entitlement to civil redress. Likewise, if reputation is protected, defamation is unlawful; if property is protected, trespass is unlawful, and so on.

French law has also developed during the nineteenth and twentieth centuries a doctrine of so-called abuse of rights. This relates to the situation where a person performs an act which is perfectly lawful but results in harm to another. If it can be shown that the act was committed not in pursuit of some lawful interest of the first party but intentionally to cause that harm, then the culpability of the act renders it unlawful. It offends against the precept *alterum non laedere*.

A distinction is also drawn in some systems between the type of damage suffered, namely whether it is material, in the sense of having a pecuniary value, or moral, in that the right harmed does not have a pecuniary value. Italian law, for instance, only allows material damage to be compensated unless the act complained of was also a criminal offence. This brings the

Italian position close to the German approach, whereby certain forms of damage are only compensatable if they were committed deliberately or recklessly. This applies for instance to non-pecuniary losses arising from physical injury, defamation or sexual offences. Generally, only material damage will be compensated, but even there, in German law, a distinction is made according to the nature of the injury. Injury to a protected right is compensatable if committed culpably, while if the harm is one based on a statute protecting certain classes of persons only, intention or gross negligence will be required, whereas if the wrong is one to public order, actual intention is always required.

The damage suffered must have been caused by an unlawful, culpable act. This gives rise to the question of what test of causation is adopted. The Roman *lex Aquilia* had originally been taken to demand that the damage have been caused directly by the body to the body, *corpore corpori*. Modern civilian systems have vacillated somewhat between requiring only that the act be a contributory factor, an equivalent cause, in the production of the damage, a viewpoint associated with the German criminologist von Buri, and the more usual insistence that the act have been a factor which could be foreseen to be likely to cause the damage and have so caused it, a so-called adequate cause, associated with the theories of another German jurist, von Kries. French law and most modern systems follow this latter view and require that the act or omission be an immediate and direct cause of the damage.

Despite the Germanic preference for strict liability, it is now generally accepted that there is no liability usually for harms caused by act of God or *force majeur*, nor by accident, the act of a third party, nor the victim's own fault, although in the latter event the extent to which the victim contributed to his harm will be calculated to assess the other party's proportion of the blame. The modern civil codes contain specific provisions for situations in which strict liability will apply, as for instance with regard to the owner's or occupier's responsibility for harm caused by ruinous buildings, the owner's or keeper's liability for dangerous animals or things, and more recently the owner's responsibility for harm caused by the circulation of his motor vehicle unless he can establish that it was being driven without his consent. Vicarious liability for the harms caused by others is also recognized; parents being liable for the wrongs of their children, artisans for their apprentices, employers for their employees, and occasionally teachers for their pupils.[23] Whereas German systems tend to see this as a form of true vicarious liability, that is a liability arising by virtue of the relationship between the tortfeasor and the defendant and bearing no stigma of blame with regards to the latter, the French-derived systems favour an interpretation which sees the defendant being made liable because of his own fault in employing or not adequately disciplining a negligent or wanton employee, child or apprentice. German law, however, in the case of employers, makes the employer liable for harms caused by his workforce, sometimes as in the case of railway companies and the suppliers of gas and electricity, without any blame attaching to either the employer or the employee, provided a harm has been caused by the activity to a lawfully protected interest of the victim.[24]

Modern civilian systems have therefore recast the law of delictual obligations, or liability for wrongful acts, according to the degree of blame attaching to the wrongdoer. This is a complete reversal of the Roman origins of delict, which concentrated upon the harm suffered by the victim, although the classification of degrees of blame is drawn from the Roman roots. However, the mediation of the mediaeval canon law has had a profound influence upon the development of this department of the law, particularly as the natural law school, which so influenced the content and structure of the modern codes, adopted the canonical approach as being in accord with their own view of obligations arising from the voluntary acts of the parties and not from fortuitous occurrences. Since the nineteenth century, this perspective has not been without its critics, many seeing the role of this department of the law as being to redistribute losses suffered within the community among its members, particularly with regard to activities from which all derive a benefit, such as industry and transport. This view has affected the development of the rules of vicarious liability but has not undermined the general civilian approach to delicts. It is sometimes amusing to note that the proponents of loss distribution have little if any inkling that they are advocating a return to the Germanic system of delictual liability within a communal rather than an inter-individual framework.

8 Quasi-Contract in Modern Civil Law

Whereas Gaius divided obligations into those which were contractual and those which were delictual, Justinian introduced two further categories, quasi-delict and quasi-contract. Quasi-delict referred to those whereby a person became liable for a wrong for which he was not to blame, and therefore covered instances which today are classified as forms of strict or vicarious liability. Quasi-contract on the other hand referred to situations in which obligations arose by which a person was obliged to make restitution to another because he had received a benefit from that other or as a result of that other's activity which it would be unjust of him to accept without compensating that other for any loss incurred by the latter on the former's behalf.

Modern civil law can be seen to be striving towards a general principle of restitution regarding quasi-contractual liability, much as has been achieved in the area of delict. The Roman beginnings were however confined to certain specific situations in which someone who had undertaken a liability on another's behalf without a mandate having been agreed could claim compensation for any loss suffered thereby. There were four main situations. The first was the classic case of quasi-contract, that of *negotiorum gestio*, where one person responds to an emergency concerning another's property affairs in that other's absence and authorizes that action be taken as though, *quasi*, acting under a mandate. Such would be the case if, during an owner's absence on holiday, his neighbour noticed that his house had a broken window and had it repaired. Provided the neighbour believed that the owner would have wished the work done and the expense incurred is reasonable, the owner will be liable to the neighbour for the cost of the work which he has borne. This has entered modern civilian systems virtually unchanged; in French law, it is called *gestion d'affaires*, in clear imitation of its Roman forebear.

A second classic instance of quasi-contractual obligation is where money has been paid under a mistake of fact. For instance, one person wrongly believes that he is indebted to another and pays that other money which is not in fact due. The person who received such a payment in Roman law was obligated to return it, a *condictio indebiti* being available to recover the sum. Again, modern civilian systems have adopted the principle virtually unaltered, French law as the *paiement de l'indu*.

Justinian also classified the relationship between curator and the owner of the property in his *cura* as being based upon quasi-contract, probably because the *actio negotiorum gestorum* was available between the parties for there had been no agreement between them, yet the curator was acting as though he had a mandate. In addition, Justinian recognized that the principle of avoiding unjust enrichment also informed certain situations in the law of property where an owner was not allowed to recover his property from another without first compensating that other for some work done on it or some interest acquired in it. Usually, the other would be able to resist the owner's *vindicatio* in such circumstances by making use of the praetorian defence of the *exceptio doli*. Thus, for instance, if a house had been built on land belonging to another, that other could not claim back the land and the house on it, which was his by *inaedificatio*, unless he paid the other for the value of the materials.

From such latter instances, the modern civilian systems have developed a principle of unjust enrichment, or enrichment without cause, under the heading of quasi-contract. The phrase quasi-contract continues in use bearing witness to the natural law school's adherence to the view that voluntary actions should found claims of obligation, although both delict and quasi-contract are in truth exceptions to that principle, accepting that it is not only the law's business to enforce agreements and remedy voluntary wrongs, but also to intervene where one person has caused a loss to another or suffered a loss for another's benefit. It was in the nineteenth century that the French jurists, Aubry and Rau, argued that *gestion d'affaires* and *paiement de l'indu* were only instances of a wider principle that none should be enriched at another's expense without cause, and this view was finally accepted by the French courts in the case of *Boudier* in 1892.[25] Domat and Pothier had referred to a maxim in the Digest which stated that it was contrary to natural law to profit from another's loss and injury, but had seen in this a rule of right conduct rather than of law. Most civilian systems have now adopted enrichment without cause as a supplementary heading of liability, not to be used if another remedy is available, allowing a person who has lost out by conferring a gain on another to recoup his losses from that other to the extent of the other's gain. The principle marks one of the most significant civilian developments of modern times, and indicates that the history of civil law has not been concluded with the production of the modern codifications.

9 Conclusions

A modern civil lawyer looking back at the Roman origins of the law of obligations can easily discern the contractual categories with which he is familiar, the classification of the degrees of fault which still subsist in the modern law and many of the individual rules which have stood the test of time. However, it is unlikely that a Roman jurist would feel as at home with the modern codified provisions. In truth, the civil law of obligations has been re-invented by the modern codes, using some of the original materials but also drawing upon the designs produced by the mediaeval civilians and canonists, who utilized their learning in the service of new political structures and the needs of expanding trade and commerce. Nor must the contribution of the Germanic legal tradition be undervalued. In a sense, the modern civil law of obligations has resulted from an application of Roman legal structures and ideas onto a new Germanic base, which ruthlessly questioned fault liability and insisted upon a very different conception of legal personality. The Germanic approach to contractual obligation has also led to a rejection of the mediaeval and modern doctrine of *causa* in those countries which have followed the German BGB rather than the French *Code civil*.

Nevertheless, the law of obligations remains one of the most Roman areas of modern civil law in its structure and content. The concept of obligations being an integral whole, with contracts, delicts and quasi-contracts being sub-parts, is unaltered, and most of the nominate contracts remain to be seen. However, there can equally be no disputing the impact of a general theory of contractual obligations which, if discernible beneath the various contractual categories of Roman law, was never developed into a systematic whole by the ancient jurists. Likewise, the modern law of civil wrongs is a unified whole owing more to the ideas of the mediaeval civilians and canonists, and their acceptance by the natural law school of jurisprudence prior to codification, than to the Roman law of delicts.

The modern civil law of obligations is a living testimony to the capacity of civil law to find itself anew, to reinvent itself, to meet the needs of a new age. Its beginnings however lay in the writings of the Roman jurists who first sought to devise theoretical structures for the jurisprudence of their time from the workings of the praetorian formulary system of actions. Something must now therefore be said of the Roman law of actions before considering the modern concept of the State in civil law countries and their systems of civil and criminal justice.

Notes

[1] See Justinian, *Institutes* III. 13. 2.

[2] See chapter 10.

[3] This was the starting point also for the development of the action of *assumpsit* in the English common law.

---

[4] This was the search *lance licioque* ridiculed by Gaius, which the praetor replaced with an action for fourfold in the event of a search being resisted, the *actio furti prohibiti*.

[5] The *actiones furti oblati* and *concepti* respectively.

[6] Harms which were due, that is lawful punishments, were just, justice being defined as giving each his due.

[7] One theory is that the literal contract by ledger entry resulted from there being no reason given for the advance; see J.A.C. Thomas, *Textbook of Roman Law* (Amsterdam, 1976), p. 267.

[8] See pp. 296 ff., 310.

[9] If the thing were not very valuable, a promise to repay its simple value, the *stipulatio habere licere*, was often employed.

[10] See H.F. Jolowicz, *An Historical Introduction to the Study of Roman Law* (2nd. Ed.; Cambridge, 1952), p. 454; M. Crawford, *The Roman Republic* (Glasgow, 1978), pp. 60, 103, 200; C. Wells, *The Roman Empire* (Glasgow, 1984) p. 94; O. Tellegen-Couperus, *A Short History of Roman Law* (English Ed.; London, 1993), p. 36.

[11] See A.H.M. Jones, *The Later Roman Empire 284-602* (Oxford, 1964), pp. 110, 237, 862 f.; Jolowicz, *Historical Introduction*, pp. 533 ff. This avoided the payment of the tax called the *collatio lustralis* which Constantine had imposed on craftsmen who sold their own products.

[12] See chapter 9.

[13] This may indeed have been the circumstances in which the *societas omnium bonorum* emerged from the *consortium*.

[14] Using either the *actio praescriptis verbis* or an *actio in factum*. See further chapter 13.

[15] See J.-B. Brissaud, *A History of French Private Law* (Boston, 1912; reprinted New York, 1968), pp. 594 ff; C. Calisse, *A History of Italian Law* (Boston, 1928; reprinted New York, 1969), pp. 782 ff.

[16] See Brissaud, *French Private Law*, pp. 507 ff; 598 ff.

[17] See R. Huebner, *A History of Germanic Private Law* (Boston, 1918; reprinted New York, 1968), pp. 568 ff.

[18] Article 54.

[19] See Exodus, XXII. 25 and Deuteronomy, XXIII. 19 f. The former text however only bans usury at the expense of the poor and the latter with one's own family. The total ban upon lending at interest imposed by the Church was as much based upon Aristotelian ideas of the barrenness of money, that is its inability to produce fruit, and also the concept of there being a just price.

[20] Diocletian's price system made the opposite rule unnecessary.

[21] Article 54.

[22] See R. Savatier, *Traité de la responsabilité civile* (2 vols., 2nd Ed.; Paris, 1951), vol. I. n°. 35, and M. Planiol, *Traité élémentaire de droit civil* (14 vols., 11th Ed.;

Paris, 1952-1960), vol. II. n°. 863, both discussed in Amos & Walton, *Introduction to French Law* (3rd Ed., Oxford, 1967), pp. 217 ff.

[23] This last head of liability was abolished in France in 1937; Loi 5 April 1937.

[24] Although the legislation concerning this is outside the BGB; see N. Horn, H. Kötz and H.G. Leser, *German Private and Commercial Law: An Introduction* (trans. Tony Weir; Oxford, 1982), pp. 160 ff.

[25] See *L'affaire Boudier* Req. 15. 6. 1892; D. 1892. 1. 596; S. 1893. 1. 281; discussed in Aubry and Rau, *Droit civil français* (12 vols., 5th Ed.; Paris, 1897-1922) and in Amos and Walton, *Introduction to French Law*, pp. 197 ff.

13 The Law of Actions

1 Introduction

The third of the three parts of Gaius' institutional scheme was the law of actions. Whereas the law of persons dealt with the issue of who could be the subject of rights and duties and the law of things what could be the objects of those rights, the law of actions is concerned with how persons can enforce their rights. It is therefore concerned with actions in the sense of the remedies that are available to uphold rights and enforce duties, and also with the process or procedure whereby the actions are conducted.[1]

The inclusion of actions within the institutional scheme emphasizes the close relation between the existence of rights and the means by which they are enforced, a relationship encapsulated in the maxim *ubi ius, ibi remedium*. It can indeed be argued that a legal duty cannot really be held to exist if there is no legal remedy to enforce it. Equally, it is commonly believed that in most legal systems the concept of a substantive right only gradually emerges as a result of the availability of remedies and procedures to facilitate access to them.[2] There has nevertheless been criticism of the inclusion of actions within the institutional scheme, some believing that remedies and procedure are subsidiary to the questions of substantive rights and duties, who may have them and over what they may be exercised. Accordingly, it has been powerfully asserted by some writers, particularly during the seventeenth and eighteenth centuries, that the law of actions is adjectival law whereas the law of persons and of things is substantive law, and this distinction should be observed. As a result, the modern civil codes do not deal with actions but confine their attention to the substantive law of persons and things, reserving the law of actions to separate procedural codes. Thus, in most modern civil law countries, the civil code is complemented by a code of civil procedure, and this has indeed been carried over into the realm of criminal law, where the law of substantive offences is dealt with in the modern penal codes but the criminal justice process is reserved to a separate and complementary code of penal or criminal procedure.

The modern law of actions has therefore become distinct from the substantive law of the civil codes, and it is appropriate therefore to discuss it in separate chapters concerned with civil and criminal justice.[3] As will be seen in those chapters, the modern law of actions has been heavily influenced by the Romano-canonical procedures devised during the mediaeval period and the reaction against certain aspects of that system during the last few centuries. It might therefore at first sight appear that the law of actions as described by Gaius has little relevance to the modern civilian approach to remedies and procedure. This however is not entirely that case as the Roman achievement in this department of the law is one of its great contributions, indeed legacies, to the jurisprudence of subsequent generations. Some understanding of the development of the law of actions in ancient Rome is therefore required, and the outline history which follows is intended to provide sufficient information for the Roman contribution to the modern law to be identified.

2 The Early History and the *Legis Actio* Procedure

The Roman law of actions may be said to have developed in three stages, the second of which, the formulary system, is the most famous, being that which is associated with the classical age of Roman jurisprudence. The final stage, that of *cognitio*, sets the scene for the emergence of mediaeval and modern systems of adjudication and procedure. The earliest stage, from which the formulary system itself may have been but a development, was that of the *legis actio*.

The *legis actio* procedure differs from the early, ritualistic procedures of other legal cultures, including the European, in that it is enacted not before an assembly of the people but before a magistrate. In the presence of such a third party, a person who wishes to claim the ownership of some thing, lays his hand or staff, *festuca*, upon it and asserts his claim in a formal phrase: "I claim this thing to be mine by Quiritary right". If his claim was not contested by the other party, the magistrate would have no option but to declare the thing to be his as he claimed, and this was the form adopted to effect formal transfers of civil law ownership, *dominium*, the method called *in iure cessio*. However, if the other party wished to contest the claim, he would make the same assertion in the same manner using the same words, whereupon the magistrate would instruct them both to let go of the thing and one party would challenge the other as to why he made his claim, the other would assert that he did so because his claim was just and the former would allege that the claim was unjust and challenge the latter to support it with a wager, the amount of which would reflect the value of the thing in dispute.[4] Once each had sworn to the justice of his cause and made the wager to back the oath, which wager and oath was called the *sacramentum*, issue between them was joined, the crucial moment in Roman litigation called *litis contestatio*. The magistrate would award interim possession of the thing to one of the parties and set a day thirty days hence for them to choose a judge to adjudicate their cause. After the month had elapsed, the parties would return and either themselves nominate a suitable third party to act as judge or *iudex*, choose one from the white book or *album* of suitable persons which the magistrate maintained or allow the magistrate to suggest a name to them or draw lots from names contained in the *album*. The *iudex* once chosen would be sworn to give a just verdict and the parties would bind themselves to accept his verdict. Thereafter, on the next day but one, the *iudex* could begin his deliberations and inquiries. He was not a professional judge, neither in the sense of being employed by the State to adjudicate nor in the sense of having qualified in the law to fulfil a judicial role. Rather he would be a person of probity within the community who could be relied upon by the parties to give them a fair and reasonable hearing and a just judgement of the issue. They having bound themselves to accept his verdict, there was no question of any appeal from his decision, although he would be liable personally to an injured party if he gave a wrong verdict through impropriety of some sort. His verdict would be that the wager of one of the parties was forfeit, that is that party's claim was not just and thereby the issue was settled. He had no means of enforcing his judgement, nor did the magistrate do so as a matter of course.

Although the archetypal form of *legis actio*, technically this was the *legis actio per sacramentum in rem*, laying claim to ownership of a thing. It could be varied so as to claim that an obligation existed, whether to perform some act or to hand over some thing or sum of money. This was the *legis actio per sacramentum in personam*, this early recognizing the distinction between actions *in rem* and actions *in personam*, which distinction influenced the subsequent juristic divide between rights *in rem* and *in personam*. This form of *legis actio* could also be used to claim that a person in bondage or slavery was lawfully free, and just as the *legis actio per sacramentum in rem* supplied the basis for *in iure cessio*, so the assertion of liberty in this ritual form provided the rite of passage to freedom called *manumissio vindicta*.

The *legis actio* procedure is clearly connected with other legal rites which in other early societies would have taken place not before a magistrate but before the communal assembly, and it is possible that in early Roman law such claims and transfers would have occurred before the *comitia curiata*, which body remained a setting for the making of wills and the adoption of persons *sui iuris* by adrogation. Indeed, it is tempting to speculate that it was with the transfer of such procedures from the assembly to the magistracy that the compilation of the customs observed in the past within the assembly became necessary, and there is for instance a fairly close correspondence between the compilation of the Twelve Tables and the creation of magistrates, the censors, with powers to manumit slaves through their office. The magistrate before whom the *legis actiones* would have originally been enacted was the consul, but from 367 BC this function was passed to the newly-created separate magistracy of the praetor in clear recognition of the amount of work involved in such administration of justice and also acceptance of magisterial authority in this area.

By that time, one would have expected the procedure before the magistrate, the proceedings *in iure* as they were called, to be seen as the precursor to getting the contentious issues settled by the judge in the stage known as *apud iudicem*. Indeed, out of the *legis actio per sacramentum*, there developed an alternative *legis actio* procedure allowing for a judge to be appointed more swiftly, the *legis actio per iudicis arbitrive postulationem*. This dispensed with the thirty-day delay before a judge was appointed, and was concerned with failure to perform a formal promise by *sponsio* and with the division of an inheritance, although it was gradually extended to other disputes requiring division of property.[5] This would appear to indicate that such cases required the services of someone to assist in a settlement rather than to give a formal verdict. Inheritance cases generally went to a special tribunal for the stage *apud iudicem*, the court of the *centumviri*, just as disputes about freedom went to the *decemviri stlitibus iudicandis*, and certain cases to a group of *recuperatores*. Otherwise, however, the *iudex* was as a rule a monocratic tribunal, that is one staffed by a single judge.

Sometime during the third and second centuries BC, another kind of *legis actio* procedure was devised, that *per condictionem*. The *condictio* lay for the recovery of a certain sum of money which was owing - *certa pecunia credita*, or else for a certain thing - *certa res*. The former kind was introduced by the *lex Silia*, of uncertain date but probably a third century enactment, and the latter by a *lex Calpurnia*, possibly that of 149 BC. The latter was an extension of the former. Although a thirty-day delay was required before the choosing of a judge, the *condictio* was unlike the *sacramentum* in that it did not require the cause of the obligation to be stated and did not involve a wager. Instead, the judge's verdict demanded the payment of the sum owed to the claimant or required that the thing owing or its value be rendered. Enforcement however did not follow, although the judgement debt replaced the debt which the judgement recognized. It was always the case that at *litis contestatio*, the claims of the parties were consumed to be replaced by any obligations which arose on the judgement.

The purpose of all the above proceedings was to ascertain the existence of a right or a duty. If the person who was obligated to pay or hand over something as a result of the judgement did not do so, the disappointed party had to commence proceedings to enforce the new obligation which had arisen on the judgement. The *legis actio* procedure for doing this was known as that *per manus iniectionem*. The claimant would complain to the magistrate that the judgement debt had not been honoured, and this being a debt of the existence of which the magistrate had cognizance, there was no room for a defence by the other party. Instead, if he wished to assert that the judgement had been obtained by fraud or that the debt had already been satisfied, this had to be achieved through the good offices of another party, the so-called *vindex*. The *vindex* however acted at his peril, for if he came forward to defend the debtor, he thereafter replaced the debtor in every way, so that if his defence was unsuccessful he became personally liable for the debt. If the debtor or the *vindex* did not pay, the claimant was permitted to seize the person of the defaulter and imprison him privately for sixty days, displaying him publicly on three successive market days in the hope that someone would come forward and redeem him by payment on his behalf. If none did so, it was open to the creditor to put the defaulter to death or sell him into slavery at his election. While there is no record of a debtor being slain in such circumstances, sale into bondage was regular, and if the amount obtained did not satisfy the debt in full, the outstanding debt remained to be satisfied.

The only other form of execution permitted by the *legis actio* procedures was that *per pignoris capionem*, whereby the creditor could seize property of the debtor to satisfy his claim, but this was only allowed in certain clearly defined circumstances in all of which the State itself had an interest. *Pignoris capio* was for instance allowed to a cavalryman who had not received his horse's ration of fodder from the party obligated to provide it; he could proceed directly against the debtor to seize the goods.[6]

3 The Formulary System

The formulary system of actions was that controlled by the urban praetor, and it is generally agreed today that it developed out of, rather than being created to replace, the procedure by *legis actio*. Indeed, it may have begun to complement the earlier system. No definite date can be given for its inception. Clearly, it belongs to the period after the creation of the office of praetor in 367 BC, and it had legitimacy conferred upon by the *lex Aebutia*, a statute probably enacted between 149 and 126 BC. During its early history it co-existed with the older *legis actio* procedure, which was not formally abolished, other than for a limited number of causes,[7] until the *leges Iuliae* of *circa* 17 BC.

The roots of the formulary system in the *legis actiones* are apparent from a number of factors, the most notable being the continuation of the split between proceedings *in iure*, before the praetor, and those *apud iudicem*. *Litis contestatio* remained of major significance under the new order, consuming the previous claim in the obligations which were to arise as a result of the judgement. As with the *condictio*, that judgement was now for a finding that something was owed or owned, and not, as with *sacramentum*, a finding as to which wager was forfeit. Some writers see the *condictio* as the basis for the development of the formulary system.[8]

The origins of the formulary system are however obscure. Some have claimed that they reside in the activity of the peregrine praetor, whose office was created in 242 to deal with causes between Romans and foreigners or between foreigners themselves while at Rome. These persons could not use the *legis actio* procedure as they were not citizens, a further sign that perhaps the procedure had its beginnings in the *comitia curiata* of which non-citizens could not be members. Others see the system as developing from the urban praetor's development of devices to uphold the civil law through supplementing the older procedure, a supplement which eventually surpassed its older relative in importance. There is no doubt that the formulary system as it has become known to subsequent generations through the writings of the jurists had its foundations in the work of the urban praetor and in particular was developed by means of that praetor's annual edict.

As the magistrate in charge of the administration of justice, the praetor developed the power to state in his edict the circumstances in which he would give a remedy during his year in office. Not only could he give actions to fulfil the civil law, he might also state that there were circumstances in which he would deny an action to a would-be litigant in that it would be an abuse of the civil law to provide it. This has parallels with the manner in which modern civilian systems are empowered to refuse a remedy which the law allows if its grant would be an abuse of the law. The praetor could also allow defences to civil law actions in order to ensure that improper claims did not succeed. In all of this, there is evidence of the Roman view that enacted law had to conform to what was just, *lex* must conform to *ius*, and the praetor appears to have worked to achieve that end. Thus, if the civil law gave a remedy in one set of circumstances but not in another similar set, the praetor could extend the remedy by granting an *actio utilis* which reached situations not covered by the strict civil law *actio directa*. Civil law actions followed the law, *in iure concepta*, but the praetor's extensions, while not permitted to contradict the law, could fulfil it by going beyond it or ensuring it was not abused. Thus, fictions could be inserted so as to allow non-owners who had just title to recover their goods in the same manner as civil law *domini*, and defences could be inserted into a claim to ensure that the plaintiff did not succeed in a civil law claim if the circumstances of the claim were in some way unfair. The praetor could also give actions on the facts of a case, *actiones in factum*, even if there were no right in civil law, if he felt that such an extension of legal protection was warranted. By all these means, he developed alongside the *ius civile* his own *ius honorarium*, enshrined in the edict of his office which was handed on in the main from praetor to praetor until its eventual codification by Salvius Julianus in the reign of the Emperor Hadrian.

Although the text of the Edict has not survived, it has been possible for it to be reconstructed on the basis of the juristic literature which it inspired.[9] The Edict clearly set out the circumstances in which the praetor would grant an action and this in turn made it possible to classify the types of action that would be given. It would appear to be on the basis of this classification of actions that the jurists of the late republic, most notably Quintus Mucius Scaevola, were able to proceed to produce a classification of rights and duties, a classification which was to be refined by later generations and to culminate in that great analytical classification of the law in the writings of the classical jurists. It is therefore not too much to claim that the foundations of Roman jurisprudence were laid in the edict of the praetor.

The legacy to modern civil law has been the whole notion of the law being divisible into the institutional categories of persons, things and actions, and even the classification of obligations into contractual and delictual, and the sub-categories of contract which have been retained as useful for so many centuries.

This is not the sole importance of the praetorian development. The formulary system is so called because the magistrate sent the *iudex* instructions as to how to decide the case by means of a written document called the *formula*. This document nominated the judge upon whom the parties had agreed (the *nominatio*), set out any facts which the judge needed to know as background to the issue which he had to decide (the *demonstratio*, often commencing with the word *quod* meaning "whereas" or "since"), and then continued with the central question for decision contained in the *intentio* or purpose of the *formula*. This clause stated the question which the judge had to determine. He was told that "If it appears...", *si paret...* , that something was the case then he should adjudge for the plaintiff and if not, not. Thus, in a *vindicatio* in which the plaintiff claimed civil law ownership of a thing, the *intentio* would state that "If it appears that the plaintiff is the owner of the thing in civil law... "; the *iudex* would have to decide whether it did so appear.

It was into this *intentio* that the praetor could insert defences or *exceptiones*. These set out the circumstances, raised by the defendant, in which, if the *iudex* found them to be true, it would not be proper to find for the plaintiff even if the central issue was decided in his favour. Thus, the *formula* might run: "Let Titius be judge. If it appears that the plaintiff is the owner of the thing at civil law, then - unless it appears that he sold and delivered that thing to the defendant - award it to him". If Titius, as judge, did indeed find that the plaintiff had sold and delivered the thing to the defendant, then, even if the plaintiff remained owner in civil law, the thing would not be awarded to him. The praetor devised other clauses to allow for the incorporation into the *formula* of other matters which had come to his attention while the parties were before him and which were crucial to the decision of the case; thus there might be a *replicatio* in response to an *exceptio*, and thereafter a *duplicatio*, *triplicatio*, etc., each representing an issue which the judge would have to resolve in order to reach a conclusion on the central matter of the *intentio*. All these issues emerged during the proceedings *in iure*; all would have to be decided on the evidence by the *iudex* in the proceedings *apud iudicem*.

The *formula* ended with the instruction to the judge to either condemn the defendant to the plaintiff if his decision on the issues in the *intentio* led to that conclusion, or else to absolve him. This clause was the *condemnatio*. In actions which required the amount of the condemnation to be assessed, there might be a clause calling on the judge to make that assessment up to, but not beyond, a certain figure, the *taxatio*. Such a clause was usual in actions for *iniuria* which went to *recuperatores*. In actions which required the division of property, such as the *actio familiae erciscundae* between co-heirs, there would be an instruction to the judge, the *adjudicatio*, to effect the division. Judgement would always be for a sum of money, never for the handing over of any thing, although payment of the sum could be in the event of something not being handed over, and the sum in such circumstances could be coercive. As with the *legis actio*, judgement did not lead automatically to enforcement. It was rather a declaration of rights and duties; enforcement required further proceedings by the judgement creditor, the judgement debt being now the subsisting obligation.

Enforcement under the formulary system remained available by *manus iniectio*, and it remained possible for a *paterfamilias* who was liable for the wrong of a child in power, or a slave or animal in his ownership, to surrender the offender to the victim to work off the value of the debt, so-called noxal surrender. However, the praetor also supplied an action on the judgement, the *actio iudicati*, to assist the judgement creditor. Once more, the debtor could not re-open the question settled in the determining litigation and, if he did not pay up, then the whole of his property could be put up for sale in order to satisfy the judgement debt, the recalcitrant debtor in effect being treated as a bankrupt. This sale of the whole of the debtor's estate was known as *bonorum venditio*, and would be carried out for the benefit of all his creditors, not just the judgement debtor. If the proceeds of sale did not satisfy the debts in full, the debtor's future acquisitions remained vulnerable for the balance owed. Only persons of rank, such as senators, were allowed to escape the full burdens of this process. If they failed to satisfy a judgement debt, then proceedings against them were directed at confiscating sufficient of their property to satisfy the debt. This limited confiscation was known as *distractio bonorum*, and contained the germs of mechanisms which were to be used in mediaeval and modern law.

The technique of the *formula* ensured that the praetor identified the issues which divided the parties and therefore required resolution. By encapsulating these in a brief, orderly and lucid written document,[10] the praetor ensured that the *iudex* chosen by the parties and whose verdict they had agreed to accept would decide the case upon the merits of those issues, each one of which he was bound to address and resolve. The *iudex*' judgement therefore was of necessity arrived at in a reasoned manner, again a harbinger of the requirement in many modern civilian systems, indeed often a constitutional requirement, that every judgement be reasoned.

Indeed, the foundation of the formulary system is its insistence that the function of the legal process is to identify the issues which separate the parties, together with the legal and factual questions which require answers for those issues to be resolved, and then to resolve them in a reasoned and structured manner. It is these tasks which the construction of the *formula*, and the focus it provides for the *iudex* in supplying a verdict, enables to be performed. Its techniques remain those which are repeated by legal systems throughout the western world, and by no means only in those with a civilian heritage. The formulary system provided a practical and efficient, and therefore typically Roman, method of adjudication, and it has provided for subsequent generations a mode of legal reasoning which has become part of the legal culture of western jurisprudence generally.

It was also during the period of the formulary system's dominance that the massively influential work of the Roman jurists was accomplished. It needs to be remembered that neither the praetors nor the *iudices* were of necessity trained lawyers, the praetors by and large being career politicians and the *iudices* remaining men of probity chosen for their reliability and fairness from among the senatorial and equestrian ranks. For specifically legal advice, both would turn to the jurists, although the decisions reached were the responsibility of the magistrate or judge.

As the *iudex* was not in any way constrained as to how he reached his verdict, other than that he had to resolve the issues raised in the *formula*, the Roman law of this period had no strict rules of evidence or really of procedure. While it was customary for the parties themselves to appear before the magistrate, advocates, trained in rhetoric rather than law, were generally employed to make opening and closing speeches before the judge. The *iudex* was however free to receive whatever evidence he deemed fit, although the parties and their family and friends were not generally regarded as competent witnesses. Oral evidence was admitted and there were no formal rules against hearsay nor regarding the different degrees of weight to be given to various kinds or sources of evidence.

One device which was used however deserves mention in that it was most definitely a precursor of a method of proof which is still important in civilian systems, although the rules regarding its operation have varied over the ages. It is the oath, and it was known to participants in the formulary system in one of three forms, two of which have proved influential, the necessary oath and the voluntary oath. The necessary oath, *iusiurandum necessarium*, featured as a possible part of proceedings *in iure*, where one party could demand of the other that they take an oath as to a crucial element in their case. If they accepted, they won; if they refused they lost. However, it was open to the challenged party to return the challenge and insist that the original challenger himself take the oath to the contrary effect. Again, if he accepted he won, but if he refused he lost. It was also possible at this stage for either party to challenge the other as to whether his claim was genuine or his contention in good faith. The oath required in this context was the *iusiurandum calumniae* which if taken destroyed the cause of action completely so that no action could proceed.

The voluntary oath on the other hand could be utilized by either party at either stage of the proceedings, whether *in iure* or *apud iudicem*, and could be used in other circumstances as well. It allowed either party to challenge the other to take an oath on the truth of his case or some aspect of it, or to seek permission from the other party to take such an oath himself. If the oath were accepted, the point was settled, and thereafter it was open for the party who had proved an issue by such means to sue on the basis of the oath or for a party who had denied an issue on oath to raise the oath as an *exceptio* in any subsequent proceedings. Neither magistrates nor judges could require parties to take oaths.

As with the *legis actio* procedure, as the parties had agreed to be bound by the decision of the *iudex*, who was the judge of their choice and not one imposed upon them by the State, there was no question of there being any appeal from the decision of the *iudex*. While a party who could show he had been disadvantaged by an improper decision, or one improperly reached, could sue the defaulting judge for having made the cause his own, *iudex qui litem suam fecit*,[11] there was no mechanism for reopening the case as against the other party. Nor did the decisions of a judge bind any but the parties to it. There was no doctrine of precedent nor of *stare decisis*, although it is likely that decisions on points of law taken upon juristic advice might become persuasive in later cases, and the opinions of the jurists, those learned in the law who advised the judges, were of course treated as a source of law. Again, there is in this a harbinger of the modern civilian position.

4 Extraordinary Cognitio

The formulary system was developed by the *praetor urbanus* for the adjudication of disputes between Roman citizens at Rome itself. It was the normal order, or *ordo*, for dispute resolution. It was not however obligatory in the provinces, although provincial governors might adopt a similar system. Their powers however allowed them to adjudicate themselves or to send cases before them for adjudication to judges delegate, *iudices pedanei*, who were authorized to determine the dispute by the governor and not by agreement of the parties. If the parties were not citizens, they might be allowed, and normally were allowed, to have their dispute settled according to their own law and methods of adjudication, the governor perhaps ensuring that enforcement would be available or at least backed by the Roman authorities in the interests of public order.[12]

Such trials did not follow the *ordo* of the formulary system and were therefore described as being *extra ordinem*, literally extraordinary. In terms of the numbers of cases decided by this means however it was probably the case during the last century of the republic that more trials took place *extra ordinem* than according to the strict *ordo*. Even at Rome, certain matters came to be decided by such extraordinary *cognitio*, as the process became known. During the reign of Augustus, for instance, when the emperor decided that *fideicommissa* should be enforced, he entrusted this task at first to the consuls and later to specially appointed praetors, the *praetores fideicommissarii*. In either case, these magistrates dealt with the whole issue before them; there was no split between proceedings *in iure* and *apud iudicem*, so that the proceedings were *extra ordinem*. The urban praetor began to entertain claims for *honoraria* for *mandatarii* in extraordinary proceedings, and during the second century AD, the emperor Antoninus Pius allowed claims for alimentary support from relatives to be tried *extra ordinem* and his successor, Marcus Aurelius, adopted the same course with regard to the supervision of tutors, appointing a special praetor, the *praetor tutelarius*, for the purpose. In all of these ways, extraordinary proceedings quietly replaced the formulary system in much litigation even at Rome. Some of the imperial magistrates also developed jurisdiction relating to their field of work using *cognitio* procedure; this was true of both the *praefectus vigilum* and the *praefectus annonae*, who were concerned with public order and safety and the corn supply respectively.

The formulary system was therefore gradually superseded by *cognitio*, which although technically the exceptional procedure slowly became the rule. It had attractions for litigants, in that once the plaintiff presented his case to the court, the court summoned the defendant to appear and could coerce that appearance. Likewise, witnesses could be compelled to attend and give evidence at the trial. This *denuntiatio* contrasted with the responsibility of the plaintiff to get the defendant to appear under the *vocatio in ius* of the older procedures, which only allowed a limited number of witnesses to be summoned by *denuntiatio* and then only in cases before the *recuperatores*. As the court tried the case itself, there was no delay before a judge was appointed, and the authority of the court to decide came from the State not the parties, so there was no obstacle to allowing appeals nor to enforcing the judgement on the court's own authority on the basis of its decision.

The extension of the citizenship, culminating in the grant of citizenship to all free persons in the empire by Caracalla in 212, meant that the vast majority of citizens were now living in the provinces, and therefore litigating *extra ordinem*, before the governor and his judges delegate. The reformation of the provincial structure under Diocletian at the end of the third century provided the opportunity to absorb the imperial city itself within a new framework of judicial administration for which the *cognitio* procedure provided the model. Each governor, or *praeses*, was expected to wield judicial authority within his own province and not, if possible, employ *iudices pedanei*, the need for such delegation having decreased in that the new provinces were smaller than their senatorial and imperial predecessors. The provinces being grouped into dioceses or vicariates, it was possible to permit an appeal from the decision of a provincial governor to the imperial vicar, and from him to the praetorian prefect of that part of the empire. Rome itself was accommodated within this new structure. Appeals could continue if necessary as far as the imperial court, the emperor himself being the highest and final appellate tribunal. It was not until the time of Justinian that the rule was settled that no more than two appeals should be allowed in any one case, thus establishing the pattern familiar in modern civilian systems of determination at first instance, followed by appeal and the possibility of further review at the highest level.[13]

The structure which emerged under Diocletian was also to be retained by the Church for its governmental and judicial functions long after the fall of the western empire. Indeed, as early as the reign of Constantine, bishops were encouraged to exercise jurisdiction within their sees over their spiritual subjects, their judgements being recognized and, if necessary, enforced by the imperial secular arm.

A plaintiff wishing to commence an action under this procedure was to request the court for one in a *postulatio actionis*, followed by a statement of his claim. This however was superseded by a system in which the plaintiff was simply allowed to present a bill of complaint, the *libellus conventionis*, which the court would serve upon the defendant, who could then reply in a *libellus contradictionis* or *responsionis*. These exchanges, mediated by the court, would continue until the issues for resolution were clear, which were still set out until the mid fourth-century in a written *formula*, although formal *litis contestatio* was no longer of such significance as under the older *ordo*. Once the issues for resolution were settled, the judge, now a State official, took charge of the proceedings, and the manner in which he proceeded was now subject to legal regulation, that is a law of evidence developed. Documentary evidence was preferred to that of witnesses, and, following Biblical precedent, the testimony of one witness alone was not sufficient, corroboration was always necessary - *testis unius, testis nullius*.[14] Although oral testimony was distrusted, the degree of reliability attached to witnesses was commensurate not only with their number but also their status. Hearsay evidence came to be excluded, and witnesses were summoned to appear by the court and examined by the judge himself with regard to their evidence. The use of oaths continued, but the judge himself was now permitted to offer a party the chance to establish a point in his case by oath in the absence of other evidence. Whereas it is difficult to say whether proceedings before the *iudex* under the *ordo* were adversarial or inquisitorial, in that there were no formal rules governing procedure and evidence at that stage, the procedure by extraordinary *cognitio* appears markedly inquisitorial in character and laid one of the foundations for the subsequent development of the inquisitorial Romano-canonical procedure of later times which is so closely associated with civilian legal systems.

Finally, although the function of the proceedings was to determine and declare rights and duties between the parties, the fact that the determination was achieved by State officials not only allowed for appeals but also for State enforcement. This was still achieved by *bonorum venditio*, although gradually the system of *distractio bonorum*, aimed at satisfying the debt rather than bankrupting the debtor, became applicable to all classes of persons.

5 Criminal Procedure

The legal processes described above were concerned with civil rather than criminal justice, for the law of actions was part of Roman private law. Compared with private law, Roman criminal law was relatively undeveloped and unsophisticated. In the early republic, criminal jurisdiction was exercised by the consuls. That this jurisdiction may have originally resided in the popular assemblies is perhaps witnessed by the survival of the right of every citizen to appeal to the assembly in Republican times against a capital or corporal punishment, a right which under the Principate became the right of appeal to Caesar. In both cases, it was known as the *provocatio*.[15]

At the beginning of the second century BC, jurisdiction over minor offences within Rome was transferred to the *Tresviri Capitales*, and by the *lex Calpurnia* of 149 BC, a special court was established to deal with cases of corruption by public officials. This court was called a *Quaestio perpetua*, and such special criminal courts were to become a feature of Roman criminal justice thereafter. Sulla created six such courts, each with a jurisdiction over certain serious criminal offences, and each to be presided over by a praetor, who was to spend his year in office as president of the tribunal allotted to him. He was president and not a judge. Adjudication within the *quaestiones* was carried out by jurors, who were drawn from the senatorial and equestrian orders, although there were periods during which senatorial involvement was distrusted and indeed excluded.[16] Proceedings before the *quaestiones* were accusatorial, and the death penalty was rarely if ever carried out, the accused person usually being allowed the opportunity to flee into voluntary exile before conviction and sentence.

During the imperial period, criminal jurisdiction also passed into the ambit of *cognitio extra ordinem*. This wrought a great change in its nature, causing it to become, like civil justice, markedly inquisitorial in character and thus setting the scene for the inquisitorial Romano-canonical approach of the criminal justice of the Middle Ages and later. The State officials, who now acted as judge as well as president within these courts, were empowered to investigate and prosecute crimes which came to their attention of their own motion, that is *ex officio*, without having to wait for a formal complaint from the victim or some other person. Here, therefore, one also sees the beginnings of the concept of the State or public prosecutor who acts as a member of the magistracy, investigating, prosecuting and determining accusations of criminality.

In both civil and criminal justice, the passage from republican to imperial government, and in particular the transition to the monarchic regime of the Dominate, marked an increase in the authority of the State in the administration of the law. The weight of State authority pressed heavily upon the legal system of the later empire giving it a decidedly baroque character. Although many of the features of this period were to be resurrected in the Romano-canonical processes of the absolutist regimes of the early modern period in much of western Europe, the Roman law of remedies and procedure also provided models and structures for legal thought and argument, as well as dispute resolution, which were much less authoritarian in character and have proved influential in the legal arrangements of much of the modern world, being by no means confined to those systems which have inherited the civilian tradition of Rome and taken Romano-canonical models as the basis for their procedural arrangements.

Notes

1 See Gaius, *Institutes* I. 8; Justinian, *Institutes* I. 2. 12.

2 Sir Henry Maine famously described this phenomenon thus: 'substantive law has at first the look of being gradually secreted in the interstices of procedure'. See H.S. Maine, *Ancient Law* (Ed.; London, 1930), p. 389.

3 See chapters 15 and 16.

4 If the thing were worth more than 1,000 asses, the amount would be 500; if less, or an issue of liberty, the wager would be for 50 asses.

5 Normally, the *actio communi dividundo* to bring to an end common ownership and the *actio finium regundorum* to determine boundaries.

6 It was also available against those who failed to pay the price of a sacrificial animal, the cost of hire of a horse knowing the money was to be used as a sacrificial offering, and those who failed to pay tax to *publicani*.

7 For instance, inheritance cases before the *centumviri*.

8 On the origins of the formulary system, see H.F. Jolowicz and B. Nicholas, *An Historical Introduction to the Study of Roman Law* (3rd Ed.; Cambridge, 1972), pp. 218 ff.

9 O. Lenel, *Das Edictum Perpetuum* (3rd Ed.; Leipzig, 1927). Lenel noticed that within Bluhme's *Ediktsmasse*, all the writers who commented on the Edict appeared to follow the same order. This he surmised was the order of the Edict itself, and on this basis he sought to reconstruct the text from the extracts.

10 Qualities which suggest some connection between the *formula* and the skills of the rhetorician as described by Cicero, *De Oratore*, 122.

11 Classified by Justinian as a quasi-delict; see *Institutes* IV. 5. pr.

[12] Thus, Pilate sent Christ for trial to Herod as he was subject to Herod rather than Pilate's jurisdiction being a Galilean; see Luke XXIII. 6 f.

[13] Interestingly, this pattern was also adopted in England and Wales at the end of the nineteenth century. The Judicature Act 1873 had intended the abolition of the House of Lords' final appellate jurisdiction, but the fall of the Liberal government and its replacement by a Conservative administration led to the retention of the Law Lords after 1876; see A.H. Manchester, *Modern Legal History* (London, 1980), pp. 177 ff; R.B. Stevens, 'Final Appeal: Reform of the House of Lords and Privy Council', (1964) 80 *Law Quarterly Review* 343.

[14] Deuteronomy, XIX. 15.

[15] It was famously used by St. Paul; see Acts XXV. 10 ff.

[16] Caius Gracchus provided that only *equites* could act as jurors in the criminal courts, but this rule was abrogated by Sulla, and Julius Caesar confirmed the eligibility of both senators and *equites*. See O. Tellegen-Couperus, *A Short History of Roman Law* (English Ed.; London, 1993), p. 52.

PART III

PUBLIC LAW

14 The Concept and Function of the State

1 Modern Constitutions

A constitution is the fundamental of the law of the State or body governed by it. All other domestic laws of the State derive their authority from being made in accordance with the constitution, both in the sense of having been made according to the methods prescribed therein for law-making and in the sense of being consonant with the principles which are enshrined in the constitution. A constitution in this sense is not simply those laws which govern the workings of the State powers. It is the fundamental law of the State in all matters.[1]

The most cursory of glances at the written constitutions of civil law countries and others will disclose a striking similarity of content. In each constitution one is likely to find a clear statement that sovereignty belongs to the people, followed by certain guarantees of fundamental rights which the people are to enjoy on an equal basis. Some of these rights pertain to individuals, others to groups. Some of these rights are political or civil in character, others economic, social or moral. The constitution will also provide for mechanisms by which laws can be made to protect and enforce those rights against other persons and against the State itself, and to provide for the punishment of those who infringe the protected rights of others. In accordance with the principle of popular sovereignty, the constitution will provide for the composition and accountability of the bodies entrusted with these law-making tasks, so that they are representative of and accountable to the people. There may also be mechanisms by which laws made by the legislative bodies which offend against the constitutionally guaranteed rights of the people can be challenged before a body competent to adjudicate upon the issue of the constitutionality of enactments. It may also be possible for the people to challenge the desirability of constitutionally valid enactments, thus reclaiming their popular sovereignty on single issues while not generally challenging the continued authority of the legislature or the government. The constitution will also provide for the structures of government at all levels from the national to the local, and guarantee the independence of the judicial power which it will establish to adjudicate upon and enforce the rights and duties which the constitutionally enacted laws protect. Methods will also be provided for amending the constitution itself, which methods are likely to be more restrictive than those which allow other laws to be made or amended.

Some constitutions go so far as to define the purpose for which the State which they govern exists. If such a statement occurs, it will probably formulate the function of the State as being to protect the individual and possibly the family and to promote the common good. It will probably also commit the State to doing this by protecting such basic goods as liberty, equality, security, peace and the development of the individual as a person. Some of these functions are programmatic, in that they involve the State in pursuing goals which are not immediately capable of realization. Other functions require that the State constantly provides the protection guaranteed.

It is manifest from the manner in which such constitutional provisions are expressed that the benefits which the State regards itself as existing to protect antedate its existence. It follows from this that insofar as laws are made under the provisions of the constitution, these benefits are not created by the law. Rather the law is created to protect them. Inasmuch therefore as these benefits are anterior to the laws which protect them, and prior even to the existence of the State itself, they are sometimes described as natural rights.

The term natural rights expresses the belief that such rights existed in a hypothetical state of nature which itself antedated the formation of human societies. According to this view, individual men and women enjoyed such rights before they ever came together to form groups for communal existence, at which time it was agreed by them according to the so-called social contract which they made that they would submit to being governed by the group for their greater protection and the advantages which group existence afforded, subject to the group respecting their fundamental or basic rights. Such ideas were current and popular during the eighteenth century and were of profound influence in inspiring and shaping the legal orders which emerged from the revolutions of the second half of that century in America and France. One of the most notable thinkers who contributed to the social contract theory was the French philosopher, Jean Jacques Rousseau (1712-1778).[2]

Although the idea that men actually entered into a social contract of the sort postulated by this theory is a myth, nevertheless the concept of there being fundamental human rights which are inalienable has proved both persuasive and durable. Statements of basic human rights have become the secular creeds of modern western societies, enshrining beliefs which are held with as much tenacity and intolerance as were religious beliefs in earlier times. To embrace political views which deny liberty, equality and the brotherhood of mankind is tantamount to heresy and to speak against those concepts a modern blasphemy. The basic ideas enshrined in the natural rights doctrine however is much older than the eighteenth century, and it is the purpose of this chapter to elucidate the extent to which the constitutions of modern civil law countries which adopt this perspective of the social order are here as elsewhere the heirs of the legal tradition in which they stand.

2 Natural Law and Natural Rights

It would be wrong to suggest that the jurists of ancient Rome held this type of view of the position of man in society. They did however express opinions which contained within them seeds from which such a doctrine could be cultivated. The Roman jurists taught that all men were governed partly by the laws of their own State and partly by laws which were common to all mankind. They distinguished these two types of law as civil law, *ius civile*, which for the Romans was the civil law of Rome, and *ius gentium*, the law of nations. When the latter term came to be used to designate those rules which were applied by the peregrine praetor in providing remedies for litigants who were not Roman citizens, a new term had to be found to describe those rules which marked the convergence of human laws. The term which came to be applied was natural law, *ius naturale*, a concept borrowed from Greek philosophy. When the extension of the Roman citizenship to all the free inhabitants of the empire in 212 AD rendered the law of the peregrine praetor superfluous, *ius gentium* reacquired its original meaning and *ius naturale* was used to describe those rules which were common to all animals and not just to all humans.[3] In later centuries, with the conversion of Rome to Christianity, it was but a small step to adapt these ideas to suit the world view of the new faith, whereby natural law was the manifestation within creation of the order which the creator willed for it, and to contrast that with divinely ordained laws which were actually revealed directly by God. It was in these terms that during the thirteenth century, St. Thomas Aquinas presented his conception of a divine law, revealed by God, as in Scripture, and natural law, also willed by God but having to be perceived by man through the use of reason. Neither was subject to change through human agency, although reason could err in its perception of natural law. Already here there are distinct precursors of the concept that there are such things as natural rights and that these are inalienable, although the eighteenth-century thinkers were not bound to St. Thomas' religious basis for these phenomena.

One of the main differences between the eighteenth-century view of natural rights and the perspectives of the ancient and the mediaeval world lies in the notion of a right itself. The Latin word *ius*, which is often translated in modern times as 'right', would not have been regarded as such a concrete legal concept prior to the Renaissance. The word *ius*, as has been seen,[4] bore a meaning in ancient Roman law of that which was right not only because it had been enacted in a *lex* but in a higher sense; it conformed with the customs of the ancestors, *mores maiorum*, and therefore the discerned will of the gods. To say therefore, as the Roman jurist Ulpian stated, that justice was the constant and perpetual wish to give each his due, his *ius*, was to look upon the content of a legal relationship from the perspective of what according to the traditions of the people was proper as between two legal subjects. It is unlikely that a Roman ever thought in terms of his having a right, in the modern sense, to compensation for an injury or the return of goods which he had lent another. He would however have thought that compensation was due to him for a wrong or that goods borrowed ought to be returned as in both instances that corresponded to the order of his world, one might even say its natural order. Such things were due to him, they were his due, but he would not have said that he had a right to them.

Much the same is true of the men of the Middle Ages. Their world view was in this respect more akin to that of the ancients than that of the modern world. Compensation for an injury or the return of borrowed goods was something which they were due in order to preserve the natural order of the world they inhabited. It was that order which ordained that promises be kept and good measure given. Human laws merely articulated and enforced that order. It was not that they had rights, but that to preserve the order of their world and the society in which they lived, some things were due to them in certain circumstances. The great change in this perspective, as in so many other things, came in the sixteenth century.

To understand the nature of that change, it is necessary to know something of the changes in the political structures of Europe which had taken place during the preceding centuries. Following the break up of the Carolingian empire in the ninth century, much of western Europe had become governed by what is now known as the feudal system. Feudalism involved landowners surrendering their estates to powerful overlords, who regranted the lands to them in return for their allegiance. Feudal lordship was in effect an agreement by the lord to protect the tenant in return for the latter's loyalty and obedience. The tenant would look to the lord for justice in the lord's court. The tenant would thus only be able to enforce obligations which were owed to him insofar as the lord was prepared to enforce them on his behalf. His liberty and security were dependent therefore upon his being under the protection, or within the peace, of his lord. The only persons who would be able to enforce the obligations which the tenant owed would be those who could claim justice from his lord.

Under such arrangements, of which monarchy was in a sense only a feudal lordship writ large, some persons might find themselves under the protection of no one and therefore unable to enforce those things due to them. Jews and foreigners found themselves in such a predicament, and thus they were often placed under the special protection of kings; they lived within the king's special peace. Gradually, during the later thirteenth and more particularly during the fourteenth and fifteenth centuries, monarchs extended their power at the expense of lesser feudal lords, so that more and more people lived as the subjects of rulers, whose rule was based upon the obedience due to them as the protectors of their subjects. Such subjects might appear to have no security in their legal relationships other than those which their rulers saw fit to grant. Absolute rule offered an alternative view of civil government to that which suggested that what was due to each person was determined in part by the natural order of their world. Instead, it would appear that all a person could expect was what the ruler chose to grant according to his pleasure. Law was what the prince willed.[5]

Having said this, it would be wrong to deduce that rulers changed the laws governing their subjects with scant regard for the obligations which the legal science of the age held to exist. Although rulers felt free to determine how they would enforce their subjects' obligations, the kinds of proof that would be demanded of litigants and the procedures which would be employed, together with the punishments that would be imposed for wilful disobedience to their laws, it would appear that they did not feel competent to alter the substance of the obligations of private law. Thus, virtually all the enactments of the absolute rulers were concerned with procedure or government and not with the substance of their subjects' dues and duties. Even in a later age when codifications of private law were published, these enactments did not alter the substance of the subjects' rights but rather sought to present the laws by which they lived in a systematic and accessible fashion.

The key question in the sixteenth century was to whom the legal protection of a particular prince should extend. That century saw the emergence of the concept of the nation state, in part as the result of the religious divisions which had emerged within Christendom as a result of the Reformation. The principle *cuius regio, eius religio* was the assertion in matters of faith of the obedience which the ruler required in return for his protection. It embodied as clear an antithesis to liberty of conscience in matters of belief as the submission demanded to the magisterial authority of the catholic Church in previous centuries. It was the enlargement of monarchical feudalism into the sphere of religious belief. To live under the protection of a Christian prince within his territory, one had to conform to his choice of religion.

This viewpoint had considerable implications for the native inhabitants of those lands which the European powers were discovering in the New World. These peoples enjoyed territorial possession of lands and possessed goods and animals, but the question was raised as to what obligations, if any, the European conquerors owed them upon their arrival. According to one view, that of the Spaniard, Sepúlveda, they were owed nothing unless they submitted themselves to baptism and thereby gained the protection of the Christian prince under whose jurisdiction the conquerors came. If they refused baptism, then they could not be within the protection of any Christian prince and were therefore unprotected by any law. They could therefore be killed with impunity and all their lands and goods taken. No respect was due to their life, liberty or property unless they were under the governance of a Christian ruler. Against this view stood another Spaniard, Francisco Vittoria, who held that by the law of nations, the Indians were entitled to their lands and possessions as first takers, and that therefore respect was due to their ownership as much as that of any Christian. Further, respect for their life and liberty was due to them as human beings made in the image of God regardless of whether they submitted to baptism. Vittoria's views of these native peoples' dues mark the beginnings of the concept that each human being has a natural right to life and liberty, and that ownership of property acquired by lawful means is also a natural right.

No longer was it sufficient to say that respect was due to a person's life, physical integrity and property; it was now being said that people had a right to expect that such respect be shown and could enforce that right against those not prepared to accord it.

It was at the hands of the Dutchman, Hugo Grotius, that this doctrine was to receive its fullest exposition. Grotius, who himself suffered deprivation of liberty and exile for failing to adopt the religion of the local ruler, argued coherently that what was due to a man, his rights, existed prior to the legal systems created by princes and republics for their protection and enforcement. Thus, even in time of war, the belligerents were bound to respect the lives and property of the enemy other than in actual battle. Although Grotius himself based his opinions upon the foundations of his own religious beliefs, he readily admitted that his views did not require a theological basis for their validity. He held that such natural rights were the heritage of all humanity by virtue of their being human. Rulers who did not respect such rights were acting contrary to natural law.

Grotius' doctrines in effect restored the rule of law in the international arena following the break up of western Christendom through the emergence of nation states. Thereafter, the notion gradually developed that these natural rights had existed in an original state of nature before men formed communities in which to live and agreed, by the social contract, to pool their resources in communal living saving always those rights which were inalienable, their fundamental human rights. These were the ideas which fuelled the opening words of the American Declaration of Independence: "We hold these truths to be self evident: that all men are created equal, that they are endowed by their creator with certain inalienable rights, among these are life, liberty and the pursuit of happiness, that to secure these rights governments are instituted among men", and also the Declaration of the Rights of Man made at the time of the French Revolution. Both revolutions drew inspiration from the idea of there being natural rights.

The natural rights which motivated the French Revolution and the laws which flowed therefrom, including the French *Code civil* in 1804, were conceived as being the rights of individuals, not of groups. Indeed, it was not long after the publication of the *Code civil* before dissatisfaction with its highly individualist agenda was expressed. It was felt that some fundamental rights inhered in groups of individuals, most notably the family, and that it was completely artificial to conceive of human society as being an amalgamation of otherwise unconnected human beings.

Throughout the nineteenth century, particularly in Germany, considerable emphasis was placed upon the need to recognize the rights of collectivities, ranging from the family through to voluntary associations, clubs, workers' groups and trade unions. It was widely believed that the individualist bias of the French laws played into the hands of capitalism, and that the French system protected the bourgeois property-owning classes at the expense of their workers, whose right to associate was not regarded as worthy of the same level of protection. Demands were heard to protect such rights of solidarity.

Thus it was that during the nineteenth century, constitutions began to guarantee not only individual rights but also those of groups, and that not only political rights, but economic and social rights, came to be protected. Alongside free speech, freedom of conscience and the right to participate in free elections, there developed the right to associate in political parties and trade unions, the right to work to earn one's living and that of one's family, and the right to education and health care, these developments accelerating during the course of the twentieth century. The list of recognized fundamental rights has grown, and in the second half of the twentieth century they have come to be embodied in international agreements, such as the United Nations Charter and the European Declaration of Human Rights as well as in national constitutions. This further illustrates the view that such rights are regarded as existing outside of national legal systems, and that such systems recognize rather than create them.

The theory of the social contract generated another important principle of modern constitutionalism, namely equality. If all mankind was originally free before entering upon the obligations of the social contract, they were also entering into that contract as equals, so that it was unfair that within society unnatural inequalities should prevail. Thus, the constitutions which developed out of the American and French revolutions have been productive of assaults upon all manner of social inequalities, based on birth, class, wealth, colour, race, religion and sex. Such differences are not permitted to form the basis of discrimination in the allocation of civic, political or fundamental economic or social rights.

The other principle which flowed directly from the theory of the social contract was that the powers of the community were ultimately derived from the individuals who sustain the contract, and that those who exercise communal power do so therefore on behalf of the population at large and must be accountable to it. This facet of the social contract gives rise to the principle that sovereignty belongs to the people and not to those who govern them.

3 Popular Sovereignty

The principle of popular sovereignty is enshrined in most modern constitutions. It stands in stark contrast to the British notion of the sovereignty of Parliament. Popular sovereignty emphasizes that the ultimate source of political power in the State is the people and that, although they may delegate powers to their elected representatives, ultimate power never leaves them. Thus, in some States for instance this is recognized by allowing referenda as of right when required, or allowing legislative proposals to emanate from the people and not just from the government or members of the legislature.[6]

The modern principle of popular sovereignty emerges into the reality of practical politics, together with natural rights and the doctrine of equality, at the time of the French Revolution. As with equality and natural rights, it was a reaction to the absolute regimes that had operated in most parts of continental Europe prior to that date. Over the last two centuries, it has enjoyed a chequered history in the countries of the civil law, with several alternating between democratic republicanism and fascist dictatorships. It is difficult not to discern in this vacillation tensions deriving from what has long been two traditions of government in the lands of the civil law.

The notion of government by popular assent is generally accorded to be Germanic rather than Roman in origin. This however places stress upon the imperial tradition of Rome, as indeed manifested in the compilations of the emperor Justinian which communicated knowledge of Roman legal science to the mediaeval world. However, as has been shown,[7] in early Rome, *leges* were made by the *comitia*, the assembly of the people. Although they did not enjoy the legislative initiative, in that only the magistrates could propose new laws, their consent was necessary for the enactment of those proposals. There is therefore a similarity between these arrangements and those of the early Germanic tribes, even as recorded by Tacitus,[8] where it was in regular meetings of the weapon-bearing men that the customs of the people were declared. However, at Rome, legislative power gravitated away from the people to the emperor and the senate, and finally to the emperor alone, beginning an association of Roman civil law with absolute rule which confirms for some the Germanic descent of popular institutions.

There can be no doubt that there is some justification for this point of view. Equally clearly, centripetal tendencies developed within the governmental arrangements of the Germanic tribes, influenced in part, but only in part, by the example of the Roman empire. All free men were entitled, indeed originally obligated, to attend the popular assembly where the laws of the tribe or clan were declared. Although such declarations would be in the main recital of the customs, the assembly could also clarify the customs when need arose, as it indeed would for the assembly also played a judicial role, disputes being settled at its meetings. Originally, the tribal chief would have been the leader in time of war, but with no power to legislate in the sense of making new rules of general application as opposed to giving orders in emergency situations. Gradually, influence and eventually power within the assemblies gravitated away from the body of free men and into the hands of the leader's most trusted lieutenants, the nobles or dukes. This development was particularly marked when the tribes occupied new territories. Thus, for instance when the Lombards had occupied Italy, although assemblies of all the free men were convened, their function became as with the *comitia* at Rome one of decision only, with no power to initiate or deliberate upon legislation. These functions became reserved to the officials of the court and the nobility. In the Carolingian empire, centralization of governmental power became even more marked. The extent of the empire made it impossible to convene meetings of all free men, so that the imperial officials represented their territories at the emperor's court. They alone introduced legislative proposals and decided upon them, the nobility having only, like the Roman senate, the right to advise. The ordinary people could attend as spectators if they wished, but had no other function than to assemble in their localities and receive news of what had been done from the imperial messengers, the *missi dominici*. In Lombard Italy, however, resistance of this exclusion of the people from their ancient right of assent was resented, and in 832, Lothar agreed at the Diet of Pavia to submit the constitutions of his predecessors to the popular assembly for approval.

The break up of the Carolingian empire before the end of the ninth century saw the end also of the centralized imperial institutions of government that had previously prevailed. As the influence of the empire weakened, so power passed to feudal magnates who offered protection to their tenants in return for their loyalty. One of the duties of these tenants was to attend the court of their lord, where governmental functions generally - legal, executive and judicial - were discharged. The custom of the lordship governed the lives of the lord's subjects and relationships within the lordship were distinctly hierarchical. Many of the humbler landholders were tied to the land they cultivated and were not free to come and go as they pleased. Freedom and other rights were very much a matter of the lord's pleasure.

Feudalism of this kind flourished in the country areas, but in the towns and cities of Italy and southern France different traditions were maintained. This is sometimes ascribed to the fact that while the Germanic invaders were primarily soldiers and farmers, the native Roman population tended to specialize in crafts, occupations which allowed them to thrive in an urban environment. The government of the towns and communes was therefore conducted upon very different lines. Popular assemblies were still held, and governing councils were elected to carry out the executive functions of the commune. By the twelfth and thirteenth centuries, it had become increasingly common for magistrates with wide executive powers to be elected on an annual basis, called consuls after the example of the Romans. Ideas of popular sovereignty, freedom and to some extent equality continued in the urban settlements. Serfdom was not practised in them and the inhabitants were allowed to come and go as they wished. The permission of a lord was not required for an inhabitant to marry nor to enter a religious order. Modes of trial such as the ordeal and battle were early abandoned in them, and there was considerable freedom to dispose of land during one's lifetime or after one's death by will. The prosperity which many of these towns attained is often attributed to the freedom enjoyed therein.

The concept of monarchical government had not however completely disappeared from view during these centuries. In particular, it had been embraced by the Papacy in the wake of the weakening of the institutions of empire. The Papacy provided the Church with central authority, and the clergy generally were a class apart with considerable powers over the lives of the Christian faithful who in turn had no say in the government of the Church. Many of the structures and institutions of the Church continued the forms of the later Roman empire. The purpose of its existence however was clearly the benefit of those whom it served and it demanded that human institutions and practices generally should be in accord with divine and natural law. If the communes therefore were the repositories of freedom during the Middle Ages, the Church can rightly be viewed as the guardian of the notion of natural law. The prevailing scholastic philosophy upheld the view that ultimate authority rested with the multitude and not with single rulers, but that whatever style of government were preferred its doings had to accord with the will of God. The people therefore always had the right to remove a tyrannical ruler.

The revival of Roman law studies in the cities of Italy buttressed the claims of secular rulers to an authority which was superior to, rather than accountable to, subjects. The emperor himself could claim against the Pope ultimate authority in the west, but it was also open for lesser rulers to assert that their domains were their empire in that they ruled by their individual *imperium*. The fourteenth-century jurist, Baldus, asserted that each king was emperor in his kingdom and held his lands only from God and by his sword.[9] Gradually, such ideas were to overcome belief in popular government in the urban centres of Italy, where the absolute rule of powerful families came to replace the democratic institutions of previous centuries. The same ideas fortified the determination of monarchs in Spain, France and the territories of Germany to assert their absolute power within their realms.

Already in the kingdoms of Spain in the twelfth century and in England and France in the thirteenth, kings had convened assemblies of their subjects to deal with legislation. The nobility, who were already accustomed to be consulted on such matters, attended in person, but representatives of the clergy and of the general population, particularly of the towns, were also summoned to attend. These meetings of the estates of the realm were taken as representing the whole kingdom, and the canonists of the thirteenth and fourteenth century devised a theory, based on the Roman law contract of mandate, to account for their capacity to bind all subjects by their action. Those who attended as representatives of others were, it was said, acting as mandatories for those they represented, capable of binding those others by their actions within the mandate until such mandate was revoked. Thus was born the modern doctrine of the mandate of an elected government as justification for its actions.

The growth of absolutist tendencies saw the discontinuance of the summoning of these assemblies of the estates. Political power became concentrated in the hands of rulers who believed themselves accountable to God but hardly to their subjects. Even in the eighteenth century, the so-called 'enlightened' absolute rulers of parts of Italy, Germany and Austria, believed that, while they should govern in the interests of their people, nevertheless it was they alone who should govern. It was government for the people, but not of or by the people. The break up of western Christendom at the Reformation accentuated this attitude, for even the faith was under the control of the prince. Not even in religion was the ruler accountable to any earthly power. This had the strange effect of uniting all the king's subjects - nobles, clergy and commoners - in their exclusion from the government of the realm. Absolutism oddly produced an odd equality among all the ruler's subjects.

If the plenitude of political power vested in the sovereign, it followed that as against the sovereign the people had no rights. Thus it was in France under the *ancient regime*, where there was no freedom from arrest or punishment, no free press, no freedom of conscience in religion, no right to associate freely, no inviolability for the home. During the eighteenth century, England was fêted by continental writers for the liberty which its inhabitants enjoyed, having secured a constitutional settlement between king and parliament after the civil wars which had ended the absolutist aspirations of the Stuart kings. On the continent, on the other hand, absolutist rule had brought feudalism to, in effect, its logical conclusion. The realm was the king's property, and he alone had rights within it. Those who lived on his land did so at his sufferance. It was a far more extreme absolutism than that which had existed under the later Roman emperors.

The social contract theory of the origins of the State was a reaction against this state of affairs. By postulating that the State was based upon the agreement of all, it rejected the notion that kings were entitled to rule by the grace of God rather than being permitted by God's grace to exercise an authority derived from their people.[10] Not until after the French Revolution, and then only gradually, did popular sovereignty successfully assert itself to occupy the position which it currently enjoys in modern constitutions. The achievement of universal male suffrage took much of the nineteenth century, and universal adult suffrage was largely the achievement of the twentieth.[11]

The victory of the principle of popular sovereignty brought its own problems. Questions remain regarding the manner in which the will of the people is to be manifested. What is to be done if the people are unhappy with the decisions of their mandated representatives? Must they wait until the mandate expires or can they reclaim their sovereignty over particular issues? What can be done if the majority of the people pursues a course of government which offends against the fundamental rights of others? What is the appropriate level within a community at which decisions should be taken by the people? These are problems which affect nations which have embraced popular sovereignty. Although the answers given to them differ from nation to nation, it is nevertheless apparent that in these answers considerable evidence can be found of the influence exercised by the historical development of the laws of the peoples concerned.

4 The Legislative Process

The legislative processes of modern civil law countries bear the hallmarks of their common legal heritage. The public law doctrine divides the process into various stages, called frequently the introductory, deliberative and decision-making phases. The first is concerned with the question of who may introduce a legislative proposal or project into the legislature for consideration. The deliberative stage is that in which the proposal in considered and debated, and amendments suggested. Finally, the decision-making phase is concerned with the manner in which the proposed law is enacted or rejected by vote of the assembly or some other mechanism.

These stages in the legislative process can be identified in the workings of most legislative bodies. Even in the case of an absolute monarchy, it is usual for the ruler to adopt legislative projects suggested by his ministers, deliberate over their content in his council or consistory, before deciding upon their enactment himself. The legislative stages were clearly identifiable in the constitution of the Roman republic, and this model was of great influence in the formation of the legislative processes which succeeded the French Revolution, as well as having been of importance in the shaping of the legislative techniques of both the Carolingian emperors and the urban communes of the Middle Ages. While a clear line of descent from ancient Rome to modern France can hardly be traced, there is no difficulty in recognizing that post-Revolutionary France returned to the Roman republic for inspiration in designing its State structures.

The constitutional arrangements of republican Rome are less therefore the common ancestor of modern legislative methods, standing at the head of a continuous line of descent leading from the ancient world through all succeeding generations to the present, than an ever-present spirit, directly inspiring each successive generation to produce anew legislative processes based upon the ideals of the republic. The legislative initiative lay with the magistrates; deliberation was for the senate; decision-making for the assembly.[12] In addition, the tribunes of the people had the power to veto enactments which were not deemed to be consonant with the interests of the plebeian class, and the *patres* in the senate had to confirm that the enactment conformed with the traditions of the ancestors, the *mos maiorum*.

All of these features recur in many modern constitutions. They were of particular influence in the constitutions which followed the French Revolution. The constitution of the Consulate, for instance, under which the *Code civil* was enacted,[13] bears witness to this. The First Consul, Napoleon, whose very title echoes the origins of his office, proposed legislation which had been prepared by his Council of State. Thereafter, the project would be debated by the Tribunate, which had, like the Roman Senate of republican times, powers to discuss but not to enact the proposal. From there, the project went to the legislative assembly, which - like the Roman *comitia* - had no right to discuss it but only to decide upon its enactment. Finally, the Senate, recalling the work of the *patres* in its Roman predecessor, reviewed the enactment to ensure its constitutionality. The influence of the Roman arrangements upon this model was direct, and not mediated by the achievements of the intervening generations.

The Legislative Initiative

In most modern civil law countries, the legislative initiative is not limited to members of the legislative assembly. Ministers with executive powers, who need not themselves be members of the legislature, have the right to introduce legislative proposals. Such persons can address the assembly, even though they are not members, but cannot vote in it unless they are also members of it. The position of such ministers is similar to that of the Roman magistrates, who introduced proposals to the Senate and the assembly.

Legislative proposals can also be introduced by members of the legislature, but provisions also exist for proposals to be introduced by regional governments and even by numbers of electors. The former bears witness to the recognition of local autonomy which has been a feature of government in civil law countries during the second half of the twentieth century, in part as a reaction to the centralizing tendencies of fascist regimes in some of them during the first half. The second phenomenon extends the principle of popular sovereignty from the choice of representatives to the choice of issues with which those representatives must deal. It is an institution of direct democracy.[14]

The impact of popular sovereignty upon the legislative initiative is a modern phenomenon. In earlier ages, such powers would not have been conceded to the governed. Although during the Middle Ages, assemblies such as the Cortes in Spain and the States General in France were vehicles by which petitions from the ordinary people could be presented to the king for the remedy of grievances or for the amelioration of some problem, such petitions were a request for royal grace and carried no suggestion that such proposals had to be considered by the ruler. Once the ruler was in office, he alone decided how to rule. A voice in government was certainly not due to the people generally. Even on the more liberal interpretation of the *pactum subiectionis*, which held that the ruler governed on behalf of his subjects and was removable by them in extreme situations, there was no suggestion that while governing competently he had to accommodate their views on individual issues.

Legislative Deliberation

The deliberative phase of modern legislative processes is restricted to the members of the legislative bodies, most of whom will have been elected by one route or another by the people. They may be directly elected to represent geographical constituencies, or may have been chosen by elected regional or provincial bodies to represent the views of that locality. They may be national representatives elected in accordance with the proportion of the total votes cast for the political party which they support.

The deliberation will either be of the whole assembly or one chamber of it, if it consists of more than one chamber. In that eventuality, each chamber will consider the proposal in turn. It is also possible for the deliberation to be delegated by the chamber to a committee or commission composed of some of its members. The process of deliberation usually involves the bill undergoing two or three readings, when its contents are discussed or debated. The idea that a change in the law should be considered on successive occasions, so that the full ramifications of its principles and details are understood, also dates back to Roman times and the provisions of the *lex Caecilia Didia* of 98 BC.

The main difference between deliberation in the age of popular sovereignty and previous times lies in the personnel who deliberate. The deliberative body in the Roman republic was the Senate, consisting originally of the patricians only and even later confined to the ranks of the aristocracy. Under the emperors, deliberation was for the members of the imperial council or consistory. Only in the Germanic popular assemblies does one encounter the notion that all the free, weapon-bearing men could participate, but it is unclear how far these assemblies can properly be regarded as legislative in any modern sense. By the time of the Carolingians, only the higher nobility were allowed to discuss the proposals of the ruler, although during the Middle Ages such consultation was seen as the due of the aristocracy. With the advent of absolutism, deliberation was for the counsellors of the king, although the decision to enact was his alone. Even under the constitutional arrangements of the Revolutionary period in France, a distinction was drawn between the deliberative Tribunate and the decision-making legislative assembly.

Unlike the deliberations of assemblies in the Greek city states of the ancient world, and possibly those of the Germanic tribes, popular sovereignty has not required admission of the people themselves to participate in the deliberative phase. Montesquieu it was who insisted that while the people were admirably qualified to choose those to whom they would give the power to deliberate on their behalf, they were not suited to discussing and managing their own legislative business. While it might be proper to allow them to participate in the decision-making phase on a single question by means of a plebiscite or referendum, their involvement in the deliberative process was not to be countenanced.

Legislative Decision-Making

It is in the decision-making phase of the modern legislative process that the principle of popular sovereignty has made its greatest impact. It is today unthinkable that laws could be made without the consent of the representatives of the people. Even when in situations of urgency, the executive government is permitted to make laws by decree, such laws are only valid for a short period, during which they must be ratified by the popular assembly. Failure to present the decree for ratification or failure of the assembly to endorse the decree renders it void *ab initio*.[15]

Popular law-making has, in a sense, returned to its starting point in Roman law. In the Roman republic, *leges* were enacted by the *comitiae*. Only as the republican institutions fell into desuetude, partly through the extension of the empire and the impossibility of assembling all the citizens together, did legislative power centralize in the hands of first the Senate and the *princeps*, and later in the hands of the emperor alone. The Germanic tribes who occupied the lands of the former western empire continued their practice of declaring laws, and by their interpretation and extension inevitably making some new laws, in an assembly of all the weapon-bearing men, not unlike the Roman *comitia centuriata*. Again, it was probably the extent of the Carolingian empire which militated against the possibility of a full popular gathering, so that once more legislative decision-making passed into the hands of the emperor and the nobility, the lesser nobility being allowed a part however in the decision-making phase although only the higher-ranking nobles were permitted to discuss the proposals with the ruler.

Although the urban communities of the Middle Ages retained popular assemblies for their legislative activities, the meetings of the estates of the realm summoned by the feudal monarchs of France, Spain and Germany were assemblies of representatives of the people rather than of the people themselves. They were however, on analogy with the courts of the feudal lords of lesser domains, regarded as being essential for the making of laws which were to be binding on all the people. While the nobility attended in their own right, the clergy and the gentry were present by representatives as were the Third Estate, consisting of the inhabitants of boroughs and country districts. These representatives were those who attended under a mandate. Elected by those whom they were to represent, they were to vote in accordance with the declared interests of their constituents, and their consent to legislation could be revoked by the latter if it was found that they had acted contrary to or beyond their mandate. This restriction upon the freedom of the States General as a body constituted an inconvenience which contributed to the reluctance of the French kings to summon it during the sixteenth and seventeenth centuries. Instead, they chose to legislate only in a manner which regulated their own kingly powers, for instance upon procedure in their courts, trade on their highways and the like. Although such laws affected all, they were not directly applicable to all subjects, thus avoiding the necessity for the States General having to be summoned for their enactment. Instead, they were promulgated by being sent to the principal law courts, the *parlements*, particularly that of Paris, for registration. The justices of the *Parlement*, however, reserved the power not to register a royal ordinance which they believed to be at variance with existing substantive law or which would be difficult to apply alongside it. They announced such objections in the form of remonstrances, which the French kings were obliged to answer. This power of the *parlements* was one of the few effective checks upon untrammelled royal power in France under the *ancien régime*.

It was this *de facto* exclusion from the legislative process to which *de iure* the people belonged that fuelled the demand for popular sovereignty. Moreover, after the Revolution, the French nation wanted an assembly which represented it as a nation and not as separate, hierarchical estates, and without the power of localities to revoke the mandate of their representatives. Instead, it was decided to control the law-making powers of the representatives by allowing the people to reclaim their sovereignty over single issues by demanding a plebiscite. According to the draft constitution agreed in 1793, but never brought into effect, a law duly passed would have to be put to a popular referendum if 200,000 voters so required within forty days of its promulgation.

The constitution of the German Weimar republic gave the head of state wide powers to call referenda on single issues where he felt that the legislature had not exercised its powers in conformity with the popular will. This presidential power of calling for a plebiscite was felt to be a weakness of the Weimar constitution. The current German basic law trusts much less to plebiscites and more to the powers of a second chamber, the *Bundesrat*, which is representative of the *Länder*, the autonomous regions from which the Federal Republic is composed. Legislative projects passed by the lower chamber, the *Bundestag*, are then sent to the *Bundesrat* which is elected not by the people directly but by the governments of the *Länder* and whose members are bound to represent the interests of the *Land* from which they come according to the instructions they are given. In other words, they are subject to a mandate of the sort that used to control the decisions of the members of the Third Estate. In the event of disagreement between the two chambers, complex mechanisms operate to effect a conciliation.[16] Other countries however have returned to the notion of a plebiscite. Italy for example allows 500,000 voters to demand a referendum on laws duly made by the national parliament if they are unhappy with their substance.

While the decision as to whether to enact a legislative proposal is generally settled by simple majority of the popular representatives assembled in the chamber or chambers of the legislative assembly, the possibility of a referendum ensures that popular sovereignty is retained on each and every issue. The mechanism is reminiscent of the tribuniciary veto over the enactments of the Roman assemblies.

Constitutionality of Legislation

The plebiscite or the intervention of a body such as the German *Bundesrat* is protection against a law being passed which is contrary to the wishes of the electorate or a substantial section of it. Such methods subject legislation to popular approval and are therefore safeguards of popular sovereignty. However, there is another danger inherent in law-making and perhaps particularly in law-making by popular will, namely that a law may interfere with those rights deemed to be fundamental and therefore enshrined in the basic law or constitution. Just as in ancient Rome, after a *lex* had been enacted by the *comitia*, it was necessary for the *patres* in the Senate to pronounce its conformity with the *mos maiorum*, so in a modern civilian jurisdiction there needs to be a mechanism which ensures that laws enacted by the popular assemblies do not offend against the basic law from which all the powers in the State, including the legislative, are derived.

Inasmuch as the concept of there being fundamental rights which States exist to protect and against which they must not offend is only a few centuries old, there cannot have been mechanisms of the kind now under discussion in earlier times. However, as has been shown, the concept of there being a higher law, a law which is based not on enactment but upon a right order in society or even in nature, *ius*, is not new. If this was what the Roman senate believed was manifested by the ancestral practices, it clearly informed their decisions albeit that it was a set of unarticulated precepts which guided their decision making. Likewise, in the mediaeval period, the Church, asserting that the right order to which human societies had to conform in order to be just was God given, acquired the power to adjudicate upon the question of whether the customs of particular regions when declared did or did not conform to this higher law, a decision upon which their validity as laws depended. With the onset of absolute rule, and the assertion that the ruler was responsible only to God and therefore not answerable to any worldly institution for his actions, the possibility for such adjudication vanished, although many individual rulers were devoutly committed to ensuring that their enactments were in conformity with natural law and the divine will.

Given the importance of the doctrine of natural rights to the legal systems which emerged in Europe after the French Revolution, one might expect that some mechanism for assessing the constitutionality of laws made would have been early upon the scene. However, after the initial experiment with the Constitutional Senate in France, which foundered when that body discharged its functions so as to enable Napoleon to assume absolute power, it was not so, for such ideas collided head on with another basic doctrine of the new legal orders, that of the separation of powers. That latter doctrine declared it anathema for the judicial power to adjudicate upon the doings of the legislature, for the legislature was after all the organ which gave expression to the popular will. Although in the United States, the Supreme Court usurped the function of adjudicating upon the constitutionality of legislation in the nineteenth century,[17] it was not until after the second world war that most civil law jurisdictions developed the institution of a constitutional tribunal with powers to declare laws null and void for offending against the fundamental rights accorded by the constitution. In France, the Fifth Republic introduced the *Conseil constitutionnel* in 1958, to which all *lois organiques* must be, and all acts of the French parliament may be, referred for review of their constitutionality before promulgation. The court has the power to declare such legislation void for offence against the constitution. It is not however possible in France to challenge the constitutionality of laws thereafter, thus preserving obedience to the popular will. In other countries however greater latitude is given to subsequent objections. In Italy, it is always open to a citizen in the course of litigation to raise the question of the constitutionality of a provision germane to the adjudication of his case, whereupon that issue is passed to the Constitutional Court for decision. This can also happen in Germany and Spain, but in both those countries it is also possible for a citizen to challenge the constitutionality of a law which it is claimed offends against basic rights at any time, that is even when the citizen is not otherwise involved in litigation on this issue. In all cases however what is being practised are methods of ensuring that enacted laws conform to a higher law at the peril of invalidity. That higher law is now that articulated by the constitution, but the concept of such conformity being necessary has a much longer pedigree in the civilian juristic tradition and indeed in the cultural heritage of Europe.

Constitutional Revision

Finally, the question of how changes to the fundamental law itself can be made needs to be examined. Again, this is not a problem that arose until after the age of written constitutions. A distinction needs to be drawn between amendments to those parts of a constitution which provide for the composition and operation of state organs such as the legislature, the head of state and the executive, and those parts which set out those fundamental rights which the State exists to protect. Most countries provide for special legislative procedures for constitutional amendments of all kinds, thus barring constitutional change by means of the normal legislative processes. It is usual for constitutional amendments to require weighted majorities in the legislature, often a majority of three-fifths, two-thirds, or even three-quarters of the members present and voting in each chamber, perhaps after the text has been approved on more than one occasion without alteration in each of two legislative chambers, or otherwise the possibility of a referendum to approve the amendment by popular decision.[18] Some countries go further than this with regard to the amendment of those parts of the constitution which deal with fundamental rights, requiring the dissolution of the legislature, fresh elections and an endorsement of the amendment by the newly-constituted legislature before submission of the text to the people for approval by referendum. The constitution of post-Franco Spain imposes such severe restrictions on fundamental changes, making them all but unthinkable in other than the clearest of cases for reform. Much has clearly been learned about the perils of constitutional change and the safeguards needed to protect fundamental rights and democratic institutions against it since the first decade of the nineteenth century when the French Constitutional Senate had powers to amend the existing constitution by *senatusconsultum*, and used them to grant Napoleon the consulate for life, to establish the empire and to abolish the deliberative Tribunate.[19]

5 Decentralization and Subsidiarity

One of the major criticisms of the legislative programme set in train by the French Revolution was its emphasis upon the individual as the source, through the social contract, of the State's rights and the primary object of the State's protection. Not enough importance, it was felt, had been attached to intermediate associations of individuals - the family, communities, trade associations - which were situated between the individual and the State. During the nineteenth century, stress was placed upon the need for the State to protect and promote the interests of such intermediate associations as well as the individual, for only through them could the full development of individual personality and potential be realized.

The duty of the State was to assist, to provide help, *subsidium*, to enable such social groups to function and fulfil their purpose. It was not the place of the State to usurp their functions and replace them. The doctrine that the State should limit itself to assisting intermediate associations to function while respecting their proper spheres of operation has become known as subsidiarity. The doctrine was set forth in an encyclical issued in 1931 by Pope Pius XI entitled, from its opening words, *Quadragesimo anno*.[20] In it, His Holiness wrote that, just as it was gravely wrong to take from individuals what they can accomplish by their own initiative and industry and give it to the community, so also it was an injustice and at the same time a grave evil and disturbance of right order to assign to a greater and higher association what lesser and subordinate organizations can do. In part, the encyclical's strong language, with talk of grave evil, was a reaction to the centralizing tendencies of the Italian fascists under Mussolini, but the reference to disturbance of right order is redolent of the natural law conception that human legal arrangements must conform to the order which the divine will has ordained and manifested for the creation. Indeed, the concept of subsidiarity articulated by Pius XI has roots far back in the Church's social teaching, and is certainly present for instance in the writings of St. Thomas Aquinas.

Modern scholarship has tended to emphasize that such notions were practised within the Roman empire. Thus it is apparent that the native inhabitants of the Roman provinces, even after having been accorded the citizenship, were permitted to regulate their relationships one with another according to their native customs and laws if they so wished. No attempt was made to force them to adopt Roman law, although of course that would govern their relationships with those Roman citizens who lived according to that law, most notably the governing authorities of the provinces, and that law would also regulate matters not dealt with under the local customs.[21] Likewise, the manner in which the Germanic invaders of the lands of the western empire allowed their erstwhile Roman subjects to continue to live by Roman law reflects the same attitude to group determination. The Carolingian emperors also distinguished between enactments which were to be binding upon all their subjects and those which were intended only for certain areas.[22] The customary laws of France, the various legal traditions of the territories of Germany and Italy, and the refusal of the kingdoms of Spain to accept a unified system of laws all evidence the extent to which legal diversity has been a continuing feature in the development of law in the civil law countries. The cantonal federation of Switzerland is a particularly clear illustration of how unity does not require uniformity, but is capable of accommodating a great deal of diversity. In Switzerland, this was especially true in the manner in which the religious divisions which occurred following the Reformation were eventually assimilated within the federal structure.

Such centrifugal tendencies did not suit the requirements of absolute rulers. Unsurprisingly, the French kings of the *ancien régime* ceased to summon the States General with its inconvenient deference to the popular mandate in the localities, preferring to issue ordinances which applied nationally by royal authority. Likewise, the Bourbon kings of eighteenth-century Spain sought to undermine the legal traditions of the different parts of the kingdom in pursuit of a central authority. The belief that human reason could produce a system of law which was suitable to all peoples at all times was as much the clear enemy of diverse legal cultures as the views of the historical school that law must manifest the spirit of the people it governed was their ally. The centralist attempts of Napoleon were therefore succeeded by law codes in Spain, Italy and Germany which attempted to accommodate the legal habits of the law's subjects. Similarly, the centralist dogmas of fascism in those same countries during the twentieth century has given way to a greater readiness to respect diversity and honour the principle of subsidiarity.

Napoleon's reforms to the administration of France involved replacing the existing territorial divisions with new, rational ones, dividing the country into departments and communes, in much the same way as, and following the example of, Diocletian's restructuring of the later Roman empire. Napoleon's reforms extended to those lands which he conquered, and, as in France, these governmental and administrative divisions, known more usually in these countries as provinces and communes - reflecting the Roman usage - have survived by virtue of their merit. Legislative power was not however accorded to such units of local government. The second half of the twentieth century has seen a renewal of the quest for legislative, as well as administrative, autonomy and decentralization, in line with the principle of subsidiarity.

This has manifested itself in two ways. Firstly, some nations have devolved limited legislative authority to a new tier of government, midway between the nation and the provinces or the departments, at regional level. Both France and Italy have created regional governments with legislative authority for certain legal matters within the areas they govern. Often, the national legislature creates the skeletal framework within which the regional legislature is enabled to create a body of law on some topic which takes into account the particular needs and sensitivities of the locality.

Secondly, some countries have established national government on a federal model. Germany is the prime example of this phenomenon in Europe, but it can also be found in other civil law countries, for instance Argentina in South America. In the same way in which the regions into which Italy has been divided in the last half century reflect some of the original states out of which the unified kingdom was established in the nineteenth century, so in Germany, the federal structure in some measure reflects a long-standing need to allow local interests substantial recognition in the structures of national government. When the first constitution for a German confederation was produced in 1849, a constitution which never came into force, it pursued a federal concept of unity. After the unification of Germany in the Bismarckian Reich and the later centralization of power under Hitler, the Basic Law of contemporary Germany has returned to a federal model for government, with considerable legislative and administrative powers being retained by the *Länder* which compose the Federal Republic, the latter nevertheless being enabled to legislate generally on a range of topics, sharing legislative authority with the *Länder* on others, but having only the right to provide framework legislation on the rest. Moreover, as has been seen, the *Länder* have considerable influence within the workings of the federal legislature through their representation in the *Bundesrat*.

The constitution of the new democratic kingdom of Spain, issued in 1977, also adopts a decentralized model. The nation recognizes the individual traditions of its component parts by establishing them as autonomous communities. These correspond to the territorial divisions of the country to a much greater extent than do the *Länder* in Germany and even the regions of Italy. Moreover, not only are devolved legislative and administrative powers given to the autonomous communities, but they are also permitted to retain their individual customs in matters of private law, so that where their *Leyes Civiles Forales* provide for certain legal topics, such as succession or family property, they displace to that extent the provisions of the national civil code. Where such a *Ley Civil Foral* exists, the court of final instance dealing with its provisions will be situated in the autonomous community which it serves, which to that extent displaces the jurisdiction of the Supreme Court of Cassation in the national capital.

The administration of justice is always highly decentralized in civil law countries. Indeed, it is one of the features distinguishing such jurisdictions from those of the common law, where traditionally the administration of justice has been highly centralized.[23] This aspect of state decentralization in the lands of the civil law will be dealt with in the succeeding chapters on civil and criminal justice.

Notes

[1] Thus, the United Kingdom does not have a constitution in this sense, although it has constitutional laws. It is not just that it has no written constitution; it has no fundamental laws from which all others derive their validity.

[2] Rousseau's *Le Contrat Social* was published in 1743, being part of an intended larger work, *Institutions Politiques*.

[3] See Gaius, *Institutes* I. 1 on *ius civile* and *ius gentium*, and Justinian, *Institutes* I. 2. pr. on *ius naturale*.

[4] See chapter 1.

[5] *Quod principi placuit legis habet vigorem*. The Roman principle referred to enacted law (*lex*) but the absolutist rulers equated this with *ius*.

[6] See T.G. Watkin, *The Italian Legal Tradition* (London, 1997), pp. 70, 73 ff., and see the Italian Constitution arts. 71 and 75.

[7] See chapter 1.

[8] Tacitus flourished from c. 56 to c. 116 AD, and described these institutions in his *Germania*.

[9] Baldus de Ubaldis, 7, *Consilia, de prob*. 4. 18; see J.-B. Brissaud, *A History of French Public Law* (Boston, 1915; reprinted New York 1969), p. 331.

[10] See Brissaud, *French Public Law*, pp. 71 ff.

[11] See O. Robinson, T.D. Fergus and W.M. Gordon, *European Legal History* (2nd Ed.; London, 1994), p. 279.

[12] See chapter 1.

[13] See chapter 7.

[14] In Italy, for example, the popular initiative is provided for by article 71 of the Constitution, while in Spain, popular *proposiciones de ley* are permitted under article 87 of the Constitution, the method of introduction being set out in *Ley orgánica* 3/1984; see P.J. Donaghy and M.T. Newton, *Spain: a guide to political and economic institutions* (Cambridge, 1987), pp. 56 ff.

[15] For Italy, see the Italian Constitution art. 77 and T.G. Watkin, *The Italian Legal Tradition*, p. 74; for France, see C. Dadomo and S. Farran, *The French Legal System* (2nd Ed.; London, 1996), pp. 26 f, 31.

[16] For details, see N.G. Foster, *German Legal System and Laws* (2nd Ed.; London, 1996), pp. 55 ff.

[17] *Marbury* v *Madison* (1803) 1 Cranch. 137.

[18] For Italy see T.G. Watkin, *The Italian Legal Tradition*, pp. 74 ff.; for Spain, see P.J. Donaghy and M.T. Newton, *Spain: a guide to political and economic institutions*, pp. 21 f.; for Germany see N.G. Foster, *German Legal System and Laws*, p. 144; for France, see C. Dadomo and S. Farran, *The French Legal System*, p. 32.

[19] See Brissaud, *French Public Law*, pp. 555 ff.

[20] Its title commemorated the fortieth anniversary of the issue of *Rerum novarum* by Leo XIII which also dealt with social issues.

[21] The use of the *mos provinciale* was specifically sanctioned by legislation of Constantine (Justinian, *Code* VIII. 53), Theodosius (*Theodosian Code* V. 22) and Justinian (Digest I. 3); see C. Calisse et al., *General Survey of Continental Legal History* (Boston, 1912; reprinted New York, 1968), p. 592.

[22] These were referred to as *capitula legibus addenda* and *per se scribenda* respectively; see C. Calisse, *General Survey*, pp. 39 ff.

[23] In England, the king's courts were based in Westminster for civil matters, although criminal courts were decentralized. Since 1972, the High Court sits outside of London, and the Court of Appeal can do so but rarely does. There are however signs of convergence with a greater readiness to contemplate the establishment of appeal courts in the provinces.

15 The Law of Civil Procedure

1 The Administration of Civil Justice

Civil procedure is concerned with the declaration of rights as between private individuals and, if necessary, their enforcement. In ancient Roman law, it was encompassed by the law of actions and regarded as one of the main departments of private law. In modern civilian systems, the law of procedure has been separated from the substantive law with which it is concerned, and in the area of private law, this is accomplished by the compilation of a separate code of civil procedure distinct from the substantive law contained in the civil code. Likewise, as will be seen in the next chapter, the law of criminal procedure has been demarcated from substantive criminal law by the compilation of two distinct codifications. The separation of procedural from substantive law was begun in the teaching of the university law faculties in the sixteenth century, primarily in Germany, and has culminated in the separate procedural codes created by the civilian jurisdictions during the nineteenth and twentieth centuries. In both civil and criminal law, the influence of the canon law of the western Church upon the development of procedure has been enormous. It is not too much to say that while the substantive law of modern civilian systems remains primarily Roman in its inspiration and raw material, in the realm of procedure, those systems are the heirs of the canonical tradition.

The courts which administer civil justice are often referred to as the courts of ordinary jurisdiction. This preserves the view that the settlement of disputes between private individuals is the normal business of the law. The jurisdiction of a court or set of courts in a civil law system refers to the area of law which it administers. Thus, the courts which administer the law contained in the civil code are those of civil jurisdiction. Those which administer the law contained in the criminal code are those with criminal jurisdiction. Although some courts may exercise both functions, the jurisdictions are distinct, and the procedure utilized when exercising the distinct jurisdictions will also be different. In some countries, there is a multiplicity of jurisdictions. Most civilian countries have separate administrative courts to deal with matters of administrative law, and as has been seen it is today common for there to be a constitutional court with jurisdiction to police observance of the Constitution even by organs of State government. Countries, such as France, with a separate commercial code may have some separate courts declaring the law, *jus dicere*, in that jurisdiction, although some countries which have a separate commercial code nevertheless allot that jurisdiction to the ordinary courts, for instance Spain. Germany has a separate set of courts with jurisdiction for each of tax law, social security law and labour law, as well as administrative courts and courts of ordinary jurisdiction with distinct civil and criminal divisions within them.

While jurisdiction is concerned with the area of law which each set of courts administers - civil, administrative, criminal, etc., within each jurisdiction courts are distinguished by their competence. Some are competent to adjudicate disputes on the first occasion that they fall for determination, while others may only hear appeals or review the decisions of other courts; these are distinctions of functional competence. Some courts of first instance, those which deal with the initial determination of cases, may only hear cases within fixed limits, based on the type of property concerned or its value; such distinctions limit their subject-matter competence. Finally, courts of first instance and of appeal will only be competent to deal with cases arising in a particular geographical division of the State, while the final court of review will probably be competent to adjudicate on cases coming to it from lower courts throughout the country; these are distinctions of territorial competence. Courts are therefore distinguished both by their jurisdiction, and within each jurisdiction, according to their functional, subject-matter and territorial competence.

Distinctions of territorial competence reflect the decentralization which is a striking feature of civilian countries. In the same manner that the country is divided into regions, provinces or departments and communes for governmental and administrative matters, so also there are divisions of the State for the administration of justice. These divisions often follow those employed for local government, although they need not conform exactly. In Italy, for instance, the appeal court districts are not identical with the State's more recent division into regions, while in Spain the autonomous communities serve as appeal court districts as well. There is general concurrence at provincial or department level.

Decentralization in the administration of justice is a manifestation of the State's commitment to complying with its obligation to provide justice for all its citizens and to make that provision on an equal basis. Justice would not be equally available for all if the law courts were all situated in the State capital, at a considerable distance from the homes of some citizens yet on the doorstep of others. Since the advent of modern codes of civil procedure following the French Revolution, the principle has been followed of ensuring that courts with general competence at first instance can be found within roughly a day's travelling distance of the homes of every inhabitant, in the equivalent of what in England and Wales would be called the county town. The day's travelling distance was measured in terms of transport which had not yet embraced a railway network let alone the possibilities of air travel. In relation to small claims, where even a journey to the local provincial capital might be an obstacle to seeking a remedy, courts with limited subject-matter competence were established in nearly every sizeable community within a province or department. Improved communications have led to a decrease in the number of centres at which such courts sit in modern times. Facilities for conciliation as a part of or instead of dispute settlement were often additionally afforded by the most local of courts.

Such decentralization has been a feature of the administration of civil justice in the countries of the civil law throughout the centuries, although the reason why justice has been administered locally has varied from age to age. There is a clear similarity between the modern structure of civil courts and the system put in place by the emperor Diocletian as part of his reforms of government in the Roman empire at the end of the third century. The administration of justice, together with other governmental functions, were entrusted to the governor of each province into which the empire was divided, and justice was to be administered at his tribunal or judgement seat. Delegation of judicial activity by him to a deputy, the *iudex pedaneus*, was to be discouraged. Appeals were however allowed from his judgements to the imperial vicar, who oversaw governmental functions including the administration of justice in the group of provinces which formed his vicariate or diocese, and a further appeal from him was allowed to one of the four praetorian prefects or to the emperor. The influence of this structure upon the modern civilian approach to the administration of justice cannot be gainsaid.

However, there has not been a direct line of descent between the arrangements effected by Diocletian and the secular courts system of modern times. As with so much else, the occupation of the lands of the western empire by the Germanic tribes broke the continuity between the civil law of the ancient world and its mediaeval and modern counterparts. The Germanic peoples typically dealt with the adjudication and settlement of disputes within the popular assemblies of all weapon-bearing men described in the last chapter. These meetings were not confined to judicial business, but also declared the laws or customs of the people, sometimes in the course of settling disputes, and took decisions of peace and war. Within them, the law was preserved in the memory of those assembled. By circumstance, they were drawn from a relatively small locality, although larger tribal assemblies would take place from time to time, for instance when the customs of the whole tribe were in need of elaboration or when they were first committed to writing.

A significant step in the development of procedure was taken when certain members of the assembly came to be regarded as having particular talents with regard to the declaration and interpretation of the customs. These individuals were not entrusted with deciding the cases before the court, but only with finding the law which was applicable to the case in question. These law-finders, or *Schöffen* as they were called in German, constituted a group of trusted interpreters of the law within the community, much as the pontiffs had been in the early Roman republic, or perhaps more accurately as the first jurists had been when the rules relating to the granting of actions were first published. Charlemagne encouraged the use of such law-finders throughout his empire, and thus are found the similar functions of the *échevins* in France and the *scabini* in the territories of Italy. Thus also was born the distinction, which is such a feature of Germanic procedure, between the *Richter*, who presides at the court and pronounces judgement, and the *Schöffen,* who declare the law upon which the judgement of the court is founded.

The law of these popular assemblies, whether declared by the whole assembly or by the *Schöffen*, was the custom of the locality. With the break up of the Carolingian empire, the localities became in large measure synonymous with the lordships of the feudal nobles under whose protection those lands came. Although the ties binding the people of those areas together were now ones of personal loyalty to the lord rather than of tribal relationship, their law remained the custom of the locality in which they lived. Eventually, the custom of the lordship became that of the territory in which it was located, and continued to be declared by those learned in it.

While the institutions of Germanic tribal and feudal justice marked a break with the judicial traditions of the Roman empire, one institution acted as a conservator in that regard. That institution was the catholic Church. It retained the structures of provinces and dioceses in its ecclesiastical administration and had, from the time of Constantine, enjoyed jurisdiction over the litigation of the faithful in courts held by the bishops and archbishops, following the pattern established by the provincial governors of the later empire. The rebirth of Roman legal science in the universities of twelfth century Europe and the development of scientific study of the canon law led to an invigoration in the tribunals of the Church. It was in the ecclesiastical courts of the thirteenth century that graduates from the law faculties first began to be employed as law-finders, acting as judges who would adjudicate according to the learned law of the Church and of the universities, namely canon and civil law. The distinction between *Richter* and *Schöffen* disappears in these tribunals, with professional judges with a legal education taking over as president and law-finder. Moreover, during the thirteenth century, the Church courts emerge as a hierarchical system of judicature, with archdeacons' courts at the most local level dealing with minor matters, in particular punishment of sins with penances, and the bishop's court or consistory court having general competence at diocesan level. Above the bishops' courts, were the provincial courts of the archbishops and, finally, above them all, at the apex of the pyramid of ecclesiastical jurisdiction, the court of the Pope, the Papal Curia, at Rome. Although litigation could be commenced at any level according to the parties' wishes, it was also possible to appeal from one level in the hierarchy to the next. Thus, many of the features of the later Roman structure were continued and many elements of the modern courts system anticipated in the arrangements of the mediaeval Church. It was the link connecting the modern system of civil justice to its ancient predecessor.

While the Church courts provided a scientific system of dispute resolution at every level from the local to the Papal, so also at roughly the same time secular jurisdiction began to utilize the new legal learning emanating from the universities. Graduates in both laws, civil and canon, were called upon to occupy judicial office in the urban centres of Italy and later in Germany and France, towns and cities which had remained free from feudal domination. There, the use of sophisticated procedures based upon those of the Church proved attractive to litigants, as was the adoption of Roman legal models to serve the needs of commerce and municipal government in these burgeoning centres of prosperity and culture.

The example and success of the ecclesiastical and communal courts spurred the monarchs of later mediaeval Europe to emulate their methods in order to enhance their authority against those of the feudal magnates. The kings of France, for instance, were in the vanguard of those rulers who adopted Romano-canonical procedures into their courts to increase their efficiency and thereby their attractiveness to litigants. At the close of the fifteenth century, the same inspiration led to the adoption of Romano-canonical procedures and the rules of the *Corpus Iuris* itself in the newly established *Reichskammergericht* of the German emperors. Although throughout Germany and France, law remained that of the locality rather than that of the nation, even in the local customary courts, law graduates from the universities began to replace lay *Schöffen* both as law-finders and as judges. From its inception in 1495, one half of the judges in the *Reichskammergericht* had to be legally qualified, the other half being drawn from the nobility.

The Romano-canonical procedure was therefore a considerable unifying factor among the emerging legal systems of later mediaeval and early modern Europe. By encouraging appeals from the decisions of the local courts to the central royal tribunals such as the *Reichskammergericht* in Germany and the *Parlement* of Paris in France, the local courts themselves became subject to royal review and inevitably sought to adopt the more sophisticated procedures themselves in order to maintain their share of jurisdiction. Among the German states, however, the role of the *Reichskammergericht* as a final court of appeal was somewhat weakened by the imperial willingness to exempt the courts of some rulers from its appellate jurisdiction. In both France and the German empire, the rulers took advantage of the right to regulate procedure in their own jurisdiction to introduce successive provisions which were in effect the first codes of civil procedure, such as the successive German *Reichskammergerichtsordnungen* and Louis XIV's *ordonnance* on civil procedure of 1667 in France.

The systems of administering civil justice which have been established in the nation states of continental Europe since the French Revolution are, therefore, in many respects the completion along rational lines of the developments that had been taking place over the previous centuries, although the structures adopted pay full homage to their origins in the legal system of the later Roman empire as devised by Diocletian. The actual procedure employed in these courts, however, is less Roman than ecclesiastical in its inspiration, being based in the main upon the Romano-canonical model of procedure devised for use in the Church courts during the thirteenth and later centuries. Testimony to the ecclesiastical provenance of the law of procedure is the fact that when it was first taught in the law faculties as a subject in its own right, it was to the professors of canon law rather than civil law that tuition in the matter fell.

The development of that area of the law of civil procedure will now be examined.

2 The Development of Civil Procedure

Avoidance of the Blood Feud

Among the Germanic tribes who occupied the western lands of the former Roman empire during the Dark Ages, the objectives of the legal process returned in large measure to those which had subsisted in early Rome at the time of or even before the Twelve Tables. According to that compilation, the penalty for the maiming of a person, *membrum ruptum*, was retaliation unless a suitable compensation could be agreed. From this it is clear that the rule was an attempt to replace resort to retaliation, with the threat of violence and disorder that that entailed, with satisfaction through the making of material redress. For lesser injuries, fixed tariffs of monetary redress had already been established.[1]

It is also clear from the Twelve Tables that no distinction had yet been made between compensation and punishment. The line between civil and criminal proceedings had yet to be drawn. At this early time, it was always up to the victim or the victim's family to initiate any action for redress or punishment; the community did not act on its own motion or on the victim's behalf. The community interest lay solely in either eliminating or regulating private vengeance and the pursuit of the blood feud between the families of the injured and the injurer.

This concentration of effort upon avoiding or at least controlling the blood feud re-appears in the legal developments of the Germanic tribes after the fall of the western empire. When a member of the tribe was injured by someone outside his kinship group, so that the issue was one for the tribe rather than the kin, it was probably not merely lawful for the relatives of the injured to retaliate, but more likely a duty incumbent upon them. The task of the community was to prevent such an occurrence rupturing the communal peace by persuading the parties to come to terms peaceably rather than by force of arms. As exacting the appropriate vengeance was probably a matter of honour, this was no easy task.

As in the early Roman situation, the Germanic tribes did not distinguish at this stage between the civil and criminal aspects of this endeavour. It being the duty of the injured parties to complain, the initiative for starting proceedings lay with them and it was satisfaction for them in terms of honour and redress which the procedure was meant to achieve. Initially, the victims would be encouraged to take their dispute before the popular assembly rather than resort to violence, and the wrongdoer would be summoned to appear before the assembly to answer the complaint. Failure to appear would be a contempt of the assembly's command and lead to expulsion from the group in the form of outlawry, being placed outside of the protection of the group's laws and therefore susceptible to being hunted down and killed like a wild animal.

The wrongdoer who appeared to answer the complaint afforded the assembly the opportunity to assist the parties to come to an agreement, compounding any liability with a payment in money or goods. At first, such a compact would probably have been negotiated, but in time sums appropriate for various injuries would be recognized and become customary payments for certain wrongs. The assembly would only thereafter need to declare the appropriate payment, other than in cases of some novelty. The initial purpose of such litigation was therefore the declaration of what, if anything, was due to the injured party. The obligation thus declared was expected to be honoured, and therefore execution of the judgement was always a separate matter.

Under the Carolingians, use was made of men learned in the customs of the communities to declare the law within the popular assemblies, *Schöffen* or *scabini* who eventually took over the task of law-finding from the assembly itself. In parts of southern Europe, particularly in the lands of the Visigoths and the Lombards, a greater remnant of Roman learning had been retained so that, for instance, the distinction between civil and criminal proceedings can be found in the Visigothic laws of the seventh century. Moreover, both the Visigoths and the Lombards regarded adjudication as a royal rather than a communal function, so that their judges and law-finders were viewed as royal rather than popular officials from an early date. The Lombards likewise were in the vanguard of those peoples who utilized those with a legal education as *scabini*; the law school at Pavia was providing such persons to the courts as early as the eleventh century.[2]

Rational and Non-rational Methods of Proof

While the purpose of litigation, whether before the assembly or a royal or popular officer, was early settled to be primarily the declaration of what was due between the parties, the manner in which that task was to be accomplished developed more slowly. The Roman formulary system had aimed at settling the issues for resolution between the parties in the proceedings before the magistrate prior to forwarding those issues to the judge of the parties' choice for determination. This settling of the issues in dispute, the *litis contestatio*, was thus a key moment in the procedure. Under the cognitio procedure of the later empire, this moment was of less significance, as the same person, the magistrate, now acted throughout the proceedings. Among the Germanic tribes, one method of avoiding the blood feud had been to formalize the combat between the parties into a judicial battle, where the issue between them was finally settled by the outcome of one contest. This necessitated the reduction, wherever possible, of the dispute between the parties to one question, capable of being settled by the outcome of one contest. Even when trial by battle gave way to other mechanisms of judicial determination, this reduction of the issues to a single question upon which the parties could stake their oaths remained a feature of Germanic procedure.

The complainant therefore would state his grievance against the other party, who could either admit the matter or contest it in whole or in part. If the defendant contested the issue, he might admit the facts as recounted by the plaintiff but question whether in law they disclosed an obligation on his part, or he could deny some or all of the facts. If the difference between the parties was solely on the question of whether by law anything was due to the plaintiff, that was simply a matter for the court to declare according to the customs administered in it. If however the facts were in dispute, then the parties would be required to furnish proof of the facts that they alleged. This could be done by producing written documents, proving that one of the parties had entered into the obligation, or by calling upon the testimony of witnesses, who could either attest to having formally witnessed the obligation being made or provide testimony concerning the facts, such as an injury, which it was claimed gave rise to the obligation. The courts usually required several witnesses to provide evidence of a fact, number and social rank being regarded as relevant to the weight to be attached to their testimony. If the judge was not convinced that the facts had been established, the final recourse was to put one of the parties to an oath to the effect that his claim or defence was true. If the party was not oath worthy, that is if his word on oath was not regarded as to be trusted, then his oath might be tested in a judicial ordeal. In this process, he might be required to carry a hot iron, or to immerse his arm in boiling water or to be placed into a river or pool of cold water to see if the water received him. If his wounds healed or the water received him, his oath was deemed true by judgement of God; if his wounds festered or the pure element of water rejected him, his oath was deemed to have been false and he would be punished as a perjurer.

These oaths, and the ordeals which followed, were supervised by priests of the Christian Church, although the practice of seeking divine judgement had been derived from the pagan past. In 1215, the Fourth Lateran Council forbade clergy to participate in such ordeals in future in that such practices were superstitious and amounted to the sin of tempting God, that is testing his involvement in creation. Other methods of determining the issues between the parties would therefore have to be employed.

Canonical Procedure

Already by 1215, the Church had been devising more rational methods of deciding cases within its own jurisdictions, and more rational methods were also making headway in certain secular courts.[3] The great step forward came with the writings of some of the Bolognese canonists on the subject of procedure in the twelfth and thirteenth centuries. Basing themselves on the Roman procedures of the later empire, as evidenced in the compilations of Justinian, they developed an elaborate but highly ordered system of procedure for the ecclesiastical courts which were being systematized at that time to administer the canon law which itself had become the object of scientific study.

Two writers of the thirteenth century made lasting contributions to the development of the Romano-canonical procedure. They are Tancred and Guilelmus Durantis. The former was a native of Bologna, where he rose to become *magister decretorum* and archdeacon, before dying at an early age. The latter was a native of southern France, who studied and taught in Italy and acquired a mastery of the canonical procedure through practical experience in the courts. Tancred wrote his *Libellus ordinis iudiciarii* in 1216; Durantis published his *Speculum iudiciale* in 1236. The works are generally referred to as Tancred and Durantis' *Speculum* respectively.

Tancred is heavily reliant upon the Roman legal sources. He divides his treatise into four books, dealing in turn with the parties to the process, the procedure up to *litis contestatio*, the procedure from *litis contestatio* to judgement, and execution thereafter, together with remedies against the judgement. This pattern was to prove of immense influence in the subsequent study of and writing on procedure. Durantis' *Speculum* is also divided into four books, but additionally into twelve parts. The first book deals with parties, but it is the second which is concerned with civil procedure as such. Its three parts reflect Tancred's division of the process into pre-*litis contestatio*, *litis constestatio* to judgement, and procedure thereafter. The third book is concerned with criminal procedure and the fourth with detailed instructions concerning specific procedural steps.

The Romano-canonical procedure as described by Tancred and Durantis is markedly different from the Germanic procedures it came to replace, harking back instead to the procedures of ancient Roman law. Knowledge of this procedure was however derived wholly from Justinian, and therefore, although there was awareness of the existence of the earlier formulary procedure, its true nature was not appreciated. Like the procedure of the later empire, the Romano-canonical usage was dominated by the use of writing at the expense of orality, with the result that the process was conducted privately rather than publicly, the role of professionals in the process became of great importance and there was considerable protraction of the time involved between the commencement of the action and its final determination. The process was very formal, being referred to as the solemn order of proceeding, *solemnis ordo*.

The requirement that the plaintiff's complaint should be made in writing and handed in to the court in order that it might be registered there and thence communicated to the defendant originated with a decree of Pope Innocent III in 1216. This also meant that the complaint was no longer a matter of public notice. Each court was now to be staffed by a single judge, rather than the plurality which had acted in the Germanic popular assemblies and the collegiate structure of courts staffed by *scabini*. The judge would be the officer of the ecclesiastic in whose court he sat, either as the delegate of that personage for a particular cause or as his judge with ordinary jurisdiction, that is the judge who normally heard causes in that court. The court also now had a clerk to deal with the writings which were an essential part of the proceedings.

When the plaintiff's statement of claim had been communicated to the defendant, the latter would be summoned by the court, not as in earlier times by the plaintiff, to appear, so that failure to appear without due cause constituted a contempt of the court's authority. Although this could lead to distraint of the defendant's property for being contumacious, it did not lead to the case going against him by default; even if he failed ever to appear, the court would still hear the plaintiff's cause *ex parte* and oblige him to furnish proof of his action before granting judgement in his favour if his proof succeeded. When a defendant did appear to answer the summons, he was permitted to present defences, called *exceptiones* after the Roman fashion, although the jurists' limited knowledge of the formulary system meant that they failed to appreciate the difference between the specific nature of *exceptiones* in Roman law and the raising of other kinds of defence. The defendant could also raise a counterclaim to the plaintiff's action. The process of pleading would continue until the parties had established all the issues over which they were in dispute. As the pleadings were in writing, it was not necessary for the parties to appear in person, and widespread use was now made of procurators to enter appearances on their behalf and perform acts for them, as well as of advocates to address the court on their behalf.

Exceptiones raised by the defendant were of two broad kinds - dilatory and peremptory. Dilatory defences are those which challenge the jurisdiction of the court to hear the cause or assert that the claim discloses no known cause of action. They therefore invite the court to strike out the plaintiff's claim. Peremptory defences on the other hand neither deny the court's jurisdiction nor the legality of the cause of action, but raise issues of law or fact to the effect that the claim should not succeed. Once the defendant has accepted the court's jurisdiction and the legality of the plaintiff's cause, he cannot thereafter challenge those issues. Accordingly, whereas peremptory defences could be raised at any stage of the proceedings, dilatory defences had to be raised during the opening stage, that is before issues were joined at *litis contestatio*.

Litis contestatio now took place when the pleadings were completed. It marked the agreement of the parties regarding the issues which separated them. Moreover, they were now required to take the so-called calumny oath to the effect that they were in earnest regarding the litigation which was about to enter its next stage and that they would not abuse the process in any way.

Once issue had been joined, it was then for the party upon whose assertions the cause depended to present the facts which he believed would establish his cause. There was no longer, with the written procedure any need to reduce the number of questions to be settled to one. Instead, the parties would make their assertions of relevant facts in the form of positions, which the other party would simply admit or deny. If admitted, the court accepted their validity; admission amounting to proof. If denied, the party making the assertion would have to prove it in some way. There was no limit to the number of positions a party could adduce. The positions were presented in writing and the other party answered in writing with a simple affirmation or denial. Further, there was nothing to prevent further positions being advanced at any stage of the proceedings until judgement, and further peremptory defences could also be raised. Proceedings could therefore be very protracted, although to abuse the process by introducing new defences or positions might always be taken as an abuse contrary to the calumny oath. The positions were in effect a set of evidential propositions leading to the conclusion that the plaintiff's claim was justified. The business of the court was to decide upon the merits of each position upon which the parties were at variance, and thereby reach a conclusion on the main issue in contention.

The court would receive evidence therefore on each position in turn, again causing the proceedings to be lengthy. The types of proof it would accept were listed by Durantis. They included the testimony of witnesses, documentary evidence, admissions, inspections, inferences from known facts and the oaths of the parties. Durantis' list is strikingly similar to those to be found in contemporary codes of procedure. It omits the testimony of experts appointed by the court, although it is clear from his account of proof that use could be made of such expert evidence.

Witnesses were suggested by the parties and questions to be put to them were also submitted by the parties although put to the witness by the judge. Immediately therefore the inquisitorial element of the canonical *ordo* comes to the fore. Either party could raise objections to the other's witness, but the witnesses when examined were not questioned in the presence of the parties, but they could suggest further questions. This again protracted the process. The judge however was not free to evaluate the witness testimony according to his own idea of its reliability and credibility. Instead, elaborate rules relating to the number and status of witnesses were devised, based on notions from the Germanic tradition, for establishing whether proof of an issue had been made. The testimony of one witness was never sufficient - *testis unus, testis nullus* - and the testimony of less credible persons was literally counted as less than that of reliable ones. The testimony of two worthy witnesses was full proof; of one, only half; of a doubtful witness, less than half. The judge's discretion in evaluating the testimony was virtually non-existent once the witness was admitted. The probative value of witness testimony was measured quantitatively, according to the rules developed, and not qualitatively, following Germanic rather than Roman models.

Documentary evidence was divided into those written instruments which were, if genuine, conclusive proof of a fact, because made in order to be such, and other forms of written evidence which only went towards proving the fact with other evidence. Letters and account books, for instance, fell into the latter category. Conclusive documentary evidence was inevitably much favoured within the written process. Considerable use was also made of oaths, which were divided into two kinds: those administered by the judge, the *juramenta necessaria*, and those demanded by the parties, the *juramenta judicialia*. The latter were derived from Roman law, being oaths relating to matters which were crucial to the decision of the issue one way or the other. One party could in relation to such an issue challenge the other to swear an oath concerning the truth of his assertions. If he swore, he won; if he refused, he lost. If however he wished, he could return the challenge, demanding that the original challenger deny the assertion on oath instead. If he accepted the returned challenge, he won; if, he refused, he lost. This oath therefore was decisive, but if at any future time such an oath was found to have been false, its swearer was of course open to a charge of perjury and liable to punishment.

The *juramentum necessarium* however was not based upon the Roman oath, but an adaptation of the Germanic suppletory and purgation oaths to suit the new methods of determining full proof. Under the older Germanic procedures, if the court was not convinced that the party's claim had been proved, but felt that it was probably the case, it could permit the party if he wished, and the matter in doubt was within his knowledge, to complete his proof by taking an oath regarding the matter. On the other hand, if insufficient proof had been established, the opponent could claim the purgation oath in such circumstances to purge his liability. The threat of punishment for perjury hung over any who chose to end a cause in this way. The new concept of full canonical proof adapted these oaths by making it incumbent upon the judge to allow a party who had made at least half proof of his case to swear an oath to make good the deficit so as to win his case, or alternatively to allow the other party to swear an oath against the assertion where less than half proof had been established.

When the evidence relating to all the positions had been gathered and it had been determined whether each one had been proved, the court then proceeded to hear the oral arguments of the parties or their counsel with regard to how the law and the evidence should be interpreted and what inferences drawn. The main points of these arguments were however reduced to writing and formed part of the *acta*, the dossier from which the judge would consider his verdict. He was at liberty to consult assessors or counsellors to advise him, but he was not bound by their conclusions. His own judgement was to condemn or absolve the defendant in clear imitation of the Roman model, but should follow the form of the plaintiff's petition in presenting its conclusions. Reasons or grounds for the decision did not have to be given. The judgement did however have to be written down, although it had also to be read aloud to the parties by the judge from the judgement seat. Appeal against the judgement within the hierarchical structure of the Church courts was permitted, the possibility of appeals only ending when a judgement had been twice affirmed by higher courts without alteration or else when the time allotted for appeals had run out. It was also possible for a disappointed party to claim *restitutio in integrum* if at any later time it was established that judgement had gone against him because of a perjured oath, false witnesses or a forged document.

The Influence of the Romano-canonical Procedure

The emergence of the sophisticated and systematic procedure of the Church courts coincided with a crisis in the administration of justice in secular tribunals caused by the Church's suppression of the ordeal. Not surprisingly, therefore, the model of the Romano-canonical procedure proved immensely influential in shaping the new procedures that perforce had to be developed in the lay courts. The process of assimilating the Romano-canonical procedure into the secular legal order began in the communes of Italy. Here, not only were the law schools pre-eminent in the development of the new learning of civil of canon law but there was also the freedom to devise laws and legal procedures suitable to a prosperous urban lifestyle. The Italian cities had obtained this freedom from the emperor in 1183 by the Peace of Constance, and their ability to govern their own legal destiny by means of their statutes was the result.

The Italian towns, however, recognized that the *solemnis ordo* of the canon law was too formal and protracted for their needs. In their statutes, therefore, they developed a less formal and more expeditious version of the order. This they did by increasing greatly the powers of the judge in the process. Whereas the canonical order upheld the control of the parties over the proceedings, both with regard to the pleadings and the admission of evidence, the Italian cities gave their judges power to admit oral statements of claim from plaintiffs, to be recorded in writing by the courts, and to restrict and control the progression of the pleadings. Moreover, it became open to the judge under their system to exclude sources of evidence which he deemed irrelevant or superfluous. Nor were the parties to be allowed to introduce new claims or defences, nor new positions or sources of evidence, once a particular item had been determined. The end result was a leaner but speedier version of the canonical procedure, bearing the signs of an increasingly inquisitorial mode of proceeding.

The Church was not slow to acknowledge the improvements made by the Italian communes. In 1306, Pope Clement V devised a speedier version of the Church's own procedure, strictly speaking as an exception to the official *ordo*, but one which was to be the basis of subsequent procedural development. From the opening word of the constitution in which it was promulgated, it has become known as the *Clementina Saepe*. The cases to which the new procedure was to apply within the Church courts were set out in the *Clementina Dispendiosam* of 1311. The new streamlined procedure incorporated the changes made by the Italian towns listed above, as well as restricting the availability of appeals. It was to prove an inspiration to the further development of procedure by Italian jurists, but was also to have immense influence in shaping the subsequent procedure of courts across continental Europe.

Developments in Germany

Despite resistance in some parts of Germany, notably in Saxony, there was a substantial welcome for the new learning in civil and canon law which was introduced from south of the Alps. The Romano-canonical procedure became well-known in Germany through the presence of the ecclesiastical courts. Moreover, from the time of Otto III, the German emperors had been clear in their claim to be the heirs in western Europe of the Roman Caesars and regarded Roman law as the proper law of their imperial courts with reference to both substantive law and procedure.

That knowledge of the Romano-canonical procedure had been assimilated rapidly in Germany is obvious from the juristic writings of the period. The early thirteenth-century *Ordo Judiciarius* sets out the new approach of the canonical procedure, and in 1405 there appeared Johannes Urbach's famous treatise on the subject, the *Processus Iudicii*, which incorporates a wealth of learning from the work of the Italian jurists. It was however with the introduction of the procedure itself in the

Reichskammergericht in 1495 that the decisive step was taken; thereafter, the history of civil procedure in Germany is a question of how the Romano-canonical approach was adapted to meet the particular circumstances and legal inheritance of the German lands. The fact that the *Reichskammergericht* was the final court of appeal from the courts of lesser territorial lords hastened the process by which those courts adopted like procedures.

The greatest resistance to the new procedure was encountered in Saxony, where the learning of the civil and canon law had made the slowest progress in previous centuries.[4] Although the new procedure was introduced there, it was subjected to modifications. These amendments addressed perceived shortcomings in the system and were themselves to be influential in shaping future developments in Germany and elsewhere. They were contained in the *Constitutiones Saxonicae* of 1572 and the 1622 Procedural Ordinance. Both sought to restrain further the protraction of the proceedings by the parties through increasing the powers of the judge. In particular, a new stage was introduced into the procedure. After the parties had settled the issues which were contested between them, they were now required to specify the sources of evidence upon which they would rely to establish the facts set out in their positions, or articles as they were more generally called by this time. Thereafter, they could not introduce new sources of evidence other than for good cause, for instance death of a previously nominated witness. When the evidence came to be taken at the next stage, once one issue was settled, it could not be questioned thereafter. This principle was known as contingent cumulation. Moreover, the judge had greater powers to decide which party should bear the burden of proof on each article or how the burden should be shared between the parties. The proceedings were becoming increasingly inquisitorial.

The Saxon legislation produced a response from the other territories of the German empire at the Diet of Regensberg in 1654. There, imperial legislation adopted the reforms made by the Saxons and further increased the powers of the judge, allowing him to investigate and interrogate concerning the allegations of fact in dispute between the parties before allotting the burden of proof to one. The inquisitorial element reached its apogee in Germany with the Prussian *Allgemeine Gerichtsordnung* of 1793-95. Under its provisions, the judge was placed in complete command of the whole process, being allowed to investigate matters which he thought pertinent even if they had not been raised by the parties in order to discover the entire truth concerning the matter in dispute. The parties were in a sense limited to commencing the litigation and complying with the judgement. While the process was in train, they had lost control of proceedings to the judge. The Prussian statute remained in force for forty years, when reforms, which were to culminate in the publication of the first German code of civil procedure in 1877, began, restoring to civil justice a greater element of party control.

The German civil process continued until 1877 to use the system of learned or legal proofs rather than the free evaluation of the evidence by the court to decide according to its intimate conviction whether proof had been made. Continued use was made of the suppletory and purgative oaths in this regard, which the court was bound to require of one or other party if full proof had not been adduced.

Developments in France

Knowledge of the Romano-canonical procedure was received into France as early as it was in Germany, and its progress in the secular courts, particularly those of the king, was considerably more rapid. The leading juristic works of the thirteenth century, such as the *Établissements de St. Louis* and Philippe de Beaumanoir's *Coutumes de Beauvaisis*, are fully cognisant of its existence. Its provisions are recounted with great learning in both de Breuil's *Stilus Curiae Parlamenti* and Boutillier's *Somme Rurale*, and it is dealt with also in the editions of the *Grand Coutumier de France*, which continued to be produced until 1539.

The procedure of a court was a matter for the lord under whose aegis it met. Thus, the procedure of the royal courts was a matter for the king alone. Not until the after the French Revolution were the people involved in legislating with regard to the procedure of the courts. Already in the thirteenth century, the kings of France moved to incorporate the Romano-canonical procedure into their chief court, the *Parlement* of Paris. Unlike the ecclesiastical courts, the *Parlement* was not a monocratic court with a single judge but a collegiate body with a bench of judges. This was to have considerable consequences for the particular shape the procedure acquired under its influence.

Once the parties had entered an appearance before the court and the issues between them identified, following the canonical model they would set out in articles the facts which they intended to prove in order to establish their cases. The kinds of proof were those used in the ecclesiastical tribunals

- documentary evidence, expert testimony, inspections, the testimony of witnesses and oaths. As in Germany, the learning of legal proofs was maintained and the court was required to request a party who had furnished half but not full proof to complete his proof by suppletory oath, and to allow a defendant with less than half proof against him to refute the claim by taking a purgative oath. Expert witnesses were appointed by the court and answered to it and not to the parties. At times, their function is difficult to demarcate from that of assessors who might assist the judges, although gradually it becomes clear that the experts are intended to address a particular item of evidence whereas the assessors are used to advise with regard to the conclusions to be drawn from the proofs made in reaching a judgement.

The most significant development made by the *Parlement* however was with regard to witness evidence. As with the Church courts, the principle of *testis unius, testis nullus* prevailed,[5] but the *Parlement* was a court in a settled location and it was a difficult matter for it to travel *en masse* to conduct inspections. Accordingly, it sent delegates to conduct such views and report back to it in writing on what they had seen. A similar device was utilized with witness evidence. Instead of requiring witnesses to travel to the court, the court sent auditors to them to hear their testimony, record it in writing and report back to the court. The parties would have identified the witnesses in the articles and the questions they were to be asked would have been drafted, but their answers and any supplementary questions would be taken by the auditors, always at least two in number, in the locality. It was on the written report of the auditors that the court would base its judgement. This institution therefore not only increased further the secrecy and written nature of the proceedings at the expense of orality and publicity, but also foreshadowed the role of the judge as investigator in an instruction phase in which the evidence is assembled and the function of the judge is to report to the court regarding the evidence upon the basis of which judgement must be made. This method, which became known as the inquest, was used also to determine questions of law regarding local customs, the auditors summoning first one and then a second *turba* from the locality to testify as to the content of a local custom. If both *turbae* agreed, the custom was proved.[6]

During the sixteenth century, the French kings began to issue the series of *ordonnances* relating to procedure in their courts. Together with the reduction of local customs to writing, which rendered the use of the *turbae* obsolete, the provisions of these enactments increased further the emphasis upon written evidence as a source of proof and therefore the written nature of the proceedings. Under the *Ordonnance* of Moulins of 1566, contracts with a value of more than 100 *livres* had to be proved by writing, and this policy was carried further by the Civil Procedure *Ordonnance* of 1667, which made writing essential for any legal transaction of that value which was capable of being so expressed, even real contracts.[7]

The *ordonnances* however had another important effect, for they were intended to govern the procedure of the king's courts throughout his realm. By this time, although France remained a land in which customary law varied from locality to locality, the administration of justice was firmly within royal control. The *ordonnances* therefore were among the first enactments amounting to national laws, and the civil procedure *ordonnance* of 1667 was in reality a code of civil procedure for the kingdom. It anticipated in large measure the provisions of the 1806 Civil Procedure Code. Indeed, the 1667 *ordonnance* was often referred to as the *Code Louis*. They left in place however, despite mounting criticism, the system of learned, legal proofs. The right of the court to reach its own assessment of the worth of the evidence according to its own intimate conviction had to wait for the 1806 Code, a code which was to prove the most influential source of civil procedure for civil law countries since the introduction of the Romano-canonical process upon which so much of its provisions were founded. The 1806 Code is in many respects the basis of subsequent civil procedure in the countries of the civil law.

3 The Modern Law of Civil Procedure

The French code of 1806 was introduced by Napoleon into the territories which he conquered. Already, in many of those lands, codifications of the law of civil procedure had been made. This was true of many parts of Italy as well as of Germany and Austria.[8] The demise of Napoleon left these lands free to return to their previous systems, but many went on to produce codes of civil procedure which were in large measure influenced by the French model.[9] Thus, the newly unified kingdom of Italy produced its first code of civil procedure in 1865, and Spain produced its own civil procedure code in 1881. The advent of the French code marked the final demise of the learning of the legal proofs. Judges were now freed to decide issues of proof according to their intimate conviction,[10] marking a return to the pre-Romano-canonical approach.

The following features are regularly present in modern laws of civil procedure.

Collegiality

The Germanic tradition of collegiate courts has prevailed over the Roman and Romano-canonical preference for the single judge. The most local courts however dealing with small claims are monocratic. This was true of the courts of the *juges de paix* in France after the Revolution and is now true of the *tribunaux d'instance* which have replaced them. It is also true of the German *Amtsgericht*, the court of the *pretore* in Italy and the *juzgados de menor cuantia* in Spain. Although single judges can and do hear some cases at the courts of major first instance, this is nevertheless regarded as the exception not the rule.

Conciliation

Before any civil cause is litigated, there must be some attempt to reconcile the parties. This principle emerged from the ideals of the French Revolution when it had been suggested that all civil disputes should be subject to reconciliation and judicial determinations abolished. Pre-procedural conciliation has proved both popular and effective in some civil law countries, often when it has appealed to prevailing cultural preferences. An example of this is Japan.[11] Until the 1990s, the most local Italian courts dealing with small claims were those of the *conciliatori*.

Pre-trial Instruction

Civil litigation is traditionally divided by commentators into three phases: the introductory phase, when the plaintiff's claim is checked to ensure that it is in order, by example ensuring that the court to which it has been submitted has territorial and subject-matter competence. Thereafter, the defendant is allowed to plead his defences and both parties to present the court with the sources of evidence upon which they intend to rely to prove their respective allegations.

The taking of this evidence takes place before the trial of the issues and is referred to as the instruction phase. Following the traditional French inquisitorial practice, this is done in many countries by appointing one of the judges to assemble the evidence in a dossier. If all of the evidence is documentary proof, this is not necessary, but where inspections are required or witness testimony has to be taken, this is normally done by an instructing magistrate. Although the parties are now allowed to be present with their counsel, the evidence is usually taken in private, not in open court. This is not so however in all jurisdictions; Germany and Spain for instance require that witness testimony at all stages in the process be attended by publicity. The sources of proof are virtually identical to those inherited from the Romano-canonical procedure. There is still a heavy distrust of witness testimony as opposed to written evidence. Witness evidence is reduced to writing at the instruction so that it can be included in the dossier. Expert evidence, if required, is proffered by an expert appointed by the court, although parties are allowed to have technical consultants comment upon such matters on their behalf. Questions are normally put to witnesses by the judge, although they can be suggested by the parties. There is no general right of cross-examination. At this stage, although the litigation is a party process, the issues being determined by the parties and the sources of evidence chosen by them, the style of this phase is markedly inquisitorial.

It is still open to the parties to challenge one another with decisory and suppletory oaths. The former can be returned as in earlier times and is decisive of the question in issue and the litigation. The latter no longer enjoys the importance it once had in the system of legal proofs. Now that the question of whether the evidence adduced has proved a particular fact is one for the freely formed intimate conviction of the court, the supplemental oath's only role is to impress the judge or judges with the swearer's belief in the correctness of the facts to which he swears.

Trial and Judgement

Where the evidence has been collected by an instruction judge, the trial amounts very often to no more than the confirmation of that evidence as presented in the dossier. The full court has no real opportunity to experience immediately the force or the weakness of a witness' evidence. While the question of proof was settled almost arithmetically under the Romano-canonical rules, this was not a problem; now that it is a matter of the court's intimate conviction, this lack of immediacy appears a defect, which can only be overcome if evidence is taken in open court as in Germany and Spain.

Where the evidence has been taken mediately and secretly, as in France and Italy, the full court is heavily dependant upon the report of the *rapporteur*, who basically guides the court towards a conclusion based on the evidence taken. Counsel for the parties are allowed to argue their clients' cases to the court on the basis of the evidence and the report. This is something of a new feature; prior to the French Revolution and the introduction of the principle of decision by the intimate conviction of the court, advocates were not allowed to address the court at the end of the process, only with regard to the evidence while it was being received. The trial phase has therefore returned to being public and oral, returning to its Germanic and Roman roots and away from the dominance of writing in the Romano-canonical process.

When the closing remarks of the advocates have been made, the judges retire to consider their verdict. This must eventually be given in writing, following the structure of the pleadings and setting out reasons for the conclusions drawn and the verdict reached. Again, this has only become necessary since the introduction of the principle of intimate conviction. Previously, while decisions had to be grounded on the proof, reasons did not have to be given. A brief experiment with giving reasons took place in Naples from 1774 but was unpopular. It is today however widespread within civilian jurisdictions.

In collegiate courts, only one judgement is given. Where there is a difference of opinion among the judges, the majority view prevails. Decisions of the courts are never binding precedents, as for them to make law would offend against the doctrine of the separation of powers. They are however guides as to the manner in which judicial decisions are tending from time to time. Their usefulness in this regard is therefore almost in inverse proportion to their age.

Appeals and Review

Appeals had been a feature of procedure by *cognitio* in later Roman law, although they were not possible under the *legis actio* and formulary procedures. The Church courts of the Middle Ages, being modelled upon the jurisdictions of the later empire, had no difficulty in allowing appeals within their hierarchical structure and did not even limit the number of appeals to two as had the emperor Justinian. Modern civilian systems of civil procedure have created a hierarchy of courts, generally allowing one appeal on the merits and thereafter a further review if there is a point of law in dispute. The only decisions which are not appealable are those relating to causes of a very small value.[12]

Appeal courts are collegiate bodies to which all the papers relating to the case at first instance are sent. The instruction phase is not repeated at this level, but new evidence can be taken if it was not available at first instance. Now that conclusions are based on intimate conviction, it is possible to argue that the lower court reached the wrong conclusion on the evidence.

Unappealable decisions, including those which have been the subject of an appeal which has been determined, can be reviewed on points of law. In most civil law countries, there is only one court of final review, charged with supervising the uniform application and interpretation of the law throughout the national territory. Often this court is called the Supreme Court of Cassation. Such a court, in its modern guise, was first introduced in France in 1790 and found in a place in the 1806 procedure. From there, the institution has spread to other countries. Its function is to review judgements which cannot be appealed and, if they are wrong in law, to quash them and remit the case to be retried to another court of equal standing with that, the judgement of which has been quashed. The retrial is usually therefore at appeal court level. The true court of cassation does not decide causes itself. It either upholds the determination of a lower court or quashes it. The *Bundesgerichtshof* in modern Germany therefore is not a true court of cassation even though it is a final court of appeal on points of law, for, if it does not uphold the decision of the court below, it disposes of the case itself rather than remitting it for a further hearing at appeal court level. In France, the court to which the case is remitted by Cassation is not bound by Cassation's view of the law. If the decision of that court is subjected to review however, the second determination of a fuller court of cassation is binding upon the third court to which it is then remitted for final judgement. In Italy and Spain, the determinations of their courts of cassation must be followed by the court to which a case is remitted, the one instance in which the decision of one court binds another.

The idea of review by cassation is drawn from the *supplicatio* of Roman law, by which the emperor could quash a decision for error of law and order a rehearing. This power was exercised by special tribunals set up for that purpose in some of the states of Italy in the later Middle Ages.[13] In France, judgements not susceptible to appeal could be the subject of special requests to the king to ask for a retrial if there had been an error of law. The court of cassation is the inheritor of these functions.

As well as appeal proper and review by cassation, it is also possible for a disappointed party to request revision of the decision if, at a future date, it becomes apparent that the decision in the case was achieved by perjury, faulty evidence or some such ground which vitiates the judgement. This is a continuation of the Roman and Romano-canonical concept that a party prejudiced by an incurably void judgement should be given *restitutio in integrum*. The Germanic notion that third parties can have an interest in the outcome of litigation to which they were not originally parties has influenced the development of so-called third-party opposition, whereby such persons can intervene if prejudiced by the effects of a judgement. This Germanic notion influenced developments under the 1667 procedural *ordonnance* in France and has retained its place in modern codes of civil procedure.

Execution and Summary Procedures

The function of the civil process, as stated at the start of this chapter, is primarily to declare what is due between the parties as a matter of law. The parties are then expected to comply with the law's demands. The court therefore has no immediate interest in enforcing compliance, and will only address that issue if the judgement creditor brings a claim on the judgement because the judgement debtor has not performed his obligation. Enforcement proceedings in civil law are generally therefore separate from initial adjudication of rights. The plaintiff has to bring a fresh suit, but all he needs to prove is the judgement. The court will not allow the defendant to contest its propriety, unless he claims he has already performed. The court will enforce the judgement if necessary by seizing his goods or some portion of them so as to coerce the defendant to satisfy the judgement debt, or else to sell them and hands the proceeds to the plaintiff in satisfaction of what he is owed. The ultimate root of this proceeding is the *distractio bonorum* of later Roman law.

Executory proceedings are also allowed however if the plaintiff in an action has documentary proof, particularly proof in a publicly authenticated document, which can be treated as equivalent to a judgement. The Italian jurists of the thirteenth and fourteenth century developed this doctrine in support of the negotiable instruments of merchants, and the concept found its way into the procedural law of Germany and France. There were already signs of documentary evidence being treated as conclusive proof and therefore entitling the holder to enforcement of the obligation rather than merely judgement in Germanic law, and it was soon settled in jurisdictions across Europe that the obligee could only challenge enforcement if he could show that the document was a forgery. Further, an unsuccessful claim of forgery would leave the obligee liable to a charge of criminal fraud, called *tricherie* by the French jurists. Such executory procedure found its place in the pre-Revolutionary *ordonnances* and in the 1654 Regensberg statute.

Executory proceedings in the sense of swift justice were also developed to protect a party's possession of property, particularly land, and to recover such property without need to establish ownership from one who had wrongly dispossessed another of it. These procedures were based upon the Roman possessory interdicts and came into the secular civil procedures via the canon law. They remain available to this day, as do procedures developed to prevent damage to one's property by the activities of others, rather than waiting to claim redress when the harm has been done, and remedies to prevent others undertaking work on their property which would harm one's enjoyment of one's own property. These are based on the Roman law *cautio damni infecti* and the *operis novi nuntiatio*.[14]

Finally, true summary procedures have always been available for small claims. Informal proceedings before local judges provide speedy remedies without the need often for legal representation. Sometimes the parties can ask the judge to decide according to his own idea of fairness rather than in accord with strict law. Such decisions cannot be appealed or reviewed.

Notes

[1] See chapter 12.

[2] A. Engelmann et al., *A History of Continental Civil Procedure* (Boston, 1927; reprinted New York, 1969), pp. 420 ff.

[3] Thus, for instance, the inquisition or jury was being employed to provide a verdict. It was widely used in common law England, had been employed by Charlemagne in his empire, and featured in France as the *turba*.

[4] This is clear from the fact that the thirteenth-century tracts from Saxony contain little of the new learning, unlike France where at a similar date there is abundant evidence of its influence; see Engelmann, *Civil Procedure*, pp. 647 ff.

[5] This began with Constantine and was based on the Mosaic law, Deuteronomy XIX. 15; see Engelmann, *Civil Procedure*, p. 41.

[6] Although it could of course be adjudged contrary to divine or natural law by the Church courts and therefore of no validity.

[7] Contracts which cumulatively amounted to 100 *livres* also required writing for their proof in order to prevent avoidance of the provision.

[8] For Germany, see above pp. 385 ff. An *Allgemeine Gerichtsordnung* had been introduced in Austria in 1781; see Engelmann, *Civil Procedure*, pp. 628 ff., and for Italy, p. 795 ff.

[9] For details regarding Italy, see Engelmann, *Civil Procedure*, pp. 795 ff.

[10] In Germany, it was not until 1877 that this change occurred, see above p. 387.

[11] See Dan F. Henderson, *Conciliation and Japanese Law: Tokugawa and Modern* (2 vols., 1964), and R. David and J.E.C. Brierly, *Major Legal Systems in the World Today* (2nd English Ed., London, 1978), pp. 501 ff.

[12] Justinian fixed a monetary limit, originally 500 *solidi*, but later changed to 10 pounds of gold or 720 *solidi*, below which the right to appeal was limited; see Justinian *Novellae*, XXIII, XXIV-XXXI, CIII; and also see A.H.M. Jones, *The Later Roman Empire 284-602* (Oxford, 1964), pp. 404; 483.

[13] For instance the *exgravatores* in Milan (1395), the *conservators* in Venice (1515) and the *syndacatores* in Genoa (1582); see Engelmann, *Civil Procedure*, p. 791. In 1870, there were separate courts of cassation in Turin, Florence, Naples, Palermo and Rome, and these were only unified in 1923; see C. Calisse, *A History of Italian Law*, (Boston 1928; reprinted New York, 1969), p. 210.

[14] See chapter 11.

16 Criminal Justice

1 Crimes and Criminal Procedure in Civil Law Countries

Criminal justice is concerned with the infliction of punishments upon persons by the law. Criminal law defines the circumstances in which such punishments are lawful; criminal procedure provides the method by which it is certified that a person merits such punishment. The conduct which justifies the imposition of punishment and the appropriate punishments for it are set out in the Criminal or Penal Code; the method by which a person suspected and accused of having committed such conduct is to be proved to have done so is governed by the Code of Criminal or Penal Procedure.

According to civil law doctrine, for a person's conduct to merit punishment, it is necessary that it should have harmed a legally protected right or interest. This may well be a right or interest inhering in another person which the law of that State protects. Thus, the State by its constitution is committed to protecting rights such as those to life, liberty, property and reputation. If someone deprives a citizen of their life, liberty, property or reputation, not only has that citizen been harmed, the State's stance of acting as the protector of the right in question has been compromised. Accordingly, a response from the State is required. The State responds by defining interference with such lawful rights as being conduct to which it will respond by punishing the perpetrator. The punishment will involve a lawful interference with the perpetrator's rights, perhaps by depriving him of his liberty for a stated period, by depriving him of property through fine or confiscation, or even depriving him of life itself. Such interference with his rights will be lawful because it is justified as a response to his conduct in not respecting the rights of others. To be lawful however the circumstances justifying the deprivation and the nature of the deprivation to be suffered must have been defined by law prior to the commission of the conduct to which the deprivation is the response.

The interference with a right or interest constitutes the harm to which the criminal law responds. Where the right or interest interfered with inhered in an individual, the harm will have been suffered by that person. Compensation may be due to that person from the wrongdoer, that is an obligation to compensate may have arisen under the provisions of the civil code. That is however a separate matter, although in many civil law countries, the person who has suffered the harm is permitted to be a party to the criminal proceedings brought by the State to punish the conduct, allowing him to obtain compensation in the course of those proceedings rather than forcing him to initiate and conduct a separate civil action.

The harm may not however necessarily be to the rights or interests of a person. The harm may be to a community interest. Thus, as the State and its legislative, executive and judicial organs exist to protect and promote the rights and interests of its subjects, subversion of the State or its institutions can amount to a harm to the collective interest. Thus, certain crimes are crimes against the State or the public good rather than wrongs damaging the interests of specific individuals. In both cases however there is an outcome to the conduct which is harmful to a lawful right or interest. Such conduct is criminal and the person who commits it is worthy of punishment. Such are the circumstances in which the State is entitled to punish an individual.

Whether an individual who has committed such conduct in a particular case merits punishment is a separate question. For the perpetrator of the conduct to merit punishment, it is necessary according to the established doctrine that he should have caused the outcome by his conduct and that his conduct was blameworthy in some way. Blame attaches to conduct which causes a harmful outcome when the perpetrator either intended to cause that outcome or was at fault in that his conduct was foreseen by him or should have been foreseen by him as risking that outcome. In some instances, conduct which produces an outcome may be punishable even where no such fault attaches to the perpetrator. Some analysts insist that there must also be an absence of lawful cause for the conduct; thus, a public executioner who, by his conduct, intentionally deprives a person of his life does not produce an outcome which is punishable. Nor would a private individual who intentionally killed another in lawful self-defence. Others would insist that this element of unlawfulness is implicit in the concept of the conduct having to be blameworthy.

To establish, where a legitimate interest has been harmed, that a particular person's conduct caused that harmful outcome and that the conduct was blameworthy and unlawful is the purpose of criminal procedure. It provides mechanisms by which it can be established that a person merits punishment according to the criminal law. In that the punishment involves interference with the rights and interests of the perpetrator, criminal procedure involves of necessity a conflict between the

State's duty to protect the rights and interests of all its subjects and its duty to respond when one of its subjects' rights have been harmed by another subject's conduct. Criminal procedure must balance the duty of the State to uphold the law and respond to the wrong done to the victim by ascertaining, identifying and punishing the perpetrator and its duty to uphold the law by protecting the rights of another of its subjects who is suspected or accused of having committed the crime. The history of criminal procedure is largely one of how the relative importance of those two goals has been perceived.

Criminal law and criminal procedure therefore is very informative concerning the State's view of its relationship with regard to its subjects. The same is very true of the punishments which the criminal law imposes for conduct which it defines as criminal. Some States, for example modern Spain, demand that punishment should be aimed at the rehabilitation of the offender, seeing punishment as part of the State's task in protecting and promoting the rights and interests of all its citizens. Italy, on the other hand, adopts a more retributive approach to punishment, regarding it as being the means of imposing a just suffering upon the delinquent. These goals are not in truth mutually exclusive; most states have elements of both approaches in their penal policy, although the retributive element obviously excludes rehabilitation in the case of capital punishment. Deterrence is another goal of some punishment systems and, as will be seen, this has been of considerable importance in the past, although it is less commonly encountered as a stated objective of punishment today in that it clearly relegates the interests of the convict to those of the State and the community.

2 Criminal Jurisdiction and the Classification of Crimes

The jurisdiction of courts in civil law countries refers to the body of law which a set of courts administers. The criminal courts are therefore those which apply the criminal law, and their proceedings in so doing are governed by the law of criminal procedure. The former will be contained in the Penal Code, the latter in the Code of Penal Procedure. As with the administration of civil justice, the administration of criminal law is markedly decentralized. Indeed, there is much overlap in many civil law countries between the courts exercising ordinary, that is civil jurisdiction and those applying the criminal law. Although the same courts may be employed for both purposes, it is important to remember that the two jurisdictions are nevertheless distinct and that different procedures govern depending upon which jurisdiction is being exercised. The personnel and nomenclature of the courts may vary depending upon whether they are acting civilly or criminally, and there are some courts of exclusively criminal jurisdiction.

As with the civil courts, the courts of criminal jurisdiction are distinguished according to their functional, territorial, and subject-matter competence. Functionally, some are competent to try offences at first instance, while others are competent to try appeals on the merits and finally there is a third instance court at national level to review points of law from decisions at appeal court level. Territorially, it is only the third instance court which is competent throughout the national territory, that being necessary to ensure that the criminal law is applied and interpreted evenly throughout the State territory. The second instance appeal courts are competent within their respective judicial districts only, these being roughly the main regions into which the State is divided, such as the *Länder* in Germany and the autonomous communities in Spain. Finally, the first instance courts, which are divided according to subject-matter competence, are to be found at community, provincial or regional level, depending upon the gravity of the offences involved.

An offence will be tried by the first instance court with subject-matter competence to deal with it. Generally, offences are classified in civil law countries into two or three categories. The main distinction is between serious and minor offences. Serious offences, sometimes called delicts in modern civil law, correspond in some measure to the mediaeval canonical concept of *mala in se*, that is wrongs which are wrongs in themselves. In the terminology of modern, natural rights theory, these are wrongs which offend against rights and interests which are inalienable and which the State exists to protect. Thus, deliberate killing, theft, deliberately causing injury and the like are *mala in se* and serious wrongs. Minor offences on the other hand, sometimes called contraventions or police offences, correspond to the canonists' *mala prohibita*, acts which are only wrong because they are prohibited by legal rules and to which otherwise no moral stigma would attach. Such conduct does not contravene a natural right. Into such category fall offences such as the breach of local by-laws and speeding or parking infringements. Minor offences are those which sometimes attract liability without fault, and for which there is no liability for attempts. They are dealt with in the most local of courts, the *tribunaux de police* in France, the *Amtsgericht* in Germany, the *pretura* in Italy and by the *juzgado del paz* in

Spain. The punishments for these offences are sometimes called by different names from similar ones for more serious offences, and custodial sentences where applicable are often served under less severe regimes of incarceration.[1]

Some legal systems further divide the more serious offences into two classes - serious and very serious, which in France are called delicts and crimes, *delits* and *crimes* respectively. Regardless of whether such a further categorization is made, there is usually a differentiation made between serious and more serious offences in that they are committed to different courts of first instance for trial. Serious crimes generally go to the provincial courts which also act as courts of first instance in civil matters, although they bear a different name when exercising criminal jurisdiction. Thus, the *tribunaux correctionelles* in France are situated alongside the civil *tribunaux de grande instance*. In Germany, Italy and Spain, however, no change of nomenclature occurs, the courts being the *Landgericht*, the *Tribunal* and the *juzgado de primer instancia e instrucción* respectively. The most serious crimes of all however are generally reserved to special courts which exercise a criminal jurisdiction only, which in some countries, such as France and Italy, are situated at appeal court centres, while in others, such as Spain, they are found at provincial level. These are the *cour d'assise* in France, the *corte d'assise* in Italy, the *Schwurgericht* in Germany and the *audiencia provincial* in Spain. A special court exists to hear appeals from the Italian assize court, but no appeals are allowed on the merits from the French and Spanish courts of this type. Spain also has a special criminal court with national territorial competence, the *audiencia nacional*, dealing with terrorist and drug offences, from which there is also no appeal on the merits.

The composition of these courts is however markedly different from the courts of civil jurisdiction, sometimes even when, as in Germany, they bear the same name. Although collegiality is regarded as the norm, the local courts dealing with minor offences are generally staffed by a single judge. However, the greatest difference lies in the use of lay or popular judges sitting alongside the professional, legally-trained judges, and forming with them what is called in civil law countries the jury. Even at the most local level, that of the *Amtsgericht*, in Germany, popular participation in the judicial process is to be found. In the *Landgericht* also there are lay judges, but generally the popular judges are present only in the assize courts. In France, nine jurors sit with the three professional judges and a majority of eight is required for a conviction with no appeal on the merits therefrom. In

Italy, six popular judges sit with two professional magistrates; a simple majority decides but there is an appeal to a similarly composed special appeal court, the *corte d'assise d'appello*. In 1995, Spain introduced trial by a jury of nine, acting with a single presiding judge.

As well as the categorization of offences into major and minor, and occasionally the further classification of major offences into major and serious, within the criminal codes offences are usually grouped into categories according to the type of interest harmed. Thus, one finds groupings such as offences to the person, to public order, to property, to the interests of the State, against religion, against public decency, and so on.

3 The Investigation and Prosecution of Crimes

One further feature of the modern criminal justice systems of civil law countries needs to be mentioned before turning to the historical development of criminal justice in those lands. That feature is the institution of the public prosecutor. Although in some civil law countries, of which Spain is an example, it is open to the victim of the wrong to initiate a private prosecution, in many, crimes can only be prosecuted by the State. A special magistrate is employed to perform this function, together with certain functions in the civil process. He is the public prosecutor, and an office of the public prosecutor is attached to virtually every court with criminal jurisdiction other than the most local. The public prosecutor is qualified in the same manner as judges, and in some countries, such as Italy, it is theoretically possible, though rare in practice, for a magistrate to move between judicial and prosecutory appointments.

When it is suspected that a crime has been committed, or if a crime comes to the attention of the authorities or is reported to them, it is their duty to inform the public prosecutor. The investigation of whether a crime has been committed and if so by whom is then a matter for him. In carrying out this investigation, the public prosecutor has at his disposal the services of the police forces of the country or locality, who when working for him are described as being the judicial police. The police work under his direction in the investigation of crime; they cannot proceed on their own initiative. He alone can authorize the detention of a suspect in custody, the search of premises and the confiscation of property as potential evidence.[2] All such decisions are therefore taken by a person with as much knowledge of the law's requirements as the judges who will hear and determine any case which results. He is obligated to investigate all crimes that come to his attention and cannot abandon an investigation or a prosecution without leave of the court. This emphasizes that he acts in fulfilment of the State's obligation to ensure that the rights and interests which it protects on behalf of its subjects are not contravened.

The public prosecutor is known by a variety of titles in the countries of the civil law. In France, he is the *procurateur de la République*; in Italy, the *pubblico ministero*; in Spain, the *ministerio fiscal*; in Germany, the *Staatsanwalt*. In Scotland, he is known as the Procurator Fiscal.

4 The Development of Criminal Law

Early legal systems do not distinguish between the civil and criminal nature of wrongs. When a wrong is committed, the victim and his family seek vengeance or retribution from the wrongdoer and his family. Such retribution can be viewed as punishment or compensation or both rolled into one, but in reality such viewpoints are anachronistic, interpreting ancient practices in the light of modern perspectives.

Retributive responses to wrongs suffered bring problems in their wake. If reprisal succeeds reprisal, the blood feud engendered will go far to disrupt the social order and undermine communal life. The group therefore has an interest in restoring peace between the parties, and the best way of achieving this is to prevent the blood feud ever occurring. The first evidence of the legal regulation of disputes in many societies, the Roman and the Germanic included, comes with the intervention of the community to regulate or prevent the blood feud by mediating between the factions and attempting to preserve the peace by effecting a compromise between them. This may involve communal supervision over the exaction of vengeance or retaliation, or, as with the Roman law of the Twelve Tables, the attempt to fix compensation tariffs which when paid buy off the vengeance of the victim's party. The penalty for maiming under the Twelve Tables was retaliation only if no composition could be agreed. Lesser injuries had their price fixed by that compilation.

A greater problem was perhaps faced when the wrongdoer was caught in the act by his victim. Thieves especially were prone to such apprehension, and the urge to inflict retribution would scarcely brook delay. Accordingly, the manifest thief of early Roman law and the hand-having thief of Germanic law were liable to summary execution at the hands of their discoverers, the law contenting itself to warn their executioners to summon neighbours to bear witness to the guilty capture lest the family of the slain thief raise the cry of wrongful killing. A posse of neighbours could also be called to pursue a thief who had escaped, and if caught on the same day or in the same neighbourhood with the stolen goods still in his possession, again there was no need for a recourse to legal process; execution followed capture. Such a wrongdoer was outside of the law's protection and paid the penalty for being an outlaw.

In Roman law, the penalty for manifest theft was tempered by the praetor. He reduced the penalty from death or enslavement to the payment of four times the value of the victim's interest in the thing stolen. This exemplary payment must in part have been an incentive to the victim to resort to the action rather than proceed to summary execution, but it was also regarded as a disincentive to thieves. Like many Roman penalties, which in effect gave exemplary damages to victims, it encouraged recourse to law and discouraged wrongdoing. A political purpose had been added to, or had possibly even displaced, the moral goal of just retribution in the Roman view of punishment. Deterrence was to continue to play a major role in the shaping of Roman legal penalties.

A similar course was followed in the development of Germanic law. There also the community stepped in to regulate the blood feud by the introduction and eventual enforcement of fixed compositions for wrongs suffered. This was achieved gradually. In the laws of the Lombard Edict, for example, the prosecution of the blood feud was forbidden where a killing, for instance, had been accidental, leaving only compensation for the victim's family as due.[3]

The concept also developed that a wrong which threatened the good order of the community was a wrong to the community as well as to the victim. Therefore, such wrongs required reparation to the community as well as to the victim and his family. The germ of the distinction between criminal and civil liability is present in this development. The Romans too had distinguished between wrongs to the community and wrongs to individuals, but had tended to base their distinction upon whether it was the interests of the individual or of the collectivity that had been harmed, rather than discerning the double element in certain wrongs. In that the ruler of a community in effect commanded that the law of the community be observed, to break that law by injuring another was a contempt of the ruler's command or his *ban*. This in itself was viewed as deserving of punishment.

This double element was accentuated by the advent of feudalism in the wake of the fall of the Carolingians. The tenants of a feudal lord lived under his protection, a situation described as being within his peace. A wrong to a tenant of a feudal lord was therefore not only an injury to the victim but also a breach of the lord's peace. Great lords, such as kings, might place whole communities or particular occasions or times of the year under their special peace, so that any wrong committed at that time was a breach of their peace and punishable by them.

Complaints that wrongs had been committed were still a matter for the victims, but the identification of a communal or more particularly a governmental interest in wrongdoing gave rise to questions as what was due to the ruler, local lord or king, if the victim made no complaint or if a deceased victim had no family to make complaint. If the ruler was aware that a wrong had been committed, or if another member of the community had denounced a wrongdoer, a penalty would appear to be due even if there was no victim or family to receive compensation. Some communities even required that compensation be paid to the State in such circumstances in lieu of there being a victim. It is in such situations that there emerge the first signs of the institution of the public prosecutor. The ruler may require an official, promover or promoter, to bring a complaint concerning a wrong where there is no surviving victim. It is likely that where there was a victim or a victim's family, they would be under a duty to bring a complaint if an injury had been done. The promover's role was to ensure that the community or its ruler did not miss out on its dues merely because there was no private complainant.

The role of the promover however was clearly to bring a complaint in the interests of the collectivity. This would mean that wrongdoers would not escape punishment merely because they had not left victims to complain. It also however inaugurated a means by which complaints could be made of actions which were deemed harmful to the interests of the community even if those actions did not harm specific individuals. Indeed, herein lay the possibility of using the criminal element thus identified in the process against wrongdoers not merely to defend the interests of the community when harmed by an individual, but also to defend the interests of the ruler in the interests of the community. Coupled with the deterrent perspective upon punishment, the criminal process was to become in the later Middle Ages a powerful weapon in the hands of rulers to maintain their rule not only in the interests of their subjects, but also against the threat of dissent or revolt among their subjects themselves. The criminal law was therefore a weapon in the struggle to retain political power, buttressing the interests of the governors at the expense of those of the governed.

This marked a profound change in the notion of crime as it had first been understood by Germanic law, and indicated also the considerable influence which Roman legal attitudes had exercised upon the late mediaeval approach to crime. In the Germanic legal order, a crime upset the balance of society and retribution was exacted in order to restore the balance. The anger which drove the urge to retaliate was but a symptom of the imbalance created by the crime; the retaliation or compensation the restoration of right order. The canonical view of sin had much in common with this. The Church saw sin as a breach of the right order of the creation, alienating man from God. Penance was the method by which the right relationship between God and man might be restored, and the function of the Church's criminal procedures was to restore that right relationship and rehabilitate the offender in the sight of God. Both systems therefore saw punishment as being a morally grounded matter, aimed at achieving justice within the social order.

The civilian jurists drew a different conclusion from the *libri terribiles*, books 47 and 48 of the Digest. To them, whereas civil wrongs disturbed the balance of justice within society, crimes were attacks upon the authority of the State and had therefore to be deterred, and if committed punished in a manner that would deter others. The Roman influence therefore favoured severe penalties, the cruelty of which was justified on the basis of the ends it served. Coupled with the absolutist notion of kingship, emphasizing that the power of the ruler was derived from God alone and not from the people, and that the ruler was accountable to God alone and in no way to his subjects, crimes were also seen as a threat to a divinely-given authority and therefore all the more deserving of exemplary punishment. The penal practices of the sixteenth and seventeenth centuries proceeded on this foundation. The fear of heresy experienced by the Church from the thirteenth century onwards led canon law also to use exemplary punishments ostensibly for their deterrent effects. The criminal jurisprudence of this age attracted the attention of some distinguished jurists, particularly in Italy. Two especially deserve mention - Julius Clarus (1525-1573) and Farinacius (1554-1613).

In many respects the high water mark of this approach to criminal law came with the French *ordonnances* relating to criminal procedure during the sixteenth and seventeenth centuries. Although they did not define crimes as such, the procedure they enshrined stressed the subjection of the individual to the State. This was particularly the case of the 1670 *ordonnance* which was in effect France's first code of criminal procedure. Even at the time of its drafting it attracted criticism for leading jurists, including Lamoignon, the eminent First President of the *Parlement* of Paris.[4] During the eighteenth century, social contract theories of society greatly increased the criticism of criminal laws which buttressed State authority at the expense of individual freedom.

In France, among those to the fore in this movement were Voltaire and Montesquieu. The latter in particular fêted British institutions as models of the protection of individual liberty and security. Not only were the British people protected by the parliamentary system of government enshrined in the settlement following their 'Glorious Revolution' in 1688-89, but they also enjoyed the right to trial by jury for serious crimes, that is a system which ensured that popular opinion rather than reasons of State determined what conduct should or should not be punishable.

Voltaire popularized in France the writings of an Italian, Cesare Bonesana, Marchese of Beccaria. Beccaria published his *Dei delitti e delle pene*, of crimes and punishments, in 1764. It is one of the most influential books on crime, criminal procedure and punishment ever written. Starting from the social contract, Beccaria holds that the only conduct worthy to be deemed criminal is that which harms the fundamental rights of others, subverts the State's ability to protect such rights or is detrimental to the common good. No other conduct should be deemed criminal. Acts which might be regarded as sinful or morally wrong in themselves should not be criminalized if they did not have the harmful effects stated to be necessary for criminal acts. One sees in this the modern approach of requiring a harm caused by interference with a legitimate right or interest.

For Beccaria, the State existed to serve the social arrangements of individuals and not the other way round. Accordingly, the State's duty was to protect its citizens from the consequences of crime by the education and civilization of its populace in order to prevent crimes being committed. If such measures failed and crimes were perpetrated, then the State was justified in punishing the perpetrator. However, before any punishment was imposed, it must be absolutely certain that a crime had been committed and that the person to be punished was the culprit. Beccaria had much to say about the kinds of proof required and how they should be obtained,[5] and he was also clear that the only legitimate function of punishments when imposed was to protect society from further crime by the delinquent and to deter others from following his example. Any punishment going beyond that would be unjust. Punishments should aim to make as clear an impression upon the minds of others of the determination of the State to prevent and punish crime as was consonant with not needlessly harming the interests of the individual punished. Punishment should not extend to confiscation of property which affected the convict's family in that they had done no wrong. Nor should the death penalty or even life imprisonment be readily employed.

Beccaria's ideas fuelled the impassioned campaigns for reform which anticipated the changes which were to follow the French Revolution. The Declaration of the Rights of Man defined the State as existing to protect the inalienable basic rights of the individual and proclaimed that only conduct prejudicial to society was to be a crime. No one was to be guilty of crimes by virtue only of their opinions, and punishments were to be limited to what was strictly necessary for the protection of the common good. Confiscations which affected the convict's family were prohibited. These principles were embodied in the practice of the first penal code to follow the Revolution in 1791, and also informed the Napoleonic code of 1810, which remains the basis of the criminal law of France.

In that Code, which has proved highly influential in other civil law countries including Germany, Austria and Italy, crimes are defined as offences against the fundamental goods which the State exists to protect - life, liberty, property and the like. Beyond that, they are classified in France into three broad groups - crimes, delicts and police offences - having regard to their gravity, the severity of the punishments imposed and also the court of first instance to which they are allocated. The three-fold classification in France goes back at least as far as Beaumanoir in the thirteenth century, although Boutillier, writing in the fourteenth century opted for a simple twofold division into serious crimes and contraventions. The Austrian criminal code of 1803 retained the twofold division, and this code was also in force in parts of northern Italy, Lombardy and Venetia, when those lands were returned to Austrian rule after Napoleon's defeat in 1815. The twofold division, which has its roots in the canonical distinction between *mala in se* and *mala prohibita*, was upheld by the jurist Garofalo in his major work on crime, *Criminologia*, in 1885, from where it has been retained in Italian criminal law to the present. On the other hand, Austria adopted the threefold division of French law when in 1852 it produced a new penal code, and Prussia favoured the tripartite approach also in its 1858 code, from where the threefold division still holds place in German law. The Spanish Penal Code of 1995, one of the most recent in the civil law world, divides crimes into *delitos* and *faltas*, subdividing *delitos* into *delitos graves* and *delitos menos graves*, all distinctions turning upon the penalty imposed, which of course reflects the turpitude of the act.

5 The Development of Criminal Procedure

Accusatorial Beginnings

In the feudal age, with no distinction being made between the civil and criminal aspects of a complaint of injury to one's interests, it was inevitable that the instigator of the steps necessary to have a wrongdoer punished should be his victim or the victim's family or liege lord. Once the issue between the parties had been settled and joined, proof would be required, which might take place by the accused purging his liability by oath with oath-helpers, who swore to his veracity, or battle might be waged between the parties or the ordeal undertaken to manifest who was telling the truth. Punishment of the accused would follow if he were convicted; punishment of the false accuser if there were an acquittal.

Proof would not be required if the wrongdoer were taken in the act or apprehended while the scent was still warm. Indeed, there would be no need for a formal accusation or trial in those circumstances; execution could follow immediately. A notorious wrongdoer could also be summoned to answer for his delinquency before the court, as could a person who was accused by popular opinion rather than by the complaint of his victim. In such cases, the prosecution appears to be instigated by the court rather than a private party, and a key element of the inquisitorial procedure falls into place, namely the court's proceeding against the defendant *ex officio*.

Inquisitorial Procedure and the Church

The inquisitorial procedure which was destined to replace the accusatorial procedure of the feudal courts was very much the creature of the canon law. It begins in the ninth century, with the readiness of certain ecclesiastical judges to proceed against a person by reason of that person's bad reputation, *infamia*, without formal complaint having been made. The *infamatus* would be summoned to appear before the ecclesiastical judge and required to clear his name by compurgation, that is by taking an oath and having a number of other persons swear to his good character as well. By the eleventh century, it is clear from the writings of Ivo of Chartres that a notorious evil liver could be condemned by a judge who had satisfied himself of the person's ill fame by his failure to clear himself. In such circumstances the judge would not only receive evidence of the accused's notoriety, but would in effect prosecute the accused himself on the basis of the evidence of his ill fame of which he had been made aware. Gratian in the twelfth century also described this process. From here it is a relatively small step to allowing the judge actively to set about obtaining proof against a person of notorious ill fame, so that the classic inquisitorial institution of the one officer acting as judge and accuser has come into being. This system was developed in a series of decretals during the papacy of Innocent III and was confirmed by the Fourth Lateran Council of 1215, the same body that deprived secular courts of their use of the ordeal by forbidding clergy to participate.

The inquisitorial procedure of the Church became its regular mode of proceeding during the thirteenth century. At first, the judge always proceeded *ex officio* from knowledge of which he was aware. Soon, however, it was permitted for private individuals to denounce the accused to the court, before leaving the court to gather evidence against the accused if it was satisfied that there was a *prima facie* case against him. However, if the proceedings began by denunciation, the accused was allowed to challenge the charge, for the denouncer had to establish that a wrong had been committed, and this the accused was allowed to contest.

The Adoption of the Inquisitorial Procedure in France

In France during the thirteenth and fourteenth centuries, the inquisitorial model furnished by the Church proved most attractive. It first emerged into the secular arena in the institution of the *aprise*. This began where, although the accused had not been caught in the act, there was nevertheless overwhelming witness testimony against him. In such circumstances, the court was allowed to proceed to sentence without offering the accused the opportunity to clear himself. He was treated as though he had been caught *in flagrante*.

The next stage in the adoption of the inquisitorial model in France came with the question of the circumstances in which the court was prepared to accept the testimony of several witnesses. Gradually, it was accepted that if one person denounced another to the court, the denouncer, although not a formal accuser, could nevertheless be allowed to promote judicial proceedings by being constituted the promover or promoter of the litigation. In effect, the denouncer was constituted civil party to a criminal inquiry. On receipt of such a denunciation, the court would set about examining witnesses to ascertain whether the charge was established. This was done by appointing auditors, as in civil proceedings, to interview the witnesses privately and reduce their testimony to writing in the form of depositions. When the depositions had been made, they would be communicated to the accused person, who was allowed to nominate witnesses to be examined on his behalf. The court would then have to reach a decision based on the evidence as adduced by the promover and the accused. This procedure, which continued as late as the sixteenth century, for it is described as a living institution by Pierre Ayrault,[6] was known as the ordinary procedure in criminal causes. It had however given precedence, rather like the Roman formulary system, to an alternative procedure which, though termed extraordinary, had in fact become the norm.

The Extraordinary Inquisitorial Procedure

The extraordinary procedure was also based upon canonical developments. During the thirteenth century, the Church was faced with outbreaks of heresy called the Waldensian and Albigensian heresies from the regions in which they occurred. To counter this phenomenon, the Church chose not to rely upon the ordinary ecclesiastical courts, which might prove sympathetic to the local people, but instead created a special tribunal to deal with the problem, staffed by militant members of the newly-created Dominican and Franciscan orders. This institution was the Holy Office of the Inquisition.[7] Unlike the usual inquisitorial courts of the Church, it proceeded *ex officio* without informing the accused persons that they had been denounced. Witness evidence was taken and the accused would then be arrested without being told the nature of the charge nor being shown the witnesses' depositions. The accused would then be interrogated concerning the evidence against him or her, the interrogation taking place frequently under torture. If proof of the charge was achieved, the judges who had investigated it and interrogated the accused as well as judging him, would pass ecclesiastical sentence and possibly hand the convict over to the secular powers for punishment. This was the Inquisition which came to be feared throughout western Christendom wherever it was allowed to operate.

By the end of the fourteenth century, this extraordinary procedure was being adopted by the royal courts in France. Its usages are described by Boutillier in his *Somme rurale*. Like its ecclesiastical forerunner, it is a secret process, the accused being kept in the dark about the charges against him, being denied sight of the evidence against him and of the opportunity of calling witnesses on his own behalf, being interrogated under oath and under torture. While it is clear that the torture was not to be life threatening or maiming, it is also clear that the secrecy involved was necessitated in order that the evidential results of the torture should be effective. It was in the context of this procedure in France that the role of the public prosecutor emerged, he being the official who would promote the public element in the case, the denouncer now being constituted if he wished as the civil party. By the 1500s, this system had brought to an end criminal trials by accusation; only civil actions or actions by civil parties within the criminal process survived from the older approach, with the civil party acting alongside the official prosecutor.

Francis I's *Ordonnance* of Villers-Cotteret in 1539 established this procedure as normative throughout his realm, with the State prosecutor from that time an essential party. Upon denunciation having been made, the suspect would be remanded in custody without notification of the charge, usually in vile surroundings. An investigating magistrate would then supervise the gathering of witness and other evidence concerning the charge, not it must be stressed solely evidence against the accused, and this would be communicated to the prosecutor. If and when the magistrate was satisfied that a charge should be brought, the accused was confronted by the witnesses and their evidence, before being interrogated on oath and then under torture. A confession under torture had to be ratified at a later date without pressure being put on the party.[8] Finally, all of the evidence, including that obtained under torture which had been later confirmed, was presented to the trial court, that being composed of a bench of judges, one of whom would act as a reporter of the evidence obtained, setting out the conclusions which appeared to flow therefrom. The court then reached its verdict. If it determined that the conduct in question amounted in its opinion to a crime, the accused was condemned. It is important to realize that no definitions of criminal conduct existed which were binding on the court; the judges had a free hand to determine that any conduct was offensive to the public good and deserving of criminal sanction. Thereafter, the public prosecutor requested what was in his view an appropriate penalty. Again, there were no defined penalties; the prosecutor could ask for the penalty of his choice and if the court agreed with his estimation, that penalty would be imposed. The individual acted at his peril where the criminal law was concerned.[9]

In France, the procedure enshrined in the 1539 *ordonnance* of Villers-Cotteret was the foundation in all but detail of Louis XIV's *Ordonnance* on Criminal Procedure of 1670, despite First President Lamoignon's protests concerning its injustices. Inquisitorial procedures had also by that time infiltrated into the legal systems of Spain and Italy, in the latter of which the use of torture had come to be developed into a virtual art. In Spain, the *pesquisa* as the inquisitorial procedure was known can be found in Book IV of the *Fuero Juzgo* as well as in the provisions of parts III and VII of the mid-thirteenth century *Siete Partidas*. The institution of the public prosecutor had also been developed in Spain. The Spanish Inquisition was employing a *promotor fiscal* from its inception before the end of the fifteenth century, and the *Leyes de recopilación* of Philip II record the presence of a secular *procurador fiscal* in 1566. An office of *procuratore fiscale* was to be found in some Italian states as early as the fifteenth century.

The institution of the public prosecutor never became a regular feature of the German legal scene during the mediaeval and early modern period, although the inquisitorial method of proceeding did become the norm. While accounts of criminal justice in the German states continue to accord a place to procedure following accusation, proceedings *ex officio* or following denunciation were more usual. In either case, whether the process followed accusation or was instigated by the court, by the fifteenth century it was a judicial investigation which followed to ascertain that a wrong had been done and to identify and collect proof against the suspect. The full panoply of learning regarding legal proof was introduced as the old *Schöffen* courts came to be staffed instead by jurists trained in Roman and canon law at the universities. The fact that many German states were governed by ecclesiastical rulers also gave an impetus to the adoption of canonical learning, procedure being categorized as a canonical subject and being taught in the German universities as a separate subject from the sixteenth century under the aegis of the professors of canon law.

The study of criminal procedure in the German universities presupposes the existence of a text, and until the sixteenth century the texts had been those of the Justinianic compilation together with the writings of the Italian jurists. The German courts however appear to have been afflicted more than most with problems caused by the complexity attaching to the law of proof.

It was to overcome these problems that towards the end of the fifteenth century attempts began to be made to produce manuals of procedure of a primarily practical nature. It was in 1507 that the most famous of these handbooks was published, that of Johann, Freiherr of Schwarzenberg, Hofmeister to the bishop of Bamberg, and it was the bishop who issued the *Bambergische Halsgerichtsordnung*. When Schwarzenberg later moved to the service of the Elector of Brandenberg, another version of his work appeared for use in those territories, the *Brandenberger Halsgerichtsordnung*.

There was however a considerable body of opinion which favoured the promulgation of a common criminal procedure for the whole of the German empire. This project was frequently discussed in the Diets of the first quarter of the sixteenth century, but it was not until 1532 that the emperor Charles V produced such a code, the *Constitutio Criminalis Carolina*. The *Carolina*, as it is generally known, was unfortunately only to operate as a supplement to existing procedural regimes in the imperial lands, but nevertheless it exercised a profound influence. It was of particular importance in that it not only addressed the procedure to be used in criminal cases but also contained provisions which defined the conduct which was to be treated as criminal. It is therefore a code of both criminal procedure and criminal law.

Its supplementary nature meant that it could not be a definitive penal code in the modern fashion. Indeed, the territorial rulers of Germany felt free, as did their absolutist counterparts in other countries in Europe, to introduce new crimes of their own authority, and their courts felt free to extend the provisions of the *Carolina* by analogy. Many criminal courts were extensions of the ruler's council. This was so in many lands; in France for example the *Tournelle* was a special sitting of the Grand Chamber. Rulers therefore controlled the workings of these courts as of right, and felt free to interfere in their work as they wished, increasing or remitting penalties imposed, and even imposing convictions without trial, as with the feared *lettres de cachet* in France. In the interests of the State, the courts had powers to impose what were called extraordinary punishments when full proof of an accused person's guilt had not been established. Although such punishments were less severe than those permitted for a fully proven crime, they were nevertheless often harsh.[10]

The Netherlands had also experienced the incursion of the inquisitorial procedure, which had all but replaced the old accusatorial methods. When the Spanish Duke of Alba introduced a particularly harsh regime of penal procedure in 1570, it did not in reality differ that much from the native model. The jurist Jodocus Damhouder of Bruges produced a famous analysis of the criminal process in the Low Countries in the middle years of the sixteenth century which was influential in shaping the penal provisions of the Prussian *Landrecht* of 1620.[11] Another very important juristic work on criminal justice came out of Saxony in 1635; this work by Carpzov was a successful blend of the provisions of the *Carolina* with Roman, the native Saxon and canon law. In all of these systems, however, the State interest in the repression of crime dominated, crime being conduct which threatened the established government of the State. All of these systems also shared the learning of legal proofs.

The Doctrine of Legal Proofs

The learning of legal proofs operated in criminal as in civil procedure, but with the important difference that as the criminal process was not a party contest, there was no room for determination according to the oaths of the parties. Nor could the accused person be permitted a purgation oath in a criminal cause as there was no longer, following the demise of the ordeal, a method of testing it, and the fear of subsequent prosecution for perjury lost its terror when the alternative was sentence of death. It was to make up the deficit caused by the unavailability of the oath that torture was employed.

Torture was of two kinds - preparatory and preliminary. Preliminary torture was the torture of convicted person in order to obtain the names of accomplices or co-conspirators. It was not limited in its ferocity and could lead to the death or permanent injury of the subject. Preparatory torture on the other hand was of an accused person against whom there was insufficient evidence to convict. The torture in this case was aimed at obtaining a confession which might, if it tallied with the depositions of credible witnesses, make up the evidential shortfall. It was not just an admission of guilt that was sought. It was confirmation of other evidence. Confessions obtained under torture had to be ratified on a later day without such pressure being applied, otherwise the proof obtained was not usable.

The kinds of evidence or proofs which were usable in criminal trials were basically those employed in civil causes,[12] with the omission of oaths and the inclusion of notoriety, popular suspicion and presumptions of various kinds. The most important kinds of proof were confessions by the accused, the testimony of witnesses, documentary evidence and presumptions. Of these, witness testimony was the most important.

To be counted as proof, the testimony had to be that of an eye-witness, who was creditable according to age, status, sex and lack of relationship with the accused, was certain of what they had seen and had been consistent in their evidence on the three occasions they were called upon to give it - when initially giving the information, when confirming the deposition to the investigating judge, and when confronted with the accused. When the testimony of two such witnesses agreed in all essentials, this was full proof. Expert testimony could therefore never be full proof as it was not eye-witness testimony. One witness was only half proof. A written document alone could not be full proof, not could the existence of a proximate presumption, as where the accused had been seen by two witnesses carrying the murder weapon from the scene of the crime. Proximate presumptions alone were not even half proof; they had to be accompanied by a remote presumption, such as the accused changing his story or looking suspicious when asked about the crime or becoming nervous when questioned about it.

Where there was some evidence against the accused but not full proof, torture was used in order to try to make up the difference. It was only usable in cases of capital crimes, but these were numerous. Accused persons might prefer the risk of dying under torture to confessing, for even though execution might be less painful, conviction would result in confiscation of property which could impoverish their surviving family. Preparatory torture was not meant to kill or maim, as it should stop short of being as bad as punishment itself. The techniques developed to cause the maximum pain within these limits were sometimes as ingenious as they were cruel.

If full proof was not obtained, there could be no conviction, but equally that did not prevent an extraordinary punishment being imposed on the basis of suspicion, and there would be no acquittal for lack of full proof. The stigma of an unproven charge could haunt a suspect for the remainder of his life. A person was presumed innocent until suspected rather than until proved guilty.

The Movement for Reform

The extraordinary inquisitorial procedures of the nation states of early modern Europe were a harsher version of the process developed by the mediaeval catholic Church. The Reformation saw religious as well as secular control of their lands pass to the princes and rulers of western Europe under the principle *cuius regio, eius religio*, which did much to buttress absolute power. This absolute power and the inquisitorial methods which protected it were both markedly more extreme than either the powers or the processes of later imperial Rome or the Roman Church.

The legists and canonists of the later Middle Ages had centred their study of criminal law and procedure upon the forty-seventh and forty-eighth books of the Digest and the ninth book of the Code of Justinian. In their writings, which influenced greatly the direction of the canon law of crime, they had stressed the importance of fault to criminal liability. The *Bambergensis* and *Carolina* both incorporated much of this Italian juristic learning, the latter especially defining in articles 104-180 the nature of criminal acts. This marked the opportunity for a new beginning in the study of penal law and practice which was taken up in the German universities. Likewise, the 1670 *Ordonnance* on criminal procedure in France presented jurists and critics with a text upon which to focus their legal science.

The dissatisfaction with absolute rule which resulted in the doctrines of natural law and natural rights led also to a powerful critique of criminal procedure. Already at the end of the sixteenth century in the Netherlands, imprisonment in penitentiaries began to be used as an alternative to mutilation and corporal punishment. In the eighteenth century, the confiscation of a convict's property to the detriment of his family was abolished in those lands. The *Carolina* had led the way with its limiting definitions of crimes, and during the eighteenth century codes of criminal law and procedure appeared, which gave notice of the conduct for which punishment was to be imposed, allowing people to guide their conduct according to the legislation. Such a code appeared in Bavaria in 1751, in Austria under Maria Theresia in 1769 - the so-called *Theresiana* - and again under Joseph II in 1787. Between these two codes, the judicial use of torture was abolished in Austria in 1776. During the same period, the criminal laws of Prussia were being systematized and rationalized under Frederick the Great.

One of the most significant reforms however occurred in Italy, where the influence of Beccaria's great work on crimes and punishments was to the fore. In 1786, Grand Duke Peter Leopold of Tuscany promulgated his code which abolished the death penalty and introduced imprisonment in penitentiaries as a rehabilitative punishment. The Digest view of prisons as places of confinement for those awaiting trial and not places of punishment was departed from significantly. The Leopold code also divided crimes into two distinct classes: those which were harmful to public or private interests were delicts; those which merely infringed regulations aimed at social well-being were transgressions. Different tribunals dealt with each category, and different kinds of penalty were employed. Italy also saw the introduction of Joseph II's Austrian code into Lombardy.

On virtually the eve of the Revolution, torture began to be abolished in France under Louis XVI, with legislation in both 1780 and 1788. By then, there was widespread demand for a criminal procedure which was open as opposed to secret, oral as opposed to written, gave free opportunity to the accused to defend himself and allowed for a full discussion and argument of the case before the trial court where the accused's fate should ideally be determined not by a State official but, following the English practice, by a jury of ordinary citizens. This inevitably meant that the jury should decide upon the accused's guilt or innocence according to its intimate conviction and not upon the basis of calculating the weight of evidence according to the technical learning of legal proofs. Reasons should be given for all judgements.

These demands were not however to be met in France until after the Revolution. The solutions achieved in France were to be the theme of much subsequent reform and development in criminal law and procedure throughout the civil law countries during the ensuing two centuries.

6 The French Revolution and After

Several attempts were made to reform the method of criminal procedure in France during the Revolutionary period, but, although the first reformed system was introduced in 1791, it was not until the Napoleonic Code of Penal Procedure was promulgated in 1810 that the foundations of the modern system of criminal justice in France could be said to have been laid. Even that system required fine tuning in the 1830s.

The model for criminal procedure adopted in the wake of the Revolution was intended to uphold the fundamental rights of the individual against the State even when the individual was suspected or even accused of having interfered with the security of the State or to have failed to respect the fundamental rights of others. The methods to be employed were remarkable for they not only hark back to ancient Rome and the institutions of the *Quaestiones Perpetuae* and draw on the inquisitorial procedures developed by the canonists, but they also seek to amalgamate that learning with the achievements of the English common law through incorporation of the jury into the proceedings. The English imput ensured that the trial should be open to the public, that it should be based upon an oral presentation of the evidence against the accused, that the accused should be given every opportunity to present his defence - or more importantly to have it presented upon his behalf by competent counsel, and that the final decision as to his guilt or innocence should lie with ordinary citizens instead of, or at last as well as, legally qualified judges. No one was to be tried for conduct which had not been clearly defined as criminal prior to the commission of the acts concerned.

Having established these basic principles, the institutions of the public prosecutor and the pre-trial investigation by a magistrate were retained. Distinct phases in the criminal process were recognized. Report of a crime necessitated action by the public authorities through the public prosecutor. Some civil law countries, for instance Italy, do not permit of private prosecution; others, for example Spain, do. The common factor in all is that most prosecutions are initiated by the State prosecutor's office, which is obligated to investigate all crimes reported to it.

Once it is established that a crime has been committed and a suspect is identified, in the case of serious crimes an investigating magistrate is appointed to identify sources of evidence and to gather that evidence for presentation at the trial. The investigating magistrate was at certain times one of those who would try the case, as in civil causes, but this practice has been discontinued in most countries.[13] Instead, the investigating magistrate submits a report to the trial court, while the public prosecutor presents the case for the prosecution. Where there is a victim, he can still be constituted the civil party and obtain civil damages for the wrong suffered as part of the criminal proceedings.

The trial however is now open and the evidence is presented to a bench of professional judges and lay jurors who are not previously acquainted with the case. They must decide the issue upon the basis of what is disclosed openly at trial, having heard at the close arguments in favour of each of the parties delivered by their advocates. Originally, in 1810, the French courts adopted the English system of having the judge sum up the case to the jury, but not orally. Instead, he submitted a list of questions to the jury, each one of which required a simple answer and as a result of which the jury was led to a conclusion on the main issue of the accused's guilt. This however was changed in 1831 to the system which prevails in several civil law countries to this day, of the professional judges retiring with the jury to consider the verdict and producing a verdict which is grounded upon the evidence received in the form of a reasoned judgement. In most countries it is not possible for a verdict of guilty to be returned without a majority or at least half of the lay jurors being in favour. Thus today in France where the jury is composed of three professional judges and nine lay jurors, eight must be in favour to produce a guilty verdict. In Italy, where two professional judges sit with eight popular judges, six must be in favour. Both professional and lay judges have an equal voice in questions of law and fact. They decide on the basis of their intimate conviction.

The distinction between the investigative or instruction phase and the trial is not followed in all systems. In Germany and Spain, the evidence is taken in open court, with full opportunity for the defence to contradict at that point. In Italy, the reforms of 1989 were intended to produce a much more accusatorial process, with as little evidence as possible being taken before the oral trial phase, only sources of evidence being identified by the public prosecutor. Spain has also since 1995 introduced a jury of nine to give the verdict in serious criminal trials.

The pattern of criminal procedure developed in France from the promulgation of the 1810 Code was adopted in many other countries. Like Napoleon's other codifications, the law of penal procedure was introduced into the lands which he conquered and influenced developments in those places long after his defeat. In Naples, where an early experiment in giving reasoned decisions took place in the eighteenth century, a code of penal procedure providing for orality and publicity was introduced in 1819, the death penalty being retained but confiscation and branding being abolished. In northern Italy, the Duchy of Parma followed the Neapolitan example in 1820. The public prosecutor made his appearance in the territories of Germany during the nineteenth century, where the individual states produced their own codes of penal procedure prior to the introduction of a code for the new *Reich* in 1877. The Austrian code of 1873 was also inspired by the French reforms, as were the codes promulgated for Belgium in 1867 and the Netherlands in 1881. Spain issued a code of criminal procedure in 1882 and the newly-unified kingdom of Italy issued its first code of penal procedure in 1865.

The history of Italy in this aspect of its legal development is in some ways representative of the experience of the civil law countries since the French Revolution. The 1865 code was replaced by a markedly liberal code in 1913, only for that to be abandoned in 1931 under fascism for a code which it has been argued emphasized afresh the protection of State interests as against the individual. That code has now been replaced since 1989 with a code which is intended to safeguard individual freedom by adopting a strongly accusatorial approach. The swing from liberalism to fascism and back to constitutional democracy has been experienced in several civil law countries during the twentieth century, Germany and Spain being further obvious examples in Europe.

Despite these dramatic political tergivizations, the changes wrought by the French Revolution in the criminal processes of the civil law countries have nevertheless been immense. Initially intended to replace the inquisitorial methods associated with absolute rule and individual subjection to the State with the accusatorial forms connected in the continental mind with the traditional freedoms of the British people, the end-result has been the production of hybrid systems, in most places partly inquisitorial and partly adversarial, drawing on both the civilian and the common law traditions. The manner in which the jury has been assimilated is particularly indicative of this, being a blend of the English institution with the lay jurors of the *Quaestiones Perpetuae* of ancient Rome and the lay assessors of earlier native systems. There is currently no normative model for a criminal process in civil law countries, other than agreement that crimes must be defined, that orality, openness, equality between defence and prosecution, and full discussion of the evidence must operate at the trial phase, and that the process be divided into distinct notificatory, investigative and trial phases. In all countries however lesser crimes are tried by summary processes, many of which retain markedly inquisitorial characteristics, including often some confusion of the roles of prosecutor and judge.[14]

The law of penal procedure in civil law countries is, in truth, still being worked out, but that working out is nevertheless according to the principles which motivated the reforms begun at the time of the French Revolution. It is a particularly fascinating development as it involves a conscious attempt to integrate not only Roman and canonical practices, but also institutions drawn from the heritage of the common law. It marks therefore a new stage in the development of law in the western world, and one the outcome of which may be of great significance to the future of western legal culture generally.

Notes

[1] See T.G. Watkin, *The Italian Legal Tradition* (London, 1997), pp. 127; 142 ff.

[2] Italy has now departed from this approach, and the power to order such searches and confiscations belongs, under the 1989 Code of Criminal Procedure, to the *giudice per le indagini preliminari*.

[3] As in the Edict of Rothari, 74, to be found in *Monumenta Germaniae Historica* (1835-1891); see C. Calisse, *A History of Italian Law* (Boston, 1928; reprinted New York, 1969), p. 275.

[4] The First President was the title of the Chief Justice.

[5] See pp. 417 ff.

[6] (1536-1601). Author of *L'ordre, formalité et instruction judiciaire* (Lyons, 1642); see A. Esmein, *A History of Continental Criminal Procedure* (Boston, 1913; reprinted New York 1968), pp. 169 ff.

[7] This was a special body created to tackle heresy, and was not the normal inquisitorial tribunal of the Church.

[8] If the accused recanted, he would go back to being tortured. The process could therefore become very lengthy.

[9] This is somewhat reminiscent of H.L.A. Hart's analogy of arbitrary judgement in sport rendering a game one of scorer's discretion; see H.L.A. Hart, *The Concept of Law* (Oxford, 1961), pp. 139 ff.

[10] In Helmstadt in 1721, a man, who had pleaded self defence to a charge of homicide and who had not been convicted for lack of proof, was extraordinarily punished by being sentenced to detention for life at moderate labour in order to safeguard the community; see C.L. Von Bar et al., *A History of Continental Criminal Law* (Boston, 1916; reprinted New York, 1968), p. 241.

[11] It is however suspected that this work was plagiarized, being said to be really that of Philips Wielant of Ghent (1439-1519); see C.L. Von Bar et al., *Continental Criminal Law*, p. 306, n. 1.

[12] See chapter 15 above, pp. 382 ff., 387 ff.

[13] In Italy, this practice was discontinued following an adverse ruling by the Constitutional Court; see T.G. Watkin, *The Italian Legal Tradition*, p. 133.

[14] As, for instance, in France and Italy. For the *ordonnance pénale* in France, see J. Pradel, 'France' in Christine Van Den Wyngaert (Ed.), *Criminal Procedure Systems in the European Community* (London, 1993), pp. 105 ff., at 130 ff. For trials before the *pretore* and other summary procedures in Italy, see T.G. Watkin, *The Italian Legal Tradition*, pp. 140 ff.

17 Administrative Justice

1 The Origins of Administrative Law

Few would dispute that the greatest contribution which France has made to civil law in the modern world was the publication in 1804 of the *Code civil*. Many however would wish to add a rider to the effect that France has also made another signal, arguably more original, contribution to modern civilian jurisprudence through the development of its corpus of administrative law, the *droit administratif*.[1] The methods and organs of administrative justice that have been developed in France over the last two centuries have proved enormously influential in other civil law countries, to the extent that the presence of a separate administrative jurisdiction alongside the ordinary courts of civil and criminal justice can now credibly be described as a feature of modern civilian systems generally. Initial reluctance to follow the French in this regard has gradually been overcome in countries such as Italy and Belgium where administrative tribunals on the French model have been established to provide administrative justice in preference to allowing the courts of ordinary jurisdiction to deal with administrative matters.

The origins of administrative justice in this sense lie peculiarly in the legal history of France prior to the Revolution. The King, acting through his ministers and his Council, the *Conseil du Roi*, had been able to intervene in disputes before the courts of justice, for instance by the issue of *lettres de cachet*. Moreover, the courts themselves had acquired a distinct tendency to intervene in executive government by questioning the actions of the executive before the *Parlements*. Both of these features of pre-Revolutionary government in France contributed to the enthusiasm with which the French embraced the doctrine of the separation of powers so eloquently advocated by Montesquieu in his *L'Esprit des lois*.[2] According to this doctrine, the executive arm of government, including the administration, should be separate and free from the influence of the judicial arm, which likewise should be immune from interference by the executive and the administration. This viewpoint was eagerly received into the Constitution of the American Republic following the Revolution there and the casting off of British rule, and was also to be a key theme in the constitutional arrangements developed in France after 1789. In the immediate aftermath of the Revolution, the judges of the ordinary courts were banned from citing members of the administration to appear before them on account of any action referable to their official functions. Instead, the organs of the administration were themselves to be responsible for adjudicating administrative disputes.[3] This however smacked of allowing the administration to be a judge in its own cause, contrary to the basic tenet of natural justice, *nemo iudex in causa sua*. Accordingly, in 1799 a special administrative body was set up to deal with administrative problems, the Council of State, *Conseil d'État*, with administrative councils of lesser jurisdiction in each prefecture.

2 The Organs of Administrative Justice

The *Conseil d'État* set up by Napoleon in 1799 was primarily intended to advise the three consuls, as joint heads of State, on the drafting and implementation of laws and administrative regulations. Eventually, it would advise the emperor as sole head of State in this regard. To some extent therefore it appears to be a successor to the *Conseil du Roi* of the French monarchy, but the resemblance is superficial. The *Conseil d'État* was at first purely an advisory body with which the ordinary justiciary could not interfere as a result of the laws passed in 1790 and affirmed in 1795.[4]

The *Conseil d'État* was divided into sections, each of which had a particular sphere of interest reflecting different ministerial responsibilities. In 1806, it was recognized that special provision needed to be made for instances where a citizen, having complained to a minister concerning one of his decisions, wished to take the matter further and appeal to the Head of State. When the Head of State received such an appeal, he sought the advice of the *Conseil d'État*, and from 1806 a special section of the *Conseil d'État* called the *Commission du Contentieux* advised the Head of State as to how he should resolve such final appeals. From 1849, the section was indeed known as the *Section du Contentieux*. Its function was to advise the emperor and did not decide matters of its own authority, although in practice the emperor always followed the advice given. It was not until the early years of the Third Republic (1870-1940) that the *Conseil d'État* acquired the power to decide such final appeals upon its own authority in the name of the French people, *au nom du peuple Français* as each judgement or *arrêt* states at its commencement. This confirmed the status of the *Conseil d'État* as an administrative court. In that it could only hear and determine appeals from complaints to ministers, it was a court of final instance, but in that it was the only tribunal which determined such causes it was also the court of first instance.

It had in the intervening decades of the nineteenth century acquired certain other features of a markedly adjudicatory nature. Most of these appeared in 1831. In that year, it became possible for parties to be legally represented before the *Conseil d'État*, and the advice of the *Conseil* was handed down in the form of a written and reasoned judgement. Like all modern civilian judgements, it was *motivée*. There also appeared in this year an extra member of the cast of characters before the court, namely the *Commissaire du Gouvernement*, who was there initially to represent the views of the government, but became the representative of the public interest, occupying a position not unlike that of the *ministère publique* in civil and criminal cases before the ordinary courts. Thus the *Conseil d'État*'s *Section du Contentieux* functioned from the nineteenth century until the Second World War. During the Fourth Republic (1946-1958), it was transformed into being primarily an appellate body of final instance, hearing appeals from first instance decisions taken at local level by newly-created *tribunaux administratifs*. These now enjoyed competence at first instance in administrative matters, the workload having proved far too heavy for the *Conseil d'État* alone to manage. Even a direct appellate competence has proved too burdensome for the *Conseil d'État* and in 1987 a further appellate tier of administrative tribunals was established in the form of the *cours administratives d'appel*, to be found in five major cities,[5] leaving the *Conseil d'État* with a final appellate role not dissimilar to that of the *Cour de Cassation* in the hierarchy of ordinary courts. Again, the typical civilian pattern of competence within a jurisdiction would appear to have been gradually replicated.

Despite the familiar structure which the French administrative courts now manifest, they are still markedly different in terms of their composition. The judges who sit in the administrative courts are not members of the career magistracy, but are instead administrative professionals drawn from the civil service. For this reason, they are never referred to as *magistrats*, but only as *juges*. Although they may possess legal qualifications, their essential qualification is that they are trained civil servants, in the main graduates of the *École National d'Administration*, an elite civil service college. They are experienced administrators therefore who understand the problems of practical government from the inside. Their careers within the *Conseil d'État* are not confined to the judicial section, but usually range between the various advisory sections and the *Section du Contentieux*, often with spells working for government ministers or in the diplomatic service. Despite the clear demarcation between these *Juges* and the professional magistracy and the other legal professions, there is nevertheless something very familiar in terms of the history of civil law in the manner in which those skilled in the art of government administration are called upon to serve the State in a combined advisory and judicial capacity.

3 The Procedure of the Administrative Courts

The process of administrative justice is again redolent of the civilian inheritance of the lands wherein it has taken root. The process can be divided into four phases, namely the commencement or introductory phase, the instruction phase, the judgement or decision-making phase, and finally the execution.

The introductory phase consists of the making of a request to the court by a plaintiff who complains of an administrative decision. It is a condition precedent for a hearing before the administrative courts that there must have been an administrative act, that is an act performed by an officer of the executive, and that a prior decision must have been made. It is not open to a citizen to complain in anticipation of an administrative act, for he could make representations in that case to the officer concerned. Moreover, it is usually necessary also to have exhausted any avenues by which the matter could be resolved through administrative channels other than the courts. Thus, the matter must have been decided executively before any litigation before the administrative courts begins. The litigant must also have *locus standi* to bring his suit before the administrative court, in that the decision must affect him personally in some way. In Italy, this has led to the development of a concept called the *legitimate interest*, an interest in what has been decided sufficient to allow the person to bring proceedings before the administrative tribunals. In addition, the complainant must have no other source of relief, else that avenue must be taken, and must commence his search for an administrative remedy in good time, without delay. In France, it is usually required that a remedy before the administrative courts be sought within two months of the decision subject to complaint.

Once the process has been commenced, the instruction phase is conducted in a manner which perhaps better exemplifies the inquisitorial method of proceeding that either the civil or criminal process of modern times. The plaintiff's complaint may be supported by written statements and these are passed to the administrative authority complained of which is allowed to reply in writing after which the plaintiff can again respond. This exchange of written pleadings continues until the issues between the plaintiff and the administration are completely clarified. The tribunal then appoints a *rapporteur* who carries out an investigation into the issues raised, gathering the written sources of evidence into a *dossier* which will eventually be passed to the college of judges for decision. The *rapporteur* presents his written report to the court at the end of the instruction and the *Commissaire du gouvernement* is then given time to consider his response and can submit a contradictory view. Although the legal representatives of the parties are asked to speak before judgement is given, they rarely avail themselves of this opportunity before the *Conseil d'État* so that the proceedings are markedly inquisitorial and written. Contradiction is however allowed and the presence of the *Commissaire* completes the remarkably Romano-canonical ambience in which administrative disputes are resolved.

At the stage of judgement, the court hands down its verdict in writing, the judgement being that of the court as a whole, no dissenting opinions being recorded. Reasons must be given. Moreover, because there is no code of administrative law, the written sources are various and the importance of judicial decisions and interpretations as a secondary source of law are very greatly increased in administrative law. Although there is no strict doctrine of precedent, nor any firm rule of *stare decisis*, the *jurisprudence* of the administrative courts, particularly that of the *Conseil d'État*, is of immense importance. Oddly therefore to some eyes, the development of this markedly inquisitorial area of the law in procedural terms is more influenced by case-law than other branches of the law in France. This is also the case with some other civil law countries.[6]

Finally, after judgement has been given, it was once the case that a successful complainant had no real means of enforcing the judgement. The lack of a formal means of execution reflected the fact that the court was part of the administration, and other administrative organs could not be commanded by it but need only be apprised of its opinion. This somewhat unsatisfactory state of affairs was remedied in France in 1963 by the introduction of a Report Commission into the *Conseil d'État*, the function of which is to keep other administrative organs informed of judgements which affect them so as to ensure their compliance. Any suggestion that enforcement proceedings could be brought through the ordinary courts would, in France, be anathema as contrary to the doctrine of the separation of powers, for the judiciary would be commanding the executive.

4 Types of Relief in the Administrative Courts

It might be thought that the type of relief afforded by administrative tribunals was in general not amenable to enforcement by the ordinary courts in any event. This however is not true of all civil law jurisdictions.

French administrative law categorizes the type of relief that may be sought in a manner that is most useful. It distinguishes four kinds of *contentieux*. Firstly, there is the *contentieux de l'annulation*, by which a citizen may challenge the validity of an administrative act. Secondly, there is the *contentieux de l'interprétation* by which a citizen requires the court to provide an authoritative declaration of the meaning of an administrative regulation. Thirdly, the *contentieux de pleine jurisdiction* exists to allow the citizen to complain that the executive has refused to compensate him for a wrong it has caused him. This *contentieux* differs from the previous two in that its basis lies in an injury to a subjective private law right of the citizen. The citizen cannot proceed against the administration for this injury in the ordinary courts as they are not permitted to entertain claims against the executive, for this would be contrary to the doctrine of the separation of powers. Instead, the citizen has to request the administration for compensation. If they accede to that request, the matter is ended; if they refuse, then their refusal is deemed to be an administrative act in itself, the propriety of which can be determined by the administrative courts, thus maintaining the distinction between the administrative courts' jurisdiction over administrative acts and that of the ordinary courts over subjective rights. Finally, there is the *contentieux de la répression* by which the administration itself may proceed against a citizen for violation of certain administrative regulations, in the main concerned with the State's property interests in roads, waterways, railways, ports, harbours and the like, which are termed *la grande voirie*. It is a sort of administrative criminal jurisdiction, but cannot lead to penalties other than fines.

This mode of categorization has not escaped criticism. The eminent French jurist Léon Duguit attacked it as being unscientific, preferring to categorize on the basis of objective and subjective remedies. According to this approach, *contentieux de l'annulation* and *contentieux de l'interprétation* are objective in that the judgement of the court is binding upon everyone and not just upon the parties to the dispute, while *contentieux de pleine jurisdiction* and *contentieux de la répression* result in judgements which concern only the parties to the litigation. The *contentieux de pleine jurisdiction* involves, as has been shown, the rights of the citizen under private law. Such rights cannot be adjudicated before administrative courts. Indeed, there exists in France a special court, the *Tribunal des Conflits*, to determine whether an issue is one of private or administrative law. In other civil law countries, the administrative courts are forbidden to touch on matters of private law in the manner accomplished in France by the *contentieux de pleine jurisdiction.* In Italy, for instance, such cases involving injury to subjective rights by the executive have to be determined before the ordinary courts, although judgement against the executive is enforced through the administrative courts. Only the validity and interpretation of administrative acts and measures fall within the jurisdiction of the Italian administrative tribunals. This is what has led to the distinction in Italian law between subjective rights and legitimate interests, the former giving *locus standi* before the ordinary courts, the latter before the administrative tribunals. Indeed, until the 1960s, Italy had no administrative courts on the French model, determining interferences by the executive with private rights in the ordinary courts and allowing administrative organs to deal with other complaints. During the 1960s, the Italian Constitutional Court questioned the propriety of administrative officers making the latter sort of determination and, as a result, in 1971 Italy created *Tribunali amministrativi regionali* on the model of the French *tribunaux administratifs*. The Italian Council of State has adjudicatory sections which act as a court of final instance from these recently-created administrative tribunals in the regions.[7]

While the question of the liability of the administration for interference with the subjective rights of citizens is not dealt with by the administrative courts in all civil law countries, where it is, as in France, concepts such as fault and risk, derived from private law, play their part. Wherever a distinct administrative jurisdiction is exercised, however, the tribunals have power to review the objective legality of administrative acts. The grounds for such challenges are fairly standard, well exemplified by the *droit administratif* of France. Firstly, the courts can rule that there is no administrative act at all, *inexistence*, if the method by which it was purportedly made totally fails to achieve that objective. Secondly, the administrative organ concerned may have exceeded its legal powers in making an act, in which the act will be set aside for *incompétence*. Thirdly, an act may be set aside as not having been made according to the correct procedure or in the correct manner, *vice de forme*, or fourthly for having contravened a hierarchically superior rule or law in its content, *violation de la loi*. Fifthly, it is possible for an administrative act to be set aside if its purpose was not really to further the policy for which the power to make it was given to the executive, so-called *détournement de pouvoir*. A classic example of this was the imposition of parking restrictions ostensibly to regulate traffic, but the underlying motive being to protect commercial interests.[8]

Linked with the concept of *détournement de pouvoir* is that of disproportionality, whereby although the purpose which an administrative act serves is proper, the range of the act greatly exceeds what is necessary to achieve the objective. This concept has been adopted by the European Court of Justice to considerable effect and is even influencing the development of administrative remedies in non-civilian jurisdictions.[9] It might be thought to carry the private law concept of *laesio enormis* into the realms of public law.[10]

The question of disproportionality raises the issue of whether an administrative tribunal is permitted to reform an administrative act so as to purge any illegality and allow what is lawful in it to survive. Again, there is no standard answer across the countries of the civil law. Such intervention is not permitted in France, where an administrative act is merely annulled and the executive has to replace it with a valid one. In Germany, however, where administrative courts were introduced in 1949, the tribunals are permitted to reform an administrative act so as to purge it of illegality. The question underlying these two approaches is whether such reform amounts to an encroachment by the judges upon executive power.

5 The Influence of Administrative Law

The development of administrative justice in civil law countries over the last two centuries is a potent example of how the civilian tradition is a living force, fully capable of producing new species which are nevertheless recognizably of the same genus. Although most closely associated with the French legal system, it has produced similar growths in other civil law countries. In 1949, Germany, which had known administrative courts in some regions since the nineteenth century, introduced a nation-wide system of administrative courts, ranging from the first instance *Verwaltungsgerichte* in the individual *Lände*, to the *Oberverwaltungsgerichte* as appeal courts of second instance, with a federal *Bundesverwaltungsgericht* as a court of third and final instance. Like Italy, which introduced administrative tribunals in 1971, the German courts do not entertain claims against the executive for injuries to subjective rights, leaving such issues within the purview of the ordinary courts. Although Belgium originally set its face against having separate administrative courts in 1831, preferring to trust to the jurisdiction of its ordinary courts, it has since 1946 established a separate system of administrative justice based on the French *Conseil d'État*. Separate administrative jurisdictions have also been created on the French model in Holland, Luxembourg, Spain, Portugal and Greece. Thus, it can truly be claimed that a system of administrative law has become a feature of modern civilian jurisdictions.

Given that the original six member states of the European Economic Community were all countries of the civil law, and systems of administrative justice were either established or being established in them, it is not surprising that the European Court of Justice of the member States has drawn upon the style and procedure of French administrative law. The proceedings before this court have been heavily influenced by those of the *Conseil d'État*, there being a staff of judges and advocates-general, whose function closely resembles that of the *rapporteur* before the French tribunals. The predominantly written procedure also reflects the influence of *droit administratif*, although it is much more common for advocates to address the European Court than is the case in the French *Conseil d'État*. The entry into the European Union of common law countries, such as England and Wales, or Ireland, or even those with a mixed heritage of common and civil law, such as Scotland, has meant that the European Court has become a point of possible convergence between the two dominant western legal traditions. There is no doubt that the European Court has, as a result, become even more case-law oriented that the administrative tribunals of France and that the common law concept of the *ratio decidendi* of a case has made inroads into the thinking of the European tribunal. There is also evidence that via the European Court, the common law courts of England and Wales have begun to be influenced by civilian administrative approaches.[11]

Meanwhile, in France itself, where the modern concept of administrative justice first made headway, the last half century has seen a development which appears to connect the modern jurisprudence of the administrative courts with the origins of civil law in ancient Rome. Since 1944, the French administrative courts have exhibited a willingness to annul administrative acts which contravene general principles of law - *les principes généraux du droit*. These general principles are nowhere to be found written down, but resemble in some measure the principles of natural justice which the United Kingdom courts have recognized in cultivating their version of administrative law. They are principles therefore not of enacted law, *loi* or *lex*, but of *droit*, the Roman *ius*, and which appear to continue to exist, albeit shadowily, behind the enacted legal order, but which must not be contravened by executive action although the legislative power has never formally recognized their content. They would probably be instantly recognizable by natural lawyers of any of the centuries in which civil law has developed. The modern administrative law of the civilian jurisdictions can therefore be seen to embody a living link with the civil law heritage as far back as Roman times, while also providing a bridge between the civilian and common law traditions. It is a fascinating area of study for those with an interest in either the past, present or future of European and indeed global legal development.

Notes

---

[1] This was the administrative law which so drew the fire of the British jurist, Albert Venn Dicey, who saw in it a challenge to the Rule of Law as understood in the United Kingdom. Modern writers have tended to discredit Dicey's views, but have perhaps failed to appreciate that French administrative law has developed considerably since Dicey wrote, and that he would probably have found those subsequent developments reassuring from his own perspective. See A.V. Dicey, *An Introduction to the Study of the Law of the Constitution* (10th Ed., by E.C.S. Wade; London, 1959).

[2] First published in 1748 in 31 books.

[3] Decree of 6-11 September 1790; see J.-B. Brissaud, *A History of French Public Law* (Boston, 1915 reprinted New York, 1969), p. 563.

[4] Loi 16-24 August 1790, art. 13, which states: 'Judicial functions are distinct and will always remain separate from administrative functions. It shall be a criminal offence for the justices of the ordinary courts to interfere in any manner whatsoever with the operation of the administration, nor shall they call administrators to account before them in respect of the exercise of their official functions.'; see John

S. Bell and L. Neville Brown, *French Administrative Law* (5th Ed.; Oxford, 1998), pp. 46 ff.

[5] Bordeaux, Lyons, Nancy, Nantes, Paris. See Décret 88-155 (15 February 1988).

[6] French decisions are, for instance, often cited in the Belgian literature on administrative law; see Bell and Brown, *French Administrative Law*, pp. 269-270.

[7] Other than from Sicily, which has its own Council for Administrative Justice; see T.G. Watkin, *The Italian Legal Tradition* (London, 1997), p. 152.

[8] See *Compagnie Pyrenéene de Transports par Taxis* (CE 10 February 1928); see Bell and Brown, *French Administrative Law*, p. 247.

[9] For instance, England and Wales; see N. Grief, 'The Pervasive Influence of European Community Law in the United Kingdom' in T.G. Watkin (Ed.), *The Europeanisation of Law* (London, 1998), pp. 90 ff.

[10] For *laesio enormis*, see chapter 12, pp. 308 ff.

[11] See N. Grief, loc. cit., n. 9 above.

18 The Legal Profession

1 Introduction

It would be difficult to speak of a legal profession in ancient Rome prior to the period of the Dominate. Jurists indeed there were, but professional lawyers in the modern sense did not appear upon the scene until the time of the later empire. The jurists were involved in the giving of legal advice, but this they did as a liberal art and disdained any notion of being hired like tradesmen for their services. They advised the magistrates, the *iudices* who under the *legis actio* and formulary systems of procedure actually decided the disputes referred to them through the magistrates, as well as giving advice to private clients. They were also involved in drafting legal documents or advising upon their content and form, as well as advising clients how to perform certain transactions in order to secure certain results. Their other major activities can be regarded as educational in that they both trained pupils who aspired to be jurists and wrote treatises upon the law for the instruction of others, works which became regarded as sources of law in themselves and through their excerpting in the compilations of Justinian have served to channel knowledge of the classical law of Rome from the ancient world into mediaeval and modern times. Under the Principate, as has been noted, the leading jurists tended more and more to gravitate into the imperial civil service where their influence upon the development of the law was considerable.

Although academic opinion, *doctrine*, is still accounted a secondary source of law in modern civilian systems, when one speaks of the legal professions in relation to a modern civil law system, one is primarily referring to those who for payment render their services to the State or to private clients. All will be legally qualified, usually according to standards which have been set by the national government. In addition, since the coming into force of the national codes of law during the last two centuries, the law in which these professionals are skilled is primarily that of the country in which they practise, although the advent of European Community law has led to national governments again requiring knowledge of a legal system which transcends the boundaries of one State.

Within modern civilian systems, the essential qualification for work as a legal professional is the law degree, which is taught in the university law faculties. Although this is a necessary qualification in most civil law countries, it is not in itself sufficient. Increasingly, for admission into the various branches of the legal profession, further training and legal qualification is required. Nevertheless entry into these branches is confined to those who have acquired a degree in law.

The choice before the graduate in law who wishes to pursue a career in the legal professions - and many prefer to go into business or administration for which a law degree is also regarded an excellent preparation - is fairly wide. A graduate can choose between becoming an advocate, a procurator, a notary, or a judicial or prosecuting magistrate. All of these are legal careers for which a law degree is essential. Although there are some other kinds of legal professional activity, these are the ones which will be considered in this chapter.[1] Advocates are those lawyers who give legal advice and are qualified to argue cases on behalf of their clients in the courts. Procurators are lawyers who are entitled to represent their clients in court in the sense of their presence being equated to that of their client and who also draw up documents on behalf of their clients relating to litigation. In some countries, the professions of advocate and procurator have been amalgamated or can be followed jointly by the same person, while in others a rigid separation of the two professions is enforced. France amalgamated the two branches in 1971, while in Italy qualification as a procurator was an essential prerequisite to qualifying as an advocate, although it was not necessary to make the progression. Most lawyers however did, but the two professions were merged in 1997. Spain still practises rigid separation.[2]

The profession of notary is entirely separate. Although also a legal adviser to private clients, the notary is also a State official, who is responsible for the drafting and authentication of certain legal documents, which by virtue of notarial authentication constitute conclusive proof of whatever transaction it is to which they bear witness, in the sense that the legal effect of the document can only be challenged by proving it to be a forgery. To be a notary requires the passing of competitive State professional examinations, and only a certain number of notaries are permitted to practise within the State or any locality at any given time. There are certain legal transactions which can only be accomplished by notarial authentication and others for which notarial authentication offers absolute probity. Notaries are required by law to perform such functions on behalf of their clients, while other transactions, such as the drawing up of marriage settlements and wills, which do not necessarily require notarial authentication for their validity, they may undertake to perform or not at their discretion.

Those who view civilian systems from the perspective of the common law are often amazed to discover that law graduates can proceed upon graduation to train as judges. In civil law countries generally, the judiciary is a career which stands as an alternative to legal practice as an advocate or notary and not as a possible development from it. Today, aspiring magistrates have to sit State professional examinations to become part of the judicial branch of the State civil service, which is how judges are viewed. These examinations are generally accounted among the most difficult of all the civil service examinations. If the candidate is successful in these examinations, he or she will thereafter spend a period as an *auditor* or listener, serving a sort of apprenticeship upon the Bench, after which he will follow a junior appointment from which a career path either will or can progress.[3] Moreover, the profession of magistrate can be subdivided into two branches, which can for convenience be called the judicial magistracy and the prosecuting magistracy. The qualifications and career structure of each are basically the same, and in some, but not all, countries it is possible for a magistrate to move between the two branches in the course of his career. The judicial magistrates are those who hear and determine cases on the Bench, in some cases in tandem with lay assessors or jurors, while the prosecuting magistrates are those who control the investigation of crimes, gather evidence for use at criminal trials and present the case for the prosecution at the judicial hearings. They are treated as being on a par with the judicial magistrates, and their offices are usually attached to the courts where their judicial brethren sit.

The structure of the legal professions in modern civilian jurisdictions reflects the influence of the manner in which the legal professions have been organized in France since the Revolution, although the modern German model has also been an influence in many countries. Japan for instance veered from an initial allegiance to the French approach to adoption of a more German structure. However, the manner in which different branches of the legal profession now deal with different functions requiring legal expertise reflects a much longer period of development, some of which have their roots in ancient Rome and others of which reflect the intervening history of civil law during the Middle Ages. It is the purpose of this chapter to give an outline of the main features of that development which have contributed to the shaping of the legal professions which serve modern civil law.

2 Advocates and Procurators

It would appear that under the *legis actio* procedure in ancient Rome, the parties had to appear before the magistrate in person and speak for themselves. Generally, neither representation nor the services of a rhetorician were allowed. An exception was made in the case of an absent owner whose property had been stolen, where another could institute the *actio furti* on his behalf, and in cases involving the bringing of popular actions, assertions of liberty and the affairs of an infant, the person instigating the action would not have a direct interest. Otherwise, *cognitores* as they were called at this time were only permitted to litigants who were provably aged or sick.

It is not clear however whether the ban on the use of advocates extended to proceedings *apud iudicem* under the *legis actiones* or whether it was confined to proceedings *in iure*. Under the formulary system, although the parties had still to appear in person before the praetor, advocates were allowed to speak for them before the judge. These advocates were orators not jurists, men trained primarily in the art of rhetoric not in the law. Although some may have had some legal training, this was neither essential nor common, nor was it the skill which they were employed to exercise on their clients' behalf. Jurists would supply the legal advice; the advocates were there to present the case with consummate oratorical skill.[4]

This division of labour changed with the growth of extraordinary *cognitio* and the new legal order of the Dominate. Representation came to be permitted at all stages of the proceedings, either by *cognitores*, formally appointed for the purpose, or by *procuratores*, appointed informally but still charged with representing the party by their presence. This representative function was demarcated from the role of the advocate who was there to speak on the client's behalf but did not represent him in the sense of taking his place before the court. Whereas the client could not disown the words or deeds of a procurator, he could dissociate himself from an advocate's arguments. By this time, the late Dominate, the advocates were no longer primarily orators but skilled legal advisers, whose education would be in the law, an education obtained in one of the formal law schools of the later empire, the most famous being at Constantinople and Beirut.

The distinction between the work of procurators and advocates, as well as the functions they served, had come to resemble their modern equivalents. Indeed, advocates by this time were organized as an order and charged fixed tariffs for their services in accordance with an imperially approved scale.[5]

It was during the Dominate also that the necessity arose of advocates enrolling at the bar of the court at which they intended to practise. The emperor Constantine insisted upon such enrolment,[6] while in 460, the emperor Leo required advocates to hold a certificate regarding their legal training before they could enrol before the court. This may have been true of all courts, but was certainly the case with regard to the court of the praetorian prefect.[7] The *iudices pedanei* used by provincial governors appear to have been drawn from the order of advocates,[8] and the assessors used by provincial governors had to be similarly qualified, and they were also employed to draft the written decision of the court, a practice which again foreshadows the modern requirement that judgements be reasoned.[9]

The level of sophistication achieved in the arrangements of the later empire did not survive its collapse in the West, and it was not until the ninth century that advocates in the shape of *prolocutores* were to appear again before the courts of the Carolingian rulers. Advocates surfaced again however before the Church courts of the twelfth century as well as before the *Parlement* of the French king. The renaissance of legal study at the law faculties of the Italian universities and at centres such as Orléans in northern Europe assisted their reappearance. The advocates began once more to form themselves into orders to regulate their qualifications, discipline and fees; in fourteenth-century France, for instance, they established the Brotherhood of St. Nicholas in tandem with the public prosecutors. The chief of the Brotherhood was distinguished by the carrying of a ceremonial staff or *baton*, and *bâtonnier* remains to this day the title of the head of the various bars before which French advocates must be enrolled. The advocates separated themselves from the ranks of the public prosecutors at the end of the fifteenth century, becoming an order in their own right during the sixteenth, by which time admission to and regulations of the affairs of the order had passed under the control of the *Parlement* itself. Although the profession of advocate was abolished in 1790 amid the fervour of the Revolution, when it was believed that under the new order men could plead plainly for themselves, it had been re-established by 1810 with a complete monopoly of pleading before the courts, in recognition of the need for litigants to be professionally advised if they were to have an equal and fair hearing before the tribunals which administered the law. The role given to advocates in post-Revolutionary France has supplied the structure and functions of the profession in much of the civil law world, in particular those which have adopted the French codes as the basis for their legal orders.[10]

The Romans had distinguished the role of the advocate, there to assist his client with advice and argument, from that of the *cognitor* or procurator, who represented the client in the sense that his presence and actions were treated as equivalent to those of the party represented. This distinction played no part in the legal arrangements of the Germanic tribes, and was not introduced into Germany until the *Reichskammergericht* was established at the end of the fifteenth century and took Roman arrangements as its own. The distinction between advocates and procurators was incorporated into the legal system of the French *ancien régime* by the *ordonnance* on civil procedure of 1667.[11]

Prior to that time, the role of the procurator, or *procureur*, had made inroads into French law. Originally, under feudal law, only the king was allowed to appear in court by a representative or attorney. Although such a limitation upon the use of attorneys was prevalent in feudal courts, it played no part before the Church courts, where the opportunity of using an attorney to enter an appearance and perform acts in law was open to virtually all litigants. Gradually, the strict feudal rule was relaxed, first by allowing attorneys to appear for litigants provided they had been appointed by charter, a requirement abolished in France in 1484,[12] and later by simply allowing attorneys to represent their clients as a matter of practice if no objection was made, so that they were widely employed before the prohibition on their use was formally abolished in 1528. Indeed, from the thirteenth century, each court in France had attached to it a corporation of *procureurs*, the members of which were available to receive mandates *ad litem* from litigants who wished to be represented before the court in question. In 1791, the *procureurs* changed their name to *avoués*, the name by which procurators have been known in French law ever since.[13] They still form a distinct profession with regard to litigation before appeal courts in France, but, since 1971, the professions of *avocat* and *avoué* have been merged in France with regard to litigation before lower courts, and the profession of *agréé*, which was equivalent to that of *avoué* but before the commercial courts, has also been incorporated into that of *avocat*.[14] In Italy, the profession of *procuratore* was merged with that of *avvocato* in 1997, although it was previously possible for a procurator to qualify as an advocate as well and serve in both roles, which most such lawyers did, the qualification of procurator being seen as an initial step to qualifying as an advocate. In Spain, however, the professions of *abogado* and *procurador* are still entirely distinct. In Germany, the *Rechtanwalt* performs both functions.[15]

In France, advocates formed a distinct sub-branch of that branch of the legal profession, *profession libérale juridique*, called the *auxiliaires de justice*. The other sub-branch of this group are called *officiers ministériels*, and *avoués* and *agréés* were members of this class. So also are notaries, and the development of their role must be the next focus of attention.

3 Notaries

The profession of notary arises from the need for documentary proof to be furnished in order to establish that certain deeds have been done. The notary initially provides an authentic record of some deed, and the document in which he provides it becomes itself known as a deed as a result. Its authenticity arises from the fact that it has been prepared by a notary.

Although the term *notary* was initially employed in the late Roman imperial civil service to designate a person who kept a record or *notae* of the emperor's deliberations,[16] the use of the word in its modern sense did not come until later. Some believe that the influence of Greek legal practices, which made much greater use of writing than did their Roman counterparts, influenced the development of post-classical Roman law in this regard when the centre of the empire became established at Byzantium.[17] Late Roman law required registration of certain transactions, such as adoptions and emancipations, as proof that they had taken place, so that writing substituted rituals as the method of proof.[18] This use of writing permeated the western empire as well, and from it played some part in the jurisprudence of the tribes which overran the western empire. Thus, when lands were guaranteed to the Ostrogoths by the Roman praetorian prefect Liberius, he gave them documents to bear witness to the gifts which they had received.[19] It was with the coming of the Lombards however that notarial authentication made its greatest progress, for they regularly employed notaries to keep a record of what was done in court, a record which thereafter was conclusive proof of what had been agreed or decided.[20] By the ninth century, Lombard law required that minutes be kept of all that occurred in the court, the purpose of which was initially so that the judge could report the proceedings and judgement to the ruler. Parties however wished to have copies of the court record to prove the rights and duties which had been established thereunder, and also to allow them to claim execution of the judgement on the basis of the court record. Initially, such a documentary record would be drawn up by the judge himself, but later it was sufficient for it to be drafted in his presence. The notaries were the court scribes who drew up such documents. Finally, they were empowered by the court to draft such documents elsewhere than in court and without the presence of the judge, but their authentication of the documents nevertheless produced the same effect. The notarial instrument had been born.[21]

When the Lombard sphere of influence in Italy had waned in the face of Frankish expansion, the Lombard duke of Benevento, Adelchi, required notarial documents if proof by writing was to be offered of a legal transaction,[22] and it was towards the end of the Frankish period, with the growth of feudalism, that the court scribes who had prepared records for the parties became established first as court clerks specifically employed to prepare documents, and from there developed the profession of notary. The practice of keeping written records of court proceedings entered the Church courts, where a distinct preference for documentary proof emerged. Only in those areas of Europe in which Germanic practices prevailed did this development not take place.[23]

It was in feudal Italy that the characteristic features of notarial practice were defined. There it was that it was first settled that such documents should always be used for certain types of transaction, that they should always be officially prepared, that is by a notary, and that the consequence of such preparation would be a special validity upon which execution could be founded.[24] It was in Italy also that during the twelfth century the practice developed of notaries keeping a register of all the documents authenticated by them. The documents were said to be *imbreviaturae*, and this practice spread, via the courts of both the Church and the emperor, to Germany where it became established during the thirteenth century.[25] In Spain, the thirteenth-century *Las Siete Partidas* contained rules on the need for documentary evidence, together with forms for its provision.

It was from the twelfth century onwards that notaries public appeared in the south of France, the *pays de droit écrit*, where they not only authenticated documents as proof of certain transactions on behalf of a court, but also acquired a degree of non-contentious jurisdiction connected with their provision of documents, so that they were able to appoint guardians and curators, perform emancipations and conduct sales of property belonging to persons who had not reached their majority.

Although the practice of actually going to court and having a transaction formally recorded in the court's records prevailed in many parts of northern Europe throughout the Middle Ages, virtually every court in the South employed the services of a notary, usually under the authority of the person whose court it was. The Pope and the emperor however had authority to licence notaries to practise anywhere in Christendom, *ubique terrarum*, which increased the attractiveness of utilizing the ecclesiastical and imperial jurisdiction as documents authenticated by papal or imperial notaries were proof before such courts anywhere. Realising the threat posed to royal authority and jurisdiction by this, King Philip IV of France reserved to himself the power to licence notaries within his realm, and required that all those practising the profession of notary should register all the deeds which they authenticated.[26] By this means, notaries became the sole source of authentication within France.

Despite some resistance to admitting written proof in preference to oral testimony as late as the early thirteenth century,[27] by the fourteenth century some Italian states were demanding written proof of certain transactions as the norm. Naples legislated to this effect as early as 1306, and other important cities such as Bologna and Milan had followed suit before the end of the fifteenth century.[28] During the sixteenth century, the use of notaries took hold in northern Europe with the Germanic Reception of Roman law. In France, the *ordonnance* of Villers-Cotteret in 1539 regulated the work of notaries, and their position was underpinned yet further by the adoption of written proof to the exclusion of other types for transactions with a value of more than 100 *livres* by the *ordonnance* of Moulins in 1566.[29] Analogous provisions can be found in the Belgian *Edictum Perpetuum* of 1611, and the *Code civil* enshrined the same practice within its provisions in 1804.[30]

Thus, the profession of notary had won an established place in modern civil law long before the advent of the national codifications. Many of the tasks which in England and Wales would be entrusted to a solicitor, such as making a will, drafting a conveyance, drawing up a settlement or creating a land charge, are the province of the notary. The relationship between the notaries' work and the widespread preference for written proof of legal transactions has meant that there has been no movement of any consequence in the civilian jurisdictions to merge the profession of notary with any other legal occupation, despite the reforms which in so many civil law countries have produced the unification of advocacy and procuratorship.

4 Prosecuting Magistrates

Already in late imperial Rome, the magistrates who were charged with the trial of criminal offences found, under the introduction of the procedure by extraordinary *cognitio*, that they were required not only to adjudicate on the question of guilt or innocence but also to investigate crimes which had been committed so as to identify the culprit and thereafter to prefer charges against the suspect by virtue of their duty, *ex officio*, to see that the law was observed and infractions of it punished. There was therefore from the beginning a link between the use of inquisitorial procedures and the duty of a public official to conduct the investigation of and prosecutions for criminal offences.

Despite this early link in Roman times between the inquisitorial procedure and magistrates prosecuting, the origins of the modern phenomenon of the prosecuting magistrate lie in the Middle Ages. Although strictly speaking, only the French king was allowed to appear by attorney before courts in his realm, in practice attorneys could be used by lesser persons provided they were appointed by charter or no objection to their use was made. It was therefore common for lords and communes to have standing attorneys and indeed advocates before the royal courts. By the end of the thirteenth century, the kings of France followed the same practice before their own courts. Although it may at first blush appear incongruous that the king should need persons to defend his own interests before his own courts, the reasons for this development are both credible and creditable. Although the judges who sat in the royal courts were royal judges appointed by the king, they were nevertheless meant to be impartial in their administration of justice even where the king's own interests were concerned. Accordingly it was not considered proper for them to seek to defend the king's interests in their deliberations, and attorneys were therefore appointed by the king to serve in his courts to defend his interests in the same way as the nobility and the communes maintained attorneys there to defend their interests. The king's justices were therefore freed from this responsibility and thereby enabled to proceed about their duties with complete impartiality.

From the beginning of the sixteenth century, these attorneys became in France public officials working exclusively for the king. With the advent of a standard inquisitorial procedure in the criminal justice of the kingdom at this time, they became interested in all matters affecting public order and with the repression of serious crimes. They also acquired a role in proceedings in which the king had an interest in his capacity of protector of those unable to defend themselves, such as absentees, wards and the poor and weak generally. By the end of the sixteenth century, advocates were employed exclusively in the royal service to argue such cases before the courts.[31]

Thus came into existence that particular hallmark of criminal justice in civilian jurisdictions the prosecuting magistrate, a lawyer who is qualified in the same manner as a judge who adjudicates disputes but who investigates crimes and prosecutes offenders, as well as acting as a guardian of the public interest in civil matters such as adoptions, emancipations and the guardianship of minors. In France and Italy, the office is known as that of the public service - *ministère public* or *pubblico ministero*. In Scotland and Spain, the original interest of this officer in protecting the financial interests of the king are manifested in his retaining the title of Procurator Fiscal or *Ministero Fiscal*. Although qualified in the same way as the judges of the bench and enjoying the same status and career structure,[32] they are often distinguished from their judicial brethren by the fact that they perform their duties in court while standing, in contrast to the judicial magistrates who remain seated to discharge their functions. Thus, in France, the *ministère public* is frequently referred to as the *magistrats du parquet* in contradistinction to the judges of the bench who are the *magistrats du siège*. Together these two categories of magistrate form that branch of the *profession libérale juridique* which is called *agents de justice* as opposed to the advocates, notaries and other such lawyers who compose the *auxiliaires de justice*.

5 The Judiciary

It is taken for granted in modern legal systems that the judges who sit in the superior courts at any rate should be legally qualified. Although lay participation in the judicial process is a feature of many modern civilian systems, whether as finders of fact alone as with the jury, *jurado*, recently introduced in Spain, or as judges of law and fact sitting together with professionally-trained judges, as in France, Germany and Italy, or as judges in small-claims courts or trying minor crimes, the norm is for the judge to be legally qualified.

This was not the case in ancient Rome, where the *iudices* chosen by the parties under both the *legis actio* and the formulary procedure were chosen for their probity, judgement and sense of justice, and were not expected to have any knowledge of the law, for which they could turn to jurists for advice. Even under the procedure by extraordinary *cognitio*, the provincial governors who were meant to preside at trials were not of necessity legally qualified, and turned to assessors, drawn from the advocates enrolled at the bar of the court, for legal support. It was not uncommon however for imperial officials such as the praetorian prefects to be highly-skilled lawyers.

With the fall of the western empire, the courts of the Germanic peoples who succeeded to the lands of western Europe were assemblies of the male population capable of bearing arms, dispute settlement being only one of their tasks. In these assemblies, the ruler generally presided and declared the judgement after a verdict had been found. Matters of fact however were frequently left to the judgement of God or the outcome of some trial of strength, so that the role of the president was solely to declare the outcome and not to himself provide a judgement. If questions of law arose, these would be settled according to the custom of the community which the assembly served, and if clarification or interpretation were needed, it fell to the whole assembly to provide it. Gradually, however, there emerged a smaller body of men within the assembly who were entrusted to declare the customs of the community. These were law-finders rather than judges and were known by a variety of names across Europe: *rachimburgi*, *Schöffen*, *echévins*, *scabini*. They declared the custom according to which the issue would be tried, the outcome of the trial being declared by the president or *Richter*.

In 775, Charlemagne provided that the *rachimburgi* within his territories should be a permanent collegial body, and in time they assumed the status of royal officials. This reflected the fact that some knowledge of imperial legislation as well as local custom was essential to the performance of their role. Coupled with the development of legal studies at the nascent university, then a cathedral school, at Pavia at which serious study of both Lombard and feudal law was commencing, this led to a preference for *scabini* and *Schöffen* with a knowledge of law derived from legal education rather than memory of local custom, so that the concept of a professional judge was born. With the further development of legal science in the eleventh, twelfth and thirteenth centuries, doctors of the learned laws, civil and canon, from the law faculties of the universities were called upon not only to advise those who held courts in the Italian communes and city states, but increasingly were asked to serve those communities in the capacity of judicial magistrate, actually using their legal skills and knowledge to adjudicate disputes according to the laws and customs of the community, but also with reference to the principles of civil law. Such legally-qualified judges were often called the *podestà* of the city or town in question, and were generally recruited from outside the community so that their impartiality was assured.

While in Italy, the office of *podestà* was by invitation and usually for a fixed term, in northern Europe, many courts continued to function with royal or seigniorial officials as their presidents, with jurists acting only as advisers and assessors. In the *Parlement* of Paris, however, the lawyers who served the king as his justices achieved very early a substantial degree of judicial independence. This was not however a development which occurred on the high ground of principle. Instead, the French kings found it lucrative to allow the office of justice in the *Parlement* to be purchased, and those who were minded to buy their position in this way would not have done so unless they were guaranteed security of tenure, otherwise they would have acquired a very poor bargain for their outlay.[33] In Germany, the crucial stage in the development of a professional judiciary came with the creation of the *Reichskammergericht* in 1495. Half of the judges of this court had from the outset to be trained in the learned laws, and eventually all were expected to have had such training. Whereas previously, legally trained *Schöffen* had advised the German courts and reference was often made to the law faculties in difficult cases for their opinion, from the sixteenth century onwards judges themselves were expected to have the requisite legal training. The professional judge had become the accepted norm throughout the lands of the *ius commune*. Thus, although the type of qualification and study required has changed in the intervening period, the principle that judicial magistrates should be legally qualified may be said to have won general acceptance by the beginning of the seventeenth century.

6 Legal Education and the Professions

The development of legal education in the lands of the civil law was both shaped by and helped shape the development of the legal professions. As soon as the cathedral school at Pavia began serious study of the Lombard and feudal laws, those who had achieved knowledge through study there were in demand to give advice and assist in the adjudication of disputes. The same was true with the growth of legal science at Bologna and the other

Italian universities. From the ranks of the graduates who had studied there were drawn the judges and jurists of the mediaeval period. The legal skills acquired in the universities were prized in the provision of legal solutions for contemporary problems. The academic lawyers of the mediaeval universities were in demand as both juristic advisers and judicial arbiters throughout the fourteenth and fifteenth centuries.

The law which they learned, taught and applied was the civil and canon law, the *ius commune*. However, with the advent of printing and the possibility of compiling definitive texts of the local customary laws, legal science was able to embrace national and regional laws as well as the traditional learned laws of Rome and the Church. The emergence of nation states at roughly the same time and the Reformation in religion also militated in favour of a switch of attention from pure study of the *ius commune* to more widespread application of its techniques to native legal systems. France in the sixteenth and seventeenth centuries saw a shift towards study of national jurisprudence; the same phenomenon of a national legal curriculum began in Germany in the late seventeenth century,[34] and the eighteenth century saw the royal, that is Spanish, law become a subject of study in the universities of Spain.[35] Although the *ius commune* largely held its place in the Italian universities, across Europe it was recognized that as lawyers and judges needed to be legally qualified, so their legal expertise had to be pertinent to the particular legal system within which they were going to practise. National legal systems were emerging together with national legal curricula, and the provision of the modern codes in a sense merely completed the former process, with the inevitable effect that thereafter, within the national territories concerned, the national laws contained in the national codes were to form the primary materials of legal study. Even in England, the eighteenth century saw the establishment of study of the native law in the universities.[36]

The emergence of the European Union in the second half of the twentieth century has caused some scholars to argue that national laws are not suited to the development of a jurisprudence to serve the supra-national Europe of the future nor the increasingly global context within which legal relations both are formed and have to be regulated.[37] This gives rise to the question of what part the civilian heritage of Europe can play in, and what contribution it can make to, the future development of a European or even global legal culture.

Notes

---

[1] For example *dottori commercialisti* in Italy.

[2] In France, the two branches are known as *avocat* and *avoué*, in Italy as *avvocato* and *procuratore* and in Spain as *abogado* and *procurador*.

[3] The Italian approach is to grant automatic promotion subject to there being no demerits; see T.G. Watkin, *The Italian Legal Tradition* (London, 1997), pp. 115 ff. This is not generally the case in civilian jurisdictions; for France, see C. Dadomo and S. Farran, *The French Legal System* (2nd Ed.; London 1996), pp. 140 ff.

[4] See W.W. Buckland, *A Textbook of Roman Law from Augustus to Justinian* (3rd Ed., by P.G. Stein; Cambridge, 1963), pp. 708 ff.

[5] See O. Tellegen-Couperus, *A Short History of Roman Law* (English Ed.; London, 1993), pp. 132 ff.

[6] See A.H.M. Jones, *The Later Roman Empire 284-602* (Oxford, 1964), p. 507.

[7] See W. Kunkel, *An Introduction to Roman Legal and Constitutional History* (trans. J.M. Kelly; 2nd English Ed.; Oxford, 1973), p. 144. The decree was actually addressed to that tribunal: *Code* II. 7. 11.

[8] Ibid.

[9] See H.F. Jolowicz and B. Nicholas, *An Historical Introduction to the Study of Roman Law* (3rd. Ed.; Cambridge, 1972), pp. 449 ff.

[10] See J.-B. Brissaud, *A History of French Public Law* (Boston, 1915; reprinted New York 1969), pp. 461 ff.

[11] See A. Engelmann et al., *A History of Continental Civil Procedure* (Boston, 1927; reprinted New York 1969), p. 717.

[12] By the remonstrances of the States-General of Tours; see J.-B. Brissaud, *A History of French Private Law* (Boston, 1912; reprinted New York 1968), p. 546.

[13] Loi 20 March 1791; see Brissaud, *French Public Law*, pp. 464 ff.

[14] The profession of *avocat* was further reformed in 1992 by incorporation of the profession of *conseil juridique*.

[15] See C. Dadomo and S. Farran, *French Legal System*, pp. 114 ff.; N.G. Foster, *German Legal System and Laws* (2nd Ed.; London, 1996), pp. 93 ff.; E. Merino Blanco, *Spanish Legal System* (London, 1996), pp. 107 ff.; and T.G. Watkin, *The Italian Legal Tradition*, p. 281.

[16] See Justinian, *Code* XII. 7; and C. Calisse, *A History of Italian Law* (Boston, 1928; reprinted New York, 1969), p. 10.

[17] See L. Mitteis, *Römisches Privatrecht bis auf die Zeit Diokletians* (1908), p. 306; and Jolowicz and Nicholas, *Historical Introduction*, p. 420.

[18] See Justinian, *Institutes* I. 12. 6 & 8; *Code* VIII. 47. 11 & VIII. 48. 6; and Jolowicz and Nicholas, *Historical Introduction*, p. 509.

[19] See Calisse, *History*, p. 15.

[20] See ibid., p. 56.

[21] See Brissaud, *French Private Law*, pp. 509 ff.

---

[22] See C. Calisse et al., *A General Survey of Continental Legal History*, (Boston, 1912; reprinted New York 1968) p. 34.
[23] See Engelmann, *Civil Procedure*, p. 50.
[24] See Calisse, *General Survey*, p. 107.
[25] See Calisse, *General Survey*, p. 332.
[26] *Ordonnance* of July 1304 relating to the South of France; see Brissaud, *French Public Law*, pp. 469 f; Engelmann, *Civil Procedure*, p. 703.
[27] In the words of Pope Innocent III: 'the word of a living man prevails over the skin of a dead donkey'; see R.C. Van Caenegem, *A Historical Introduction to Private Law* (English Ed., trans. by D.E.L. Johnston; Cambridge, 1992), p. 189 ff.
[28] See Van Caenegem, *Historical Introduction*, p. 190.
[29] See Calisse, *General Survey*, p. 264; and Van Caenegem, *Historical Introduction*, p. 190.
[30] Art., 1341.
[31] See Brissaud, *French Public Law*, pp. 465 ff.
[32] This is not the case in Scotland where senior judges are recruited from the Faculty of Advocates.
[33] Royal legislation established the practice: *ordonnance* of 1344, and *lettres* of 21. X. 1467; see Brissaud, *French Public Law*, pp. 459 ff.
[34] See Calisse, *General Survey*, p. 430 ff.
[35] Ibid., p. 677.
[36] This was when the Vinerian Chair of English Law was established at Oxford and the Downing Professorship of the Laws of England at Cambridge.
[37] See, for instance, R. Zimmermann, 'Savigny's Legacy - Legal History, Comparative Law and the Emergence of a European Legal Science' in T.G. Watkin (Ed.), *The Europeanisation of Law* (London, 1998), pp. 1 ff.; and B. Markesinis (Ed.), *The Gradual Convergence: Foreign Ideas, Foreign Influences and English Law on the Eve of the Twenty-First Century* (London, 1994).

Conclusion : The Future of Civil Law

The history of how the civil law of Rome, having served the needs of a great empire in the ancient world, was revived in the university law faculties of mediaeval Europe to form the basis of the codified legal orders of the vast majority of nations in modern Europe and of many farther afield, is truly one of the most, if not the most, remarkable stories in the legal history of the world. It is important however to bear in mind that it is a story which does not as yet have an ending; the progress of the civil law has not been arrested. It is true that the compilers of the modern codifications believed that they had achieved legal systems which would endure within their nations for generations. Indeed, the compilers of the French *Code civil* believed that their work was suitable to govern the legal affairs of all nations at all times by dint of its rational content. However, Justinian also believed that his compilations could replace all pre-existing laws, and doubtless the compilers of the XII Tables in the early Roman republic had high hopes and aspirations for their handiwork. With the benefit of hindsight it is clear how optimistic these over-confident expectations all were, those of Napoleon no less than those of Justinian.

This is not to deny the enduring qualities of the achievements of all of these law makers in their several generations. Each produced a legal text of exceptional clarity, a clarity achieved not only by virtue of the rational content of their work but also because of its systematic presentation. The certainty of written law lends it a permanence which allows it to endure as an object of study as well as for application. Allied with the lucid system given it by the institutional scheme, the various compilations of civil law have proved exceptionally resilient to the processes of time.

One can indeed discern a kind of cyclical development in the history of the civil law. It appears to proceed from codification to juristic analysis and back to codification, but on each occasion extending the ambit of its influence. The XII Tables were compiled for a city state in central Italy, but by virtue of the development of the law they contained first by the pontiffs and then by the jurists and magistrates, their law became the Roman *ius civile* which was to be the proud possession and inheritance of the citizens of a great empire. Likewise, the edicts of the praetors and curule aediles came to be, in effect, codified by the jurist Salvius Julianus in 130 AD, and thereafter subject to further extensive juristic treatment. Then again in the sixth century, the emperor Justinian sought to reduce the great mass of enacted laws and juristic writings into a manageable compass, resulting in the works which the world has come to know as the *Corpus Iuris Civilis*.

The decline of classical Roman law in western Europe after the fall of the western empire is the one hiatus in the dominance of Roman civil law upon the continent. The survival of Justinian's compilations through the Dark Ages to be revived as a subject of academic study in the universities of northern Italy in the eleventh century is the great piece of good fortune in the history of Roman jurisprudence. Thereafter, the cycle continues, with the Digest undergoing intensive study at the hands of the Glossators and then having its contents adapted for application in the contemporary world by their juristic successors, the Commentators. At the same time, the adoption by jurists serving the western catholic Church of the techniques fashioned in the service of the Digest to produce a systematic and rational presentation of canon law marked the beginnings of an awareness that the science of the civil law could be applied to other bodies of law as well as the Roman texts. Thus, in a sense, Roman civil law, by virtue of the example of its reason and order, conquered other legal systems in terms of how their laws should be composed and presented, thus gaining territory through intellectual power rather than armed might.

Just as the humanist scholars of the Renaissance began to doubt the claims of Justinian's work to be the true classical law of Rome, so too the tools of Roman legal science came to be turned upon the raw materials of legal systems native to the various lands of Europe. In France, in particular, the reduction to writing of the manifold native customs allowed for their analysis and systematic presentation according to the institutional scheme. This not only offered the opportunity to assess the qualities of the native product in relation to its learned competitors, but also created the chance to compare the native rules with their Roman counterparts and gauge their similarity or otherwise. Eventually, it was possible to accommodate native and civilian elements in a synthesis made possible by the refined methods and structures of the learned law.

It is from these efforts that the modern national codifications were born. Although each marked the culmination of a great feat of assimilation and reconciliation within the lands it governed, there is a sense also in which they have fragmented the civilian legal heritage. Each country now has its own law; in some countries, such as Spain, each region can have its own system. Yet there remains a unity in this diversity. Each code proclaims renewed faith in the reduction of laws to writing; the juristic doctrine of each nation manifests continued belief in the possibility of maintaining a systematic unity and harmony throughout the legal order.

In the second half of the twentieth century, the nation states of Europe have again been moving towards a greater union and their common legal heritage in the *ius commune* is a precious unifying factor. It is again appreciated that, despite the different national legal traditions which currently obtain among the civil law countries, the juristic tools are still in place to fashion therefrom a new unity, in the same manner as the mediaeval Glossators 'restored' the systematic unity of Justinian's Digest and the jurists of sixteenth-century France produced principles of French law from among the disparate native customs. So once more there is an opportunity to work by time-honoured methods towards a new harmonization and systematization of the European legal orders.[1]

Moreover, as again has been proved in the past, the analytical clarity of the Roman institutional scheme permits of its application to bodies of law which are outside the family of civil law systems. By bringing bodies of law into systematic conformity with the civilian model, the opportunity is afforded thereafter to work towards a reconciliation of substance as well as form. The efforts of Bracton in the thirteenth century and Blackstone in the eighteenth illustrate how even the English common law can be assimilated in this manner. The experience of 'mixed' civil and common law systems in Scotland and South Africa encourages the belief that such an assimilation is a practical possibility.[2]

Nor need this enterprise be confined to Europe. The civil law can no less be an instrument of legal globalization as well as of Europeanization. Already, in the wake of the nineteenth-century national codifications, countries in Africa and the Far East have adopted civilian models to govern all or part of their legal affairs. Some such adoptions reflect the aftermath of empire, but others were freely undertaken, for instance the adoption by Japan of a civil code on the German model at the end of the nineteenth century. The fact that the institutional scheme permits native traditions to be expressed in a supra-national manner makes the civilian model very appealing to states which are endeavouring to bring their legal systems into closer proximity with those of their global neighbours without having to forfeit distinctive national or even regional characteristics. The Spanish experience of allowing the autonomous communities their distinctive *leyes civiles forales* is a powerful exemplar of how the civilian approach permits of diversity within a unified system. Indeed, it should be remembered that recourse to local customs was permitted to provincial citizens within the Roman empire when dealing one with another in their native lands. Further, as the history of civil law in the ancient and the mediaeval world illustrates, the learned law is capable of working in a non-national context, that is it predates a world consisting of nation states and can work in an inter-institutional society, as witness for instance its role within the mediaeval Church and among men of commerce from different lands. The learning and methodology of the civil law has much to offer therefore in a world which is becoming more inter-institutional than international in terms of its social composition.

Whatever the future holds for the Europeanization or the globalization of law, one thing is certain; the heritage of the civil law will have as active a role to play in its formation as it has an honourable place in its history. For the fullness of its potential contribution to be realized, the history of how it has supplied the legal needs of past generations must be both known and appreciated. It is an achievement of such magnitude and distinction in the history of human society that nothing less is its due.

Notes

[1] See for instance R. Zimmermann, 'Savigny's Legacy - Legal History, Comparative Law and the Emergence of a European Legal Science' in T.G. Watkin (Ed.), *The Europeanisation of Law* (London, 1998), pp. 1 ff.

[2] See Bracton, *On the Laws and Customs of England* (Ed., G.E. Woodbine; trans. with revisions and notes, S.E. Thorne: 4 vols., Cambridge, Mass., 1968-1977); Sir William Blackstone, *Commentaries on the Laws of England* (1st Ed., London, 1765-1769; reprinted Chicago, 1979); R. Evans-Jones (Ed.), *The Civil Law Tradition in Scotland* (Edinburgh, 1995); R. Zimmermann and D. Visser, (Ed.), *Southern Cross: Civil Law and Common Law in South Africa* (Oxford, 1996).

Select Bibliography

The following list of books contains suggestions for further reading on the development of civil law from its Roman origins to the present day. It is not in any way designed to be exhaustive and in particular is confined to works available in English. It is divided, for convenience of reference, into five sections dealing respectively with works on Roman law, Roman history, the legal history of the mediaeval and modern periods, the general history of those times and, finally, introductory works on the major contemporary civilian systems.

1 Roman Law

Birks, P.B.H. and G. McLeod (ed.), *Justinian's Institutes*, London, 1987.
Borkowski, A., *Textbook on Roman Law*, 2nd Ed., London, 1997.
Bradley, K.R., *Slaves and Masters in the Roman Empire*, Oxford, 1987.
Buckland, W.W., *A Textbook of Roman Law from Augustus to Justinian*, 3rd Ed., by P.G. Stein, Cambridge, 1963.
Corbett, P.E., *The Roman Law of Marriage*, Oxford, 1930; reprinted Aalen 1979.
Crawford, M.H. (ed.), *Roman Statutes*, 2 vols., London, 1996.
Crook, J.A., *Law and Life of Rome*, London, 1967.
Daube, D., *Aspects of Roman Law*, Edinburgh, 1969.
Earl, D., *The Moral and Political Tradition of Rome*, London, 1967.
Gardner, J.E., *Women in Roman Law and Society*, London, 1986.
Gordon, W.M. and O.F. Robinson (ed.), *The Institutes of Gaius*, London, 1988.
Greenidge, A.H.J., *Infamia*, Oxford, 1894; reprinted Aalen 1977.
Honoré, A.M., *Emperors and Lawyers*, Oxford, 1994.
Honoré, A.M., *Gaius*, Oxford, 1962.
Honoré, A.M., *Tribonian*, Ithaca, 1978.
Honoré, A.M., *Ulpian*, Oxford, 1982.
Johnston, D.E.L., *The Roman Law of Trusts*, Oxford, 1988.

Jolowicz, H.F. and B. Nicholas, *Historical Introduction to the Study of Roman Law*, 3rd Ed., Cambridge, 1972.
Kunkel, W., *An Introduction to Roman Legal and Constitutional History*, 2nd Ed., Oxford, 1972.
Lawson, F.H., *Negligence in the Civil Law*, Oxford, 1950.
Leage, R.W., *Roman Private Law*, 3rd Ed., by A.M. Prichard, London, 1964.
Lee, R.W., *The Elements of Roman Law*, 4th Ed., London, 1956.
Mommsen, Th., P. Krueger and A. Watson (ed.), *The Digest of Justinian*, 4 vols., Philadelphia, 1985.
Moyle, J.B. (ed.), *The Institutes of Justinian*, 2 vols., 5th Ed., Oxford, 1913.
Nicholas, B., *An Introduction to Roman Law*, Oxford, 1962.
Saller, R.P., *Patriarchy, Property and Death in the Roman Family*, Cambridge, 1994.
Sandars, T.C., *The Institutes of Justinian*, London, 1962.
Schulz, F., *Classical Roman Law*, Oxford, 1969.
Schulz, F., *History of Roman Legal Science*, Oxford, 1967.
Sherwin-White, A.N., *The Roman Citizenship*, Oxford, 1973.
Staveley, E.S., *Greek and Roman Voting and Elections*, London, 1982.
Tellegen-Couperus, O., *A Short History of Roman Law*, London, 1993.
Thomas, J.A.C., *Textbook of Roman Law*, Amsterdam, 1976.
Thomas, J.A.C. (ed.), *The Institutes of Justinian*, Amsterdam, 1975.
Thomas, Ph. J., *Introduction to Roman Law*, Deventer, 1986.
Treggiari, S., *Roman Marriage*, Oxford, 1991.
Watson, A., *Roman Private Law around 200 BC*, Edinburgh, 1971.
Watson, A., *Roman Slave Law*, Baltimore, 1987.
Watson, A., *The State, Law and Religion: Pagan Rome*, Athens, Ga., 1992.
Watson, W.A.J., *The Law of Obligations in the Later Roman Republic*, Oxford, 1965; reprinted Aalen 1984.
Watson, W.A.J., *The Law of Persons in the Later Roman Republic*, Oxford, 1967; reprinted Aalen 1984.
Watson, W.A.J., *The Law of Property in the Later Roman Republic*, Oxford, 1968; reprinted Aalen 1984.
Watson, W.A.J., *The Contract of Mandate*, Oxford, 1961; reprinted Aalen 1984.
Zulueta, F. de, *Digest 41, 1 & 2*, Oxford, 1950; reprinted Aalen, 1979.
Zulueta, F. de, *The Institutes of Gaius*, 2 vols., Oxford, 1969.
Zulueta, F. de, *The Roman Law of Sale*, Oxford, 1945.

2 Roman History

Bonner, S.F., *Education in Ancient Rome from the Elder Cato to the Younger Pliny*, Berkeley, 1977.

Brown, P., *Authority and the Sacred: Aspects of the Christianisation of the Roman World*, Cambridge, 1995.

Brown, P., *Power and Persuasion in Late Antiquity: Towards a Christian Empire*, Madison, Wisconsin, 1992.

Brunt, P.A., *Italian Manpower 225 BC - AD 14*, Oxford, 1987.

Brunt, P.A., *Social Conflicts in the Roman Republic*, London, 1971.

Burckhardt, J., *The Age of Constantine the Great*, New York, 1989.

Carcopino, J., *Daily Life in Ancient Rome*, London, 1941.

Chadwick, H., *The Early Church*, London, 1967.

Crawford, M., *The Roman Republic*, Glasgow, 1978.

Dupont, F., *Daily Life in Ancient Rome*, Oxford, 1992.

Jones, A.H.M., *The Later Roman Empire 284-602*, 2 vols., Oxford, 1964.

Ogilvy, R.M., *Early Rome and the Etruscans*, Glasgow, 1976.

Pallottino, M., *A History of Earliest Italy*, London, 1991.

Rostovtzeff, M., *The Social and Economic History of the Roman Empire*, 2 vols., 2nd Ed., Oxford, 1971.

Scullard, H.H., *A History of the Roman World 753-146 BC*, 4th Ed., London, 1980.

Scullard, H.H., *From the Gracchi to Nero: A History of Rome 133 BC to AD 68*, 5th Ed., London, 1982.

Wells, C., *The Roman Empire*, Glasgow, 1984.

3 Mediaeval and Modern Legal History

Alvarez, A., L. Duguit, J. Charmont, E. Ripert et al., *The Progress of Continental Law in the Nineteenth Century*, Boston, 1918; reprinted New York 1969. [*Continental Legal History Series*, vol. XI].

Bellomo, M., *The Common Legal Past of Europe 1000-1800*, Washington D.C., 1995.

Berman, H.J., *Law and Revolution: The Formation of the Western Legal Tradition*, Cambridge, Mass., 1983.

Bonfield, L., (ed.), *Marriage, Property and Succession*, Berlin, 1992.

Brissaud, J.-B., *A History of French Private Law*, Boston, 1912; reprinted New York 1968. [*Continental Legal History Series*, vol. III].

Brissaud, J.-B., *A History of French Public Law*, Boston, 1915; reprinted New York 1969. [*Continental Legal History Series*, vol. IX].

Brundage, J.A., *Law, Sex and Christian Society in Medieval Europe*, Chicago, 1987.

Brundage, J.A., *Medieval Canon Law*, London, 1995.

Calisse, C., *A History of Italian Law*, Boston, 1928; reprinted New York 1969. [*Continental Legal History Series*, vol. VIII].

Calisse, C. et al., *A General Survey of Continental Legal History*, Boston, 1912; reprinted New York 1968. [*Continental Legal History Series*, vol. I].

Chambers, D.S. and T. Dean, *Clean Hands and Rough Justice: An Investigating Magistrate in Renaissance Italy*, Michigan, 1997.

Davies, W. and P. Fouracre, *The Settlement of Disputes in Early Medieval Europe*, Cambridge, 1986.

Engelmann, A. et al., *A History of Continental Civil Procedure*, Boston, 1927; reprinted New York 1969. [*Continental Legal History Series*, vol. VII].

Entrèves, A.P., *Natural Law*, 2nd Ed., London, 1970.

Esmein, A., *A History of Continental Criminal Procedure*, Boston, 1913; reprinted New York 1968. [*Continental Legal History Series*, vol. V].

Evans-Jones, R. (ed)., *The Civil Law Tradition in Scotland*, Edinburgh, 1995.

Goody, J., *The Development of the Family and Marriage in Europe*, Cambridge, 1983.

Helmholz, R.H., *The Spirit of Classical Canon Law*, Athens, Ga., 1996.

Hucko, E.M., *The Democratic Tradition: Four German Constitutions*, New York, 1987.

Huebner, R., *A History of Germanic Private Law*, Boston, 1913; reprinted New York 1968. [*Continental Legal History Series*, vol. IV].

Kamen, H., *The Spanish Inquisition*, London, 1997.

Kelly, J.M., *A Short History of Western Legal Theory*, Oxford, 1992.

Lea, H.C., *The Ordeal*, Philadelphia, 1866; reprinted, 1973.

Meeston, M.C., W.D.H. Sellar and Lord Cooper, *The Scottish Legal Tradition*, Edinburgh, 1991.

O'Connor, D.J., *Aquinas and Natural Law*, London, 1967.

Peters, E., *Torture*, Oxford, 1985.

Phillips, R., *Putting Asunder: A History of Divorce in Western Society*, Cambridge, 1988.

Radding, C.M., *The Origins of Medieval Jurisprudence*, New Haven, 1988.

Robinson, O.F., T.D. Fergus and W.M. Gordon, *European Legal History*, 2nd Ed., London, 1994.
Schrage, E.J.H., *Unjust Enrichment*, Berlin, 1995.
Stein, P.G., *Regulae Iuris*, Edinburgh, 1966.
Stein, P.G., *Roman Law in European History*, Cambridge, 1999 (forthcoming).
Ullmann, W., *Law and Politics in the Middle Ages*, London, 1975.
Van Caenegem, R.C., *An Historical Introduction to Private Law*, Cambridge, 1992.
Van Kleffens, E.N., *Hispanic Law until the End of the Middle Ages*, Edinburgh, 1968.
Vinogradoff, P., *Roman Law in Medieval Europe*, Oxford, 1929; reprinted Cambridge, 1968.
Von Bar, C.L. et al., *A History of Continental Criminal Law*, Boston, 1916; reprinted New York 1968. [*Continental Legal History Series*, vol. VI].
Watson, A., *Failures of the Legal Imagination*, Edinburgh, 1988.
Watson, A., *Slave Law in the Americas*, Athens, Ga., 1989.
Weisser, M.R., *Crime and Punishment in Early Modern Europe*, Brighton, 1982.
Wieacker, F., *A History of Private Law in Europe*, Oxford, 1995.
Wijffels, A. (ed.), *Case Law in the Making*, 2 vols., Berlin, 1997.
Zimmermann, R. and D. Visser, *Southern Cross: Civil Law and Common Law in South Africa*, Oxford, 1996.
Zimmermann, R., *The Civil Law of Obligations*, Cape Town, 1990; Oxford, 1996.

4 Mediaeval and Modern History

Bloch, M., *Feudal Society*, 2 vols., London, 1975.
Boswell, J., *The Kindness of Strangers: The Abandonment of Children from Late Antiquity to the Renaissance*, New York, 1988.
Burns, J.H. (ed.), *The Cambridge History of Medieval Political Thought c.350 - c.1450*, Cambridge, 1988.
Byron, R., *The Byzantine Achievement: An Historical Perspective AD 330-1453*, London, 1929; reprinted 1987.
Chadwick, O., *The Reformation*, London, 1964.
Cobban, A., *A History of Modern France*, 3 vols., Harmondsworth, 1985.

Collins, R., *Early Medieval Spain: Unity in Diversity 400-1000*, London, 1983.
Daniel, N., *The Arabs and Mediaeval Europe*, 2nd Ed., London, 1979.
Dockès, P., *Medieval Slavery and Liberation*, Chicago, 1982.
Duby, G., *France in the Middle Ages 987-1460*, Oxford, 1991.
Duby, G., *Rural Economy and Country Life in the Medieval West*, London, 1968.
Gierke, O., *Political Theories of the Middle Age*, Cambridge, 1900.
Halperin, S.W., *The Separation of Church and State in Italian Thought from Cavour to Mussolini*, New York, 1971.
Hearder, H., *A Short History of Italy*, Cambridge, 1991.
James, E., *The Franks*, Oxford, 1988.
James, E., *The Origins of France 500-1000*, London, 1982.
Kertzer, D.I. and R.P. Saller (ed.), *The Family in Italy from Antiquity to the Present*, New Haven, 1991.
Kiernan, V.G., *The Duel in European History*, Oxford, 1988.
Llewellyn, P., *Rome in the Dark Ages*, London, 1993.
Lynch, J., *Bourbon Spain 1700-1808*, Oxford, 1989.
MacKay, A., *Spain in the Middle Ages: From Frontier to Empire 1000-1500*, London, 1977.
Morris, C., *The Discovery of the Individual 1050-1200*, Toronto, 1972.
Oakley, F., *The Crucial Centuries: The Mediaeval Experience*, London, 1979.
Pullan, B., *The Jews of Europe and the Inquisition of Venice 1550-1670*, Oxford, 1983.
Roberts, J.M., *The French Revolution*, Oxford, 1978.
Robinson, I.S., *The Papacy 1073-1198: Continuity and Innovation*, Cambridge, 1990.
Sayers, J., *Innocent III: Leader of Europe 1198-1216*, London, 1994.
Sigmund, P.E. (ed.), *St. Thomas Aquinas on Politics and Ethics*, New York, 1988.
Southern, R.W., *Western Society and the Church in the Middle Ages*, London, 1970.
Tabacco, G., *The Struggle for Power in Medieval Italy: Structures of Political Rule*, Cambridge, 1989.
Tierney, B., *The Crisis of Church and State 1050-1300*, Toronto, 1988.
Ullmann, W., *Medieval Political Thought*, London, 1965.
Waley, D., *Italian City Republics*, 3rd Ed., London, 1988.

Wickham, C., *Early Medieval Italy: Central Power and Local Society 400-1000*, London, 1981.

5 Modern Civilian Legal Systems

Amos and Walton's Introduction to French Law, 3rd Ed., by F.H. Lawson, A.E. Anton and L.N. Brown, Oxford, 1967.

Bell, J.S. and L.N. Brown, *French Administrative Law*, Oxford, 1998.

Bell, J.S., *French Constitutional Law*, Oxford, 1992.

Bell, J.S., S. Byron and S. Whittaker, *Principles of French Law*, Oxford, 1998.

Certoma, G.L., *The Italian Legal System*, London, 1984.

Dadomo, C. and S. Farran, *French Substantive Law*, London, 1996.

Dadomo, C. and S. Farran, *The French Legal System*, 2nd Ed., London, 1996.

David, R. and J.E.C. Brierly, *Major Legal Systems in the World Today*, 3rd Ed., London, 1985.

Donaghy, P.J. and M.T. Newton, *Spain: A Guide to Political and Economic Institutions*, Cambridge, 1987.

Foster, N.G., *German Legal System and Laws*, 2nd Ed., London, 1996.

Horn, N., H. Kötz and H.G. Leser, *German Private and Commercial Law: An Introduction*, Oxford, 1982.

LaPalombara, J., *Democracy Italian Style*, New Haven, 1987.

Merino-Blanco, E., *The Spanish Legal System*, London, 1996.

Nicholas, B., *French Law of Contract*, 2nd Ed., London, 1992.

Oda, H., *Japanese Law*, London, 1992.

Sassoon, D., *Contemporary Italy*, 2nd Ed., London, 1997.

Villiers, C., *The Spanish Legal Tradition*, London, 1999 (forthcoming).

Watkin, T.G., *The Italian Legal Tradition*, London, 1997.

West, A.D., Y. Desdevises et al., *The French Legal System*, 2nd Ed., London, 1998.

Wyngaert, C. Van Den (ed.), *Criminal Procedure Systems in the European Community*, London, 1993.

Index of Persons and Places

General Index